1976

This book may be kept

FOURTEEN DAYS

THE NEW LOOK

1. "RE-ENTRY INTO CIVIL LIFE", 1945–46: Trying on a "demob. suit" in one of the Dispersal Centres. There was also a hat, shirt with two collars, cuff-links and studs, two pairs of socks and one of shoes, a 14-Day Emergency Ration Card— and a pamphlet of advice.

Harry Hopkins

THE NEW LOOK

A SOCIAL HISTORY
OF THE FORTIES AND FIFTIES
IN BRITAIN

"For that matter, what is History about? . . . The conclusion I reached was that the real central theme of History is not what happened, but what people felt about it when it was happening; in Sir Philip Sidney's phrase, 'the affects, the whisperings, the motions of the people', in Maitland's, 'men's common thoughts of common things', in mine, 'the conversation of the people who counted'."

—G. M. Young, Preface, *Portrait of an Age*, 1952 Edition.

BOSTON

HOUGHTON MIFFLIN COMPANY

The Riverside Press Cambridge

1964

To My Father

Contents

Introduction   11

PART ONE: THE AFTERMATH

1. "In the Picture"   15
2. Clean Break   27
3. Chain Reaction   37
4. "Fair Shares"   42
5. Third Force?   53
6. Keeping Left   64
7. The Climate of Crisis sets in   73
8. The Manager   82
9. New Look?   95
10. The Englishman's Burden   105

PART TWO: MORE EQUAL THAN OTHERS

11. Horny-rimmed   113
12. Shaking the Bottle   125
13. That Other Revolution   136
14. Eleven Plus—What?   143
15. The Endless Middle   153
16. Free-for-All   162
17. Grass Roots   176

PART THREE: STILL SHOOTING NIAGARA

18. Human After All   193
19. The Everlasting Maybe   206
20. Vital Statistics   220
21. Culture and Anarchy   234

PART FOUR: BETWEEN PAST AND FUTURE

22. The Shadow of the Bomb   255
23. "Contemporary"   268
24. New Elizabethans?   285

PART FIVE: THE NEW LOOK

25. Not Marx, but Marks   307
26. "Housewives' Choice"   320
27. Semi-detached, Open Plan   338
28. The Subtle Terrorism of Words   358

PART SIX: NIAGARA SHOT

29. "Flying Saucers—OFFICIAL"   383
30. Triumph of a Salesman   399
31. Teenage Trajectory   423
32. The End of the Beginning   441
33. Fog Lifting   458
34. The Heart of the Matter   472

Bibliography   493

Acknowledgements   504

Index   505

Illustrations

facing page

1. "Re-entry into Civil Life"   *frontispiece*

2. Sir William Beveridge at the Central Hall, Westminster   32

3. "Union Jack" keeps the troops 'in the picture'   32

4. Winston Churchill's election campaign, 1945   33

5. Middle East troops Mock Election, Cairo   33

6. Labour Ministers and King George VI   44

7. Nylons!   45

8. Squatters hold out in Abbey Lodge, St. John's Wood   45

9. The New Look reaches London   74

10. The Fuel Crisis: East Enders queue for coke   75

11. The troops take over on the docks, 1950   75

12. The dilemma of Sir Stafford Cripps, *Vicky* cartoon from the *News Chronicle*   128

13. John Belcher reads Lynskey Tribunal Verdict   128

14. TEN PER CENT MORE . . . Government productivity campaign   129

15. TRY BARRACOUTA FOR BREAKFAST—Ministry of Food advertising   129

16. Gilbert Harding in the Brains Trust, 1948   158

17. Gilbert Harding in "What's My Line?", 1951   158

18. LOW on the cost of Korea, *Evening Standard*   159

19. LOW on Anglo-American relations, *Evening Standard*   159

20. The Dome of Discovery rises   196

21. The birth of the "Contemporary" style   196

22. British Lion, 1951 Model   197

23. The Ubiquitous Spiv   197

24. The Queen comes Home   224
25. Franta Belsky's "Joy Ride", Stevenage New Town   225
26. The Bentley Case: Execution Eve   256
27. The Craig-Bentley Case: headlines in the Press   256
28. West Indian immigrants arrive Victoria   257
29. Coronation night in the Mall   288
30. Prince Philip tries out the Comet   289
31. Disaster overtakes the Comets: headlines   289
32. Cummings, *Express* cartoonist, on Commercial TV   322
33. The advance of Television: pocket cartoon   322
34. Philip Harben makes *Soupe à l'Oignon*   323
35. Sabrina   323
36. Edwardian elegance at Mecca Dance Hall   352
37. *A Streetcar Named Desire*: scene   353
38. *Look Back in Anger*: scene   353
39. Morrison congratulates Gaitskell on way up, 1955   384
40. Churchill leaves Downing Street, 1955   384
41. Georgi Malenkov visits the Mansion House, 1956   385
42. Suez demonstrators clash in Edinburgh   416
43. Suez front page, *Evening Standard*   416
44. Juvenile skiffle group   417
45. Pick of the Pops: record-buyers   417
46. *Mirror* cartoon by *Zec*, 1945   448
47. *Mirror* City Page, 1960   448
48. Peckham Secondary School for Girls   449
49. Tower Bridge School   449
50. A nuclear disarmer on the march   480
51. The New London: Thorn House   481

Introduction

THE AIM of this book is to document and in some degree chart the "social revolution" of the last twenty years or so, a process of change so swift and many-sided that we have not yet been fully able to grasp it. I describe it as a "social history" because its point of departure is change that reaches into the lives of ordinary people, and, in doing so, affects the whole stuff and quality of life. But since social history does not exist in a vacuum, one has to go beyond the level of description, to economic, technological and political causes: and, in fact, explore a process. As this is *contemporary* social history one is exploring the process from inside it. This is a not a wholly disadvantageous position. Political history may have to await the "opening of the archives". But social history is organic. It needs, to live, the moods, thoughts, flavours, significant incidents and memorable occasions, shifting perspectives which, once passed, can rarely be accurately recaptured.

A contemporary social history deals with trends. At what point a trend moves from emergence to dominance, it is rarely possible with certainty to say. Statistics only help to a limited extent. The English may still consume vastly more suet pudding than *apfelstrudel*, yet *apfelstrudel* may embody the *zeitgeist* in a way that roly-poly does not. Therefore, if I report, for instance, that we became less insular, I do not imply that we were still not capable, on occasion, of finding "the Continent isolated", or if I find us becoming less hypocritical I mean *less* hypocritical. My quest, in short, is for perspective, indispensable, but remarkably hard to come by today.

History does not, of course, neatly divide itself up into decades: the trends that shaped these years did not originate with them. Yet often the pace of their development accelerated so greatly as to produce differences of kind rather than merely of degree. Visible since 1918, the decline of British power reached a point where even the most purblind were at last forced to acknowledge it and begin extensive and painful psychological adjustments. Expanding down the years, the social services now attàined such breadth and scale that they lost the lingering flavour of charity and became what their name claimed. At the same time, the standard of living of the "workers" which had been rising intermittently over many years reached a level where it began to transform the whole character of our society.

In this transformation, the part played by science and technology was visibly greater and more immediate than ever before. It not only set us in a new environment, but enveloped us in an atmosphere. The hydrogen bomb was more than just one more step in that steady increase in the power of explosives which was already causing alarm in the Thirties. In 1948, the "dual" (business and university graduate) vote was abolished. Political democracy in its classic form of one vote per person had finally reached its logical conclusion. But now a force more powerful than constitutional change was at work. The complex influence of science, sometimes advancing the ends of social democracy, sometimes frustrating them, emerges as one of the two key themes of these years. The other derives from the intricate and shifting relationship or balance between community control and the concept of public good and the drives of private profit. For science and technology, in part self-generating and self-directing, are also harnessed and directed with formidable effect to dubious ends.

A contemporary social history inevitably measures by the more recent past. Equally inevitably, it hints at the future. *Hints* only, however. For this is not a book designed to outline a particular path along which civilisation is travelling to perdition. It merely seeks to show the factors at work, the currents and the cross-currents, and the "incidence of accident", aiming to serve as an *aide-memoire* by means of which the reader may look back over the way we came and reflect on some of the extraordinary experiences that have befallen us in these crowded years "since the war".

PART ONE

THE AFTERMATH

"Our task is to work out a system of a new and challenging kind which combines individual freedom with social justice. The task which faces not only ourselves but all the Western democracies requires a Government inspired by a new conception of society with a dynamic policy to accord with the needs of a new situation."

—C. R. Attlee, broadcasting in January, 1948.

1. "In the Picture"

"*When I get my civvy clothes on,*
Oh, how happy I shall be!"
—Soldier's Song, World War II.

"Bottled up in men are great
emotional forces which have got to be
given an outlet which is positive and
constructive and which warms the
heart and excites the imagination."
—Field-Marshal Viscount Montgomery, *Memoirs*.

ON FRIDAY the 4th May, 1945, Stuart Hibberd, the
B.B.C.'s Chief Announcer, began the six o'clock news
for the last time with the familiar formula "Here is
the News—and this is Stuart Hibberd reading it". Berlin had
fallen the day before and the B.B.C. did not lose a moment
in re-embracing its normal impeccable anonymity which had
been reluctantly abandoned only as a precaution against
enemy saboteurs.

That evening and all next day people stayed glued to their
radio sets. But the news for which they were waiting did not
come. On Sunday the news bulletins told of the Patriots'
Rising in Prague and their radio call for help. In the afternoon
New York Radio broke into its programmes with news of the
German Armed Forces' surrender at Rheims. But General
Eisenhower's Headquarters issued a prompt disavowal. In
London, flags were flying, planes zooming overhead. Crowds
were beginning to gather. But it was Monday evening before
the B.B.C. was able to announce that next day would be
celebrated as V.E. Day and that Mr. Churchill would broad-
cast to the nation at three o'clock.

On the General Forces' Programme the familiar voice, deep,
rumbling, yet slightly sibilant, was carried across the world.

In the Naafis of Cairo and Benghazi and Tripoli men crowded around radios more usually vibrating with the "request" songs of Vera Lynn, the Forces' Sweetheart, or the interminable adventures of the Robinson Family. Some of the Eighth Army men who heard the Prime Minister's broadcast had crossed into Austria the day before after their dogged two-year advance up the spine of Italy; others listened in Athens, reoccupied in October, in liberated Denmark, or in the rubble of Hamburg which the tanks of the 7th Armoured Division, the famed "Desert Rats", had entered on the evening of the third.

Spoken with great deliberation, the words fell slowly on the listening air: "Today perhaps we shall think mostly of ourselves . . . tomorrow we shall perhaps pay particular tribute to our Russian comrades. . . ."

One silent listening group gathered around a crackling radio truck in the garden of a house in the battered and deserted city of Rangoon which they had reached five days before, some by invasion from the sea, the others racing down the Irrawaddy. On Singapore Island, the news, picked up on radios secreted under floors and boilers in Changi Jail, breathed new life into 7,000 sick and weary prisoners.

For these, and for others, it was still a long way home. "Japan, with all her treachery and greed," as the Prime Minister said, remained unsubdued. Well, one had waited this long; one could wait a little longer. But henceforth it would be a different kind of waiting, more sharply felt, more grudgingly measured.

For although he had worn uniform for so long the British citizen soldier had somehow still contrived, as ever, to retain his amateur status, to remain, within his private self, a civilian. And, happily, a civilian, this time, who was in surprisingly good shape, better physically and often better mentally too than when he left home. Penicillin—first used on Battle of Britain pilots—blood plasma, new anti-shock and surgical techniques, successfully healed injuries which twenty years earlier would have left men life-long cripples. Despite the horrific prophecies of the Thirties, this war of movement had produced only one-third of the casualties of the mud-bogged trench warfare of 1914-18. D.D.T. (discovered in Switzerland and passed to the Allies in 1942) and the new scrub typhus vaccine had largely eradicated typhus and other insect-borne diseases. American-style "K rations" and vitamin pills had vastly reduced the dangers of malnutrition even in long-drawn-out jungle warfare. When the use of mepacrine was enforced, casualties from malaria had dropped from a disastrous 740 per thousand in 1943 to 26 per thousand in 1944.

But it was not only the speed of scientific advance that was illuminated by the profound contrast between the temper and conduct of the two world wars. The extent of social change that had been going on in the inter-war years, often concealed beneath a little-changed surface, was sharply revealed also. In 1914 the Army had still functioned as almost an independent Estate of the Realm, a semi-feudal position underlined by the status of Kitchener and later of Haig in direct and secret communication with the King. Civilian criticism appeared little short of treason, and even Lloyd George with all his energy and guile and popular following had found himself powerless to effect the changes in the High Command that were so patently needed.

In 1939 there had been indications that these anachronisms might persist. Early in 1940, the energetic, popular, reforming War Minister, Leslie Hore-Belisha, was peremptorily dismissed by the Prime Minister, Neville Chamberlain, under pressure from the Generals. Belisha, who had established the idea of a New Model democratic army ("Carpets for Conscripts") and, incidentally, introduced battledress, had shown inadequate deference, committing the unforgivable offence of addressing himself directly to juniors and Other Ranks. With the Chamberlain Government in power, it looked as if the hierarchy retained its old sureness of touch.

In the event, the distance between 1915 and 1940 was to be unforgettably demonstrated. An upsurge of anger at the muddle and failure in Norway and the "business as usual" conduct of the "phoney war" swept Chamberlain from power in May. The Generals who had got Hore-Belisha out were themselves sacked shortly afterwards by a "Politician and Civilian". Backed by an all-party coalition which was the clear embodiment of the people's will expressed openly through Parliament and not, as in 1916, the result of a backstairs intrigue, Winston Churchill was able to secure through the new device of the Chief of Staffs Committee, civilian, and—since Churchill was a devoted Parliamentarian—in the last resort Parliamentary, control over the direction of the war.

If this came about partly by accident—the coincidence of the moment and the man—it was also an early and critical victory for social democracy which was to set the stage for many others. The *Daily Mirror*, however many frowns and even threats of suspension it might attract, was not (like the *Daily Mail* in World War I) burned on the Stock Exchange.

The Conscription Bill had received its Third Reading in May, 1939, three months before the war began. The Labour and Liberal Parties opposed it. Had not Keir Hardie described conscription as "the badge of the serf"? In the event, at this stage in Britain's social evolution, conscription proved powerfully democratising. The existence of systematic call-up from the outset was reflected in the whole tone of the war, substituting for the Rupert Brooke-ish romanticism of the Elect in 1914-18, with their strange yearning to be "under fire", an earnest, patient, practical acceptance of an unpleasant but necessary job to be done by the nation-in-arms.

It meant also that—especially after the break-up of the B.E.F. at Dunkirk—it became progressively more difficult to maintain unchanged the old military-social patterns and attitudes. "The Army as I know it," Gort told Sir Walter Elliot, "has completely disappeared. What we have is an enormous, very raw, very inchoate Militia." It was for these men that Hore-Belisha had proclaimed the ideal of a "Citizen Army"—and proclaimed it just in time. The circumstances of the war assisted its realisation. The war's global swing, its immensely varied conditions, the tempo of modern technology pacing its development from the start, broke the Regular soldiers' instinctive resistance to change and produced an elasticity, even an inventiveness, in sharp contrast to the "nothing-like-a-well-bred-horse" mentality of World War I. At the outset in 1940 the Army was still despatching men to tropical fronts in narrow drill trousers, tunics brass-buttoned to the neck, and immense Wolseley helmets. In Malaya and Burma the Japanese, infiltrating through the jungle in sloppy green denims and plimsolls, or advancing swiftly on bicycles, made the necessary point with force and speed. No modern war can have been fought in such variety, and often informality, of costume—the proud and particular mark of that *corps d'élite*, the Eighth Army.

But it was not the Army, but the most junior and most technological arm of the Services, the R.A.F., which in many ways set the tone of World War II as it also originated its characteristic slang and humour. And the R.A.F. had very clearly been made neither in the elementary schools nor "on the playing fields of Eton", but in the grammar schools and technical colleges. Its rapid expansion brought high command to many very young men—"R.A.F. types"—who shared its breezy irreverence and relatively classless approach. It sounded a new note which was to make itself increasingly heard in England in the years ahead. And as war weeded out the more incompetent, and provided opportunities for the able, the Army, too, became more mixed, cohesive and democratic.* Battledress, worn by Generals and privates alike—and echoed at home in the uniforms of the A.R.P., the A.F.S. or in the Prime Minister's "siren suit"—accurately reflected the new solidarity and singleness of purpose.

This new sort of war—and the National Service soldier who was fighting it—demanded a new approach from commanders —and in due course received it. The time had gone now for the silent Father Figure like Kitchener, for the Gentleman like Haig. There was a new phrase going the rounds, spreading downwards and outwards, "putting you in the picture". "Every single soldier," ruled Montgomery, "must know, before he goes into battle, how the little battle he is to fight fits into the larger picture, and how the success of his fighting will influence the battle as a whole." Most men had gone through World War I without ever seeing a major commander; distance and dignity were then studiously cultivated. In World War II, by contrast, a well-publicised nickname, a

* In this and other matters a comparison of the favourite cartoon characters of the two world wars is instructive. Cf. for instance Bruce Bairnsfather's long-suffering Old Bill, dumbly seeking his "Better 'Ole" with Jon's jaunty and irrepressible Eighth Army "Two Types", who were officers, although not that one would have noticed it.

good brand symbol (Monty's black beret and twin badges was the classic example) an effective man-to-man style, an un-wearying readiness to jump on to a box and put all around "in the picture", were among the essential accoutrements of a well-equipped General.

It was odd to recall that only a year or two earlier the War Office had been frankly horrified by Hore-Belisha's introduction of Press conferences. "Public Relations" then had been an odd quirk of the Post Office or such esoteric bodies as the Empire Marketing Board. Now, suddenly, under the impetus of the common purpose, public relations departments pro-liferated both at home and on the war fronts.

Mr. Duff-Cooper was later to explain the 1945 election with the comment: "The private soldier always votes against the sergeant-major." But this time it went a little deeper than that. This was, in the full sense, Britain's first national citizen army and history shows such a body to be a powerful accumulator of the forces of change. In the Forces in these years the social revolution and the scientific-technological revolution which were to form the twin themes and driving forces of the Forties and Fifties declared themselves and demonstrated their potent and many-sided inter-action.

It was, in a quiet English sort of way, a revolutionary army. The sergeant-major was not only voted against, but was under orders to document that vote. It became axiomatic, for instance, that every front must have its newspaper, often run by a staff of full-time soldier-journalists, served by a central War Office-M.o.I. news-service. From the *Arctic Times* and the *Midnight Sun* to *SEAC*, the air-dropped daily of South-East Asia Com-mand, the staple of the army papers was news from home. But their most important feature was their correspondence column, full of soldiers' complaints and sardonic queries. Many a letter appeared which in the First World War would have got both writer and editorial staff court-martialled. Now there would merely be a printed "explanation" or sympathetic comment from G.H.Q. Welfare and the letter-writer would be left in hope that the offending authority had "got a rocket" (which indeed it sometimes had).

In one way or another the rights of the citizen soldier were being stressed hardly less than his duties. Communication ran upwards now as well as down. In this "New Model" army, as in Cromwell's, it was theirs ("approved" doctrine ran) not only to "reason why", but to know, and a vast apparatus of Army Education, Morale and Welfare was built up to further this knowing. The social Grand Inquisition of the later Thirties had been largely confined to the intellectuals of the Left. Now in the classes and pamphlets and wall-diagrams of the Army Bureau of Current Affairs its issues were reduced to simple terms and dramatised in earnest discussion of all the plans for a New Britain that were being drawn up at home.

A.B.C.A. was not only a bold and imaginative experiment in constructive democracy, it was also a successful one. For if some commanders regarded its compulsory classes as a "bind" and some soldiers saw them as an opportunity for sleep, others —with a chance for the first time in their lives to let their minds run free—were stirred and drawn together. The B.B.C. now encountered so formidable a demand for information (the "pukka gen") that it was driven to devise for the Forces Programme a new type of radio feature, at first entitled "Any Questions", but soon to be rechristened "The Brains Trust".

Modern war creates vast deserts of boredom; but for many it also offers periods of once-in-a-lifetime stimulation. For many the old slogan "Join the Army and see the World" had proved true enough. Young airmen had trained in Canada, in Texas and Australia. And at this point, in May, 1945, Indo-China, Japan, and the Dutch East Indies were still to be added to the Serviceman's world tour. And though the British soldier was apt to cling fiercely to his "egg-and-chips" from Rome to Tokio, rejecting all alien ways, nevertheless a war brides' club in Sheffield after the war contained seventeen nationalities. So much travel, so much experience, reflected upon in tranquillity, inevitably brought a new flexibility to many minds. The bounds of the possible had stretched. Many thousands of men in cloth caps who had for years punched the same time-clock at 7.30 every morning, men in bowlers who had for years caught the 8.5 to the City, had discovered the world. What was perhaps more important, they had discovered each other.

II

These educational experiences in the Armed Services had their counterpart on the Home Front. For this time "Home Front" was no mere figure of speech. Sixty thousand civilians had been killed in air raids. Conscription had been industrial as well as military. Many thousands of middle-class girls whose horizons would otherwise have been bounded by office, tennis club and holiday cruise had discovered a vast new world without even leaving England. Around mobile canteens in the Blitz, in the war factories and rest centres and air raid shelters and hostels, old barriers of caste and convention were shattered. A million and a half mothers and children had been evacuated from threatened towns. Vast numbers of those children whom the Minister of Health had referred to not many months before as the "bud of the nation", were now suddenly dumped in middle-class residential areas, and were seen to be dirty, often verminous, ill-nurtured and miserably clad. Many set out on their journeys wearing plimsolls, with no overcoats to protect them from the winter. The newspapers were full of the horrific details. Nice middle-class housewives were shaken to the core to discover that the little girls from Manchester and Liverpool who were billeted on them did not wear, and had never worn, knickers under their frocks. Countless "evacuee stories" spread across garden fences and along shopping queues in the more comfortable suburbs, some shocking, others pathetic, but all in their way revealing. And if some people merely shuddered, many others felt the compulsion of elementary human need and did what they could. There was, James Drawbell, Editor of the *Sunday Chronicle*, noted in his diary on the 24th July, 1940, beginning to be a "picknicky, comradely feeling" around.

With this fund of shared experience to draw on, the Home Front and the war fronts were linked as never before by the new communications. The reassuring voice of the B.B.C. reached out across the oceans and the jungles and the deserts. "Here is the News—and this is Stuart Hibberd reading it." The lugubrious tones of that great leveller, Mrs. Mopp, girdled

the world in the mad half-hour of ITMA—It's That Man
Again, *that man* being Hitler (and Tommy Handley). Airliners
and the R.A.F. flew out air lettercards and newspapers. From
Rangoon to Tobruk, from Naples to Baghdad, men could keep
a check on the day-to-day state of undress of "Jane" in the
London *Daily Mirror*.

The Home Press, like the Army, had responded to a climate
of the times, the *Daily Mirror* with a surer instinct and a
greater gusto than most. After Munich the *Mirror* had set
about the "treacherous upper-crust riff-raff" who had made a
darling of the "pale spy Ribbentrop". Now it cast itself with
striking success in the role of the fighting man's champion.
It was the trick the *Daily Mail* had carried off in the First
World War; but this time there were significant differences.
There was no patronising of the "Tommy". In "flaying"
"Blimps", "Army foolery", etc., the *Mirror* did so much in the
ordinary soldiers' idiom, reflecting the natural radicalism
—or 'bloody-mindedness'—of the ranks. "RUSSIA BLEEDS
WHILE BRITAIN BLANCOES", it roared in black type, inches high.
It was, wrote Cecil H. King, later its Chairman, "a raw crude
medium, very typical of its day". When Churchill protested
against the *Mirror's* unseemly jeers, King countered: "Loyalty
to the future involves not only scanning the horizon for new
ideas and ideals which may shape the world, but also the
discrediting of the men who made the period 1919-39 such an
ignoble page of English history. This is not done to humiliate
them, but to impress on the young people growing up (who
read our papers) that that is an era which must not recur."

The Mohammedans, King explained, plunging into history,
had conquered the Middle East with sword in one hand and the
Koran in the other—"and who will deny the Koran was the
more important weapon?" At that moment, he concluded,
England needed, above all, her Koran.

Authority, coached by its multiplying morale and public
relations officers, was not unaware of the need.

As the war wore on and the various Reconstruction committees set up by the Coalition Government issued their reports,
the *Daily Mirror* was able to add to its weird but potent mixture

of sex, sensation and righteous indignation, a strong stiffening
of economics-and-social-reform-made-easy, a sort of civilian's
A.B.C.A. In Naafis or works canteens, at home or abroad, the
Mirror reader could now turn from the contemplation of
"Jane's" lingerie to a discussion of the National Health
Service (foreshadowed in the "Willinck" White Paper of
February 1944) or of the massive Abercrombie Plan for
Greater London (which recommended fourteen new towns),
or to an exposition of the policy of Full Employment (another
White Paper in May), or to the implications of "Secondary
Education for All" to be realised through the Butler Act of
1943.

But it was left to a creative civil servant to produce the
missing Koran. The Beveridge Report, a highly technical
document of 200,000 words, was a runaway best-seller from
the start. Long queues formed at the Stationery Office to
purchase it; Army commanders urgently demanded supplies
for their troops. There were two main reasons for the phenomenal enthusiasm the report aroused. The first was that Sir
William Beveridge, from long experience in the social field,
clearly possessed a rare grasp of the difficulties facing ordinary
people in their lives, and an equally obvious and highly practical sympathy with them. Beveridge obviously both knew and
cared. The second reason was that as an imaginative humani-
tarian in a great Liberal tradition (like Attlee he was a 'graduate' of Toynbee Hall), Beveridge was able to capture and
reflect, almost perfectly, the spirit of that time and the peculiarly English blend of practicality and evangelism.

The Coalition Government, having ordered what it thought
was an innocuous technical survey of social insurance, thus
found itself saddled with what in effect was a declaration of
Human Rights, a manifesto and a programme. Not only were
the "five Giant Evils" (paragraph 456), "Want, Disease,
Ignorance, Squalor and Idleness", indicted, but the means to
remove them were boldly proclaimed. There was to be a truly
comprehensive system of social insurance, enjoyed not merely
by industrial workers, but by all citizens, *as of right*. The
principle of a National Minimum was put forward. "Assumption A" of the report postulated a comprehensive health service
freely available to all. "Assumption B" looked to the family

and called for children's allowances. "Assumption C" made "Full Employment" the essential basis of the whole system. Thus, concluded Beveridge, should we show that we were fighting "not for the glory of rulers and races" but for the "happiness of the common man".

In the Beveridge Report the radicalism of the Home Front and the radicalism of the Armed Forces—soldiers and workers—found a common cause. From being an obscure academic, Beveridge became a popular hero overnight. "Though not a good speaker, he can overfill any hall in the country," an American correspondent reported. A Gallup Poll showed that nineteen people out of twenty knew of the Beveridge Report, an unusual state of public knowledge indeed. From all over the country letters poured in to Sir William from ordinary people who wished to thank him personally. From Plymouth, an old-age pensioner apostrophised him:

> At last there is a saint on earth
> An angel he would be
> If only he could have his will
> And make the Commons pass his Bill.

When Authority, taking alarm at commitments so specific, ordered the withdrawal of the Army Bureau of Current Affairs' pamphlet on the Beveridge Plan, so great was the outcry that it was obliged to reissue it with interest. Sir William Beveridge had accomplished the miracle of getting a Blue Book into the hands of tens of thousands of ordinary people—a landmark in the advance of British democracy and once again striking evidence of the stimulating powers of war.

Nor could the spectre of Bolshevism this time be used to obscure the sharpening vision of a "New Britain". The powerful myth of the Russian Revolution once again nourished the Utopian dream. The Left, it seemed, had been right about Russia after all. At any rate, the Bolsheviks were "our valiant Allies" now; Stalin, the bloody-handed ruffian of Mr. Churchill's 1919 tirades, was—whatever misgivings the Prime Minister might be expressing privately—"the supreme Commander-in-Chief, Marshal Stalin, this truly great man".

For some time, as the Russian armies rolled westwards—as when they had taken the whole shock of the German onslaught in 1941—the cartoonists had been drawing their Red Army men larger than life, looming out of the page with outstretched hands. On the morning of 26th April, 1945, the papers came out with pictures of the link-up of the American and Russian soldiers on the Elbe. The revolution of the New World and the revolution of the Old saluted each other over the ruins of Europe, and, for a moment, it almost seemed that the vision of Wendell Willkie was about to be realised. Willkie's book, *One World*, a plea for human brotherhood founded on his globe-girdling flight in the *Gulliver* as President Roosevelt's personal envoy, had sold over a million copies since its publication in 1943. In Russia, Willkie told Americans, he had been repeatedly reminded "of the romance of our own Western development". This time the United States must not turn her back as she had in 1920. "When I say that peace must be planned on a world basis, I mean quite literally that it must embrace the earth. Continents and oceans are plainly only part of a whole, seen, as I have seen them, from the air . . . The Peoples of the East . . . would like the United States and the other united nations to be partners with them in this great adventure. They want us to join with them in creating a new society of independent nations, free alike of the economic injustices of the West and the political malpractices of the East."

2.   Clean Break

"Rejoice and be glad! For this is the
Day of the People."
—*Daily Express*. July 5th, 1945.

"It is terrible—they have elected a
Labour Government. The country
will never stand for it!"
—Lady overheard in Claridges.

IN 1918 only one Serviceman in four had managed to cast
a vote; in 1945 the proportion was to reach almost 60
per cent, two million Servicemen and women voting by
special air post or by proxy. The troops, war correspondents
agreed, were nevertheless finding it all a little baffling. An
election address with a candidate's complacent face on the
front was apt to read oddly in the ruins of Cologne or under a
Burmese palm-tree. But then it was an unusual election in
every way, this first General Election in Britain for over nine
years, held now in the twilight between war and peace, its
campaign headlines in bizarre juxtaposition with lurid details
of war's aftermath . . . "HAW-HAW FOR TRIAL: CLAIMS TO BE
GERMAN"—"ONLY THREE UNOPPOSED RETURNS"—"RIBBENTROP
FOUND IN BED IN HAMBURG"—"NINETEEN DAYS TO POLLING"
—"THE DEAD DOKTOR [Goebbels] ON VIEW TO ALL".

Mr. Eden and Mr. Attlee flew back from the San Francisco
conference where the United Nation's charter was being
hammered out. Each day when his campaign meetings were
over Winston Churchill returned to his headquarters in a
special train where he worked on his telegrams into the night:
the war with Japan still made heavy demands on his attention.
Yet if exhausted, he could look back on his five-day tour of
Britain with satisfaction. The *Daily Mail* had summed it up:
"V.E. DAY ALL THE WAY." Everywhere—except in a few parts
of London where there had been organised booing—"Good

Old Winnie!", the Man Who won the War, had been eagerly acclaimed. Between Coventry and Birmingham the crowds had been so dense that his car had taken three hours to cover twenty miles. In Glasgow, "Red Clydeside" of 1919, the streets had flowered overnight with flags and bunting; people stood on the roofs of houses, packed every balcony, filled every window. As Churchill's car left, the loudspeakers roared: "Will ye no come back again?" and the vast crowd took up the refrain.

On the walls of every town the familiar face looked out from posters boldly captioned: "HELP HIM TO FINISH THE JOB—VOTE NATIONAL." Half the Conservative candidates used the portrait on their election addresses. ("Don't let HIM down.") Despite the indications of the Gallup Poll (a new institution in British politics) most political observers took the Conservatives' return for granted. Three days before polling day, the *Daily Express* announced: "Socialists decide They Have Lost", and Mr. Attlee has since admitted that as far as he was concerned this was true enough. The most unorthodox prophets did not predict more than a draw.

Veteran campaigners remarked that it had been a strangely quiet election with little about it of the old rough-and-tumble of the hustings—save, that is, for the efforts of Mr. Churchill himself which had struck a discordant note. A Tory Democrat of the old romantic-paternalist order, still visualising an election as a sort of joyous demagogic joust, his attempts to make the flesh creep with a picture of his late Cabinet colleagues resorting to a Socialist *Gestapo* or with dread forebodings of the dictatorship of Mr. Harold Laski and the "shrivelling away" before one's eyes of that "nest egg . . . by thrift and toil accumulated", were better attuned to the aftermath of Lloyd George's and Horatio Bottomley's and Kitchener's war than to this strangely serious new A.B.C.A.-R.A.F.-Beveridge public.

In the coalition Committee of Reconstruction, the Conservatives had participated equally with Labour in outlining the key postwar reforms. But they had given the impression of dragging their feet*—an impression now confirmed by their "Four Year Plan" which seemed vague and lacking in con-

* In February, 1943, there had been a heavy protest vote in Parliament against the Government's refusal to promise forthwith Beveridge, the whole Beveridge and nothing but Beveridge.

viction beside Labour's *Let Us Face the Future* with its confident root-and-branch commitment on the Beveridge Plan, Full Employment, housing, and public ownership of the coal mines, inland transport, gas and electricity, the iron and steel industry. "Labour," the manifesto insisted, "will plan from the ground up."

Nor was patriotism any longer the exclusive electoral property of the Tory Party. Labour Ministers had worked long and ably in key positions in the war years. The real zealots of the joint production committees had often been their Communist members. In 1942, with Russia fighting back valiantly under the German attack, membership of the British Communist Party had soared to more than three times its 1938 level. Some of the residual enthusiasm now went into the campaign for a "People's victory" at the polls. Fervour was also heightened by the crusading Radicalism of Sir Richard Acland's Common Wealth Party which had risen to fame in the war years by winning by-elections during the coalition parties' electoral truce. An expression of wartime stirrings in a section of the middle class, Common Wealth boldly declared for that "real" Socialism which by removing the corruption of the Profit Motive would enable men to extend the brotherhood of the war years into the years of peace.

Millions of men and women under thirty were voting for the first time. Candidates observed that questions seemed to be asked to gain information rather than to embarrass. Twenty-six party addresses broadcast successively for twenty-six nights—with one ten-minute talk apiece for the Communist and Common Wealth parties—were listened to by 44 per cent of the potential audience, a proportion normally secured by only the most popular variety programmes. The people, said some Labour candidates, were thinking.

Were they? And *what* were they thinking?

Even at the conclusion of the poll, the answer to this tantalising question was not immediately available. The ballot-boxes were not opened for a count, but were taken away in the custody of the returning officers, there to remain for the nineteen days allowed for the Services' postal vote to come in.

Mr. Churchill, who took the opportunity to snatch a few days' painting on the Basque coast before going to Potsdam, has since confessed that there were moments on that holiday when unwelcome speculations about the secret of the sealed ballot boxes intruded.

On the evening of the 25th he flew home from Potsdam in an aircraft of Transport Command. Next morning he did not rise till rather late and by the time he reached the Map Room in the Cabinet Offices the first results had already begun to come in. They were not encouraging.

By 10.25 the first Minister—Harold Macmillan at Stockton-on-Tees—was out. By 10.40 it had become clear that the great industrial city of Birmingham, a Tory stronghold since the days of Joseph Chamberlain, was falling. By noon, the London suburbs were going Labour.

And the Labour gains went monotonously on. Bradford, Hull, Leicester, Plymouth, Stoke, Wolverhampton, Cardiff . . . all captured entire, without a single Tory in. Labour won seventy-nine seats which had never before returned a Labour Member.

When the final results came to hand, they gave Labour the overwhelming majority of 145 over all other parties. For the Conservatives this was not merely a lost election, it was in the words of the historian, R. B. McCallum, one of "the three great defeats of Conservative history", comparable with those of 1906 and 1832. McCallum added: "It may be that it leaves them in a weaker position for recovery than on the two previous occasions."

At 7 p.m. that evening Winston Churchill, still flourishing his cigar, drove to Buckingham Palace to tender to the King his Government's resignation. Half an hour later Mr. Attlee's small Austin with Mrs. Attlee at the wheel drove into Palace Yard.

II

Whatever consternation the news might arouse across the Atlantic—and according to one correspondent it "landed in the United States like a giant V2"—London continued to face the future with its customary calm. Within a very few days the event had taken on the inevitability of history.

4. Winston Churchill's 1945 election tour of Britain was a triumphal progress. But the cheers were for the man—and the nation—not the party . . .

5. . . . the results (*below*) of a Middle East soldiers' Mock Election, held in Cairo in 1944, suggest that the troops at least had already made up their minds about *that*.

RESULT	
LABOUR	119
COMMONWEALTH	55
LIBERAL	38
CONSERVATIVE	17

2. Mid-summer, 1943: The Beveridge Plan focused hopes for a Better Britain after the war. Supported by the Archbishop of Canterbury (William Temple) and the Bishop of London (Dr. Fisher), Sir William Beveridge (seated) explains his Principles and Assumptions to a meeting at the Central Hall, Westminster.
3. (*Below*) Army newspapers, like North Africa's *Union Jack*, edited by Capt. Hugh Cudlipp, keep the troops "in the picture".

Plainly, the old garments no longer fitted; new cloth was being cut.

It was a process hearteningly visible at many points. British films, for instance, had begun to show a maturity and integrity worlds removed from the stilted drawing-room dramas that the words "British film" conveyed before the war. Informed by the compassionate detachment learned in the school of wartime documentary such films as *Next-of-Kin*; *The Gentle Sex*; *San Demetrio, London*; *Brief Encounter*; *The Way Ahead*—whose co-author was a young soldier-actor, Peter Ustinov—had established a large and lively school of British directors—David Lean, Thorold Dickenson, Carol Reed, Michael Powell, Charles Frend, Sidney Gilliat, Harry Watt—whose work was as essentially English as the films of the Italian "Neo-Realists", soon to become fashionable in London, were essentially Italian. Theirs were films about real people, accurately and, sometimes, tenderly, observed, in real situations; their tone was quietly assured, with little formula emotion and no mock heroics. "Britain," conceded Sam Goldwyn, "has stopped trying to imitate us. They have begun to use a method of their own, applying a broader viewpoint and getting closer to the people."

This renaissance of the British cinema had been accompanied by stimulating developments in the other Arts. For artists, as for the public at large, the war had brought a breaking down of old compartments and cliques. Employment as a war artist had offered many a promising young man unique opportunities. Huddled in shelters, sharing the common life of blackout and Blitz and for most of the time cut off from Europe, artists had returned to more native ways of feeling and there had come that strange upsurge of "Neo-Romanticism", symbolised for most people by the pictures of John Piper and Graham Sutherland, with their dark, tumbled blocks of masonry, their brooding ruins, sombre red glow, and twisting steel—eloquent rather than anguished—under lowering purple skies.

Nor had the theatre been left out. With the backing of the war-founded, State-supported, Council for the Encouragement of Music and the Arts,* under the chairmanship of J. M.

* Inspired by Tom Jones, chairman of the Pilgrim Trust, and started with an initial grant from that body which the Treasury later doubled.

B

Keynes, the Old Vic had had four or five companies on the road taking Shakespeare, classical plays, opera and ballet to enthusiastic audiences in remote industrial areas where there had been nothing but cinemas for years. Bombed out of its traditional home in the Waterloo Road, the Old Vic's London company had established itself at the New Theatre with an accomplished group of players, and in the summer of 1945 Ralph Richardson and his co-director, Laurence Olivier, released together from the Fleet Air Arm, were putting on a series of brilliant productions—Chekov, Shakespeare, Sheridan —which were causing some of the more sanguine drama lovers to announce that a rebirth of the English theatre, too, was at hand.

Even H.M. Treasury could not remain wholly impervious to the spirit abroad in 1945: it now resolved to continue into the peace its financing of C.E.M.A., henceforth to enjoy institutional status as the Arts Council of Great Britain.

"I do not believe it is yet realised what an important thing has happened," rejoiced J. M. Keynes, in a B.B.C. broadcast. "State patronage of the Arts has crept in. . . ."

III

By August, when heavy bombers were pressed into service as transports, Servicemen on leave were pouring into London in their thousands. For many this was the first sight of England for four or five years, and there was much in the long-imagined scene that was strange. The railings had gone from the London squares. Great clumps of rose-bay willow-herb and yellow rag-wort grew over the bomb-sites. People paused on their way about the City to watch adventurous ducks which had alighted on static water tanks. And where Rennie's famous old Waterloo Bridge had been, the shallow white arches of a handsome new bridge—to be officially opened in December—skimmed across the river.

In some ways civilian and army life seemed surprisingly alike: the queues were different, that was all. One went into a Lyons and found that the Nippies with the little white starched aprons had vanished; one had to take a tray and get into line.

Or one found oneself at a trestle table in one of the communal feeding centres, the British Restaurants (there were five of them even in Bournemouth) which had been improvised in all sorts of buildings—an old Tube station, a millionaire's flat in Park Lane, a Turkish Bath, a warehouse, a museum, or in the peeling splendour of the Fishmongers' Hall.

Trains were dirty, jam-packed and hours late. They had no dining-cars, and the queues on the platforms for tea or "Bev" in chipped cups were enormously long. Shop windows were still boarded up; one had to look into them through peepholes. From the walls Mr. Chad still offered his ironic comments. People seemed shabby and tired and, although they had escaped all serious epidemics, their faces were set in serious lines.

If the returning soldier wanted to take out a girl-friend his difficulties became formidable. Taxis were all but unobtainable. If—it was a considerable if—he could find an unoccupied table in a restaurant he had to order from a menu whose items were starred, double-starred, and footnoted to indicate permissible permutations under the three-course 5s. meal limit order. The theatres still started at 6.30 and it wasn't easy to get tickets. Backers of plays were enjoying the usual wartime bonanza and with the help of trusted playwrights and well-tried formulas were establishing new long-run records all over the West End. *Arsenic and Old Lace* was in its third year at the Duchess Theatre; Terence Rattigan's *While the Sun Shines* was getting into its stride, and Noël Coward's *Blithe Spirit*—he had three productions concurrently running on the London stage—was going through its fourth year with undiminished *élan*. In August, Lupino Lane had successfully revived the breezy Cockney *Me and My Girl* at the Victoria Palace; Ivor Novello's *Perchance to Dream* was packing them in at the Hippodrome; at the London Casino, a relatively new comic star, Sid Field, was making a big hit as "Slasher Green", a Cockney "wide-boy"—the word "spiv" had not yet come into fashion—in a loud-checked waistcoat.

The country had the atmosphere of one huge transit camp. *Forever Amber*, 800 pages of Technicolor sex in period costume, still passed rapidly from hand to hand and was considered enormously daring. The staccato chatter of ITMA still rolled from the radios, and a million breakfast tables still vibrated with the gruff, rumbling tones of the Radio Doctor—not yet identified as Dr. Charles Hill and certainly not visualised as a Minister of Health—genially discoursing on the workings of the bowels or the care of carbuncles. Demobilisation had been started with a flourish in June, two weeks before Polling Day. But the "groups" coming out were Groups 1 to 3, men aged between thirty-eight and fifty. To the younger soldier unable, after repeated tracings of a finger along the age-and-length-of-service tables, to make his own group lower than 28, deliverance still seemed infinitely remote. And despite the mysterious workings of PYTHON, the War Office's much-boosted scheme for home leave after long-service overseas, "repat" seemed for many thousands hardly more real than "demob".

3. Chain Reaction

"This is the dawn of a new day and in the light of it we are going to march forward to those things of which we have dreamed for years past."
—George Isaacs, Minister of Labour.

"THE BOMB THAT HAS CHANGED THE WORLD"
—*Daily Express* front-page headline, 7th August, 1945.

I F IN retrospect Labour's triumph at the polls in 1945 appears as confirmation of change that had already largely taken place, Churchill's rejection then was nevertheless as decisive an event as Churchill's installation in 1940 had been. Both were resounding victories for social democracy, signally celebrating its onward march.

When on Wednesday, 1st August, the new House of Commons met for the first time to elect its Speaker, there were many on the packed Labour benches who were deeply conscious of being participants in a climactic moment in English history, the culmination of a process of political evolution and education stretching back to the great Reform Bill of 1832, the People's Charter and beyond. Fifty-three years after that other historic August afternoon, when Keir Hardie, defiantly wearing his working-man's cloth cap, had taken his seat in the House of Commons, the Labour Party had succeeded to the government of Great Britain, with a majority for the first time absolute and unchallengeable.

On both sides of the House the number of new faces was altogether exceptional, but on the Labour side in particular the transformation was spectacular. In the last Parliamentary Labour Party—numbering 164 against the present 393—half the members had been trade union-sponsored candidates and, despite its sprinkling of "intellectuals", the party had seemed as decisively working-class as tripe-and-onions.* The new party looked very different. The familiar veterans were still there, of course, Ernest Bevin, an ex-drayman, George Tomlinson, the former weaver who was to be Minister of Works, Herbert Morrison, a London policeman's son. But now beside these self-educated men who had made their way via chapel, trade union branch and town council, sat many Labour M.P.s of a very different sort—professional men, technicians, businessmen, many of them young. A check revealed 44 lawyers, 49 university and school teachers, 26 journalists, 15 doctors and dentists, 16 managers and technicians—150 white collar Members in all. The "middle class" Fabian Society could now have boasted—had it ever boasted—of having no fewer than 229 Members on the Labour benches in the House.

Some few were ambitious young men who had chosen Labour because the future now seemed to lie there. Others, like Hugh Gaitskell, the new Member for South Shields, while themselves public-school men from the comfortably-off middle class, had developed their position from the study of British economic and social history of the interwar years. There had always been a few such men in the Labour Party—the new Prime Minister (Haileybury and Oxford) was one of them. So was Dr. Dalton, the new Chancellor. But now they were being reinforced by the grammar school boys, men like the new Parliamentary Under-secretary at the Ministry of Works, Harold Wilson, products of the educational "ladder" set up between wars, stretching, still shakily, from the council schools to Oxford and Cambridge, where they had been able to fill out the Hammonds' 19th-century history-with-a-moral from their own and family experiences. In yet another way, Harold Wilson seemed to strike a distinctively postwar note: he was a professional economist. Able, adaptable, relatively classless, uniting in their persons the two streams that had come together to form the Labour

* In the 1945 Parliament trade union-sponsored members, made up 30 per cent of all Labour M.P.s. But, of these, only two-thirds were trade union or other paid officials. Though the miners' union representatives were, as usual, outstandingly strong: there were 39 of them.

Party, the "intellectual" and the "proletarian", the advent of such men seemed to signal a new stage in the politics of the Left as well as in the development of the nation.

The new tone of the party was echoed, distinctly but more faintly, by a new note in its electoral support. It was the suburbs as well as the soldiers that had put Labour in. A survey* suggested that about half the middle-class votes of 'Blackcoatia' and about one-third of those of 'Suburbia' had gone to Labour, which could not have won either without them. The "lower middle class" of "lower professionals and office-workers" had favoured the Labour side only a little less than the Conservative. Yet at deeper levels the old class gulf was preserved. For if the Parliamentary Party had a more middle-class face, it was the trade unions which had paid 80 per cent of the cost of its election, as it was the trade unions which wielded 80 per cent of the votes in the Party Conference.

Confusions were to arise from this curiously contrived and uneven partnership in the future as they had in the past. But on this first Wednesday in August, 1945, all were fraternally united in enjoyment of this moment of triumph and fulfilment. As their defeated leader, Winston Churchill, entered the Chamber, the Tory benches rose to their feet to roar: "For he's a jolly good fellow!" A counter-demonstration followed. Conducted by George Griffiths, the new Labour Members burst into the Red Flag, giving a spirited if slightly self-conscious rendering of two verses, before a smiling Speaker intervened to observe that he had been elected to preside over the House of Commons, not a musical show.

It was noticed that several Labour Ministers at first rose to sing, then apparently thought better of it, and sat down. In retrospect, their sense of the appropriate appears well founded. The Labour Party was the party of revolt; but what was being celebrated that afternoon was not revolt, but full establishment.

Yet, that August afternoon, with a thousand election perorations still echoing over the Labour benches, a certain revolutionary flush was understandable enough. Nor had it subsided two

* John Bonham, *The Middle Class Vote*, using Gallup Poll material. The same survey showed that the white-collar swing-back began between 1945-50 and that by 1951 the lower middles were voting 2:1 in favour of the Conservatives.

weeks later when the House met again to hear the King's speech. As they listened, rapt, to that sonorous roll of vast projects, that masterful design for the creation of a new Heaven and a new Earth, it seemed to many that, somehow, all they had fought for through so many long and weary years was at last about to be fulfilled. England had indeed arisen and the long, long night was o'er.

In fraternal co-operation with Soviet Russia—for "Left", as Ernest Bevin said, could surely "speak to Left in comradeship and confidence"—a regenerated, reconstructed Britain would lead a regenerated Socialist Europe firmly and steadily along the path to Peace and Plenty in this dawning age of the Common Man.

Few then were in the mood to pay overmuch heed to the clipped, dry voice of Clement Attlee warning of the "difficult years" that lay ahead. Yet within a matter of days—indeed of hours—events had occurred which made it clear that the Prime Minister had not over-stated the dangers, and that if this was indeed a new dawn, it was likely to be a chilly one.

II

The first of these events had already occurred between the first meeting of Parliament on 1st August and the State opening on the 15th. On Sunday, the 5th August, as the British enjoyed their Bank Holiday week-end, the first atomic bomb had fallen on Hiroshima.

"SMOKE HIDES CITY SIXTEEN HOURS AFTER SECRET WEAPON STRIKES". . . . In the *Daily Mail* the Science Editor carefully explained with the help of the paper's staff artist just what "nuclear fission" amounted to, what a "chain reaction" was and what President Truman had meant by his statement that "British and American scientists had harnessed the basic power of the Universe". An impressed reader wrote to a newspaper to suggest the new bomb be called "The Churchill".

A "chain reaction" of a somewhat different kind had, in fact, almost at once been set in motion.

Broadcasting at midnight on the 14th, the day before Parliament met to inaugurate the New Britain, Mr. Attlee announced the precipitate surrender of Japan. Next day was to be celebrated as "V.J. Day".

That night a hundred thousand people swayed and danced in Piccadilly circus to the music of six barrel organs. Searchlights swept the sky. At midnight a vast crowd gathered outside Buckingham Palace. There was a great surge of relief and joy that, at last, at last, it was all over.

On the same Bank Holiday on which President Truman had announced the dropping of the Bomb a meeting of British and American Treasury officials had been hurriedly summoned by John Maynard Keynes in London. Its purpose was to sketch plans for peacetime financial aid to replace wartime Lease-Lend on which Britain (drawing 25 per cent of her imports from America and 20 per cent from Canada) was utterly dependent. It was a few days too late. On the 19th, before a new arrangement could be improvised, Washington announced that with the cessation of hostilities all Lease-Lend Aid had terminated.

On the very morrow of victory, Britain's bankruptcy was starkly revealed. Her overseas investments were largely dissipated, almost half her merchant shipping at the bottom of the sea, the exports on which her existence depended shrunk to less than a third their prewar volume. A new debt of £3,000,000,000 to India, Egypt, and others hung around her neck to frustrate any efforts at recovery.

There was, it now appeared, scarcely enough cash on hand to ensure the next meal.

Only slightly less dismaying was the behaviour of Mr. Molotov, the Soviet Foreign Minister, who was astonishing his British and American colleagues by advancing a succession of unexpected and unyielding demands while consuming day after day in point-scoring procedural argument. At the beginning of October the Foreign Ministers' Conference which had met in London three weeks earlier to prepare the peace treaties finally collapsed in a welter of recrimination.

"Perhaps," reflected Ernest Bevin, "we were a little too close to two great victories." Perhaps in spring when the Foreign Ministers met again it would be different.

4. "Fair Shares"

"Grateful thanks to the Sacred Heart, Divine Infant of Prague, Our Lady of Perpetual Succour, St. Anne, St. Anthony, St. Jude, Little Flower, Holy Souls, for obtaining a house."

—Personal column, Newcastle *Evening Chronicle*, 1946.

As CHRISTMAS approached, the American Loan Agreement was debated at length in Parliament amid much wailing and gnashing of teeth. "We have sold the Empire for a packet of cigarettes," cried Robert Boothby. But most ordinary Britons just then were relieved to hear that the cigarettes, anyhow, were safe. "In a tobacconist's shop these days," reported a journalist, "it is bad manners to use the word 'cigarette'. You talk about THEY, you say 'Have THEY come in yet?'" Most tobacconists avoided such embarrassments by placing bold NO CIGARETTES signs at their doors. In some ways this first Christmas of peace promised to be a pretty dim one. Because of the danger of swamping the railways, leave had been severely restricted. In London bus conductors and clippies had made their own "No Standing" rules and there were many reports of brisk engagements with passengers. A wine merchant estimated that there would be a bottle of wine for every 200 applicants, but added that the shortage of bottles was such that they might have to take it away in jam-jars. In Trafalgar Square the children could be taken to admire a new feature of the London Christmas, a magnificent spruce newly arrived by ship from Norway, the gift of the Norwegian people. But filling the stockings was difficult. In one shop 200 surplus R.A.F. kites, price 24s. 6d., were sold in an hour; model planes used in training the Observer Corps, and ex-R.A.F. rubber dinghies, were bringing £5 each. The more desperate parents combed the second-hand shops. A pair of roller skates (prewar value

3s. 1d.) was bid up to £3 in an auction; for ladies a roll of parachute silk (two coupons) was understood to be highly acceptable.

Increasingly ominous stories of starvation in Europe were seeping through, but the Minister of Food, Sir Ben Smith, boldly casting himself in the part of British bulldog, refused to yield up any crumb of the island's meagre rations. And meagre they undoubtedly were. Many butchers, having issued the week's rations, shut down for five days each week. "The housewife, seeking food, has to acquire some of the attributes of the primitive hunter," announced the Ministry of Health's psychiatric medical inspector, Dr. E. A. Hamilton Pearson. For the successful huntress, an egg—one a month was the ration—might be the reward. Dried or "reconstituted" egg had become a central prop of the British cuisine: its threatened disappearance from time to time made front page headlines. In a Bath newspaper an embittered soul advertised: "Wanted: Egg-timer, sentimental reasons. Wanted: Egg, same reasons."

On 31st December, too late for Christmas, the first shipment of bananas to reach Britain for six years arrived at Avonmouth and was welcomed in a dockside ceremony by the Lord Mayor of Bristol. But for many months to come England was full of children who had never peeled a banana. There were many such odd, inconsequent, shortages, frustrating gaps in the familiar apparatus of life. There was no pepper; no elastic; vinegar mysteriously appeared and mysteriously vanished; and if there were piles of canned sardines on the shop shelves, it was merely because someone had neglected to provide the necessary openers.

The one thing the housewife did not lack was advice. The Ministry of Food, constituting itself a sort of universal aunt, poured out through the advertising columns of the newspapers an endless stream of Tips for Healthy Living. A typical advertisement, recommending salads as "Nature's Beauty Foods", told in picture strips the touching story of Sandra who was a "wallflower" ("He didn't even seem to see me") until she started gorging on lettuce, after which, a radiant figure bursting with vitality, she is seen in the final panel besieged by importunate admirers. "GREEN FOR GO!" urged the Ministry, driving the moral home.

Whatever the virtues of lettuce, many people yearned for sweet things—even for the sight of things that looked like sweet things. The empty slot machines gaped mockingly. Only the milk bars, their counters piled with highly coloured pastries, offered hope of relief—and the milk bars were jammed. They were springing up everywhere, particularly conspicuous among them those of a young member of an Anglo-Italian catering clan, named Charles Forte, who combated the postwar gloom and the dreariness of dirty mackintoshes by painting his milk bars in red-and-white stripes and dressing his counter girls in a red-and-white (freely adapted) "Puritan" costume. The old London tea-shops that had preserved a little of the "muffins-under-a-silver-cover" cosiness of the Victorian era had vanished from the scene for ever.

II

As the months went by more and more men passed through the Dispersal Centres and were to be seen, in battledress for the last time, waiting on station platforms or walking bemusedly through the streets carrying under their arms the large flat cardboard box which contained a "demob suit", a shirt, two collars, two pairs of socks and one of shoes, a pair of cuff-links, a tie and a hat. As they went off with their last Army ration of cigarettes on their paid Resettlement Leave (eight weeks with an extra day for every month of overseas service) each carried in his pocket a booklet directing him to the nearest of 400 Resettlement Offices, and detailing the steps he should take "in order to re-enter civil life".

It was a point on which few men felt that they required much instruction. Yet many were to discover unsuspected complications. Under the "Reinstatement in Civil Employment Act", provided he notified his old employer of his intention to return by the fifth Monday after his release, an ex-Serviceman was entitled to have his old job back. But five years had intervened. The former junior clerk sometimes returned a Wing Commander, accustomed to running an Air Station ten times the size of the firm. Some jobs had simply disappeared. Other men, demobbed in their early twenties, had never had a job nor

6. 16th August, 1945: Ministers of Britain's first majority Labour Government meet the King. (*From the left*) Herbert Morrison (Lord President of the Council), C. R. Attlee (Prime Minister), King George VI, Arthur Greenwood (Lord Privy Seal), Ernest Bevin (Foreign Secretary), A. V. Alexander (First Lord of the Admiralty).

7. "Genuine American nylons, lady! Only 35 bob!"—a hasty deal in Oxford Street.

Most things were short, but nothing was shorter than nylons. The Board of Trade might classify them as "non-essentials": women took a different view.

8. The Government announced that housing was to be treated as a "military operation". The Squatters had their own interpretation, descending in force on vacant flat blocks and camps. They are here seen holding out in luxury flats at Abbey Lodge, St. John's Wood, under siege by the police.

a chance to gain any professional or occupational training. Nor was this great human general-post confined to men and women from the Services. At the end of 1945 there were still 8,500,000 men and women awaiting release from the war factories; it was estimated that manufacturing industry would need to recruit 5,000,000 to restore exports to prewar levels. Here, as at so many other points, the authorities had learned much from the unfortunate experiences of the First World War. Despite the vast scale of the operation, redeployment proceeded comparatively smoothly. For Servicemen there were training schemes covering over twenty trades. Most ex-officers were only too ready to put aside rank with uniform and, with the help of the Appointments Offices of the Ministry of Labour, settle for some modest post with prospects. For the promising young man whose education had been interrupted by the war there was a free business training course, organised by Mr. Frederick Hooper, former managing director of Lewis's, the departmental store organisation. A sign of the times, this, a type of training largely new to Britain designed to produce the professional manager.

But to many it seemed that the great lottery of war had merely been succeeded by the great lottery of peace. House-hunting, flat-hunting, room-hunting, occupied a fantastic proportion of many peoples' lives and thoughts; in every quarter of London people were to be seen scrutinising the postcard advertisements pinned up on boards outside newsagents and sweet shops, making furtive notes on bits of paper. It took weeks to get an advertisement into the classified columns of the evening papers: *Dalton's Weekly*, a hitherto obscure sheet given up wholly to advertising, grew fabulously in size, each week vanishing from the bookstalls within minutes of its appearance.

Houses worth £1,000 in 1939 were now selling at more than four times that figure, and the "Agony" appeals of young couples waiting to marry were a regular feature of the advertisement boards outside the shops. If, by some miracle, they achieved both living space and privacy, setting up house was itself something of a feat. The system of "Utility" specifications for mass-produced furniture, available only to newly-weds or bombed-out families, against dockets, would ensure that the place could be decently furnished at reasonable cost. But delivery might take eight months, and many essential household articles were virtually unobtainable. As demobilisation gathered pace, the male clothing ration, too, became difficult to meet. A shirt of a particular size might involve a long search; to get it back from the laundry might take eight weeks.

III

Destruction on the late war's scale was something new in the experience of the English, hitherto safe behind their Moat. It was announced that re-housing was to be treated as a "military operation". Flying squads of building workers were being formed. The Royal Ordnance factories would turn out baths and other "bottle-neck" items. Meanwhile, on the cleared bomb-sites the colonies of "prefabs" visibly multiplied, odd stunted little boxes, yet—another sign of the times?—well designed and equipped with stainless steel "kitchen units" which were a vast improvement on anything most of their tenants had ever known before.

But the building industry with its innumerable small units was difficult to organise. As many thousands of war workers and evacuees drifted back to the cities the situation grew worse: by November it was estimated that a million and a half had come into London since the war. It was becoming evident that the figure of 758,000 new houses which the 1944 White Paper had said would be needed to give every family a separate dwelling had been very far short of the mark. It was at last being realised that nobody really knew the dimensions of this problem. Time as well as the Luftwaffe had taken its toll. Three million houses were over eighty years old—and there had been no housing census for seventeen years.

But the political philosophy of the Government was in many ways well matched to the war's long aftermath. The elaborate and now well-run-in system of controls—both quantitive and qualitative—that had been devised to meet the scarcities of war was continued firmly through the beleaguerment of peace. And despite Press and Opposition agitation, the public, by and large, appreciated its value and its necessity. The Utility Scheme, under Board of Trade supervision, by insisting on good simple design and specifying materials, had made it difficult to cover up shoddiness in furniture and clothing, in prewar fashion, with mouldings or trimmings. The points system, if it complicated housekeeping, had been an excellent school of social discipline. Rationing had started, not as in 1914-18 after the third year of war, but early in 1940, and by 1945 its advantages—when combined with subsidies to keep prices low —declared themselves. In the First World War the infant mortality rate, "the most sensitive index of a nation's health", had risen steadily; between 1941 and 1946 it had dropped 28 per cent.

Thus in the still potent name of "Fair Shares" licences could be—and were—denied for all but the most socially necessary building. Almost all new houses were built by local authorities for letting rather than by private builders* for sale to whoever could command the price. And as the new "accommodation units" came into existence the local authorities scrupulously allocated them through an elaborate "to-each-according-to-his-need" "points" scale of priorities.

To those who found that their "number would come up" in ten to fifteen years, the consciousness of "fair shares" remained, nevertheless, a distinctly limited consolation. Especially during that summer of 1946 when it rained everywhere and almost all the time. As month by month the frustrations mounted, as the returning soldier ran through his gratuity, and his dreams of "Civvy Street" were inexorably replaced by the civilian life of dreary reality, as the ex-W.A.A.F. wife peered into shop windows still dark because of the fuel shortage, collected her "egg allocation" or urged her husband to take the landlord before one of the new Furnished Rents Tribunals —as the relatively free-and-easy life of the Services was re-placed by existence in small crowded rooms with no prospect of relief—quiet desperation overflowed in one of those rare, spontaneous, yet often strangely orderly movements in which the English, pushed beyond endurance, take the law into their own hands.

* Theoretically, local authorities might license low-priced private enterprise houses for sale in the proportion of one to every four local authority houses built for letting. In practice in many places even this proportion was not attained.

The squatter movement—and the speed with which it spread across the country—took the Government by surprise. Like the 17th-century Diggers exerting the fundamental right of the People to the soil by turning over with their spades the squire's park, the Squatters proceeded with equal conviction and assurance to demonstrate an even more fundamental right by simply taking possession of the living space denied them. Pushing their babies and household goods in perambulators before them, from Durham to Widnes, from Sunderland to Salisbury, the squatter families broke down barriers and moved into old Service and Government camps, setting up homes in the Nissen huts. At Prestwieh one night urgent messages recalled R.A.F. men from dance halls and cinemas just in time to forestall a column of squatters about to move into their billets.

By early September, squatters had become, like spam, an accepted part of the life of the times. Then, suddenly, squatter news shot into the headlines again. With something of the old flair which had prompted them in the Thirties to move the unemployed into the Ritz, the Communists had taken over.

On Sunday, 8th September, 700 squatters, travelling by taxi, bus and train from all over Greater London, formed up at a prearranged rallying point, and then marched off through the rain to Kensington and Marylebone. Here they proceeded to occupy luxury flats, empty pending "rehabilitation" after Service occupation. Once inside, they elected "block committees", set up bedding depots, and generally prepared to resist a siege. Bread and milk were hauled up on strings. The electricity supply had been cut off and, as night came, candles and storm lamps glimmered in the high windows of the flat-blocks.

It remained a "revolution" with an unmistakably English flavour. "The policemen were most helpful," Mr. Lou Kenton, a Communist Party organiser, was quoted as observing. "They got the Army Service Corps to provide tea and told us to ring up the station if we were in difficulties." Several of the rightful tenants turned up and pointed out that they wanted the accommodation for their own families, so would the squatters please leave—and sometimes they did. The Press on the whole was sympathetic, though not failing to point out that this was

England, and that in the words of the popular song, "You can't-do-that-there-here".

Thus fortified, the Cabinet secured eviction orders in the Vacation Court; and after about ten days in enjoyment of this bizarre "luxury" most of the squatters, getting rather tired of the whole business—the Communists had recruited many of them by displaying advertisements for "unfurnished flats"— packed their pots and pans and children into their prams and quietly faded away.

Their gesture had not been wholly in vain. The true desperation of Britain's housing situation—the legacy of a century of neglect—had been vividly illuminated. The complacency of officialdom was shaken. The requisitioning of unused houses was pushed ahead. Local authorities took over hundreds of abandoned Service camps and put them in shape as temporary homes, and the Government launched a new drive to "get the roofs on".

IV

At the end of September, 1946, the War Crimes Tribunal at Nuremberg began to deliver its 80,000 word judgment. The trials which had now dragged on for almost a year had for the British public the piquant but short-lived interest of some grotesque charade. Hess's mad eyes, staring out from beneath the black brows, had flickered across the front pages. The "pale Ribbentrop" who, it was said, had once given the Nazi salute at Buckingham Palace, had been picked out with interest. And even in the dock, that old rogue Goering, it was noted with grudging admiration, retained his massive domineering presence. But the British newspaper reader had quickly wearied of this long-winded over-rhetorical drama and it was finally firmly relegated to the inside pages.

In this curious interregnum between the end of the war and the full resumption of "normal" living—the "phoney peace" to match the period of "phoney war"—there was much to occupy the attention of ordinary citizens without looking across the Channel. For women there was the feverish, unremitting and almost hopeless pursuit of "nylons"—the new synthetic, semi-miraculous fabric which had flashed around the world on the legs of U.S. Servicewomen. A rumour that a store had a consignment in would produce a queue several thousands strong outside its doors at 7 a.m. and the small stock would melt away in minutes. Although the grim international news and the Government's massive programme filled most of the four-page newspapers, room was still found for many a strange domestic item. In mid-March a strident body calling itself the Vigilantes' Action League, and alleged to be a cover for a resurrected British Union of Fascists, had taken the Albert Hall for a meeting. This was a fiasco. But fears continued to be expressed about a "recrudescence of Fascist activities", although, apart from being a social nuisance,* the minute groups concerned were mainly significant as psychiatric case-material. Meanwhile at Stevenage in Hertfordshire, old residents were up in arms at the proposal to turn their village into a "New Town", already christened "Silkingrad" by local wags, after the Minister of Town and Country Planning. Schoolmasters complained that the new ballpoint pens would be the ruination of good handwriting. And the newspapers hinted that the Government, confining them to four pages, ostensibly because of the "dollar gap", was in fact deliberately preventing them from performing their duty of informing the public.

Then, in the early autumn, newsprint control was eased a little—just in time to enable the papers to accommodate the full, instructive details of the trial of the psychopathic sex murderer, Neville Clevely Heath. An ex-Borstal boy, Heath had twice been commissioned in the Air Force (and twice cashiered). It was his custom to wear an R.A.F. tie and to affect that devil-may-care nonchalance which, in the popular imagination, was identified with the "RAF Type". His nails carefully manicured, his hair set in waves, he cultivated a casual, blue-eyed, slightly decadent charm. His characteristic costume was brown sports coat, flannels, suède shoes; his natural background the roadhouse *thé dansant*. When arrested, he was staying at the

* The social nuisance became more grave in the following year, 1947, when the British League of Ex-Servicemen and Women provoked almost weekly riots with its anti-Semitic meetings at Ridley Road in Dalston. Sir Oswald Mosley duly officially "returned" to head a new Union Movement in 1948, when the nuisance was abated by banning all demonstrations and processions in the East End.

Tollard Royal in Bournemouth under the name of "Group Captain Rupert Brooke". There was a flavour of the *Zeitgeist* about Heath, which perhaps accounted for the fascination exerted by the trial. It was the *Zeitgeist* of war's aftermath—but of the Twenties, perhaps, rather than of 1946. In the dock, at his trial, Heath kept up his jaunty man-of-the-world air. To his parents he wrote: "My only regret at leaving the world is that I have been damned unworthy of you both."

But not all the news was sordid or dispiriting. In the autumn there was the wonderful mirage of the "Britain Can Make It" exhibition, designed by a young Scottish architect, Basil Spence, to show off 6,000 products from 1,300 firms newly switched over from war work. It was the first big popular display organised by the new Council of Industrial Design established by the Government in 1944, and few debuts can have been so spectacularly successful. Queues of colour-starved Britons, six deep, wound around the Victoria and Albert Museum where the exhibition was staged, waiting patiently for a chance to feast their eyes on fabrics and materials that had come into existence since the war—and to read on almost every article the neat label: "FOR EXPORT ONLY."

And in the autumn, too, appeared the romantic question-mark so intriguingly and continuously visible to most of the female population on the island: Princess Elizabeth had been seen dancing with this young man; at the theatre with that.

Who was it to be?

And then, steadily, one name—a rumour originating in Monarchist circles in Greece as early as the autumn of 1945— had moved up to the front. In September, the London *Star* had boldly come out with it; the question now, it implied, was not who, but when.

Buckingham Palace issued a dignified denial, the first of many. Unabashed, the *Sunday Pictorial* conducted a poll of its readers: "Should Elizabeth marry Philip?" 62 per cent, it reported, were "for"; 32 per cent against.

The rumours multiplied. Lieut. Mountbatten's comings and goings from the Naval Petty Officers' School at Corsham, Wiltshire, where he was an instructor, were carefully charted. He was at Balmoral again: it was "on". No—they were not seeing each other, it was "off".

On 18th March, the *London Gazette* cryptically announced that Prince Philip of Greece and Denmark had been granted British nationality and would henceforth be known as Lieutenant Philip Mountbatten, R.N.

On 11th May the Royal Family returned from its South African tour. And then the contents bills proclaimed it: "THE RING." The *Daily Worker* alone dissenting, the Press voted it an ideal match. It was explained that although born in Corfu of Danish and Greek royal stock and thus nominally a "foreigner", "Mr. Mountbatten"—as *The Times* called him— had been to school in Britain and was "almost an Englishman". He could not, it was reassuringly pointed out, even speak Greek. Moreover, he was six feet one, almost incredibly handsome, had a breezy, friendly way with him, and looked very dashing in his naval uniform. There was hardly a woman in Britain who did not, once in a while, deliciously imagine herself in the shoes of the Princess.

5.   Third Force?

"Famine, like Peace, will be found to
be indivisible."

—John Strachey, Minister of Food,
   31st May, 1946, in House of
   Commons' debate foreshadowing
   bread-rationing.

"Particularly when the Labour Party
is in office, foreign policy becomes the
last refuge of Utopianism."

—Denis Healey, *New Fabian Essays,*
   1952.

"SOCIALISM CAME to Britain in giant strides yesterday,"
reported the *Daily Express*, detailing the plans which the
Government had just published for the nationalisation of
Cable and Wireless Ltd. and the setting up of the three State
airlines. The Bill to nationalise the Bank of England (BANK
BOOKS WILL STILL BE SECRET) had been introduced two days
earlier.

And the "giant strides" continued with a regularity that
seemed scarcely human. The "Beveridge" National Insurance
Bill, a monumental structure requiring two explanatory White
Papers, was closely followed by Dr. Dalton's Investment Control
Bill; five days later Emmanuel Shinwell moved the second
reading of the Coal Nationalisation Bill, a complex document
which attracted to itself no less than 400 amendments in twenty-
four days of debate. In March, 1946, came the text of the
National Health Service Bill; in April the New Towns Bill,
and in May—to remind M.P.s that Britain was in the throes of
a scientific as well as a political revolution—the Atomic Energy
Bill. At the same time the Minister of Supply, John Wilmot,
invited and received the approval of the House for the nationalisation of "parts of the steel industry".

Bleary-eyed and blue-jowled, M.P.s. sat through night after night. "Whatever Members' physical endurance—and many of them showed quite astonishing endurance," wrote *The Spectator*, "this kind of thing wears human beings out. The whole thing is completely inexcusable."

By June, nine months after the Labour Government's entering office, Mr. Attlee was able to hearten the faithful at the Party Conference at Bournemouth with the news that seventy-five Bills had been introduced and fifty-five had received the Royal Assent. "In previous Parliaments," he said, "any one of these would have been thought a full meal for a year."

The vast expansion of the sphere of Government that had taken place in the war years was now, it seemed, to be permanent. Activity in Whitehall was hardly less intense than at Westminster. There was a mighty drawing up of organisational charts as complex and far-reaching as Biblical genealogical tables. There was need for speed. For, far from being "doctrinaire"—as the Opposition alleged and the Socialist rank-and-file hoped—this nationalising activity was, in the main, an urgent salvage operation. In the capital-starved, semi-derelict mines and railways, the Government confronted —as in other areas of basic national capital equipment—an appalling mess, a collapsing patchwork of inadequate structures whose extraordinary self-defeating complexity derived from the interwar reluctance to interfere with private property rights.

Both in the coal mines and on the railways the problems had, in fact, been carried over from 1919 when there had been a failure to persist with the radical remedies the urgencies of war had enforced. But the Second World War, reinforced by the managerial and scientific revolution, had at last brought about the necessary change of climate. The Reid Committee, set up by the Coalition Government with a "capitalist" coal technician as chairman, had in March, 1945, recommended the root-and-branch reorganisation of coal-mining under "an Authority" to be established by Parliament. Nine months later, in December, 1945, the Heyworth Committee on the Gas Industry whose Chairman was also chairman of Unilever Ltd. was ready unequivocally to advise public ownership. After the vast expansion in demand of the war years electricity likewise clearly called for a radical approach: nationalisation had been recommended by the Scott Report in 1942. As for State aviation B.O.A.C. had been established in 1939* while if transport was to be co-ordinated, the nationalisation of long-distance road haulage was merely the logical consequence of the nationalisation of the railways.

The organisational model almost automatically chosen was the national board or corporation, so dear to the heart of the Webbs and much admired in the Thirties when Herbert Morrison had provided a bright and successful example in the London Passenger Transport Board and Sir John Reith reigned at the B.B.C. Whatever the wisdom of this choice, the task of simultaneously reorganising a succession of complex and nation-wide industries proceeded with remarkable smoothness and speed. The British Electricity Authority took over 550 independent undertakings, organising them under fourteen area boards, each with its system of districts, divisions and consultative councils. The Road Haulage Executive of the new British Transport Commission formed 3,000 firms into a thousand-odd depots and sub-depots.

The result was an impressive addition to the number of industrial monoliths, the creation—notably in the case of the mines and transport—of undertakings—and bureaucracies—which were amongst the very largest in the world. Obviously, it was easier to outline such towering structures than it was adequately to clothe them. Hence a certain bite in the Opposition jibe—"Jobs for the Boys". Yet the political fight against nationalisation remained curiously half-hearted. The Road Hauliers' campaign, the antics of a strange organisation known as the Housewives' League, nominally run by a suburban vicar's wife, the lament of the doctors, the continuous denigration of the Tory Press, might be irritating, but bore little resemblance to the expected sabotage of the social revolution by "Capitalists, Fascists and Vested Interests" which had been the subject of much feverish Socialist discussion in the Thirties.

Possibly the Conservative Party was still dazed from the knock-out at the polls, "the Capitalists" still punch-drunk from

* But the Coalition Government's "Swinton Plan" would have created, in place of B.E.A. and British South American Airways, two "private enterprise" companies run by consortiums of shipping and railway interests.

the war years when they had been "concentrated", "zoned", "sponsored", their raw materials bulk-purchased and allocated, their production standardised by Whitehall with the assistance of recruits from their own ranks. But the calm, it seemed, went deeper than that. The cool voice of the professional manager, of the business bureaucrat and committee man, was increasingly heard in the land. "We recognise that the control of industry is no longer a matter solely for its proprietors," conceded the President of the Federation of British Industries, Sir Clive Baillieu. "We want a broad area of agreement."

Meanwhile, could there really be much objection to the State buying out, at public expense, the owners of bankrupt railway companies and derelict mines? It was not until later, when Labour at last seemed to mean business about national-ising the modern and profitable iron and steel industry, and the even more profitable industrial assurance industry, that one was able to detect in the distance the rumble of Capitalism's heavy artillery.

But for the moment, with or without a satisfactory counter-revolution, Labour had no intention of being deprived of the emotional values attendant upon this moment of entry into the Promised Land. "The Treasury," announced Dr. Dalton, introducing his Budget—"with a song in my heart" —was "no longer to be a curb, but a spur". Jim Griffiths, a former miner, outlining his Ministry's National Insurance (Industrial Injuries) Bill, told of boyhood memories of buying a threepenny raffle ticket to purchase a peg-leg for a miner, mutilated in the pit. "It is insecurity that destroys," he cried with Welsh fervour. "It is fear of Tomorrow that paralyses the will. It is the frustration of human hopes that corrodes the soul!"

Even rationing was endowed in those months with the glow of high idealism. Thanks to school milk, Town Hall fruit juice, cod-liver oil and the wholesome National Loaf, English doctors, Dr. Edith Summerskill liked to point out, had to go abroad if they wished to study malnutrition. A Bill was introduced to make the wartime British Restaurants*—now to be renamed Civic Restaurants—a permanent feature of our towns. The

---

* This name was Churchill's, suggested as an improvement on "Communal Feeding Centres". "They may as well have the name if they cannot get anything else," he minuted.

Ministry of Food, citizens were assured, would also become a permanent national institution, eternally dedicated to the golden rule of "Fair Shares" and the building of a Better Britain.

II

The sabotage of the "New Britain", though it was to come from an unforeseen direction, nevertheless came. It came from without, rather than from within; and it was totally disinterested.

If indeed "Left could speak to Left", there were, it now seemed, nevertheless, certain acute difficulties of accent. What was developing in Europe and the Middle East seemed suspiciously like the old "power politics", as naked as ever.

In Persia, Russia was backing the "rebel" Azerbaijan republic. "What is the motive for wanting to get across our throats?" demanded Ernest Bevin, with his characteristic touch of truculence and Grand Guignol. From the Council of Foreign Ministers ("We have been here four weeks," growled Bevin in Moscow, "and we have done nothing") the scene shifted to the Security Council, clamant with charge and counter-charge over violations of Greece's frontiers; from the U.N. Atomic Energy Commission, deadlocked over the Baruch Plan for Atomic Disarmament to the acrimonious Peace Conference of the twenty-one nations.

This indeed was a new diplomacy—the diplomacy of public insult and verbal attrition, of open slanging matches, openly conducted.

Drought, storms and monsoon failure, coming on top of the dislocations of five years of war, had brought hunger and chaos to much of Europe. The newspapers carried pictures of hollow-eyed German children, of old people dying among the rubble heaps. As an Occupying Power, Britain could not avoid responsibility for the 24,000,000 Germans in her Zone. In May, to provide more grain for Europe, the Government brought in a smaller, darker loaf. Since this implied a cut in feeding stuffs it meant less poultry, bacon, eggs for the British.

But it was not till July that the true desperation of Europe's position was brought home by the rationing of bread in Britain. Bread-rationing had been avoided in both world wars. It carried overtones of catastrophe. The new Food Minister, John Strachey, was booed by the Master Bakers when he addressed them at the Central Hall. "Rebel vanmen," were reported to be threatening to stop deliveries if required to collect "B.U."'s (bread units).

Some newspapers reminded their readers of Belsen. Why should we deprive ourselves to feed the Germans, whining away again in their well-known Teutonic fashion? But that old-horse, though tentatively flogged, refused to run; the Morgenthau Plan for Germany's "pastoralisation", agreed in 1944, had been quietly forgotten by 1945; and Lord Vansittart gained small response to his elaborate arguments in pamphlets and innumerable letters to editors that the German race was inherently and irredeemably evil. Everybody was agreed, of course, that the "re-education" of the Germans must be pushed ahead; one must lose no time in eradicating their unfortunate militarism. But there was little hatred. Victor Gollancz's "Save Europe Now" crusade packed the Albert Hall and 60,000 individuals responded with offers to reduce their own rations to make up food parcels for the Germans.

Yet if, this time, there was no howl for revenge, the confusion of aim which seems inseparable from the aftermath of great wars was not avoided. The falling of what Mr. Churchill now called—in a phrase revived from 1920—"the iron curtain" across Europe had undercut all previous economic calculations which had been based on inter-zonal co-operation. Nevertheless, reparations on the Potsdam scale continued. Despite rioting in Hamburg, dismantling of the Bloem and Voss shipyards, on which thousands were dependent, continued. It was unthinkable that the Germans should ever again possess aviation or ships larger than fishing boats. In the Ruhr, too, Allied dismantling squads were engaged in removing German war—and incidentally industrial—capacity. British Cabinet Ministers were now hinting that the support of Germany was bankrupting us, yet we went steadily on making it progressively more difficult for the Germans to support themselves.

Nor was it in Germany alone that victory had exposed our nakedness. All through the summer weeks of 1946, Sir Wilfred Eady of the British Treasury had been out in Buenos Aires, trying, against the mounting exactions of the portly Señor Miranda to barter the British-owned railways there for the meat which before the war had been piled high in our cut-price butchers' shops. The Argentinos were eating their own meat now—and to give an extra twist to the lion's tail were claiming the Falkland Islands.

In 1939 it had still been possible to think in terms of Empire. Britain had put India, the "keystone of Imperial Defence", into the war without even consulting her; in 1942 the British Ambassador in Cairo had surrounded the Abdin Palace with armoured cars and presented the King of Egypt with an ultimatum. Under its heading "Old and True" *The Times* in 1941 had quoted the late Lord Lloyd: "The moral and material resources of the British Empire are virtually inexhaustible."

How remote all that seemed now.

In India, as the Constituent Assembly arranged by the British Cabinet Mission met, the Raj was going down in a hideous twilight of communal rioting, tramcar burning, acid-throwing through Bombay, Bengal and Bihar. In Burma, chaos seemed all but complete. In Egypt, negotiations for the renewal of the 1936 Anglo-Egyptian Treaty were again dead-locked. There were anti-British riots in Alexandria and Cairo.

But of all Britain's ordeals in these immediate postwar years her experience in Palestine was the most baffling and the most humiliating. For though continuing to bear the burden of the Mandate as we had since 1920, we no longer controlled the situation. The United States had been admitted to partnership without responsibility through the Anglo-U.S. Committee of Inquiry, and President Truman—who had the New York vote to consider—was insisting on a Jewish immigration rate of 100,000 a year. For many months British soldiers, civil servants and policemen, striving only to keep the peace and to reconcile the irreconcilable, had been shot at, blown up, kidnapped— and in one notorious case flogged—by the highly efficient terrorists of the Stern Gang and Irgun.

Wherever one looked about the world that year the *Pax Britannica*, which in the unconscious of many Britons was still almost a part of the order of Nature, was breaking up under one's eyes. Everywhere there was a sliding and loss of control.

By December the burden in Germany had become insupportable: the fusion of the British and U.S. Zones was announced. Two months later, Ernest Bevin informed Washington that Britain's economic position would no longer allow her to continue her financial and military support to Turkey and Greece.

Here, too, under the new-minted Truman Doctrine the Dollar and the G.I. were about to take over.

III

First the thought was voiced in private, then ruefully, persistently—almost masochistically—debated: Was it *Great* Britain any more? Could we still consider ourselves a First-Class —or even a Second-Class—Power?

According to prejudice and temperament, people responded to the situation in a variety of ways. But two responses were well marked, and characteristic of the time. For the loyal Conservative, it was easy: the scapegoat was to hand. The long decline in Britain's relative world position since the 19th century could still be ignored, the debilitation of the last six years could be forgotten. Even easier was it to shut one's eyes to the resurgence of Asia. The country had been brought to this sorry pass by one thing only—the pusillanimity of the Labour Government with its policy of "scuttle"—a phrase, significantly, which went back to Gordon and the loss of the Sudan. Given a "firm hand" as of yore, the helpless millions would still—in Churchill's words—"dwell in peace and justice and contentment under British rule".

Labour, equally, was able to turn events to the service of sentiment and prejudice. If, in the Cabinet, the reaction was orthodox enough—the continuing of peacetime conscription, the manufacture of the atom bomb—to some ardent spirits of the rank-and-file the loss of power appeared almost as a deliverance. When the Foreign Office had been thoroughly cleansed and democratised, the field would be clear for a "Socialist Foreign Policy" which would look to peoples rather than rulers, rely not on guns and gun-boats but on the force of moral leadership and example.

In these matters, it was felt, Britain had much that was uniquely valuable to offer. And she could start at once by offering it to Europe.

The rediscovery of Europe on which the British now embarked —though the stresses were variously placed—in fact spanned the political spectrum. Churchill, who became Chairman of an all-party committee to launch the United Europe campaign, placed the stress on the common heritage of spiritual values, seeing Europe with a characteristic robust historicism as a redoubt of Western civilisation against the barbarian hordes. Some Labour pundits, on the other hand, like G. D. H. Cole and R. H. S. Crossman, visualised a regenerated Europe as the core of a "Third Force", a zone of sanity, between the rival fanaticisms of Washington and Moscow, a haven of British-type Socialist Freedom-with-Planning. Some saw in Europe the answer to Britain's pressing balance-of-payments problem; others again, in an older vein of the Left-wing idealism, pointed to the absurdity of Europe's multiple frontiers, so obstructive of the Brotherhood of Man.

Yet for all the enthusiasm, it was to prove that—as usual on these European excursions—the British had taken a return ticket, short-dated at that. As the European Movement gathered momentum and the logically minded French began again to construct their federal constitutions, British insularity and British empiricism reasserted themselves. "To take a homely test," Winston Churchill, so lately the champion of European unity, was to tell a puzzled Assembly beneath the green-and-white "United Europe" flags at Strasbourg, "we may just as well see what the girl looks like before we marry her."

In fact—though they had gallantly averted their eyes during the arrangements—the British *had* seen. What the Conservatives saw, just across the Channel, was a drifting, unstable France, with a Communist Party mustering five million votes. What Labour had seen was a Germany in which, far from the basic industries having been socialised, as Ernest Bevin had promised, the outlines of American-style capitalism were daily more apparent.

Suddenly conscious of the fate so narrowly averted, Britain drew back amid the usual recriminations against Perfidious Albion. Henceforth, when any supra-national European authority was in question the return half of her ticket was openly displayed: her method was to send "observers".*

Yet for all her apparently permanent detachment Britain's involvement with the Continent grew deeper. The common dollar shortage dictated economic co-operation and in 1947 the Marshall Plan in whose formulation Ernest Bevin played a leading part provided a solid foundation. As Marshall Aid or "E.R.P."—the European Recovery Programme—gave birth to the Organisation for European Economic Co-operation, the European Payments Union, and a whole alphabetical armoury of European planning agencies,** the coming and going became routine and continuous.

Yet was there not, after all, a more satisfactory arena than Europe for the exercise of Britain's moral leadership, a firmer foundation for the building of the Third Force? If the curtain had fallen on the Empire, had it not risen again almost immediately to reveal the multi-racial Commonwealth—as striking evidence as could be wished of Britain's continuing political genius?

While in futile efforts to turn back the clock to 1939 the French and the Dutch struggled bitterly and endlessly in Indonesia and Indo-China with tragic wastage of energies and assets, the Labour Government—prepared by its philosophy to accommodate change in Asia as well as at home—was hurrying Pakistan, India, Ceylon and Burma along the final stage of the road to unconditional independence, enacted for all four in 1947-48. Whatever its immediate cost in India, this swift and decisive severing of the knots of Empire in Asia was an inestimable service to the nation, possibly the Labour Government's greatest. It was the first full and ungrudging acknowledgment of the true nature of the revolution in Asia and of the drastic changes in European attitudes it must imply.

* As, for instance, when M. Robert Schumann was struggling to build the European Coal and Steel Authority in 1950.
** The Treaty of Dunkirk concluded between Britain and France in March, 1947, widened out, bringing in the Netherlands, Belgium and Luxembourg via the Brussels Treaty for economic, social and cultural co-operation, and via Western Union for defence.

Because of this rare act of insight and statesmanship the name of Britain stood high through a vast area of the world at this time. Former rebels, released from jail, had become our firm supporters and friends. And if Burma did not join the Commonwealth, merely signing a treaty of friendship, here, too, as in the other new nations of the East, the "New Britain" of Clement Attlee and William Beveridge shone forth like a good deed in a naughty world.

For "progressives" at least it was thus not difficult to feel that—"Great Power" or not—Britain still disposed of a unique moral authority in the world, ideally qualifying her for the all-important role of holder of the balance between the—in the phrase of Mr. Konni Zilliacus—"two muscle-bound giants of East and West".

If no longer the hub of the world, we might still serve as its skilfully self-adjusting fulcrum.

6. Keeping Left

> "Sometimes we feel as if our destiny
> hangs on the decisions that come
> from a three-ring circus. Congress-
> men who have never given a morn-
> ing's serious thought to world problems
> may hurry to register votes that
> ruin half a continent. Columnists
> in search of a scoop casually blast the
> plans of half a dozen countries. Pri-
> vate feuds we in Europe know nothing
> about shape our lives."
>
> —J. B. Priestley in *Reynolds's News*.

WHILE THE role of Redresser of the Global Balance and far-sighted Marshal of the Third Force had its satisfactions, when one turned from the world power-conflict and looked inwards upon the domestic scene, the consequences were apt to be odd and even disconcerting. Through these years of Britain's "social revolution" the main topic—and polarising force—in British politics derived for long periods not from anything being done at home, but from attitudes to the policies and character of the U.S.A. and the U.S.S.R.

After America's isolationism in the Twenties and Thirties, the emergence of 1945 had about it something of the character of a fabulous sleight of hand. Quite suddenly, Americans in uniform and out, official and unofficial, were everywhere. In battered old Europe they had a fresh-minted, larger-than-life look which suggested an invasion not so much from another continent as from another planet.

Reactions were apt to be complex—especially inside the Left. When in November, 1946, during a Commons debate on foreign affairs an amendment was placed on the Order Paper deploring the Labour Government's "subservience" to the United States, no less than 100 Labour M.P.s signified their agreement by ostentatiously abstaining.

In the years that followed it was the Americans who were to

provide the main focus—a focus of frustration—for the residual radicalism of the Labour Party as the "anti-subserviens", challenging Dollar Imperialism, coalesced into the "Keep Left" group which in due course developed into that complex and elusive neurosis known as Bevanism.

The classic 1946 motion regretting the Government's "subservience" to the U.S.A. was counterpointed by equal and opposite regret at that same Government's failure to co-operate with the U.S.S.R. For despite Mr. Molotov's hard-bitten attitude and Soviet enthusiasm for the veto in the United Nations Security Council, the goodwill generated at Stalingrad had not yet been wholly dissipated. There were still many Britons who were prepared to make the allowances that had been recommended in the Army Bureau of Current Affairs pamphlet (No. 103A), *Portrait of an Ally*. "Next consider the differences in personal background", the Note for Officers conducting the session had suggested. "Few people should need reminding that a Soviet citizen in the forties would have lived through two invasions and a revolution. . . ." As for the disturbing news from the Balkans, the *New Statesman* now pointed out almost weekly that it was naïve to suppose that parliamentary democracy could have any meaning in those primitive feudal societies. A vast social and economic revolution was in progress out there, a new life dawning for the long-down-trodden common people: that was the thing to remember.

Nor should anyone find it surprising that Soviet Russia was anxious to have friendly governments along her vulnerable frontier. Had not Churchill, the old arch interventionist of 1919, already intervened with British troops in Greece in 1944 in support of "reactionary Monarchists"? And in March, 1946, at Fulton, Missouri, had not the same Churchill returned to the attack, calling for the military collaboration of the "English-speaking peoples" with the "joint use of bases all over the world" against the "growing challenge and peril [of Communism] to Christian civilisation"? A year later, under the Truman Doctrine for the "containment" of Communism the Americans had moved into Greece and Turkey.

That a Socialist Foreign Minister should support—indeed actively promote—such manœuvres seemed to many of Labour's rank-and-file frankly incomprehensible.

c

To complement its portrait of the Russian ally, the Army Bureau of Current Affairs had issued a companion pamphlet (No.102A), *America and the Future*. But few Britons were disposed to make the parallel allowances suggested for "our American cousins". For whereas Private Ivan was only seen, heroically, on the news-reels, "G.I. Joe" had been with us for many months and there had been times when morale sections of the British Army overseas had been more preoccupied with the effects of "Yanks" on the Home Front than with that of the "buzz-bombs". From Rainbow Corner to Yalta war experience had strikingly demonstrated the deadly accuracy of the old aphorism about being divided by our common language.

And when peace came the first great issue had been the American Loan. At the moment of victory, after a long and exhausting war which Britain had for a critical period sustained alone, the Loan debate mercilessly exposed the bitter facts of our ex-Imperial condition. To some it seemed to offer the alternatives of subjugation or starvation. At best the Loan appeared an over-sharp return to commercial practice. Not only had our American allies declined to make it interest-free as Lord Keynes had pleaded in Washington, but they had also insisted on attaching vastly hampering doctrinaire provisos insisting on non-discrimination, multilateralism and a grace period of only one year before the return to the convertible pound.

It was true that we had embraced the ideal of world free trade in the Atlantic Charter, accepted it in the Mutual Aid Agreement, and, in 1944, with a more dangerous particularity, in the arrangements agreed at the United Nations Monetary and Financial Conference at Bretton Woods. But whereas the Americans continued to inhabit this large and airy world, Britain was now hard up against the intractable realites of Europe. It was a classic source of New World-Old World friction and the emergence of America on the world stage merely exacerbated it. For as they pushed out everywhere with their astonishing wealth of equipment, the oilmen in the Middle East, the businessmen and administrators in Germany and Japan, the road-builders in Greece and Turkey, the "information officers" everywhere, the Americans showed themselves almost totally insensitive to the traditions, prejudices and complex situations of their new provinces. Within the narrow confines of Europe they continued to propagate the American Way of Life with the "hard-sell" loud-hailer approach attuned to their own open spaces. For the British there was perhaps a certain poetic justice in all this: if so, few fully appreciated it.

For Roosevelt the British had cherished an almost proprietary affection. But F.D.R. of "Destroyers for Britain" and the "Four Freedoms", F.D.R. with his heartening voice and generous smile (whatever lay behind it!) was dead. Now, through Britain's postwar years of trial came a steady flow of globe-girdling senators, often of phenomenal ignorance and inexperience, loudly demanding to know why Uncle Sam should go on pouring out his hard-earned dollars to underpin "Communism" and support in luxury the obviously work-shy British.* These gentlemen firmly pronounced Britain dead and done-with and on the whole appeared to consider the clearance salutary.

II

In Britain the debate about the true nature of Russian Communism was still on a largely academic level, illustrated possibly with references to Arthur Koestler's *The Yogi and the Commissar* (1945) or his earlier *Darkness at Noon*. *I Chose Freedom*, the revelations of Victor Kravchenko, a Soviet official who escaped from a Russian purchasing mission in New York, might sell millions in many countries, but in Britain still appeared too melodramatic for truth. It was as an "amusing satire" that George Orwell's savage attack on Soviet "democracy", *Animal Farm*, a best-seller in 1945, appealed to most British readers. Even the trial of Dr. Alan Nunn May, convicted at the

* Cf. the *Wall-Street Journal* on the pre-devaluation crisis of 1949: "The U.S. is financing a régime that shows itself determined to make a large part of the world conform to its own poverty-stricken standards." Or the full-page advertisements announcing a new Scripps-Howard newspaper series, by a "senior editor-reporter", after a six-week tour: "UTOPIA ON THE ROCKS: How Millions of Our Money have been Poured Down the Drain of Political Exploitation —How Crippling Taxes and Soaring Living Costs, Resulting from High Wages and Low Production are bringing the British People to their Knees. . . ."

Old Bailey in 1946 of scientific espionage for Russia, seemed little more than some strange freak, entirely failing to communicate any sense of alarm. The term 'crypto-Communist', though increasingly heard, still raised a smile.

Mr. Molotov's barracking of the Marshall Plan for European economic aid in Paris had, it was true, been disquieting, and Czechoslovakia's clearly reluctant withdrawal from the forthcoming feast at Russia's insistence even more so. But then if the United States aid was truly disinterested, why wasn't it dispensed through the United Nations? Might not the Marshall Plan be just another case of "Dollar Imperialism", of the same old dollar diplomacy which was now busy turning Germany into a Capitalist free-for-all and which had attached to the U.S. Loan conditions disastrous for Britain but favourable to American policies? "America has swung Right when the rest of the world is going Left," complained the authors of the pamphlet *Keep Left* in 1947.

In their relations with the British the Americans received the worst of both worlds. British Radicals and Labour men who would have responded to the Americans' democratic approach were alienated by their proselytising capitalism. British Tories, professedly sharing the Americans' faith in tough individualism, were smoulderingly resentful both of their failure to observe the public school code and of their native anti-Imperialism, the George III and the Redcoats' complex which the publication of the *Roosevelt Papers* was soon to show to be still far from dead. Though, in public, upper- and middle-class Tories would refer in the most ingratiating terms to the Anglo-American alliance, their private conversation was more than ever larded with veiled but well-understood sneers at these insufferable, cultureless, adolescent parvenus who had so monstrously succeeded to the proconsular positions they themselves had once held. They hated the Americans' guts in a way of which Labour was hardly capable—and with excellent reason, for events were to prove that the "American Way" was a more formidable underminer of the class and value system of the Raj than Mr. Attlee's Socialism could ever be.

On both sides of the House at this time the dilemma was apt to appear both cruel and inescapable. We couldn't live without the Americans and their Loan. Equally, we couldn't live with them.

III

Earlier in the 20th century, when certain niggling doubts
about Britain's dominant position in the world had begun to
appear, Sir Halford Mackinder had assisted them by "invent-
ing" the science of geopolitics. By the middle of the century it
was becoming clear that, over much of the world, for adequate
diagnosis and prognosis, the logic of geography would henceforth need to be complemented by the findings of national
psycho-analysis. Only psycho-geopolitics would suffice to explain, for instance, why the British, having in 1946–47 rediscovered Europe, unveiled the New Commonwealth, balanced
the U.S.A. and the U.S.S.R. in skilful equipose, suddenly once
again took up the Dark Continent.

Nobody, probably, could say just how or when it started,
but somehow the idea of Africa as a new Eldorado capable of
removing all Britain's nagging problems steadily grew until it
had all the sharpness and conviction of a collective hallu-
cination. "JUNGLE LANDS WILL GROW YOUR FOOD!" exclaimed
the *Daily Herald*. "Chance for Young Empire Builders",
pointed out the *Daily Express*. Leader-writers waxed lyrical
about "Britain's new garden in Africa", that vast empty land
that could so easily fill our gaping larders. Feature-writers flew
to Nairobi and came back with stories to rival Rider Haggard.
"Gold, diamonds, coal, lead, copper, phosphates and almost
every mineral known to man are to be found in East and Central
Africa if Britain wants to come and get 'em," wrote Graham
Stanford, presenting an "up-to-the-minute documentary" in
the *Mail*.

All parties shared in the rediscovery of the Dark Continent
as they had in the rediscovery of Europe. If the Conservatives
saw this new Africa as the beginning of a "Fourth Empire"
rising triumphantly on the ruins of the Third in the well-known
British tradition, Labour was now enthusiastically remodelling
the White Man's Burden (henceforth carried by fork-lifters)
on Socialist lines. The new evangel was most strikingly embodied in the Colonial Development Corporation, set up in
1944, whose most imagination-catching projects—such as an

£820,000 poultry farm (20 million eggs a year) for the Gambia —had Africa as their setting. "ROAD BACK TO PLENTY", proclaimed the *People*, quoting Lord Trefgarne, the C.D.C.'s Chairman: "Expect little for two or three years. But by then we should be really under way, employing hundreds of thousands of young workers in the colonies."

In this surge of optimism a few elementary but obstinate facts—agricultural, climatological, economic, sociological— were overlooked. These oversights, however, were to be brought sharply and memorably to public attention as a result of a roneo-ed memorandum which in the first days of April, 1946, was circulating around certain Ministries in Whitehall.

The author of the memorandum was a certain Mr. Frank Samuel, managing director of the United Africa Company, and it proposed the clearing of 2,555,000 acres of Central Africa, at a cost of £8,000,000, for the mechanised cultivation of *arachis hypogaea*, otherwise known as the groundnut.

Since the groundnut was an important source of fat and the meagre margarine ration was at that very moment about to be cut, the memorandum circulated with unusual speed. An expert mission was flown to Tanganyika to examine the practicability of the proposals. The following February it issued the document which became known as the Wakefield Report.

Five thousand square miles, equal to "the combined area of Hampshire, Surrey, Sussex and Kent", was to be cleared of bush and made into "the biggest Government mechanised farm in history". A hundred miles of new railways would be built. There would be new towns, schools, reservoirs, a new port. Not only would this great plan provide one-third of Britain's fat supply but, explained John Strachey, the African would be uplifted, too. "Each worker," announced the *Herald*, "will have his home and half acre of garden and will be encouraged to develop village crafts." Here, indeed, was a veritable "African TVA". The vision of the Bright New Africa, so lately conceived, was already about to be realised.

More than 100,000 British men and women applied to join what was soon being called the "Nut Army". And the scheme was indeed in the great pioneering tradition, carried through with the same sort of fanatical vision and faith that at a somewhat earlier date had carried *hevea braziliensis* from South America to Asia to turn the jungles of Malaya into one vast rubber plantation.

The price of such pioneering is always high. Events were soon to suggest that in the postwar condition of Britain and the world it might be unsupportable.

Launched under extreme difficulties, the venture was dogged by misfortunes and misjudgments from the start. Shipping was short. Rolling stock was scarce and supplies of tractors were inadequate. The beaches of the Philippines, Hawaii and Honolulu were combed for old bulldozers. When the machines at last arrived, the sunbaked ground broke their prongs. Tree-roots proved cruelly obstinate. Major-General Harrison, Mountbatten's Chief Engineer in Burma, who had been brought in to run the job, imported Sherman Mark III tanks. But Nature herself seemed to be conspiring against the pioneers. A prolonged drought attacked the few groundnuts (one-tenth of the acreage scheduled) that had actually been planted. Baboons dug others up.

The tragi-comic "Groundnut" serial story ran through the Forties and into the Fifties, a story of hope renewed and hope deferred, of Utopian visions and bitter realities, that seemed somehow to reflect—in a distorting mirror—the life of the British through those years.

In the spring of 1949, Mr. Strachey was still claiming that the "revenue of the scheme . . . may well add up to anything up to twice the original estimate". But soon the truth had to be faced. For the first season's planting 4,000 tons of groundnuts had been ordered as seed. By mid-1949, after two years of labour by thousands of men, the clearing of the jungle, the building of new settlements, the construction of railways and the expenditure of £25,000,000, 2,000 tons of groundnuts had been harvested.

In 1950 yet another "Working Party" reported. But more eloquent was a brief news-item that appeared later that year. It announced that "18,000 bottles of spirits surplus to requirements of the groundnut scheme" were being disposed of at Dar-es-Salaam. Nevertheless, in December, 1951, the prospect was still being described as "encouraging", though results in the Kongwa area were "disappointing".

Not indeed till 1953, when it was absorbed into the decent anonymity of "East African Industries Ltd.", was the last heard of the great Groundnut Scheme which was to have done such tremendous things for both Britain and Africa.

By that time the sum written off had reached £36,500,000.

Yet if *arachis hypogaea*—the peanut, monkeynut or groundnut —was to provide some of the deadliest political ammunition of the century, what this mainly proved was the extreme chanciness of political life. If the details went awry and the stresses were not always rightly placed, the larger idea behind the Groundnut Scheme was to become one of the key world themes of the future.

7. The Climate of Crisis sets in

"From today, Britain will be living on her wits."
—City Editor, Sunday newspaper, 21st August, 1948.

THE PROCESS of transferring two or three million British workers from the employment of the old Capitalist "Boss" to the service of "the People", an entity presumably benevolent but as yet insubstantial, continued.

"THE PEOPLE'S PITS: 11 a.m. is Deadline for Great Change-over", rejoiced the *Daily Herald* on 1st January, 1947, "vesting day" under the Coal Mines Act. Nowhere had the struggle of organised labour for recognition, decent conditions and pay been harder fought or more bitter than in the pits. If national-isation had been in the end technologically dictated, for the miners themselves it remained the fulfilment of a dream made all the more poignant by its long deferment.

The day, said Mr. Attlee, in a printed message delivered to every miner, "would be remembered as one of the great days in the industrial history of our country". From the Rhondda, a *Herald* man reported how, "an hour before dawn today, miners' wives took their children, some still asleep, and carried them, Welsh fashion in flannel sheets, up the starlit road to the Penallta Colliery to show them something they would remem-ber the rest of their lives. . . . They saw chains of 'glow-worms', hundreds of miners in steel helmets and pit-clothes, fathers, brothers, cousins, each carrying his lamp, winding out of the colliery yard. A band was playing under the shadow of a pit-shaft. The blue flag of the National Coal Board was hoisted and 'Bob' Silcox wearing a khaki battledress jacket, shouted into a microphone, 'Private enterprise has had it!'

"The valley rang with cheers.

"As the last of the night-shift reached the surface, Last Post was sounded.

"Then came reveille, and Sir Reade Godwin-Austen, Chairman of the South-West Regional Coal Board, passed under a 'Welcome' notice the miners had erected for him and told them that the future of the coal industry would be that of serving one another."

Even the *Daily Mail* could not remain impervious to the ozone of human brotherhood in the air that week, reporting a few days later that the "new team spirit" in the mines was "boosting output". Such a boost was badly needed, for coal, which had been dangerously short through the war years, still represented the greatest threat to Britain's recovery.

By the end of 1947 this recovery was in many ways striking. Four million men had been demobilised and settled in industry. Exports were running above the estimates and had already reached twice the 1938 figure by value. Whether by new construction, in prefabs or by repairs, 300,000 families had been housed.

But as the new householders switched on their electric fires, as factory output soared, neither the prewar power stations nor the coal supplies could meet the demand. Already before Christmas, a very seasonable one, there had been warning signs. Several cotton mills in Lancashire had shut down for lack of fuel.

On 20th December, the Birmingham Electricity Undertaking manager, drawing attention to his fast dwindling coal stocks, warned: "We are moving towards a national calamity."

In the curious bemusement of those days, few found it possible to believe him. If the feet were in the gutter the head was apt to be somewhere in the clouds. One day Lord Hyndley was promising the miners that the Five-Day Week would start in May; the next, the Austin Motor Company was shutting down for lack of coal, throwing 14,000 workers out of work. One day an unofficial strike of lorry-drivers was putting the meat ration in jeopardy; the next Sir Stafford Cripps was announcing a 50 per cent cut in coal for factories—a severe reduction on the Shinwell allocation programme, then only a fortnight old. The boom on the Stock Exchange went happily on.

In this advanced industrial society, it took the most primitive force of all, the weather, to introduce a note of realism. It had been getting colder for several days, and, on the 27th January, the thermometer suddenly plummeted. Villages were

9. The arrival of the New Look in Austerity Britain gave rise to astonishment and consternation.

10. As Britain shivered through the Fuel Crisis of February, 1947, East Enders (*above*) queued outside the local gasworks in hope of getting a little coke.

11. Despite nationalisation and the unions' new status, strikes of dockers, miners, transport workers often made black headlines. Twice (1950, *below*) the Labour Government ordered the troops on to the docks "to keep the rations moving".

reported "cut off in Arctic Britain"; the newspapers discovered that it was colder in Britain than Iceland.

But it was not till the 30th—the day before the Royal Family was due to board H.M.S. *Vanguard* for their South African tour —that the Elements were fairly launched upon what was to prove the most bitter and sustained assault the British Isles had known for half a century. Power-cuts were now long and total. Trams and electric trains stopped. The Riviera Express, slowly thrusting her way through the snowdrifts from Cornwall, was 8½ hours late. Reaching Paddington at last, her famished and shivering passengers ran to the refreshment room to be confronted by a notice: "No Tea, No Coffee, NO GAS!"

On the 5th February a blizzard with mile-a-minute winds swept over a vast area of the north. It cut Manchester off from Sheffield. It isolated scores of villages in Yorkshire. On the railways points were frozen solid. In many districts the miners could not get to their pits. A hundred and twenty-five colliers with fuel for London were stormbound in the Tyne.

The Ministry of Fuel and Power conceded that "a most serious situation had arisen". For "the next few days" no electricity could be supplied to any industrial user in London, south-eastern, midland, and north-western areas of Britain. In the home, electricity would be cut off for five hours a day.

If consumers did not co-operate "the country would find itself in a position of complete disaster within ten days".

Thus began for a large part of the nation a strange half-life that was to become part of the collective experience of post-Imperial Britain—cold breakfasts by candlelight, blacked-out streets (the lamps, at first half on, were finally wholly extinguished), motionless escalators at the Underground. At the office typists, muffled in overcoats and rugs, tried to operate machines with cold-numbed fingers. In the newspapers Home Page editresses explained the art of cooking by haybox "as Grandma used to do".

But as frozen day succeeded frozen day it seemed doubtful whether there would long be anything left to cook. The price of cauliflowers soared. Many shops ran out of dehydrated potatoes. Candles quickly became scarce, so women went to ecclesiastical shops and bought small altar candles. "Such candles," noted a newspaper helpfully, "are not blessed."

All eyes watched the thermometer for some sign of relief. None came. "COLDER! COLDER! COLDER!" cried the headlines on 1st March; and on 5th March "FREAK BLITZ NIGHT: FROZEN RAIN: TREE ICICLES."

The B.B.C. "did its bit" by suspending TV—not a great hardship since there were only 20,000 licence holders peering into miniscule screens. To save fuel the weekly magazines were forbidden to print; the dailies offered the hospitality of their columns to the weekly journals of opinion. At the Covent Garden Opera House, recently reopened, fashionable women, intent on reviving the grand tradition, shivered valiantly in evening dress.

"Do you want to see how a besieged city looks?" wrote the correspondent of *France-Soir*. "Then take a walk through Central London today. . . ."

There was, indeed, a chill in the air that was more than meteorological. Two million men and women had been thrown out of work by the closing of the factories. As the first of the sahibs and soldiers returned from Nehru's India, they found a Britain whose clocks were plastered over with strips of brown paper, whose fires were out, whose streets were dark, whose railway services were sketchy and uncertain. There was, for some, the sense of a once great nation running down.

Yet the reaction of the *Daily Express* was different from that of *France-Soir*. Wrote its leader-writers with characteristic Beaverbrookian verve: "Hard weather—well, what of it? Britain's climate, our foreign admirers—and we still have some of them —have always said, has helped to mould our national character. The Englishman is heir to the tradition of great deeds done in the worst weather."

And the old cliché about the British showing up best in adversity was, indeed, being vindicated once again. Railwaymen laboured long hours in appalling conditions to get the trucks moving. Miners volunteered for Sunday work. People, put on their honour not to switch on fires during the prohibited hours, complied on the whole with remarkable discipline. Cheerful improvisation was the order of the day. In Norwich a baker cooked in his ovens the Sunday dinner for a hundred households for a nominal charge of 3d. per house. At the

Rolls-Royce works at Crewe workers used car engines to generate emergency power. And, as in war, there was the inevitable, the ritual, snoot-cocking, note. Troops sent to help at the pitheads loaded coal on to Army lorries chalked all over with slogans: "MONTY'S BEVIN BOYS" . . . "YOU WANT IT—WE'VE GOT IT!"

II

And after the Great Freeze-up came the Great Flood. Rivers, from the Bristol Channel to the Wash, overflowed their banks, an assault on the senses that reached its Wagnerian crescendo on the 31st March when the River Wissey broke out, inundating a vast area of the Fens. In a wet and cheerless Easter, giant cranes were brought from Holland and naval landing craft assembled to fight the rising waters.

Had the British still been followers of the Old Testament they might surely have believed that Jehovah was resolved to chastise them for their lack of humility, their worship of false gods. And there was indeed a sense in which the Winter Crisis was, as the unfortunate Shinwell assured the House of Commons, a "blessing in disguise". Part of Britain had been living in the majestic Past, part dwelt in the splendid Future; the icy winds of February, cutting through the warm veils of illusion, recalled all sharply to the urgent needs of the Present.

That summer and autumn the British public was to become all too familiar with the language of economic beleaguerment, "the Battle of the Dollar Gap", the "Economic Dunkirk", "Equality of Sacrifice", "Austerity Now for Stability Later". The "Sterling Balances" were proving an ever-present threat to the precarious balance of payments, and the handy little word "cut" made now frequent appearances in the headlines. In March, to "cut" absenteeism mid-week football and greyhound racing were prohibited. In the Budget that year the tobacco duty was doubled. Two months later there was another round of "dollar import" cuts, including one in newsprint that brought a return to four-page papers.

The American Loan Agreement contained a clause inserted at the insistence of J. M. Keynes making it possible after consultation to postpone the date (15th July) fixed for the return to sterling convertibility. It was characteristic of the "Daltonian" "easy money" optimism of this period that no attempt was made to invoke it. The boast was that the Pound would, and the Pound could, "look the Dollar in the face".

The confrontation duly took place. Three weeks later a further round of "cuts" was briskly summed up in a headline across the *Daily Express* front page: QUARTER OFF THE MENU, and Mr. Attlee shocked the House of Commons with the news that the U.S. Loan—which had been expected to last till 1950—would run out that year.

Though irked by the "cuts", few people were disposed to lose much sleep over the nation's alleged plight. Factories were busy, jobs were superabundant, pay was rising. And it had turned out a glorious summer after all. On Saturday, 20th August, most Britons were sprawling in deck chairs in parks or gardens, lying beside the rivers, or on the beaches, thawing out the last of the February ice. Or they were using their painfully accumulated petrol ration to take out their cars for the week-end. In any case, the "Problem of the Dollar Gap" did not figure prominently in their thoughts.

At 9.15 that night Dr. Dalton, the Chancellor, went on the air in a surprise broadcast. The run on the pound by foreigners eager to convert into dollars had reached frightening proportions. From midnight—five weeks after it had been introduced —convertibility would be suspended. The doctor concluded on a characteristic note of pontifical but ominous benevolence: "God bless you all and your families. Get all you can of happiness and health and strength out of the sea and the sun and the fresh air and then go all out in a great effort to help our country."

It was about this time that the cartoonist Giles introduced to his readers the "Crisis Family" whose multiple frustrations he would henceforth depict. His timing was excellent: the climate of crisis was about to set in.

III

For it was not only in domestic affairs that the cocoon of illusion was now torn open. As Britain shivered through January, 1947, Mr. Mikolajczyk, leader of the London Poles, was protesting from Warsaw that scores of Peasant Party candidates in the forthcoming elections had been terrorised or murdered. All attempts to send independent observers to these first "free elections"—as agreed at Yalta and Potsdam—had been blocked. In May, M. Ferenc Nagy, the Hungarian Prime Minister and secretary-general of the Smallholders's Party, resigned after "confessing his guilt"; in September Nikola Petkov, the Bulgarian Agrarian leader whose party, despite all pressures, had won one-third of the votes at the elections, had been hanged in Sofia after another "confession". From Rumania it was reported that the veteran Peasant Party leader, Juliu Maniu, had been put on trial. At the same time, fierce dock and transport strikes—obviously centrally directed and aimed at preventing the distribution of relief grain under the Marshall Plan—had erupted in France and Italy.

Even in Britain the "cold war" was no longer a merely rhetorical expression. There were still many, however, who were reluctant to accept its inevitability and the "Keep Lefters" continued to plead for an understanding, non-provocative, approach to Russia. In Europe thousands might be living in daily consciousness of the Soviet tanks and divisions massed so few miles away, ready to roll across the open plain. But behind the British Moat such notions were still apt to appear melodramatic. Despite the Bikini tests, and the 200,000 dead in nine seconds at Hiroshima, the atom bomb still entered the consciousness of many mainly as a bright new objective— the "Atomic" dry-cleaners, "Atomic" hair-restorer, even "Atomic" pudding. In the face of militant Russian Communism and militant American Capitalism, many Britons were inclined—with a strange echo of America before the war—to reject "all foreign-isms".

And then, at the end of February, 1948, came an event which changed the whole climate overnight.

Czechoslovakia could not be dismissed as merely another primitive Balkan State. Created at Versailles in 1919, modern-minded and energetic, a synthesis of East and West, by her mere continuing existence under the presidency of the re-assuringly familiar Dr. Beneš, Czechoslovakia had seemed— despite everything—to hold out hope for the future of a Europe organised on Western liberal principles.

And then, in two days in Prague, in a *coup*, swift and expert—and all the more horrifying for its comparative lack of violence—the iron curtain had come clanging down here also.

With the discovery, shortly afterwards, of the body of the Czech Foreign Minister, the jovial Jan Masyryk, so well known in London, spreadeagled beneath his window in the Czernin Palace, the phantasmagoria of ideological war came stealing at last over the neat privet hedges of England.

Even "British common sense" now seemed powerless. The maps of Europe, half white, half black, studded with small flags indicating numbers of divisions now became almost daily feature of the newspapers. The cold war, we were warned, might last for years: we must learn to live with it. This, this state of cataclysmic suspense, must henceforth be considered normality; this *was* the peace we had been waiting for.

Everywhere now the lines were hardening. In May the twenty-one Labour M.P.s who had sent a well-wishing telegram to the veteran Italian Socialist, Pietro Nenni, then fighting an election in alliance with the Communists, were carpeted by the Party Executive. Konni Zilliacus and one or two others who refused to repent were expelled. In November the T.U.C. issued its "Defend Democracy" statement, urging unions to stop Communists filling key positions or acting as delegates. Arthur Horner, the Miners' Communist secretary, who had pledged N.U.M. support for the French miners' strike, was repudiated by his Executive. By 1949 the World Federation of Trade Unions, created in 1945, was splitting. There was little room for idiosyncratic opinion, for "Third Forcers" or "Keep Lefters" now. Insensibly, all thinking, almost all published writing, was being forced into the single mould of "East" or "West". Everything started out from the same, narrow, curiously distorted, set of "givens".

In June, Tito was expelled from the Cominform. All pretence of Four Power co-operation in the Berlin Control Council was given up. Road and rail communication from the West to Berlin across the Soviet Zone had been suspended from time to time in the mounting "war of nerves". Now it was finally severed.

Already in experimental operation, the Anglo-American "Air Bridge" was stepped up to full strength.

As the R.A.F. Wellingtons, the American Globemasters, landed, minute by minute, with their loads of coal and flour, victualling the beleaguered city, all Europe watched as in a nightmare this strange and desperate struggle at its heart.

England watched with them. For months past local authorities had been carting away the rusting Anderson air-raid shelters from the bottoms of back gardens, demolishing the ugly brick shelters which still obstructed many a street corner.

In October, 1948, they received a communication from the Home Office which called a halt to the removals.

8. The Manager

"Targetology . . . at precisely what stage the word 'target' infiltrated under the cover of the more noticeably luxuriant verbiage to seize the commanding position which it now holds probably none can say for certain."
—Leader in *The Times*.

"10 Per Cent More Will Turn the Tide."
—Government advertisement, 1949.

THE TIME had gone now for the doctrinaire unction of a Dr. Dalton; in our small, overcrowded island for ever poised on the brink of crisis, the traditional class 'militancy" of a Shinwell seemed increasingly wide of the mark. Through the dismal weeks of that cold-numbed February of 1947, a new name, that of the President of the Board of Trade, Sir Stafford Cripps, had been steadily moving to the fore; in early October, Cripps was appointed to the newly created co-ordinating post of Minister of Economic Affairs; in November, by the fortunate chance of the minor pre-Budget indiscretion that led to Dr. Dalton's resignation, he succeeded to the Chancellorship and thus gathered into his hands all the financial and economic controls of the nation.

In domestic, as well as in foreign, affairs, a new note of realism now began to be heard. A new political terminology was coming into being. Politicians began to speak of " the public sector" and "the private sector": whatever the Nationalising Acts had created, it began to be realised, it had not been "Socialism". If the public sector had been enlarged—and now gave occupation to nearly one-quarter of all in civil employment—the private sector was much larger and still crucial. The "New Britain" was not, after all, the New Jerusalem, but the "mixed society"; the Socialist Government's function not to abolish the profit motive but to guide Labour and Capital in double harness in their mutual interest—no easy feat, considering that Socialism had so long nourished—and been nourished by— the belief that no such mutual interest either existed or could exist.

To the complex and curious structure of Socialist ideology and symbolism in England was now added a new feature at once simple and bizarre, the Theory of the Cake. Why, Ministers tirelessly—and rhetorically—asked, should capitalist and worker waste time squabbling over the size of each other's slices? It was, after all, really so simple. Let them just concentrate on making a *bigger* cake—then *everybody* would have a larger slice.

But of course, the cake—the gift of J. M. Keynes—must be *planned*: and that clearly was the task of the Government, now the greatest single participant in the economic affairs of the nation, and, under the Keynesian canon, maker of the economic climate.

As a Party shibboleth, "Planning" was now progressively moving up into the place formerly occupied by that older panacea, "the common ownership of the means of production, distribution and exchange". During the war years—with energetic assistance from Keynes himself*—Keynesian ideas had permeated the Treasury. A number of economists had been brought into the Civil Service from the universities. The War Cabinet had acquired an Economic Section and a new Central Statistical Office had calculated, among other things, the National Income. In the matter of food production and import, labour deployment, munition manufacture, agriculture and land use, central control had become indispensable. A Government Social Survey had been set up to work with the Departments. With the minimum necessary data and machinery at last available—and the relatively clear objectives of wartime— overall planning had for the first time been seriously attempted.

Cripps built on these foundations. At an earlier stage, a central joint planning staff had been established with Sir Edwin

* He guided for instance, the Mutual Aid Agreement and inspired the anti-inflationary device of "deferred payments", euphemised into "Postwar Credits".

Plowden as Chief Planning Officer. Now export targets were allocated to each industry, and to all industry. The list covered 153 items or groups of items. The ether and the headlines became congested with statistics of O.P.M.H. (Output Per Man Hour), percentage productivity increases, economic White Papers and surveys.

What appeared to be the characteristic organs of this new Planned Mixed Society now began to emerge. There were the "Working Parties", set up to run the modernising rule over cotton, furniture, pottery, hosiery, and thirteen other old British industries ("to help them to win through to *real* efficiency," as Sir Stafford briskly informed their directors); the Development Councils* which were planned to arise out of the Working Parties; the Anglo-U.S. Productivity Council founded in August, 1948, and its satellites; the National Production Advisory Council, the Regional Boards of Industry, and, on the lower levels, the many joint production councils, and productivity, consultative, and works' committees.

In form this was little more than the "Tripartitism" which had developed in both world wars, and which had continued fitfully as "Whitleyism" after the first one. But whereas Whitleyism in the Twenties had lacked conviction, now with Labour in power and Keynesianism and "economic planning" accepted (and demonstrated both in the war and in the American New Deal) Tripartite organisation quickly came to seem almost a part of the natural order of things.

Yet such success as it enjoyed and the rapidity with which it became established owed much also to the unique combination of qualities possessed by Cripps himself. As an earnest Churchman who had been brought to Socialism by a desire to translate the precepts of Christianity into daily life, he was able to give these rather pedestrian arrangements an aura of moral purpose which almost made them seem a part of "Socialism's" great design. A brilliant advocate, with unusual powers of assimilation and of exposition, he was able to hold the "sides" together

---

* These Statutory Development Councils, however, proved a disappointment. Owing to opposition from industrialists, now apparently getting their second wind, it was only possible to get them established for four industries, including Cotton where little more than a change of name was involved.

by the sheer cogency of the case he presented. As a young man he had trained as a scientist under Sir William Ramsey, and this—and industrial experience in both world wars—had given him a grasp of technology, rare indeed in English politics, which well fitted him for the central role in the advancing managerial society.

Flanked by his young economists, Cripps travelled incessantly, conferring with trade union leaders, exhorting industrialists in some provincial city, constructing and co-ordinating the plans necessary for the due attainment of each target. Probably never before in modern British history had a single individual in time of peace exerted a direct effect on such a diversity of individuals. The newspapers were full of anecdotes about this new Socialist superman—how he would rise at 4.30 a.m., hold a conference of officials each morning on the stroke of nine, work fourteen hours and more per day. Civil servants were reported dazed by the speed with which the powerful brain digested papers. The newpapers printed photographs, arrowed and labelled, of the Spartan Crippsian lunchtray: the shredded carrot, the cheese, the apples, the walnuts and almonds, the brown bread and butter.

It was, we were told, "the Cripps Era". "Sir Stafford Cripps," wrote the *Daily Mail*, typically, "made a speech designed to revolutionise the age-old economy of Britain."

Cripps' leadership was indeed accepted with gratitude by people of all parties. He brought a stirring in many long stagnant places; a clearing away of a good many mental—and physical —cobwebs and an unprecedented degree of co-operation between obstinate individualists in the common interest—most notably perhaps when he succeeded in persuading both employers and trade unions of the necessity of a prolonged standstill on dividends and wages.

II

Despite the blinding clarity of Stafford Cripps' exposition, the reign of Reason remained somewhat less than universal. If, on the highest levels, trade unions, major industrialists and Whitehall could work—somewhat sketchily—together, their decisions remained dependent for their execution on thousands of ordinary unregenerated bosses, millions of normal, obstinate, unconverted workers. If the bosses could often be rendered amenable by Whitehall's control of licences and many sorts of scarce materials, the co-operation of the workers was less easily secured. Despite the acute and visible need, "voluntary absenteeism" in the coal mines was running at almost twice the prewar level. Houses, too, were being built more slowly than before the war. Bricklaying statistics were solemnly and endlessly bandied about, proving, it was said, that the "British working man" was no longer giving a "fair day's work for a fair day's pay".

Economists, publicists, miscellaneous self-appointed experts, tirelessly debated what was called "The Problem of Incentives". The miners already had higher pay and the five-day week. A monetary incentive bonus system had at last been introduced in building. But in a heavily rationed island extra money in the pocket was apt to have a hollow ring. Furthermore, as consumers a large part of the British working class still appeared heavily circumscribed by class tradition. The miners, in particular, isolated in bleak pit villages in their "rows" of free or low-rent cottages with few or no "mod. cons", were hardly ready for full membership of an acquisitive society. Endeavouring to discover, in the late Forties, just what miners would do with more pay if they had it, Ferdynand Zweig could find no objects of further expenditure beyond drink, tobacco and gambling—and further indulgence in these was not worth the extra effort.

At the same time, full employment meant that in the unlikely event of anyone getting the sack there was always another job, possibly at better pay, just around the corner. Socialism and the Welfare State, concluded the *Economist*, coining a phrase that was to be repeated *ad nauseam*, had taken away both "the stick and the carrot".

How then to make sure of all the Crippsian "targets"? Even if the workers worked hard and long, how induce enough of them to enter the "undermanned industries"—cotton, coal, iron-founding, farming—on which the precarious balance of trade now depended?

"A Wages Policy", Labour intellectuals never tired of pointing out, was the obvious answer.

But, apart from many other difficulties, a "wages policy" was precluded by the trade unions' fears for their independence. Economic planning thus remained, in the jargon of the subject, "permissive" rather than "positive".

It was not enough. In the grim circumstances of the autumn of 1947 as the basic petrol ration was abolished (and with it all pleasure motoring) and the foreign travel allowance was wiped out, Direction of Labour—without precedent in time of peace—was brought in.

The incentives now would be—as the headlines put it—"£100 Fine or Three Months Jail"—awardable to workers refusing to do the Ministry of Labour's bidding.

Was British Socialism, then, about to take the "Road to Serfdom"—that "inevitable" path which, with Continental logic, Professor F. A. Hayek had predicted for it in 1945, in a celebrated book of that title?

There were few signs of it. The planners, having made their gesture, seemed content. Direction, the Minister apologetically promised, would be used "sparingly, courteously and decently". It would apply only to workers changing jobs and these would always be offered several alternatives in their own line. It was, concluded the *News Chronicle*, after some weeks of it, "demure direction". And before long the whole episode had sunk into oblivion, a curious and characteristic footnote to the history of the times, the high-water mark which the incoming tide of Planning touched briefly before ebbing in the years that followed, though never again to retreat completely into the old anarchic British sea.

So the "problem of incentives" remained—and with it the problem of how to create Mr. Attlee's "system of a new and challenging kind" which should "combine individual freedom and social justice".

Once again the groping search for a social dynamic led back to the war years. General Montgomery had put the troops "in the picture" in war. So why should not Sir Stafford Cripps now put the citizens "in the picture" in peace?

Using an expository technique similar to that developed in the war by the Army Bureau of Current Affairs the annual

White Papers on the economic state of the nation were now translated into eye-catching sixpenny editions with "animated" statistics, photographs and parables. Within the staid confines of the Treasury was set up a central Economic Information Unit under S. C. Leslie, an Australian professor-turned-publicist who had distinguished himself by creating that genial sprite, "Mr. Therm", for the Gas Light & Coke Company. The fact that Leslie's salary, £3,500 a year, was equalled in Whitehall at that time only by the Head of the Civil Service came in for a good deal of Press comment and did indeed shed an interesting light on the changing priorities of a developing social democracy.

Cripps' fortnightly Press conference was now complemented by a "Report to the Nation" appearing regularly in the advertising columns of the newspapers. "RECORD OUTPUT—but Problem of World Prices", Report No. 5 was encouragingly headed. There was a "Report to the Women of the Nation" in the women's magazines; broadsheets went to 18,000 factories, and a series of exhibitions succeeded in attracting large crowds. One, called "On Our Way", included "Learnalot's Mammoth Amusements", with comic distorting mirrors making points about exports and imports.

As Sir Stafford Cripps' "productivity drive" got under way the flow of "pep-talk" leaflets, "putting-you-in-the-picture" advertisements and posters became a flood. "What good will Productivity do *me*?" a typical leaflet asked, and answered itself with professional fluency: "Most people agree with the general idea of using your head to save your hands and feet— and that's what increasing Productivity really amounts to. . . ." Below, a small drawing of a housewife putting something into an oven rammed the point home. "By cooking two courses in the oven at the same time you increase Productivity in the home."

On one side of the "Report to the Nation" appeared a "Credit Column", itemising meritorious achievement by named workshops and workers. Now and again there would appear something very like a "Stakhanovite". A certain Glamorganshire miner, Ted Greenslade, "the £30 a Week Miner", was much photographed and starred in advertisements after "hewing 120 tons of coal in six consecutive shifts". In the same spirit of "Socialist emulation" the N.C.B. spent thousands of pounds on purchasing flags to be run up in triumph at pit-heads when the miners there "surpassed their target".

Amateur publicists felt it their duty to "tell the People", too, and a day rarely went by without some national or local figure explaining with a condescension due to infants that we were "living on tick", suffering from "too much money chasing too few goods", and must bake a "larger cake".

Described by Cripps as "a fundamental part of our great experiment", this new departure in the art—or science—of democratic government in Britain enjoyed a limited success.* But its main effect perhaps was to underline once again the profound difference between being "Up Against It"—as the Treasury's posters had it—in peace, and up against it in war; between an "economic Dunkirk" and the real one.

And whereas in war "defeatists" and dissidents were easily contained ("creating alarm and despondency"), in 1948 Governmental efforts at "putting you in the picture" might appear alongside bold editorial declarations that "planned poverty" was "leaping ahead". The *Daily Mail* greeted the suspension of the foreign travel allowance with the declaration that Britain was being turned into "a concentration camp" overnight, and, when the Government, as it increasingly had since the war, used social surveys to provide an accurate foundation for planning, the *Daily Express* warned its readers: "SNOOPERS (17 Kinds) MAY CALL."

III

And still it seemed that almost every week brought its black load of "cuts"—"lashings" as the newspapers now ecstatically called them—cuts in sugar, and cuts in tobacco, and cuts in house-building, and cuts in factory-building. . . . In hotels ration-books now had to be surrendered after two days instead of four; the profits tax had been doubled at a blow; purchase taxes raised all round; a tax clamped on the pools and tote-betting at "the dogs". With the enthusiastic assistance of the

* For instance a Government report in 1948 claimed that cotton industry recruitment had been notably aided.

cartoonists, the stern unbending figure of Sir Stafford Cripps, "Britain's Economic Dictator", loomed daily larger, thick eyebrows arched in remonstrance, arms raised in exhortation, the Prophet of Austerity Now for Better Times Later.

Nevertheless, by the spring of 1949, it had begun to look as if the planners' discipline was working. In February the Economic Survey showed our external trade account balanced at last, with exports running at record levels, though the "dollar gap" was not yet closed. Then, in March Mr. Harold Wilson was photographed tearing up his clothing ration book; in April, men, women and children made a dive for the chocolate kiosks as sweets were "freed" at last. Sweets consumption, in those first derationed weeks, was reported to be running at 7s. a head; adults wrote to the papers complaining that children were hogging supplies. One child riposted, also in the correspondence columns, that, on the contrary, it was the sweet-crazed adults who were storming the shops. The charge received circumstantial support from a reporter who described how, "at one stall, a mustachioed major ordered four Mars bars, gravely tucked them into a folded copy of the *Sunday Times* and marched away".

And then—as if no one and nothing could stop it—the all too familiar pattern reasserted itself.

Stocks slipping on Wall-Street . . . in London a slide in Gilt Edged . . . in Europe, a whispering campaign against the pound . . . the gold and dollar reserves melting away . . . a heavy wave of selling in the City. . . .

In July, another dollar standstill—and a new round of cuts. And one more hurried flight to Washington.

Sweets, having disappeared "under the counter" went back on the ration. But that summer record numbers of people did manage to get abroad. In mid-September thousands of these were enjoying their brief escape from Austerity in various parts of Western Europe when suddenly they found themselves stranded and penniless. The banks had closed against them. The money-changers refused their pounds. The British devaluation—from 4·03 dollars to 2·8 dollars to the £—much more drastic than had been foreseen—had thrown Europe into turmoil. In Brussels, British tourists queued for hours outside the banks; from Rome they were reported to be selling gold watches; in Geneva a holiday-maker approached a resident and offered to sell him three pairs of silk socks.

While at home a mixed bag of moralists debated in the *Manchester Guardian*—a correspondence initiated by a critical Bishop of Carlisle—whether Sir Stafford Cripps' repeated denials of an intention to devalue had, or had not, been a "necessary untruth", Mr. Attlee was quietly going before Parliament with yet another round of "cuts".

This, he told the House gravely, might be the last opportunity of restoring the country's position as a trading nation without a drastic lowering of the standard of living.

"LESS . . . LESS . . . LESS", cried the *Daily Express* in a headline stretching bleakly across its front page.

IV

The giant posters which had now become a part of the British street scene looked down mockingly from the hoardings. "WE'RE UP AGAINST IT! WORK OR WANT!" It seemed not impossible that we might have to do both. Outside the Dominions immigration offices, long queues filled the pavements. An international Gallup Poll revealed that 42 per cent of Britain's population—58 per cent if one kept below the age of thirty—would emigrate "if free to do so"—a far higher proportion than in any of the other seven countries tested, and spread fairly evenly over all income groups. Over half a million* would-be emigrants were in fact on the waiting lists. But even here there was frustration: there was shipping for only a fraction of them.

Even among the faithful now there was a nagging sense of disillusion. The war-born sense of community and social purpose which had swept Labour to power in 1945 was gone; the fund of emotional capital which had been at the Government's disposal then had melted away. In *The Linden Tree*, J. B. Priestley's drama of contemporary life then drawing crowds to the Duchess Theatre, old Professor Linden sadly told his disgruntled middle-class family: "We are trying to do a

* Emigration was not in fact greatly out of line: between 1922 and 1931 almost 1½ million Britons had emigrated.

wonderful thing in this country of ours—but, somehow, not in a wonderful way. There is a grey chilly hollowness inside when there ought to be gaiety, colour, warmth, and vision." There were many in Labour's ranks to say "Amen" to that.

Certainly there had been no lack of energy or dedication. A vast programme of social and economic rehabilitation had been swiftly carried through despite the strains of an unforeseen cold war and swift, disconcerting global shifts in the pattern of power. There was more than a touch of heroism about the whole thing. Ernest Bevin and Stafford Cripps literally worked themselves to death in the service of the country. Rarely can a Government which served the nation so well have received so little credit.

Yet devotion and energy just then were not enough. "Credit columns" in the newspapers and silver cups for norm-exceeding pits were no substitute for that instinctive imaginative leadership which could strike a chord in the nation and which Britain had known in war. It was the misfortune of the Labour Government of 1945-50 that for one reason or another none of the three remarkable men who principally determined its character were able to offer this sort of vision. Ernest Bevin, who perhaps possessed the necessary intuition and imaginative breadth (but not the command of words), was preoccupied with his formidable task at the Foreign Office, where his main achievement, bringing the United States firmly into Europe, ran counter to the traditional sentiments of his party. Stafford Cripps, who possessed the command of words to an almost dangerous degree, was all too clearly an "intellectual" who lacked the common touch. Attlee, whose cool and steady judgment and integrity were the Government's hidden strength, shared the characteristic inhibitions (as well as the virtues) of the professional middle class from which he came. A sort of orator in reverse, he took great events, rich themes, and in that dry clipped voice reduced all to the level of the most pedestrian cliché. In such an atmosphere, the flights of a Bevan began to seem "bad form" not only on the Conservative side of politics, but on both.

No doubt the time for demagoguery was past. But so, too, was the time for the stance of Toynbee Hall. Labour in power was still, ironically, the victim of the class system its declared purpose was to abolish. Trapped in the very processes of social change it promoted, it could address effectively neither "one nation" (which did not yet exist) nor what Ernest Bevin used, nostalgically, to call "my people". Even within the Cabinet itself the dilemma of transition was sharply illuminated: the diversity of social background and prejudice was so great that misunderstanding and distrust flourished.

In any event, some degree of deflation was unavoidable. A "Movement" which becomes a government is that much less of a movement; the reality inevitably falls short of the Dream. Nor could endless ritual incantation of the phrase "Full Employment"—a fragment of Keynesian economic jargon—really enable it to blend with the soaring notes and harmonies of Blake's "Jerusalem". In the cold light of peace even the Beveridge Plan, an actuarial concept, had turned out to be something less than "Beveridgism".

Communication between the Movement's heart and the Movement's head had long been uncertain. There had been moments—many of them—when it had indeed seemed doubtful whether both could belong to the same body. Now when that body was required to function, it was perhaps inevitable that it should be the Webbs-ian Intellect rather than the Morris-ian Intuition or the Methodist Soul that prevailed. There was a certain humourlessness, a heavy governessy quality about the régime. At the Ministry of Food, like some formidable and symbolic Mother, Dr. Edith Summerskill ordered the nation to eat it up at once because it was good for it, insisting that butter and margarine were indistinguishable, or stigmatising as self-indulgence a desire for cheese of other than the permitted processed "mouse-trap". Meanwhile, at the Ministry of Fuel a young ex-don named Hugh Gaitskell won equal fame by solemnly supporting his Ministry's "Four-Inches-Only-in-the-Bath" campaign with a speech deprecating the unnecessary luxury of bathing.

Yet the matter went deeper than the temperament of Ministers. If men asked for Hope, and Mr. Herbert Morrison gave them the Monthly Digest of Statistics, it had to be admitted that the statistics just then were a crucial requirement.

During the war years the advance of science and technology appeared to be reinforcing the advance of social democracy. In the years of peace it began to appear that, having brought social democracy to this moment of fulfilment, technology might now be about to take over and dictate its own terms. The post-Keynesian world was an economists' world. Government began to look more and more like a specialist process, as the air became thick with "fundamental disequilibriums" and "serious imbalances", "unrequited exports" and "price mechanisms", not to mention inflation, deflation, reflation and disinflation. Churchill, a man out of his time, had led the nation in war—a time out of time—as a person, by his presence. Cripps, a man in his time, led it, in war's aftermath, as a co-ordinator of the Experts. Whereas Churchill invited "blood, sweat and tears", Stafford Cripps, via innumerable expert committees (and "Learnalot's Mammoth Amusements"), invited an export target of 140 per cent of 1938 by volume, an advance in Output Per Man Hour, a rise in the ratio of capital investments. He also, it was true, frequently called for "faith in the Divine purpose"; it was not his fault that this, too, was in somewhat short supply.

In the meantime, the newly nationalised industries—which not long ago had been seen as the instruments for the realisation of true social democracy—were proving to be merely one more means by which the economists, the technologists, the managers, the experts, entered yet further into their kingdom.

After Cripps, British Socialism could never be the same again. It had lost its innocence. The managerial revolution had overtaken the social revolution and would henceforth lead it into paths far from the realms of William Morris and Keir Hardie.

9.   New Look?

"All spivs, says Mr. Alfred Cope, have
one thing in common: no visible
means of support."
—Peterborough's Diary, *Daily Telegraph*, 30th July, 1947.

"I am like a second Livingstone,
discovered by Stanley."
—Mr. Justice Lynskey.

WHEN IN 1947 the "New Look" arrived in London from
Paris, its long, swirling skirts, Renoirish curves and
flounces, its wasp waist and bustle, were roundly voted
not only frivolous and absurd, but in flagrant bad taste in the
context of the times. The volume of the outcry at what was
basically merely a return to traditional feminine lines was
indeed a remarkable tribute to the grip which the puritan
discipline of Austerity and Fair Shares had gained on our island
life.

The chorus of disapproval grew as it became known that the
new fashion required thirty to forty metres of material, not to
mention new corsets, still firmly classified by the Board of
Trade as "luxury garments", and possibly such aids as
"hipettes" which the newspapers announced would shortly be
in the shops at 25s. 6d. the pair. There were indignant questions
in the House. The Government was rumoured to be considering
legislating against the new skirt length. In the meantime, Sir
Stafford Cripps made an appeal for moderation, receiving
emphatic support from Miss Mabel Ridealgh, M.P. for North
Ilford. The New Look, declared Miss Ridealgh, was "too
reminiscent of the 'caged bird attitude'. I hope our fashion
dictators will realise the new *outlook* of women and give the
death blow to any attempt at curtailing women's freedom."
But M. Christian Dior had been right and Miss Mabel

Ridealgh was wrong. The women of 1947, unlike their sisters after that other war, no longer needed to *declare* their Emancipation with short skirts and "flapper" lines; the emancipation they craved just then carried a small 'e' and was of an altogether different character.

This they now proceeded to make clear. Within a year the New Look was everywhere. Opinion polls showed an astonishing *volte-face*. A young office worker was reported as noting: "It is bringing into my vision a bevy of rather attractive females ..." A student ardently agreed: "It is pleasant walking through the town to see the young women discarding their squarish fashions and wearing garments that let you see they have a curve here and there."

Probably no new fashion had ever before spread with such mechanical efficiency and economy, or transformed the British street scene from Mayfair to Mile End, from Perth to Paignton with such astonishing speed. And yet, in a sense, it was Crippsian Utility—or postwar Egalitarianism—that had prevailed. For the New Look that now flowered across the country was a New Look shorn of its *Rue de la Paix* extravagances, a New Look severely modified for Liverpool Street in the rush hour, a new-old look of bottleneck shoulders and rounded hips which would allow its wearer to hop on a bus or travel home from the office in a jam-packed Tube train.

For any who could read it, here was a sign of the times. In a world in which its old clientele had been all but super-taxed out of existence, *haute couture* was henceforth to find its most important function as a high-powered publicity mechanism, a generator actuating a mass-sale ladies' garment industry, that was already beginning to boom impressively, as successive developments of the New Look, the large dominant collars, the "plunging neckline", the vast tent coats, multiplied themselves with ever-increasing speed and thoroughness on the pavements of Britain. The "little dressmaker" of prewar days had disappeared in the war and would not be back.

And in the newspapers—with that instinct for major social change which popular journalism sometimes shows—"New Look" ("the Government's 'New Look' policy") had already begun to replace the long jaded "New Deal" as a metaphor of all work.

II

The confusions of the new fashion's reception were in some ways a reflection of the many contrary pulls to which our poor battered island and its poor battered citizens were at this time subjected. There existed, side by side, often overlapping in baffling fashion, an England of 'plain living and high thinking', and an England of high living and distinctly low thinking, an England of 'Reality' and an England of 'Escape', the England of Sir Stafford Cripps, of equality of sacrifice and the export drive, and the England of the black market restaurant, the expense account, and Mr. Sidney Stanley, "the Pole of Park Lane".

To some extent this was the perennial dialogue between the Puritan vein in the British character and the older, underlying, Rabelaisian vein; to some extent also—and this, too, was no new process in our history—the one England had given birth to the other. For this was the time when a jungle of petty restrictions reminiscent of the medieval sumptuary laws positively invited evasion; when a West End milliner found herself in court for the "crime" of embroidering roses and butterflies on cami-knickers; when the length of men's shirt tails was legally limited; double cuffs specifically and firmly prohibited. A vast complex of strange, illicit cravings had thus been created and England just then was not lacking in men who knew how to supply them. It was estimated that in London alone there were 10,000 deserters from the British and American forces. Such men had often served a thorough-going apprenticeship in the mechanics of the black market in the back-streets of Hamburg or Naples. Nor did every Control Commission employee emerge or even go in (for the bottom of the barrel of manpower had to be scraped) with integrity unimpaired.

Much easy money was to be made from a wonderful variety of major or minor dishonesties, ranging from the "fiddle" of a small builder carrying out repairs without a licence to some spectacular sleight of hand with surplus military stores. Rolls of "export only" worsted, consigned to San Francisco, might pursue a strange and devious course before arriving, in a plain

D

van at some discreet little tailor's not many miles from their place of origin. Whisky, matured with phenomenal rapidity, would somehow get into bottles bearing world-famous labels. In North Staffordshire scores of small pot-banks, often set up in private houses, turned out illicit *decorated* china. The waiting list for new cars stretched into infinity; yet twice or three times the list price, cash down, might work wonders—and there was always the man who knew where he could get a gallon or two of petrol without coupons, just as there was always the woman who knew the little shop where chocolates—"as many as you want"—were to be had "under the counter", or the farm in the country where eggs were available—at a price.

And thus it came about that "New Look" was not the only addition to the English vocabulary that gained currency at this time. Questions about "spivs" appeared in Hansard. The sedate columns of the *Daily Telegraph* were given up to a lengthy discussion of the word's dubious origins and precise connotation. It had been coined, it seemed, among the race-course gangs of the Nineties, lying there doggo like some unpleasant virus waiting the moment of weakness when it could overrun the body. And now, spectacularly, it had done so.

For Britain at large there was a new topic of conversation as reliable as the weather: the latest tricks and outrages of the spivs. Was there no rock for kiddies at Blackpool? Instantly the newspapers produced the explanation: "SPIVS HAVE THE ROCK." Were bananas elusive? The spivs would sell them only if one also bought 2 lb. of apples and five of tomatoes. There were stories of spiv master minds who drove around in enormous cars, collecting thousands of pounds from the fleets of spiv carts and tricycles which dispensed watered ice-cream to a trusting population. The B.B.C. offered a special programme featuring a spiv explaining his black market deals. When police inquiries cast doubts on the subject's authenticity, a B.B.C. spokesman explained: "We thought he was a genuine spiv. We have no further interest in him."

In the form in which he had taken possession of the British imagination the spiv was, of course, an abstraction, a figure in a modern morality. The convention was rapidly established by the "pocket cartoonists" whose single column comments on life were one of the livelier creations of newsprint-rationing: the peaked shoulders, the wasp waist, the dazzle tie, the hoarse behind-the-hand whisper, "Nylons!" In the drama of the bright new Welfare ("Fair Shares") State, the spiv personified the anti-social forces: the Man Who jumped the Queue. For this, the supreme enormity, he was held up to heavy and continuous obloquy. When it was announced that "Direction of Labour" was to be applied, not only to those who had jobs and wanted to change them, but also to those to whom it had never occurred to seek them, to the "spivs and drones" (a category now expanded by Mr. Isaacs, the Minister of Labour, to include "eels and butterflies") public glee was great. For weeks the newspapers carried gloating headlines: SPIV DRIVE—POLICE GET NEW POWERS . . . NIGHT CLUB SPIV HUNT . . . MONTH'S NOTICE TO ALL DRONES. . . .

Yet an observer might have been puzzled to note that the spiv nevertheless managed to draw as many indulgent smiles as frowns. For if the British were now the People of the Queue, it had not always been so.

Here was a conflict which even Sir Stafford Cripps could not wholly resolve. Sir Stafford might confidently assure the public that social justice now reigned supreme; that the rich—idle or otherwise—had been abolished; that there were in the United Kingdom no more than thirty-seven persons whose incomes, after tax, exceeded £10,000 a year. But anyone who read a newspaper at this time was familiar with items about hordes of bank notes, cached away in biscuit-tins under the floor, and now brought to light by burglary or fire. There were legitimate 'easy pickings' too: massive tax-free capital gains were being freely made. Large numbers of family businesses were being capitalised and floated on the flood-tide of postwar markets; the Stock Exchange was booming; demand, pent-up by war was lucratively supplied.

Nor did it go altogether without notice that, despite a foreign currency allowance limited to £50, thousands of Britons were somehow to reside almost indefinitely in luxurious Riviera hotels. And for the less successful émigré who couldn't quite manage France or Belgium (whose fabulous shop-windows were much featured in the Press) there was always Eire, just across St. George's Channel, with bacon-and-two-eggs as large as life on the plate the moment one landed, and unlimited steaks and butter in O'Connell Street afterwards.

These confusions and conflicts were deepened in that the old hierarchical certitudes, which had proved so durable, were now so visibly disappearing at home as well as abroad. As returning Indian Army colonels abruptly discovered when affably addressed by bus conductors as "mate" (and their mem'sahibs as "ducks"), "respect" was now no more automatically accorded in Bayswater or Bermondsey than Bombay. There were new men, new manners and—just possibly—a new code.

But who were they? And what was it?

In the late winter of 1948 these obscurities were suddenly illuminated by the proceedings of a judicial tribunal set up to inquire into persistent rumours of Ministerial corruption that had been linked with the activities of a "certain alien" who, however, bore the reassuring name of Stanley.

As through five November and December weeks the Tribunal presided over by Mr. Justice Lynskey probed the infinite complexities of the affair, the two faces of the New Britain confronted each other bizarrely across the oak-panelled Hoare Memorial Hall of Church House, Westminster.

On one side were ranged such solid figures of the postwar social revolution as George Gibson, the first trade unionist to be appointed a director of the—now nationalised—Bank of England. At the age of twelve a 3s. 6d. a week errand boy, later an asylum attendant who had organised his colleagues in a trade union, George Gibson had come to politics via the Trades Union Congress. Self-made, self-educated, a person of note in the councils of Labour, he had, after 1945, moved on to the wider national stage, a director of the Bank of England, a member of the North-West Regional Board for Industry, finally, in 1947, chairman of the N. W. Regional Electricity Board at a salary of £4,000 a year. A typical member, some cynics were already saying, of a new "ruling class".

That might go, too, for John Belcher, who shared Gibson's ordeal before the tribunal. A former G.W.R. railway clerk, Belcher had ascended the political and social ladder by a different, though equally traditional, route—diligent night study, steady self-improvement, the taking of a London University diploma, a career of earnest endeavour which, after 1945, had been rewarded by the post of Parliamentary Secretary at the Board of Trade.

And then, on the other side, confronting these new men, a figure from an older world, adapting its skills to the new situation, that "certain alien", "the man known as Sidney Stanley", king—by his own account—of "contact men", those tactful guides through that no-man's-land where the new world of the planned society met the old world of big—and sometimes curiously ill-defined—business: where the England that queued met the England that did not queue.

Labour politicians, coming to office, were traditionally on their guard against the "aristocratic embrace". But times had changed: as the tribunal proceeded, it became evident that the perils of a wholly non-aristocratic embrace had not always been adequately realised.

And the embrace of Mr. Sidney Stanley was in a class all by itself. When that irrepressible little man stepped up to the lectern which at Church House served as a witness stand, the whole tribunal, Ministers of the Crown, the massed brains of the English Bar, high Civil Servants, important business men— all became enveloped in his boundless good will, swallowed up in clouds of Caliph-like benevolence in which fact and fantasy became indistinguishable.

Attorney-General (Sir Hartley Shawcross): *Sidney Stanley, what is your address?*—No. 4, Aldford House.

How long have you gone under that name?—Over twenty-five years that I know of.

You have enjoyed (if that is the correct expression) a number of other names during the period?—Not that I know of, except Stanley Rechtand.

Under what name were you born?—I do not know.

Do you not? Do you know what your father's name was?—My father's name was apparently Kohsyzchy.

Right through the war you acted as a commission agent to promote contracts?—I would not say promoting contracts.

Assisting?—Assisting and completing contracts.

You changed your sphere of activity?—I did.

What did you change it to?—Well, I wanted to go back and start selling dresses and so on, but I did not get a chance to do so, so instead I started, to begin with, trying to buy and sell stores.

Buy and sell what?—Stores—departmental stores.

You changed your activity from selling dresses to selling stores?—May I say once again, sir, when you say selling dresses, I was never interested in selling ten or twenty dresses; I always sold thousands. . . .

In the Strand the newspaper sellers were joyfully chalking on their boards: ALI BABA AND THE FORTY THIEVES. And there, again, was the underlying ambivalence of Crippsian England. Stanley was manifestly a super spiv—a drone, an eel and a butterfly, yet, in his astonishing audacity—or incredible cheek —his ever-active imagination, his absurdity, the little man had irresistible appeal. The Great British Public took him, temporarily at least, to its heart. Had he not intimated—in one of those astonishing, casually tossed-off asides of his—that he would "sink or swim with England"?

The "great breakfast serial", as the wags were soon calling it, had everything—wit, pathos, famous names. Its subject matter ranged impartially from football pools to the Bank of England, from pin-tables to the steel shortage; it had more twists, red herrings and exotic clues than Phillips Oppenheim himself could have provided. There was the strange affair of Teper the Tailor and three 35-guinea suits . . . of the "very charming gift of sausage" . . . of the "bunch of ten or twelve bananas". There was the enigma of the telephoned warnings, "Keep Off the Grass!" . . . of that pocket roll of £30,000 in one-pound notes . . . of the precise nature of the icing inscription on John Belcher's birthday cake. . . .

It was, no doubt, a sign of the times, that the majestic power of the State had to be deployed to deal with the petty intrigues of this intrinsically ridiculous little man who was not even a British citizen. Yet, when all was over, when the million words had been transcribed, the evidence of the sixty witnesses weighed and the tribunal's report issued, it was the England of Cripps and Fair Shares that prevailed. By Continental standard

Britain's black market was revealed as no more than faintly tinged with grey; beside the "war profiteer" of the Twenties the "spiv" of the Forties held merely amateur status. And if—rather from carelessness than venality—two men had been obliged to retire from public life, what had mainly emerged from it all was the continuing high standard of British public life and the jealousy with which this was still guarded.

III

And yet uneasiness remained. There were still many moments in the late Forties—as there were to be other, very different, moments in the Fifties—when to many Englishmen this seemed an England they could scarcely recognise. Identity cards still had to be carried and shown at a policeman's demand. The streets were still drab, unpainted and dim-lit. In the West End, Oxford Street seemed to have become a succession of pin-table arcades and garish sideshows, offering such attractions as a REAL LIVE MERMAID IN A TANK OF GOLDFISH . . . CRIME DOES NOT PAY—THE CLEFT CHIN MURDER CASE . . . or Epstein's *Jacob and the Angels*, billed as THE SHOW THAT WAS TOO HOT FOR BLACKPOOL.

In the first half of 1948 there were still thousands of German prisoners of war around in their chocolate battledress and old peaked Wehrmacht caps, now and again breaking into the headlines when one of them, working on the land, married some girl in an English village. And in the autumn, the G.I.s were back, leaning in gum-chewing rows against the walls in Piccadilly Circus, or dating the girls on some English market square. Among us, too, were the 40,000 "Displaced Persons", now renamed European Volunteer Workers and mainly from the Baltic States. And the Poles were always with us, the stocky, square-faced peasants from General Anders' Army, drafted from the Polish Resettlement Corps to building sites, or the lean and craggy ex-colonels, haunting South Kensington cafés or growing mushrooms profitably in cellars.

Nor, at the start of each day, was any reassurance to be found on the British breakfast table. The Ministry of Food, sweeping the world for potential articles of human consumption, proudly laid at the feet of the British housewife a succession of bizarre items. Whale meat came and went; so did nectarines and Russian tinned crab (which, hideously suspect, piled up in the shops) ; and snoek, a South-African canned fish that sounded like something from pre-history. To a worried reader, the *Church Times* replied discouragingly: "G.F.—We have no authority to decide whether whale steaks should be reckoned proper Friday fare. Ask your bishop."

In small things as well as large, the mould seemed broken, the old values overturned. England needed her sense of continuity as she needed air; yet as the decade moved towards a close there were some to whom it seemed that what we were now facing was a permanent—and possibly fatal—hiatus.

10. The Englishman's Burden

> "This gift of a common tongue is a priceless inheritance. . . . I like to think of British and Americans moving freely over each other's wide estates with hardly a sense of being foreigners to one another."
> —Winston Churchill, at Harvard, 9th September, 1944.

> "Thanks, pal. Must be pretty quiet on Broadway with all you boys and girls over here."
> —British comedian, in gutter, begging dollar from American performer, Lee cartoon, *Evening News*, 1948.

POSTPONED BY the war, the Olympic Games were held in London in the summer of 1948. On its progress from Mount Olympus, the Olympic Flame became extinguished on its first contact with English soil—an incident which, it soon began to appear, might have been some sort of omen. For if records were broken with "monotonous regularity", they were not broken by citizens of the host country. The eclipse of the Sporting British appeared all but complete. The Americans won thirty-eight events; the British won three.

The venerable cliché was trotted out again: we British didn't just play to win; with us "the game was the thing". But it was becoming a little too obvious that we *had* to be "good losers". At Lord's in 1949 England failed to defeat New Zealand in one of the four Tests; next year, the West Indians were celebrating their triumphs with calypsos. At Wimbledon, record crowds sought in vain for some hint of a new Fred Perry or Dorothy Round while the Press photographers focused mainly on the non-Utility under-garments of America's publicity-conscious Miss "Gorgeous Gussie" Moran. Another year—and

Britain's two world boxing titles were lost. Great hopes had been built on the British heavyweight Bruce Woodcock. But these, too, plummetted when at the White City he met the American, Lee Savold, and went down in the fourth round. At football, the game we had taught to the world, our pupils ignominiously defeated us. Successively—and, it seemed, almost automatically—we were trounced by Russia—the Moscow Dynamos in 1945, Sweden, Switzerland, Spain, the United States, Uruguay, Hungary. . . .

Even Channel swimming—the gallant Captain Webb must have turned in his grave!—appeared to have been surrendered to the ever-buoyant Egyptians who now lined the beaches at Dover each summer.

With more than a touch of self-pity, we blamed our meagre rations. But that deceived no one: it clearly went deeper than that. Our sport had been founded on the idea of the "keen" amateur—the natural complement of the "born gentleman", and in our Victorian hey-day the world had "played the game" our way—or pretended to. In the world of the technocrat our way was plainly obsolete. The "keen" amateur, had been replaced by the dedicated professional, backed by all the resources of science and Big Business and frequently by the apparatus of the State. Between America and Russia and the satellite "People's Democracies" sport had become one more front in the world conflict of systems.

Once again, it was becoming inescapably evident that, long and splendid as the road might have been, Britain was reaching the end of it.

II

As, in our economic weakness, the regenerating transfusions had come from across the Atlantic, so now, at this nadir of our national morale, it was again the Americans who revived us.

In April, 1948, A. P. Herbert and Vivian Ellis's pretty and tuneful *Bless the Bride* had opened at the Adelphi Theatre and had been well received. Four days later, the all-American *Oklahoma!* exploded across the vast stage of Drury Lane, and in the words of the sober critic, Harold Hobson, shook "London up more than anything that has hit it since the first flying bomb". Thirty-eight days later, *Annie get Your Gun* opened at the Coliseum.

For two years, through the dismal succession of "cuts" and crises, these two robust American musicals with their zestful dancing, youthful high spirits, and bright primary colours cast their spell over the London scene. Between the Convertibility Crisis and the Devaluation Crisis, *Oklahoma!* cheered up 2,200,000 British citizens—and continued to pack them in. Whistled by bus conductors, booming from radios, reverberating in bathrooms, "Oh, what a beautiful morning!", "Doin' what comes nat'r'lly", "The Surrey with the fringe on top" echoed on down the Forties and into the Fifties.

By 1949, it began to seem that in theatrical terms at least Britain was now on the way to becoming the 49th State. American productions were having an electric effect on the "legitimate", as well as on the musical, stage. As poor Blanche du Bois in Tennessee Williams' *Streetcar Named Desire*, as Willie Loman in Arthur Miller's *Death of a Salesman*, Vivien Leigh and Paul Muni exhausted themselves nightly and left audiences as shattered as if they had been under artillery bombardment.

American theatrical "invasions" were certainly not new. The letters of schoolmasters and others protesting against the inroads of "American slang" had been a perennial feature of the newspapers in the inter-war years. Perhaps the point was that they wrote no longer. The peculiar psychological condition of the British at the end of the Forties, suspended between the old England that was dying and the new England that was yet to be born, had endowed the American article with a quite peculiar potency. By their freshness and gusto, by their air of being "about" something, most of all by their unforced demotic expressiveness and lack of class inhibition, the American productions struck the British at this time with the force of revelation. They at last succeeded in showing up the standard English drawing-room drama and the English "musical" of the Ivor Novello or Jack Buchanan tradition for what they were— something of a moribund world.

In the thirteen years after the end of the war over 100 music halls closed down in Britain. Undermined in the Thirties by radio vaudeville, by the end of the Forties the Empires and the Hippodromes—and with them one more lively, nation-spanning tradition of our hey-day—were finally collapsing in a welter of peeling stucco, grubby gilt and inept and tawdry "girlie shows" boasting titles like "STRIP! STRIP! STRIP! HOORAY!"

When, therefore, in 1948, Val Parnell, impresario of the London Palladium began to cast around for some way of putting variety in England back on its feet, he almost inevitably turned to the United States. There he signed up, among others, a young comedian, Brooklyn-born, of Russian parentage. Under the professional name of Danny Kaye the young man had appeared in a cabaret at the Dorchester in 1938 without attracting much attention. He had since starred in three films; but his debut at the London Palladium was still thought to be something of a gamble. A member of the audience on his opening night wrote: "He was obviously nervous when he walked on; a good-looking slightly stringy, young man with unruly marmalade hair and carelessly wandering hands. He gave a high-pitched giggle, and said, 'I'm shaking like a leaf, honestly.' Then he smiled. The effect was miraculous. People began to clap and cheer and the gallery girls called their welcome."

When the curtain came down, it descended on a personal triumph such as the British music hall had not seen for a quarter of a century. Next day, Danny Kaye had become the talk of the town. *The Times* printed his photograph on its back page; Cabinet Ministers flocked to the stalls; Royalty went round to the dressing-room. Ticket spivs reaped a rich harvest from queues that stretched around the building. Standing-room tickets changed hands at £3 and stalls from anything up to £20.

As the Forties ended, it seemed that the long-vacant throne of King of the British Music Hall had been filled; that the missing successor to the line of our great popular comedians, Dan Leno, Harry Lauder, George Robey and the rest, had been found.

And that he, too, was an American.

As the sportsmen found a scapegoat in food rationing, some critics laid the blame for America's theatrical 'walk over' on the "Welfare State". What could Shakespeare himself have made of the society of the docile queue, social security, and the teabreak?

Critics of this school might, however, have done better to have followed the sport-writers still more closely—to the amateur/professional dichotomy, that conflict of social and value systems still so persistent on our side of the Atlantic though scarcely visible on the other. Educated to inhabit a technological democracy, bred to the Machine, the Americans could unembarrassedly mingle their art with science; felt no shame at all in their intense devotion to "know-how".

But whatever the correct diagnosis, in the years After Kaye there was no lack of opportunity to study the evidence. An endless procession of American stars of "stage, screen and radio", marched into the spotlight, hugged the microphone, and made their little speech about how fine it felt to be back again with the "wunnerful English people" who could "take it" in the Blitz. Most of them received a rapturous welcome. Yet if the offerings were greedily consumed, they nevertheless left a curious, indefinably unpleasant, after-taste. For there were "explanations" which were rarely voiced, much less put into print, but yet rose unbidden in the mind. Might it not, after all, merely be that we were old and weary and they were young and vital and full of the joy of living! That their society was adapted to the times it had played so large a part in forming, while ours was obsolescent, fatally weighed down under the burden of its glorious past? That this, in short, was more than ever the American Century?

As military, financial, cultural bonds grew tighter, and "Anglo-American" became an ever more valid adjective, the old love-hate relationship grew more tortuous, intense and ever-present; the old strand in the pattern of our history flared out in new and angrier colours. Resentment about the money the American performers were taking out of the country was loudly voiced. British reporters, interviewing visiting American sportsmen, would inquire caustically about the poundage of steaks brought over in their baggage. In a jaundiced book entitled *What the English think of Us*, Fred Vanderschmidt, London correspondent of *Newsweek*, estimated—and opinion polls bore him out—that one in every three Englishmen were "more or less antagonistic to anything that came from America from Buicks to businessmen".

Odd to reflect that there had been a time when Henry James had complained of the special "burden" that afflicted the American writer since, "he *must* deal more or less, even if only by implication, with Europe, whereas no European is obliged to deal in the least with America".

PART TWO

MORE EQUAL THAN OTHERS

"England, a pioneer of religious and political equality, has known little of their economic and social analogues. Her history, so rich in other lessons, supplied no large body of experience by which to judge the more distant effects of her recent, unspectacular turn towards them."

—R. H. Tawney, Revised 1952 edition of *Equality*

11. Horny-rimmed

"Today the Trade Unions are the
Fourth Estate of the Realm."
—Young cliché of the late Forties.

"You might as well say that the
Transport and General Workers
Union is our employer now."
—Two London bus conductors, cited
in Pilot Papers inquiry, *Closed
Shop.*

HE REAL service to the nation of the Labour Government
of 1945-50 lay in its ability to assimilate, at home as in
Asia, the long-term social changes which the war had
brought to a head. It was uniquely able to do this because the
Labour Movement itself was so very much a part of these
changes: it stood, in 1945, in the mainstream of history.

The most obvious example lies in the manner in which the
Labour Government was able to gain swift acceptance for the
wartime transformation in the balance of power between
Capital and Organised Labour. The war had turned the former
General Secretary of the Transport and General Workers into
the Minister of Labour. For five years in this position Ernest
Bevin—a monument in his person to the new status of the trade
unions in Britain—had enjoyed enormous power over the lives
of all British citizens between 14 and 64. And when peace
came, the same Ernest Bevin, speaking now with all the
authority of the Foreign Secretary of Great Britain, had been
able symbolically to confirm this silent wartime shift in the
social balance by the repeal of the hated Trade Disputes Act
enacted after the General Strike.* "I am fighting," he said,

* The Act made "sympathetic" strikes beyond the limits of one
industry illegal. In fact, despite its repeal, ALL strikes remained
illegal under the wartime National Arbitration Order until 1951
and striking gasworkers and dockers were prosecuted by the Labour

injecting his characteristic note into the stormy (and cloudy) debate, "to remove the stigma the Tory Party put on me in 1927 as a leader of a trade union."

In fact, though the gesture of repeal in 1946 was not an empty one,* the Trade Disputes Act already seemed to belong to a vanished world. Between 1939 and 1945 under the State-held umbrella of the Essential Works Orders the trade unions had become deeply involved at all levels, on equal terms with Capital, in the running of the industrial machine. A firm generally needed their approval before being granted the status of being "engaged on essential work"; a citizen needed it to get a permit to buy an alarm clock. In the ten years between 1938 and 1948 the trade unions' new power had been both reflected and reinforced by a growth in their total membership of more than 50 per cent.

After 1945 the trade unions' new status, symbolised in Labour's victory at the polls, was swiftly and smoothly incorporated in the nation's institutional fabric. In 1946 Arthur Deakin could boast: "We have an open door in relation to all State Departments", and under Cripps, the Tripartite (Union-Government-Employers) organisation of wartime began to take on the character of a feature of the British Constitution. In 1939, the number of Government committees on which unions were represented had been twelve. By 1948-49 it was sixty. Five years later, with the Tories in power, it was eighty-one.

In the newly nationalised industries compulsory trade union consultation at all levels was written into the founding Statutes. As if this were not safeguard enough, the trade unions succeeded in installing their former officials and other nominees in executive posts at all levels from Area to National Board. Since the T.U.C. had finally rejected the notion of "workers' control"

Government. In addition, by replacing "contracting-out" by "contracting in" the Trade Disputes Act had, in theory at least, compelled each trade unionist to make a personal decision whether or not to contribute to Labour Party funds. It had also redefined more restrictively the law on intimidation, prohibited the civil service unions from affiliating to the T.U.C. and Labour Party, and local authorities from forcing a union "closed shop" on employees.

* Among other things, it increased the number of contributors to union political funds by 50 per cent, thus swelling Labour Party resources.

in 1944, these jobs, mainly in welfare and "industrial relations", were theoretically non-representational. But the effect in introducing new attitudes to labour was obviously substantial— particularly since almost a quarter of the total civil labour force of the nation now worked in the public sector where the new "model" standards applied.

In addition, the Agricultural Wages Act (1947), the Catering Wages Act (1943), the conversion (1945) of the old trade boards into Wages Councils and their extension to $1\frac{1}{4}$ million workers in retail distribution, now brought $4\frac{1}{2}$ million workers under statutory wage regulation—again with trade union participation.

In this new climate, many large private concerns now came to favour full trade union membership for their employees. For this not only conferred a reputation for enlightenment but was also administratively convenient. Often their attitude brought about what, in effect if not in name, was a "closed shop".

Speakers in all political parties who valued a reputation for alertness were now discovering in the "great trade unions" a "fourth estate of the realm". By the late Forties the meta-morphosis of the "labour agitator" into the "trade union statesman", horn-rimmed rather than horny-handed, black-Homberged and brief-cased, appeared all but complete. For such men knighthoods began to seem almost as inevitable as for high Civil Servants. And the knighthoods were forthcoming, thirteen of them, in the first postwar ten years, spanning the spectrum of Toil from boots-and-shoes to boilermaking.

But the change in the status of labour was not confined to the institutional level. Postwar economic pressures powerfully reinforced the egalitarian spirit of 1945 to bring about a dramatic revaluation of the labourer also.

There were many weeks in the immediate postwar years when the survival of Britain seemed to depend on the efforts of her ordinary workers as clearly as it had on the morale of her private soldiers in the war. If the dockers could turn round the ships a little faster . . . If the bricklayers could just lay a few more bricks . . . If, above all, every miner could dig a little more coal . . .

"Be generous when you think of the miners," the *Daily Mirror* commanded its readers, "be a little humble before these men who spend their lives underground." The blizzards of 1947 had made their point. Nylons and scarce dress fabrics were directed to the mining towns for the miners' wives. Extra rations were theirs. From being a half-submerged, shockingly underpaid, coal-blackened helot from whom the lowliest white collar clerk shrank in disgust, the miner shot up to the heroic proportions of Soviet proletarian statuary.

Such notions were highly novel in England and their sincerity was inevitably open to doubt. Yet the "social revaluation" was accompanied by an impressive monetary revaluation also. In 1948 the *Economist* calculated that in the preceding ten years the real net level of wage earnings had risen by 10–35 per cent while, in the same period, salary income had fallen by 20–30 per cent. That year the President of the National Association of Local Government Officers warned his members: "You and I have been brought up in a world which recognised without question the social ascendancy of the white collar . . . and its undisputed right to a preferential salary. Have we realised that that world has gone for ever?"

By 1955 the average manual worker had drawn level with the average bank clerk of twenty-eight and was considerably ahead of the local government clerk of the same age.* The manual worker, furthermore, was being ardently wooed by employers with the offer of "pleasant surroundings", music, cut-price or free refreshments and—for Lancashire or Yorkshire "mill-girls"—"free hairdressers on the premises".

In 1890 the Radical politician Sir Charles Dilke wrote: "There is reason to expect that the worker will become king in Britain as he is already king in the British countries of Australasia."

Sixty years later it had begun to seem to many that this day might be at hand.

II

Perhaps the first intimation that these large developments might still fall short of that "industrial democracy" envisaged

* *The Blackcoated Worker* by David Lockwood, 1958.

in Socialist theory came with the strike at the Grimethorpe Colliery in the summer of 1947.

It was, ironically, the direct result of the new dispensation. In order to facilitate mechanisation and ensure that no coal production was lost through the inauguration of the five-day week, it had been agreed between the N.U.M. and the N.C.B. that "stints"—the yardage at each working-place to be completed in a single shift—should be reassessed. The carrying out in detail of this agreement was an obvious task for the new "democratic" consultative system. And thus it came about that one August day a sub-committee of four, two officials from the National Coal Board, two from the National Union of Miners, arrived at Grimethorpe in Yorkshire, visited the Melton Field, and after weighing local conditions, decided that 2 feet should be added to the 21-foot stint in force there.

A modest enough demand, it might have been thought. But the 104 miners who worked in the Melton Field did not think so.

Did not their pit already do better than most in the district?

Why, then, this punishment?

Burning with indignation, they trooped out on strike. Traditional "solidarity" ensured that when the news reached them the 2,500 other miners at Grimethorpe downed picks also.

The country was teetering on the edge of the Convertibility Crisis; Mr. Attlee had just called for a "national effort comparable to that we developed during the war". Union leaders, honoured names, travelled to Yorkshire to plead with the striking miners. Will Lawther, their President, appealed to them; so did Jim Bowman, Arthur Horner. They would bring down the Government, *their own* Government, cried Horner. The men remained obdurate. Other pits came out, over forty of them, 60,000 miners.

Without strike pay—for the stoppage was "unofficial"—the miners worked in the harvest fields. Let them just give the new stint a trial, pleaded the management and their own union officials. If it proved too hard, it would be revised.

A typical bosses' trap, retorted the men beneath the bright new N.C.B. flags fluttering from the pitheads.

The "Stint Strike" gave birth to miles of baffled reportage and discussion of the miner and his problems (and the Problem of the Miner). But in that grim Yorkshire colliery village, with its two pit-rows bleakly confronting each other, the miners turned dour faces on the swarming reporters and continued to hold out.

Ministers journeyed up to Grimethorpe. Tom Williams, Minister of Agriculture, an old miner. Emmanuel Shinwell, Minister of Fuel and Power. "This country is hanging by a thread—make no mistake about it!" shouted Shinwell in the Miners' Hall, as he appealed to the men to "play the game by the nation".

More men came out: 70,000 now, with 54 pits affected. Gas production fell so low for lack of coal that the lights went out in West Riding towns. In Sheffield, steel production had to be cut back.

PIT SLAVES INTO PIT PARTNERS had run a *Daily Herald* headline on Vesting Day. In an adjoining column, a leader-writer had adjured his readers to STRIVE ON! Had readers been in an analytical frame of mind it might have occurred to them that in the annals of the Movement "striving on" had associations somewhat different from those of business partnership.

After Grimethorpe, such emotional conflicts were to become increasingly visible. "I found," ruefully wrote Arthur Horner, the N.U.M. Secretary, "that men's minds did not change because the circumstances of their life were changing", and went on to quote Lenin on the need for three decades of adjustment. In South Wales, in the Yorkshire and Scottish coalfields— where traditions were bad and working conditions difficult— friction was continuous. In both 1947 and 1948 there were 1,500 colliery strikes; in no prewar year had there been more than 500.

On the docks, the massive de-casualisation scheme—hailed by Bevin as "the fulfilment of a lifetime's dream"—had just been given statutory enactment. Yet three times the Emergency Powers Act was invoked against striking dockers, with all the melodrama of "sending in the troops to keep food supplies moving".

Nor had the embroidering of neat B.R.(E.)s or B.R.(W.)s on railway antimacassars brought the expected glow of loyalty to railwaymen's hearts.

III

But the strikes, if numerous and concentrated in a few industries, were generally also short. In the first three postwar years workdays lost amounted to less than one-twentieth of those lost through strikes in the same period after the First World War and they were only a minute fraction of those currently being lost in the United States.

These postwar British strikes which became so much a part of the curious climate of the times were, in fact, worlds away both from the solid Galsworthy-esque class-against-class strikes of earlier days and from the prolonged "split-the-take" tussles between Capital and Labour which were a feature of life across the Atlantic. They were more like outbursts of exasperation, explosions of protest—in every sense of the term, "unofficial". It was sometimes said they were expressions of boredom. Certainly it seemed possible that the historian of the future might see them as a visible symptom of the profound structural change taking place in our society. This process of change was far from new. But it was now both accelerating and consolidating. The individual, with less and less room to manoeuvre, every year—every week—felt himself more and more solidly hemmed in, began to feel in his bones that there was no escape, that the whole vast process was utterly irreversible.

There were moments of panic.

In Grimethorpe in the old days under the coal-owners, it had been the custom in some pits that if the men could finish their "stint" in five hours they could pack up and go home. In the bright new world of the National Coal Board that sort of "rule-of-thumb" was out. In the old days, "rag-outs" were often settled in rough-and-ready fashion with the Boss on the spot. Now the smallest squabble might all too easily become a matter for a complicated, impersonal, nation-wide, conciliation machine: one of the Grimethorpe strikers' bitterest complaints had been that the union representatives who assessed their "stint" were not *Yorkshire* miners!

But it was in the docks in the late Forties that this clash between worlds achieved its classic expression. In the days when the docks were—in Sir James Sexton's phrase—the "Sargasso Sea of all the flotsam and jetsam of industry", the "liberty" the dockers enjoyed had certainly often enough been the liberty to go hungry. Yet equally, in good times, it had included the liberty to work like mad for five or six days—and then take a week off to enjoy the proceeds if one felt so inclined. However low in the social scale such dockers might be, they could nevertheless feel that they were, in an important sense, their own men.

Under the new régime, meticulously administered by the National Dock Labour Board, the dockers had representation at every point from the top downwards, official registration, a regular job; they had welfare officers, canteens, football teams, a docks' newspaper. Ships or no ships, they had a guaranteed weekly wage, the "fall-back"—on condition that they attended twice daily at stated times at their stated Dock Centre to get their official dockers' cards officially stamped "A.P."— Attendance Proved.

They had thus exchanged "demoralising anarchy" for a "privileged" status. As Arthur Horner wrote of the miners: "Things we never dreamed possible became perfectly feasible."

Were they, then, well content?

It hardly seemed so. Perhaps somewhere, deep down in this great inarticulate mass of men smouldered a resentful suspicion that the new "Equality" was being bought at too high a price— the price of the old "Liberty" still more familiar and perhaps also dearer to most Englishmen.

In the complicated new machinery of decasualisation on the docks, the dockers' spokesmen, the 'officers' of the Transport and General Workers' Union, were now permanently enmeshed cogs. The local district secretary might be also chairman of the ruling authority, the Dock Labour Board, sitting cheek-by-jowl with the stevedoring employers. In the ponderous multi-tiered structure of conciliation and rate-fixing, union officials would serve on the disciplinary committees trying and sentencing transgressors. The cry against "trade union bureaucrats" was far from new; but now that bureaucracy was institutionalised.

The wave of nationalisation, adding spectacularly to the

rising number of mammoth concerns, strengthened the central-
ising tendencies of the great trade unions. One of the
earliest acts of the new National Union of Mineworkers, formed
in 1945 from the old looser Federation of thirty-nine District
Associations had been to crush the small clerical and winding
enginemen's union. Meanwhile, product of fifty-eight earlier
amalgamations, the Transport and General Workers—within
whose domain most of the newsworthy strikes occurred—had
reached a membership of 1¼ millions, with funds totalling
£5–6 millions, and a paid staff of 1,200, covering twelve trade
groups and thirteen territorial areas.

Power was the law of the unions' existence, and for union as
for State, power meant numbers, revenue, territory—a fact
neatly symbolised at the Labour Party Conference each year
when Mr. Arthur Deakin, using the T.G.W.U.'s one million
block-vote, could, in a moment, cancel out the votes of nine-
tenths of the constituency parties. Monolith confronted
monolith; the N.U.M. meshed with the N.C.B., the T.G.W.U.
with London Transport or the organised port employers.
Ex-trade union knight or peer, now pillar of some nationalised
industry, conferred with trade union knight across the Board
Room table, beneath the new crest and armorial bearings,*
supplied by the ever-busy College of Heralds. No doubt they
conferred, drawing on their capacious memories, about the
welfare and the interests of their brother-workers. If so, their
brother-workers were unappreciative.

IV

To all this, the theoreticians of the New Britain had their
answer pat. "Industrial Democracy" must be carried through
all levels to the factory floor—as provided for in detail in
the nationalised industries. The spirit of the wartime joint

* Tactfully selected, of course. The National Coal Board's *Ex
Tenebris Lux* seemed unimpeachable, but it is doubtful whether such
gestures as Lord Calverley's (Mr. George Muff's) in forming his
escutcheon from "two miners' picks in saltire and a miner's lamp all
proper" made their expected contribution to the brotherhood of
labour.

production committees* must be recaptured, the rule of "We"—
the natural corollary of a Labour victory and public ownership
—substituted for the bad old régime of "Them" and "Us".

The sturdiest optimists could not deny that these admirable
aspirations confronted a number of very awkward facts. Even
within the trade unions themselves "industrial democracy" was
more honoured in the breach than in the observance. It was
pointed out *ad nauseam* that only a tiny minority of members,
probably 3-4 per cent, attended branch meetings of the
T.G.W.U. and that even in the relatively skilled A.E.U. only
about 10 per cent troubled to vote in elections for their National
Executive.

Nor was this wholly a matter of proletarian apathy. The times
now seemed firmly set against this sort of small-scale democratic
activity. Even at the grass roots of British democracy, in local
government, the technocrats and centralisers were now taking
over in force. In these early postwar years the elected munici-
palities suffered—in the name of technological logic—the loss of
service after service which they had built up with proprietary
pride, their hospitals, their gas works and electricity undertakings, their (for non-county boroughs) independent police
forces, their secondary schools and fire brigades. . . .**

Thus while the old "Gas and Water Socialism" had been
supported by local pride, nourishing—and nourished by—the
sense of community, the "nationalising" Socialism of 1945 was
cast on stonier ground. At the same time, the attempt to devise
new democratic forms to clothe the hard technological outlines
—the "industrial democracy" of "joint consultation"—faced
heavy odds in the England of the Forties. Even in the
"reformed" territory of the N.C.B., a middle-aged colliery

---

* In the late war, joint production committees had been set up
in over 3,000 factories and by common consent had played a useful
part in developing the national effort. After the war they had been
set up on building sites to speed the houses. But again, there was a
world of difference between the pressures exerted by an "economic
Dunkirk" and the other one.

** As with the trade unions, the decline of democracy here was in
some measure due to failure to adapt the old organisational structure
to correspond with mid-century realities. Here, as in the unions, the
extraordinary tangle of conflicting vested interests inhibited radical
reform.

manager who had "slaved" to "raise himself" might not take kindly to explaining—even debating—his actions to men elected from the ranks to the pit consultative committee. Equally, workers might well find themselves having to choose between attitudes of self-conscious obsequiousness or of class-conscious aggression.

Like so much else in Britain in these years "industrial democracy" thus stood in danger of falling into the gulf between the Old England that was dying and the New England that was conceived but hardly yet born. The trade unions themselves—straddling new and old worlds both in their structure and their ideas—often seemed to resemble a man who has just put on bifocal spectacles and is chronically uncertain through which half to look. The consequent patches of fuzziness, the baffling switches of focus, formed one of the characteristic phenomena of the Forties and Fifties.

At one point, in their obsolescent craft jealousies, narrowness of vision and rigid conventions—the ossified apprenticeship system, for instance—the unions would seem to be living still in the world of the medieval guilds; at another point, they might be found deeply involved in the startling new "no frontiers" world of the chemical engineer, the nuclear scientist, the electronic magician. At one level, they might embrace the Theory of the Cake, collaborating on Sir Stafford Cripps' Productivity Committees or sending shop stewards on Work Study courses organised by the T.U.C.'s new Production Department; simultaneously, somewhat further down the scale, other shop stewards—or the same ones!—might be waging the traditional war against the Speed-Up and the Class Enemy, and obstructing, with an almost Luddite fanaticism, the introduction of such elementary aids as fork-lift trucks, automatic gear-cutters or bulk-loading equipment.*

The trade unions were, in essence, faced by the central dilemma of democratic Socialism in Britain in a particularly acute and immediate form. In the name of Equality they eagerly espoused "Socialist planning"; in the name of Liberty

---

* Obstruction—on the docks in particular—often took the form not of refusing to operate the machines but of insisting that the same number of men be employed on each job as before the machinery was installed.

they as enthusiastically denied it, clinging desperately to absolute union sovereignty, the rule of the market and the hard brute bargain by which they lived. On the one hand they might accept "wage restraint" from Cripps as a temporary expedient; but in the next breath they would fiercely repulse the Socialist intellectuals' demand for a national wages policy which would make it possible to substitute economic design for economic accident. "We will have none of that!" cried Arthur Deakin.

Even the T.U.C. was not permitted to attempt to regulate to any degree the rich anarchy which the trade unions inhabited, one of the largest preserves of *laissez-faire* now left in Britain. Nevertheless, as the unions grew in size and wealth and consolidated their "Fourth Estate" status it was inevitable that the planners and managers would push in there, too. It was already clear that this would not remove the unions' perplexities; their dilemma was not to be solved merely by "getting up-to-date". The historic mission of the unions—and of British socialism—was to give significance to political democracy by realising economic and social equality. But it was now becoming unpleasantly evident that in modern industrial society the organisation needed to raise a man's status as a worker might dwarf him as an individual; that the technology which delivered him from "feudalism" might yet subject him to the new serfdom of technocracy.

In the "new dawn" of 1945 the idea of Equality had still possessed the potency and the glow of an absolute and self-evident truth. By 1949 this truth was veiled over in a dismaying elusiveness and something of the frustration and confusion and even heartache that would attend the effort to work out this simple and self-evident idea in the complex conditions of industrial society was becoming apparent.

It was a theme that was to be illuminated from a bewildering number of directions and in a bewildering number of lights in the years ahead.

12.   Shaking the Bottle

"The first duty of the Government is to protect the country from external aggression. The next aim of national policy must be to secure the general prosperity and happiness of the citizens."

—White Paper on Social Insurance, September, 1944.

"Why is it that wherever I go to speak the people seem to be interested in nothing but their social security and their dentures?"

—'Tall, exasperated Conservative M.P.' quoted in *Time* magazine.

"ON MONDAY MORNING," a *Daily Mail* writer assured readers one day in July, 1948, "you will wake in a New Britain, in a State which 'takes over' its citizens six months before they are born, providing care and free services for their birth, for their early years, their schooling, sickness, workless days, widowhood, and retirement. Finally it helps defray the cost of their departure. All this, with free doctoring, dentistry and medicine—free bath-chairs, too, if needed—for 4s. 11d. out of your weekly pay packet. You begin paying next Friday."

The British public was by no means unaware of the imminence of this particular new dawn. For months past a stream of 'family guides', announcements and explanatory leaflets ("Further, you should, in your own interests, report anything which may lead to an increase in your family allowance . . .") had been thrust into their hands or through their letter-boxes by the new Ministry of National Insurance, maternally anxious that none should miss any of the fourteen different forms of pension, benefit, grant and allowance to which they would become entitled under the four great Beveridge Acts.

And rarely can official literature have found more eager readers. For to most people the heart of the "social revolution", the true gospel of 1945, lay—as it had always lain—in the Beveridge Reforms. This must have been puzzling to anyone unfamiliar with Britain's social structure because the Beveridge programme in fact contained little that was really new. For the most part it was merely building on the foundations laid by Lloyd George (and Beveridge) in 1911. It was true that by 1949-50 the effect had been to raise social service expenditure to a level more than twice that of 1936, at adjusted prices. But redistribution of this sort had also now been going on for a long time. The true potency of "Beveridge" was to be sought elsewhere; the secret of the Acts was psychological and political rather than fiscal. It could by summed up in the single word "comprehensiveness".

"The scheme as a whole," the 1944 White Paper on Social Insurance had insisted, "will embrace, not certain occupations and income groups but the entire population. . . . In a matter so fundamental it is right for all citizens to stand in together without exclusions based on differences of status, function or wealth."

That was the authentic Beveridge note—and 1948 was to show that it had been no mere rhetoric. Since the benefits offered under the Acts now covered a wide range of normal contingencies and since all males and single women of working age from Mayfair to Mile End were now obliged to stick their stamps on their cards—or have them stuck on for them—it was no longer possible to think in the old "two-nation" terms of "the dole". "Old Age Pensioners", lately a small category for semi-charity and pity, became the universal 'pensioners'. The people, said *The Times*, had joined together "in a single national friendly society for mutual support during the common misfortunes of life".

And at this stage in Britain's social evolution the fact of membership was more important than the cash benefits; whatever cynics might say the promise of full citizenship and no exclusion bulked larger than security *qua* security.

This promise, crystallised by Beveridge, in fact pervaded the whole of 1945's new deal of which social insurance was but a part, and was so attractive that few noticed that the Beveridge guarantee of a National Minimum "as of right" was not in fact being adequately met and that benefit rates, calculated by actuaries rather than idealists, had been fixed at a level which would compel many people to eke out their benefits with National Assistance Board allowances.

Yet, this body, too, now approached its task in a notably different spirit from that of the old "relieving officer". "The primary business of the Board," it declared, "is to ensure that people applying to them have sufficient income and have it in the majority of cases with as little trouble and inconvenience to themselves as possible."* The new war-born social philosophy remained in being.

At this critical point maturing social democracy was reinforced by the developing social sciences. Under the new wide roof of Beveridgism a new professionalism of approach,** rapidly grew up, replacing the notion of semi-charitable ministration to "the poor" by the idea of the servicing of many varieties of human need in a "clientele". Health visitors, child care organisers, housing managers, psychiatric social workers, industrial rehabilitation officers, almoners, youth leaders, and many other "specialists" proliferated, though (inevitably!) far short of the need.

From the workhouse at one end of the social scale to the Bar and the Courts of Law at the other the flavour of social service was seeping in. The old workhouse casual wards or "spikes"— reduced in number from 371 prewar to little over a hundred —were metamorphosed into "Reception Centres", with welfare officers whose duty it was to woo the tramps, their "clients"— the new social workers' phrase—to (in the words of the Act) "a more settled way of life".

By 1950 even the Courts of Law were losing a little of the old reproach that they were "open to all like the Ritz Hotel" as

* In prewar days financial inquisition was extended to relatives; now an applicant was allowed to own his own house and possess a fair amount of capital, and children were not required to contribute.

** Though voluntary organisations continued to play their part, these, too—as for instance the W.V.S.—had become immensely more expert and "professional" in their approach.

the new British Equality gingerly touched hands with the old British Liberty in the State-financed Legal Aid and Advice Organisation, designed to replace the haphazard patchwork of Poor Man's Lawyers. Five years later it had handled 70,000 divorce petitions and recovered a total of £7,000,000 in damages in High Court actions initiated on behalf of litigants of small means.*

Thus the human claim to Equality asserted in the new status of the horny-handed worker and his horn-rimmed union 'officer', received restatement in more universal and less directly political (if sometimes somewhat clinical) terms.

II

If for most people the heart of the "social revolution" of 1945 had seemed to lie in Beveridgism, that part of Beveridgism which had really captured the popular imagination was its assault on "the Giant Disease". This proved an excellent judgment, for it was the National Health Service that was to push out the bridgehead from which the idea of comprehensive all-class social service could be advanced on other fronts.

It was, from the first, a bridgehead that was hotly contested.

The British Medical Association had long campaigned for a comprehensive health service which would, in the wartime White Paper's words, make available, "all medical facilities to all the people". With the Royal Colleges, the B.M.A. had, in fact, played a leading part in the wartime Medical Planning Commission upon whose recommendations the Beveridge health proposals had been built.

Yet the moment the White Paper was out, and the harness of social purpose had come fully into view, the medical horse—so long accustomed to graze at large—had taken the bit between its teeth and bolted.

The White Paper's proposals, eight doctors complained in a

* By 1955, the Legal Aid system had been extended from the High Court to the County Courts, and by 1959 to the criminal courts, and to legal advice without litigation. The income limitations of the scheme were, however, still low, and breach of promise and libel and slander cases were excluded as offering too powerful a temptation to the litigious.

12. Sir Stafford Cripps "Between the Devil and the T.U.C."—a comment by *Vicky* in the *News Chronicle*, April, 1950. Cripps called for wage and profit restraint and stern dedication to duty and "Fair Shares"; but the Lynskey Tribunal revealed another, "under the counter" world of luxury flats, expense accounts and "contact men". 13. (*Below*) John Belcher, a junior Labour Minister, involved in the inquiry, reads the Tribunal's verdict.

14 and 15. The Opposition sneered at "a policy of exhortation", but the Labour Government proudly called it "telling the People"—a new stage in the evolution of a democratic society. Only there was so much to tell—and so many to do the telling—from the Treasury on the hoardings (*above*) to the Ministry of Food in the advertising columns (*below*).

This is the first of a series of Barracouta recipes

FOOD FACTS

Try BARRACOUTA
for breakfast!

Delicious Fish Cakes

Fish Cakes

These can be made overnight and re-heated.

Ingredients: 1 can barracouta, 8 oz. mashed potatoes, 2 level tablespoons finely chopped onion, 1 level teaspoon thyme, salt and pepper

BARRACOUTA is helping out with breakfast in many homes to-day. This economical smoked fish, now off points, makes temptin', and savoury dishes such as Fish Cakes and Toasts. Barracouta comes in ½ lb. cans, price 1/-. All recipes are for four people.

Barracouta Fritters

Ingredients: 4 oz. self-raising flour *or* 4 oz.

joint letter to the *Sunday Express*, would "undermine the priestly quality which is inherent in medicine". It was a chord frequently struck and poignantly held. And vital to this priestly quality it was now rapidly made clear was the right—which the White Paper proposed to abolish—to buy and sell practices (and thus patients).

Even more frantic was the profession's alarm at the small "basic salary" (£300 a year) written into the scheme to enable young doctors to exist while building their lists. This, the doctors declared, was "the thin end of the wedge" in a conspiracy to deliver them into State bondage.

For four years the medical neuroses were poignantly and publicly paraded. The tragi-comedy of the doctors' revolt against Lloyd George, launching the first health insurance scheme in 1911, was re-enacted with another Welshman, Aneurin Bevan, in the villain's role. Negotiations were broken off, restarted, broken off again. In their attitude to the honourable role promised them in the service of the "New Britain" the doctors indeed appeared to be suffering from personalities as distressingly divided as those of the dockers and miners.

Four months before the service was due to start, as citizens were being exhorted by the Ministry to choose their doctors in good time, the B.M.A. announced that in its most recent plebescite on the Act (which had become law fourteen months earlier) 40,814 doctors had voted *against* working the Scheme; 4,735 in favour.

In April—two months to go—the newspapers carried the third answer of the nation's doctors: in favour 14,620; against, 25,842.

Three weeks later—history repeating itself once more—a B.M.A. meeting recommended the doctors to sell themselves into bondage after all. By the appointed day, the great majority were safely signed up with their Executive Councils.

"THE DAY IS HERE", proclaimed an ecstatic *Daily Mirror* across its front page. But what exactly, after so remarkable and sustained a heralding, all those eager citizens who on that first Monday morning in July streamed off towards their chosen doctors' surgeries really expected to find when they got there

E

must remain a subject of speculation. We have, however, the testimony of a bank clerk who that day called in the doctor "under the Health Scheme" for his baby son: "I felt mildly surprised when the doctor arrived at the house and behaved precisely as he had always done." The turn-out remained impressive. A vexed Hammersmith G.P. complained to a reporter: "One would think the people saved up their illnesses for the first free day".

For a while there was indeed a faint air of the bargain sale about many a surgery. Some doctors in a first flush of National Health enthusiasm prescribed such medical "comforts" as whisky, stout, and even champagne, until neighbouring, less liberal, practitioners made bitter complaint. The number of prescriptions, announced the Minister of Health, had been "phenomenal". He appealed to people to use the National Service "prudently, intelligently and morally". "People must not rush to doctors who do not require doctors."

But as the pilgrimage for "free teeth" and "free glasses" gained momentum, dentists found themselves booked solid for many months ahead. Oculists ran through the £2,000,000 estimated to last nine months in the first six weeks of the service. With a five-month wait for spectacles, myopes who broke their glasses were now faced with effective disablement. Meanwhile, operating for twice the estimated number of hours—and sometimes, unfortunately, at about twice the rate—the dentists were achieving incomes that became the envy of the country. In Lanarkshire, the Chairman of the County Health Service Executive revealed that one dentist had earned £25,000 in eleven months, and that eleven were making £1,000 a month.*

Artificial legs, arms, eyes, surgical boots, trusses, belts, invalid chairs, and other appliances, freely available now to those needing them, provided the Press with an inexhaustible source of "human stories". But the article that appeared to exert on reporters and sub-editors a really irresistible fascination was the "National Health" wig, prescribable for conditions which "would unfit a person for acceptance in normal work or

* In 1949 the gloss was taken off this dental bonanza by an emergency regulation *halving* earnings above £4,800 a year—an action duly stigmatised by the British Dental Association as "an attack on the liberty of the individual".

society". "GRANNY, 94, IS GETTING SILVER CURLS FROM BEVAN" ran a typical headline. "At first I didn't much like the idea," the old lady was reported as saying. "It seemed like cadging. We've always paid for everything. . . . But so many people seem to be wasting National Health money that it won't do the country much harm if I have my little fling."

Another item, also allegedly illustrative of the New Britain, recorded that 400 National Health patients a month were receiving treatment in the Roman hot spring at Bath "exactly the same" as that for which "gouty colonels and rheumaticky dowagers" paid impressive sums of money.

III

Beneath the persiflage, the battle continued; the bridgehead, though widening, was still under attack. Officially, the Conservative Party approved the National Health Service. Unofficially, it became the main target for the Party's rearguard guerillas, providing a Wailing Wall against which class spleen could be vented and the bitterness of defeat could be purged.

The service was presented as a sort of malingerers' benefit, the news assiduously combed for items pointing conclusively to the persisting depravity of human nature—an attribute, it went without saying, that belonged principally to the working classes. Dark stories were exchanged of free corset-cadging (corsets were prescribable for 'viscenoptsis' or fatness), of multiple wig-hoarding, of high-altitude flights to cure Johnnie's whooping cough, of N.H.S. spectacles already detected in pawnshop windows. Then of course, there was the concomitant depravity of foreigners. Continental fishermen and lascars, it was alleged, were demanding free spectacles, dentures and wigs at every port of call. The nation—upon whom this gross parasitic body now preyed—was being bled white—an assertion to which colour was lent by the fact that the Health Service's cost, estimated at £140,675,000 a year, emerged in its first year at £208,000,000 and had by 1950 reached £358,000,000.*

* As the national income was rising and money values falling, the cost of the N.H.S. as a proportion of the national income remained relatively steady—at around $3\frac{1}{2}$ per cent, hardly wild extravagance.

On a more elevated—sometimes almost terrifyingly elevated
—level, the service was represented as tarred with the noxious
brush of the "Welfare State", that insidious sapper of the
national moral fibre, protector of the feckless, underminer of
the old British virtues of self-reliance and independence. The
Welfare State was deepening the prevailing materialism, creating a debilitating appetite for security, and had removed
Britain from the list of "dynamic societies".

In the Labour camp, the news was scrutinised with no less
zeal, the evidence deployed to form a very different picture.
In 1939, it was pointed out, there had been in Britain six million
people who needed spectacles, but did not possess them. Of
those who had spectacles, something like half had picked them
up from the sixpenny-store counters. Equally, the awful state
of British mouths had long been notorious: most women who
attended local authority clinics had half or more of their teeth
useless or gone. Again, half a million people had formerly had
both their efficiency and happiness reduced by deafness. If,
then, there was a rush for dental attention, or spectacles
(17 million pairs dispensed in the first two years), or if the white
ear-pieces of the N.H. Medresco hearing aid were suddenly
everywhere, what this really established was the depth of prewar neglect. Quite clearly, the question was not: "Can we
afford it?" but "Can we afford not to afford it?"

From 1944, when the doctors fired the opening salvoes, the
battle over the National Health Service was to continue, with
intermittent lulls, for more than a dozen years. Yet its outcome
had been decided almost as soon as it was joined. Apart from the
vitality and "social logic" of Beveridgism, the inauguration of
the service happened to coincide with a steep rise in medical
costs which made private treatment for any sort of serious illness
something few families could face with equanimity. So for the
middle class—as well as for the working class—the worth of this
particular "equality" was starkly evident from the first. The
Beveridge principle of comprehensiveness, however assailed
in words, was welcomed in practice.

The change here was dramatic and crucial. Before the war
only about half the G.P.s had "panel" practices, which
embraced 24,000,000 insured workers, and had a decisively
working-class flavour. The Beveridge scheme, by contrast,

embraced 97 per cent of all G.P.s and enrolled all but 3 per cent of the population as patients. "The local aristocracy have joined the N.H.S.; they wait their turn in the surgery with the rest," a wondering Home Counties doctor told a medical investigator.

Similarly the flavour of class-conscious charity no longer pervaded the hospitals. Of a total of around 240,000 hospital beds—excluding the minute number of private hospitals—only around 6,000 were now "pay-beds"* for consultants' private cases.

The old "two door" (or "two nation") approach to doctoring had become impracticable. The National Health Service was, as its name claimed, national.

IV

As, in mixed areas, the new middle-class N.H. patients encountered the dreary conditions and sometimes cursory treatment inherited from industrial panel practice, as they made their voyages of discovery into the public hospitals and met their often barrack-style regimentation, their cries of dissatisfaction caused a stir no less salutary than that aroused by the evacuee experience of the war.

For the first time authority began to take a purposeful look at the nation's medical servicing. A survey of general practices undertaken in 1951 by the B.M.A.'s own assistant-secretary, Dr. Stephen Hadfield, revealed nearly one-quarter of the surgeries "lacking in some essential or below standard". Some horrific details came to light and the B.M.A. set on foot a process of surgery inspection by its own local committees who were to persuade defaulters to bring their standards into line.

Here and there now, stylish panels of glass bricks began to appear in place of the old surgery shop windows of the

* The much criticised provision of these "pay-beds" appears to have been a sop to win over consultants—now, curiously, both well-paid pensionable permanent Civil Servants *and* private proprietors. The growth, over the years, of private health insurance schemes, which by 1957 covered 2 million people, might conceivably offer a greater threat of a return of the dual standard of medicine in the future, though, at this stage, this did not seem very likely.

"sixpenny doctor" tradition; modern chairs to replace benches, potted house-plants to brighten waiting-rooms as doctors came into line with the new middle-class—the new all-class—standards.

Yet in the deeper sense the doctors failed dismally to respond to the challenge of Beveridgism. They could not respond to what they did not feel. The high cost of qualifying and establishing oneself in practice before the war had ensured that almost all England's doctors came from a small social class. Blinkered by prep and public school, their horizons had been further shuttered by a long and intensive technical education which took little account even of the social and psychological background of disease. Nor were their social sympathies enlarged by induction into a professional guild whose power has been built on a mystique of exclusivism and secrecy. Again the effort to build the new society was undercut by class attitudes carried over from the old one.

But now the tide of change was flowing too strongly to be halted. Whatever medical misgivings, a minimum of central social planning had been accepted, and this slowly took effect. "Over-doctored areas" like the pleasant, rich southern seaside towns were closed to new entrants who were encouraged, financially and otherwise, to put up their plates in those long chronically "under-doctored areas" at the heart of industrial Britain. While, at the outset it had been necessary to permit N.H.S. lists exceeding even the official maximum of 4,000 per doctor, by 1951 it had been possible to cut the maximum to 3,500, and in the following three years the number of people still in "under-doctored areas" was more than halved.

But more important than any of the relatively small changes in the general practitioner's surgery was the redeployment and development of the nation's medical resources behind him. Before the war there had been large areas of Britain, including quite important towns, where there were no consultants, and where none ever came. Now that consultants were State-salaried, and no longer had to work in the great teaching hospitals to build up their private connections, their more systematic distribution over the country became possible. Now, too, they could go out from the hospitals to visit patients in their homes, whether fee-payers or not. In 1950 alone, 165,000

N.H.S. patients in all parts of Britain received visits from specialists, summoned by their G.P.s.

This was merely one aspect of the slow, massive, reorganisation of the "grotesque patchwork"—the 1944 White Paper's phrase—of Britain's prewar hospitals into a properly staffed, equipped and distributed nation-wide system. As it proceeded, nurses—hitherto sweated by almost bankrupt Voluntary Hospitals living precariously on flag-days and subscription schemes—achieved at last more reasonable pay and conditions and increased in numbers; diagnostic departments, laboratory and medical auxiliary staffs, were strengthened; beds increased in numbers and more patients passed through them more quickly.

In its wide range, its comprehensive structure, the National Health Service was perhaps the greatest single achievement of the postwar "social revolution". It was a social invention which Britain pioneered and other nations admired, even envied. Yet for Britain herself it was more than this. It was her first genuinely classless social service. The drugs prescribed by National Health doctors, the teeth filled by National Health dentists, the hearing aids dispensed by National Health audiometrists—even those wigs—doubtless did much to increase that "general prosperity and happiness" which the White Paper of 1944 set forth as the second duty of Government. But it was early evident that the most important of the National Health Service's nostrums might prove to have been contained in neither bottle, nor pill-box, nor ampoule; that it might prove to be an idea.

That Other Revolution

"It is not too much to say that
progress [in Medicine in these postwar years] has been greater than in
all preceding periods combined. . . .
Medicine has undergone little short
of a revolution."

—Dr. Ffrangcon Roberts, *The Cost
of Health,* 1952.

". . . hospitals in the London area
were asked to stop all but emergency
admissions so that they could deal
with the mass of cases arising from
the recent smog. In Glasgow and the
Forth-Clyde area four days of continuous smog had also filled the
hospitals."

—News-item, the *Observer.*

MASSIVE AS was the expansion of social responsibility that
had been set on foot, it was still in its very early stages.
The ugly gaps in the fabric of the "New Britain" were
more visible than the work proceeding on the foundations.
Where, for instance, was that nation-wide network of "gleaming" Health Centres much publicised in 1944 as the pivot of the
"Great Health-for-All Plan"—all those pleasant, well-equipped
buildings, where the New Model family doctors, working in
co-operative groups, were to marshal the latest diagnostic aids,
local authority preventive services and the diverse skills of
the specialists, in a grand assault on Sir William's "Giant
Disease"?

They had proved no less a mirage than the ground-nut
tribute of Africa. Whether they ever stood much chance of
coming into being is an academic speculation: shortages of
material and money ruled them out from the start. And the

reality which replaced that splendid vision was that of ever lengthening out-patient queues, hundreds of thousands of unhappy people clutching often cursory and even enigmatic notes of introduction ("Abdominal pain, please examine") overflowing the gloomy waiting-rooms of hospitals which were themselves generally "in an advanced state of obsolescence"* almost half having been built before 1891. At the same time, the G.P.s who despatched the patients thither, often for almost every trouble which was neither obviously trivial nor obviously routine, complained that they were being reduced to the status of "underpaid clerks", human pillar-boxes and fillers of forms at the beck and call of every petty bureaucrat.

The complaints had some justice, but were scarcely new. If the National Health Service had brutally underlined the change in the G.P.'s status, it had not originated it. The doctors were the victims not so much of Aneurin Bevan as of science. The reign of the bedside oracle was over. Abernethy himself would no longer have dared to stand alone at the bedside, pronouncing judgment from a glance at the tongue or a tap or two on the chest—without, that is, first being buttressed and insured by X-ray plates, electrocardiographs, an array of lab. reports, the opinions of the appropriate specialists—the whole vast panoply of modern scientific medicine. Thus, the inevitable consequence of the failure to realise the concept of the health centres** at this critical point in medical history was that the hospitals, designed for the treatment of a disease, became, paradoxically, the true heart of the National Health Service. And from these vast, isolated and forbidding fortresses of science, which swallowed up his patients, documented and processed them and converted them into "cases", the general practitioner was, in the main, excluded.

From presiding Godlike—artist, philosopher, integrator— over human life and destiny, the family doctor saw himself becoming, in the phrase of Kenneth Walker, "a kind of medical travel agent", consigning patients, properly ticketed, to clinic, laboratory and chemist. In short, he both shared the fate of

* The phrase of the Guillebaud Report, 1956.
** In 1957 there were still fewer than a score of health centres at work: some like those at Harlow, financed, as pilot schemes, by the Nuffield Trust.

many of his patients and sharply illuminated the mid-century predicament.

II

The ambivalence of science, as experienced by the ordinary man in the mid-twentieth century, was most evident in medicine which touches life at many points. At some levels science appeared to be a disintegrating force, breaking down the old forms and values without having yet shown the way to effective new ones; and yet simultaneously at other levels, the social revolution and the scientific revolution again appeared powerfully to reinforce each other.

Thanks to the first, the doctor was at last free to prescribe without anxious calculation of the patient's means. Thanks to the second, and more particularly to the pharmacologists' new ability to synthetise an ever-widening range of antibiotics and other drugs selectively aimed at particular bacteria, he had come into possession of a curative arsenal of unprecedented precision and power. Almost without leaving his chair, the G.P. could now confidently deal with many potentially serious conditions which would have defeated his father or himself before the war.

The great redbrick fever hospitals, the sight of which had once filled many a child with the secret dread of being "taken away" there, were now mostly empty or converted to other uses. Many young doctors had never seen a case of diphtheria. Progressively declining, year by year, it was by 1956 down to 53 cases, compared with 65,000 in 1938. In the same period the incidence of pneumonia, which had also lost much of its melodrama, almost halved.

But probably the most satisfactory of the largely postwar achievements was the victory over T.B. In 1948 there had been long waiting lists at all the sanatoria. Eight years later there were many spare beds, the death-rate from respiratory tuberculosis had sunk to one-quarter of the 1945–49 figure, and the medical authorities were hoping and planning for the disease's total elimination. Here, the social revolution and the scientific revolution worked powerfully together in a many-pronged, sustained and socially directed attack which included nation-wide mass-radiography, the new chemotherapy, the B.C.G. vaccine, T.T. and pasteurised milk, welfare foods for infants and mothers, school meals and milk, rationing by "Fair Shares" instead of by price, priority municipal housing . . .

The chemists and biologists, working now on a vast, industrial scale, had prepared the way for a hardly less spectacular break-through in the field of surgery. The anti-shock treatments developed in the war, penicillin, the new anaesthetics and muscle relaxants, injected rather than inhaled, aids like radio-active isotopes, extending the possibilities both of diagnosis and treatment, new techniques like hypothermia, chilling the body to reduce the need of oxygen, ingenious substitute mechanical organs, like the kidney machine or the Melrose heart-lung machine, these and many other converging advances, had enabled the surgeon to advance confidently into new territory. Delicate and protracted operations inside the brain, heart and lungs, unthinkable before the war, became routine. The newspapers—with good reason—were full of stories of "the Miracles of Modern Surgery"; how holes in hearts were being repaired; how sections of diseased arteries were being replaced by graftings; how plastic aortic valves were being fitted to defective hearts apparently as casually as a plumber replaces a washer on a dripping tap.

Old people could now be operated on and put back on to their feet with astonishing briskness. Statistics, it is true, still administered something of a cold douche, showing that the "expectation of life" at sixty-five had advanced only slightly over the last 100 years. But figures could not render the colour and quality of those years, and for all who could remember the prewar days, the change challenged the eye: people in their seventies, still full of vigour, even doing a good day's work, were everywhere. Spritely octogenarians had become commonplace. "The old" became "the elderly".

Meanwhile, at the other end of the life-span, vital statistics alone had a dramatic story to tell. By 1956, the maternal mortality rate, if still slightly higher than that of Sweden or Norway, had fallen to half what it had been only ten years ago—and one-sixth of the 1938 figure. The infant death rate, also steadily falling, was by 1956 half that of the immediate prewar years. And this was an improvement which visibly continued through childhood: the puny, weedy child, once so common, was becoming a rarity.*

III

But if, at both ends of life, there was so much striking evidence of the value of scientific medicine, in the working years between —when men and women might have been expected to come fully into their heritage—its shortcomings were amply demonstrated. Statistics suggested that most adult workers were "on the sick list" as often in the Fifties as in the interwar years.** Rheumatism still afflicted in one way or another two-thirds of the population over forty; no less than half of it suffered intermittently from bronchitis, "the English disease", and the elusive and unpredictable influenza virus continued to ravage the country from time to time.

Worse, two major diseases had become fearful cutters-off of males in their prime. Coronary thrombosis was now killing two out of every seven men who died between the ages of forty-five and sixty-four.† The death-rate from lung cancer had doubled in the ten years after 1945 and its graph-line continued to rise with frightening steepness. Cancer in its many forms remained the last great plague, the last fearful unknown. Science had unlocked the atom, but had not yet plumbed the secrets of the living cell—though there were some who were confident that it now stood upon that tremendous threshold.

Again, if many diseases of the body had been eliminated, the afflictions and vagaries of the mind increasingly thrust themselves on the attention. A working party of the newly established College of General Practitioners reported as "generally ac-

* In 1950, after examinations of around two million school-children, the Chief Medical Officer of the Ministry of Education reported that the condition of only 3½ per cent was "poor"; five years later it was 1½ per cent. As a corrective against over-optimism, in 1955, 268,000 (of all schoolchildren) were reported "vermin-infested".

** Dr. J. N. Morris, M.R.C. social medicine research unit, in address to industrial medical officers, 1958.

† 1958 figures.

cepted" that around 30 per cent of the patients consulting G.P.s were suffering from "psychological illness"—"one of the most pressing matters confronting the medical profession today". One-tenth of all drugs prescribed were now sleeping pills; in addition, the British public were getting through ten million aspirin tablets *per day*, a number which represented twice the prewar rate—and was still rising.

Contemplating these things, as the Forties gave way to the Fifties, a cynic might have reflected that progress consisted in little more than an exchange of diseases; a moralist or theologian might have been stimulated to renewed reflection on the subject of Original Sin. The latter, indeed, would certainly have noted that the "new" killing diseases appeared largely man-made. They were, it was often pointed out, diseases of stress, the characteristic diseases of modern industrial civilisation.

Two-fifths of the population of England and Wales now lived in six gigantic conurbations, six Great Wens which had swallowed up towns and villages alike in their grey, dirt-laden enormity—vast *reductio ad absurdum* of technological civilisation. On jam-packed human conveyor-belts one million people each day travelled into central London to work—and every year 20,000 more joined them, every year travelling further and longer as new housing spread out along the railway lines. Loneliness, reported the Women's Group on Public Welfare, had become so widespread and so distressing a phenomenon that it might be well to revive the wartime street warden. There was the vast lost legion of the "bed-sitters", the life that revolved around the gas-ring and the "built-in wash-basin". There was the even more desolating loneliness that lurked behind the neat curtains of the new estates where families were "decanted"—the official term—from the over-crowded old working-class areas. More and more, normal social and human communications seemed to be breaking down.*

---

* One of the more bizarre pointers to this breakdown was a strange postwar boom in Marriage Bureaux. There were over fifty of these "introduction agencies" registered in the U.K. with an expanding clientele of all ages and classes. In addition newspapers and magazines were flooded with letters asking help in locating a life partner.

Science, which could do a miraculous repair job on the tortured arteries, which could soothe the jittering brain with the new tranquilliser drugs, or, in hard cases, with a quick, neat, prefrontal leucotomy, seemed powerless before the larger situation.

This, perhaps, was hardly remarkable since it was the application of science—inadequately checked by earlier criteria —that had done so much to produce it.

And again, the mid-century state of medicine itself sharply illustrated the predicament and pointed the moral. For as the science of medicine devoured the older art of healing it had proliferated into innumerable sub-divisions, each smaller than the last, each intelligible fully to a narrower and narrower circle of specialists. Though postwar medical students spent two extra years in training—seven in all—in order to cram their heads with the appalling burden of technical detail that now appeared necessary, as practising doctors they quickly discovered that a large part of their technical journals was unintelligible to them. Complexity seemed to have reached the point of no return, producing problems of communication and of physical and intellectual organisation as acute as those of the great conurbations.

Medicine, insisted Sir John Charles, Chief Medical Officer at the Ministry of Health, needed to treat the "sick society" as well as the "sick person". It was an excellent, if comprehensive, diagnosis. But unfortunately the medical books were largely silent on methods. That Victorian Titan, the town Medical Officer, who had performed such prodigies of life-saving and life-making, was now reduced to the stature of a mere administrator. Nor were the new plagues to be banished by any such simple expedients as laying streets and drains. At a glance, it looked as if a useful preliminary prescription might be: "Physician, heal thyself!" It was occasionally ungratefully remarked that science (aided by Beveridgism) had now given us a good National Disease Service. What we had really wanted was a National Health Service.

This seemed likely to take a little longer.

14.   Eleven Plus — What?

"Such, then, will be the three main
types of secondary education, to be
known as Grammar, Modern and
Technical. . . ."

"Such diversity must not impair the
social unity within the educational
system which will open the way to a
more closely-knit society. . . ."

—White Paper on Educational
Reconstruction, July, 1943.

IF THE "equality" of the National Health Service and the
sick bed gained on the whole speedy acceptance and the
"equality" of the trade unionist received at least lip-service,
the concept of equality contained within that other foundation
deed of the "New Britain", the Butler Education Act, 1944,
quickly became entangled in a web of cherished prejudice and
sacrosanct tradition. It was one of the characteristic ironies of
the time that the massive, liberating programme summed up
in the wartime slogan, "Free Secondary Education for All",
and hailed as a great advance towards a unified, modern
society, should, in its enactment, have provoked a sharper,
grittier, more particularised, consciousness of class and social
inequalities than had perhaps ever before existed in Britain.
The violence and duration of the reactions offered some index
of the depth and novelty of the social change set on foot.

Certainly, the pains of transition were made more acute
by the grim circumstances of the Forties. Five thousand schools
had been damaged in air raids. Even without the extra school
year, the wartime "birth-rate bulge" would have put a heavy
strain on the long grossly inadequate schools that remained.
So that when, one bleak morning in January, 1947, the
Government announced that the raising of the school-leaving
age to fifteen would go ahead in April, not everyone felt able
to echo the *Daily Herald*'s enthusiastic declaration that

"historians may marvel at the British people's audacity in making this gesture of faith in the future almost at the peak of their economic difficulties". An eminent Oxford Professor of Economics wrote to *The Times* to protest that it was "flagrantly foolish" to rob the nation of the labour of 300,000 fourteen- year-olds who might otherwise have been helping in the Export Drive.

This was no new note in Britain where for many years the public educational system had been the automatic victim of any and every economic setback, and it was fortunate that the Ministry of Education at this critical point was in the charge of a tough and resolute old campaigner. The daughter of a Lancashire cotton operative, herself a former teacher and "scholarship girl", Ellen Wilkinson was possessed by that fierce missionary faith in Education—with the capital 'E'—that had shone through the old Labour Movement. To Ellen Wilkinson, and those who felt like her, it seemed that it was now or never; this extraordinary pretence that Great Britain could not afford a decent educational system had to be knocked on the head now, once and for all.

And thus was launched what the Press was soon calling "The Battle of the School Place Gap" ("Gaps" like "Cuts" being part of the basic vocabulary of the Forties). Hundreds of concrete H.O.R.S.A. ('Hutting-Operation for the Raising of the School-leaving Age') hutments began to spring up in school playgrounds and on bits of wasteland, equipped with the bright new products of S.F.O.R.S.A. ("School Furniture Operation for the Raising of the School-leaving Age").

All over Britain in the summer of 1947 posters appealed— "MAKE TEACHING YOUR CAREER!" By April of that year, 2,000 new teachers were trained, 11,000 more were in training, and 15,000 more awaited admission to forty-eight Emergency Training Colleges hastily improvised in country houses, orphans' homes, hutted hospitals, Army camps.

Many of the new teachers were in their thirties; some forty and over. Interviewing panels had gone out to the theatres of war. In a single training college were to be found men of thirty-eight different former occupations, bus drivers, French polishers, engineers, clerks, local government officers. . . .

Something of the old wartime sense of purpose and camaraderie still survived in all this. Lecturers were often astonished at the enthusiasm with which these men and women attacked the one-year course. Theoretically this was to be followed by two years' part-time study. But by general consent, what the new teachers lacked academically they often more than made up in the breadth of experience they brought to the often closed-in world of the classroom.

Never before, in fact, had so strong, invigorating and continuous a breeze blown through the cobwebby structure of the British education as was to blow through it in these years. All over Britain local educational authorities, at the behest of the Ministry, were drawing up the elaborate Development Plans required to realise the concept of universal free secondary education. By the summer of 1949 new school places were being brought into being at the rate of 300 a day. Children were moving into their new schools with the bricklayers, painters and carpenters still working around them.

II

Anywhere but in England it might have seemed extraordinary that a nation should embark on this vast process of educational expansion and change without first getting quite clear the sort of schools it required; even more extraordinary that there should have been so little appreciation that the matter transcended pedagogic considerations and must profoundly affect the whole tone and shape of English society.

In this instance the customary obfuscations of English empiricism were increased by the fact that while Mr. Churchill's Coalition had issued the White Paper on Educational Reconstruction and a Conservative Minister had embodied it in the Act of 1944, it fell to a Government of a radically different political philosophy to translate this key reform into practice.*

For all the difference it made, the political change might hardly have happened. With its innumerable caddis-wormlike

* The Act itself merely said that the new schools should be "appropriate" to "the different ages, abilities and aptitudes of the pupils"; whereas the earlier White Paper had specified a "Tripartite" division of schools into Grammar, Modern and Technical. The Labour Party's official policy was to establish Comprehensive Schools. When it had come to office, however, "The Nation's Schools"

accretions down the years, its infinite local variations and embattled sectarian enclaves, the English education "system" was a maze of such denseness, complexity, and, occasionally, richness, that radical reconstruction would have defeated any but the most determined iconoclast. The "Tripartite" organisation of secondary education that emerged was the result of the "incidence of accident" far more than of any deliberate choice. Behind the screen of a series of reports by committees of inquiry,* largely sanctifying the *fait accompli*, it had for over twenty years been growing in characteristic English fashion out of a past which by 1948 was at many points hopelessly out-distanced.

Nevertheless, with the ozone of 1945 in their nostrils, the Governmental educationists enthusiastically proclaimed the tripartite division of secondary schools into "grammar", "technical" and "modern" as the new revelation—a sort of educationists' equivalent of the wonderful new health service. Not only would this arrangement provide careers for all talents, it would bring social equality also. All schools, they pointed out, must, under the Act, have gymnasia, libraries, playing fields, arts and crafts rooms, assembly halls in equal numbers and of equal dimensions. For all alike, regulations specified a maximum of thirty pupils per class. All schools must, and indeed would, enjoy "parity of esteem".

There were, however, from the beginning those who found neither conviction nor comfort in this curious guilt-laden phrase. Even as the Education Act was passing into law, Britain's largest educational authority, the London County Council, Labour-controlled since 1934, was voting down

and other Ministry of Education expository literature, enveloped the whole issue in clouds of generalised educationists' goodwill, mentioning and enthusiastically explaining almost everything, while in effect promoting "tripartitism".

* The Hadow Report (1926) had recognised the "Bipartite" arrangement of Grammar and Modern (then, senior elementary) schools; the Spens Committee (1938) added the secondary technical school (in recognition of the achievements of the junior technical schools); the Norwood Committee (1943), chaired by a public school headmaster, advocated Tripartitism, which was accordingly written into the White Paper (1943), though omitted from the Act. All these variants in fact derived from the old "two nation" system of grammar schools and elementary (3R) schools.

Tripartitism and cleaving to the Comprehensive school, the common high school, which had long been the rule in such democratic countries as the United States and Scotland.

"When the aristocracy of wealth went out of fashion," ran the L.C.C.'s manifesto on the subject, "we created a new one which we were pleased to think was an aristocracy of Brains— that is, of those who excelled in Book Learning. We need to create a much wider aristocracy—of those who excel in the art of social living."

In its zeal for "social living" the L.C.C. proposed to swallow up some of the old London grammar schools in the chain of gigantic new comprehensive schools it was planning.

The attack on the Public Schools as fortresses of privilege had been familiar ground since the Twenties. The indictment of the grammar schools—*their* entrenched privilege based now on I.Q. ratings rather than directly on money—was new and distinctively postwar. It called forth the briskest reactions.

The great Comprehensive *v.* Grammar School Row, was to rumble on for well over a decade. In its own rather absent-minded, intellectual-weekly way, it went to the heart of things in Britain at this time far more than most of the conventionally 'political' issues before Parliament. For the comprehensive school represented about the most unequivocal statement available of that egalitarianism which in one form or another, had powered most of the social reforms of the Forties. It boldly asserted the simple human claim ("a man's a man for a' that"); it stood for the quintessential equality whereas the Tripartite system merely stood for equality of opportunity—in practice unrealised and unrealisable. The one aspired to "the classless society"; the other appeared to believe this to be not only impossible but also undesirable.

In these vast barns of comprehensive schools, protested these traditionalists, the nation's clever boys, its "alpha plus types", its "high flyers", were to be sacrificed to the false and shoddy gods of envious egalitarianism. The tone would be that of the Lowest Common Denominator, of the feckless, reckless plebs. Gregory Peck would oust Plato! Donald Peers replace Pythagoras! To accept such schools was to surrender to the barren cult of mediocrity.

The champions of the comprehensive schools mounted a no

less passionate attack on "outmoded class distinctions" and the besetting English vice of snobbery which the old school system encouraged. The "creaming off" at the age of eleven of those small boys who were—as the Ministry's booklet, '*The New Secondary Education*' put it—"attracted by the abstract approach to learning", to undergo in a grammar school that "stern intellectual discipline" appropriate to the future mandarinate was every bit as bad for them as it was for their less brainy coevals who were summarily excluded.

The debate continued, filling miles of correspondence columns in a great variety of journals. But if accent and example were novel, the debate itself was no new one. It was the old dialogue, still somehow going on, between the traditional "representative democracy" of Burke and the rotten boroughs and the squirearchy and the up-and-coming "count-heads", one-man one-vote, greatest-happiness-of-the-greatest-number England of the Utilitarians and the Chartists and Birmingham and the Labour Movement and 1945 and Dr. George Gallup and his poll. It was the old time-bomb, planted under English society since the French Revolution, which had, unaccountably, never gone off, but of whose continued ticking the English became intermittently aware.

But now the Great Comprehensive School Row signalled a new phase. For the bridging of the Atlantic, the approach of the cultural democracy of the electronic soap opera, was bringing a renewed sharpness—even a note of desperation—to what for most of the time had been a lofty, often academic, debate, stripping it of literary trappings to recast it in terms of a stark choice between the class society and "the mass society".

If choice there were any longer.

III

The debate on the schools was prolonged and complicated by the fact that the rival systems existed in England at this time in their advocates' imaginations only. The score or so local authorities who had adopted the Comprehensive School principle included a few of the largest and most vigorous in the country. But the schools themselves existed only on the drawing board.* As for the Secondary Modern school, by which—since it would take two-thirds of the nation's children—the Tripartite approach must stand or fall, there were a few showplaces, many more where a new spirit was stirring in ancient buildings, but many, too, where all that seemed to have happened was that one more euphemistic title had been tacked on to some decrepit "Senior School" (ex-Board School) long ago "reorganised" under the prewar Hadow Plan.**

Worse, there were still at this time a million children in "unreorganised" "All-Age" schools—a sinister statistic which, together with that for "illegal" over-thirty classes, continued to cast its shadow over the Fifties.

The neglect of a generation was not to be repaired in two or three years. But the Education Act of 1944 had at least done one thing. If Equality of Opportunity was still beyond its reach, it had gone a significant distance towards securing Equality of Lack of Opportunity. It had abolished fees in "maintained" grammar schools.† And of all the factors making up the "social revolution" of 1945 it was probably this quite small step that came nearest to justifying the word "revolution".

Though the number of fee-carrying places in these schools had been declining, it had still remained large enough‡ before the war to enable that part of the middle class which did not aspire to the boarding school to take grammar school education more or less for granted.

Suddenly, this was no longer so. With all places free, and

* Even by the year 1958 there were still only forty-six comprehensive schools in being in England and Wales.

** By 1939, two-thirds of the nation's eleven-year-olds had in fact been "reorganised" in such "senior schools"—in preparation for the institution of universal secondary education and the raising of the leaving age. The Technical side of the alleged Tripartite approach was equally sketchy, there being only one technical school to four grammar. Two-fifths of local authorities possessed no technical schools at all.

† By one of those totally illogical anomalies that seem inseparable from England's most "sweeping" reforms, 165 "Direct Grant" grammar schools, by virtue of receiving their public funds from Whitehall direct rather than via the local authority, were permitted to continue to charge fees for half of their places.

‡ About a half—but with wide local variations. Some local authorities had abolished fees before 1944.

maintenance grants available, the simple right of class and purse was abruptly replaced by an annual pitched battle of childish wits and nerves. And this at least was no "quiet revolution"— the anguished protest of 'scorned' middle-class parents filled the suburban air and the newspapers. To many it now began to appear that "ruin" came not from bankruptcy or matrimonial disaster or defalcation or drink, but from having had the misfortune to have conceived a child who "failed" the Eleven Plus.

Eleven Plus cram books poured from the presses; the advertisement columns of local papers all over Britain offered extra coaching. The Eleven Plus's simple intelligence tests acquired a nightmare quality and teachers, goaded by desperate parents, were forced into coaching children to grapple with them. When one local authority proposed to rely instead on teacher's opinions, the teachers refused to write these down unless guaranteed absolute secrecy. Otherwise, they complained, the fury of rejected parents would force them to leave town.

Never was the class structure of the nation and of its educational system more nakedly exposed. For even if the alternative Secondary Modern school was a good one whose pupils wore their new badges and blazers with an air, many parents openly regarded it with a revulsion that they would in decency have hesitated to show to a leper colony. Since most of its children left at fifteen, it was unlikely in any case to provide the new General Certificate of Education to which employers had now perversely become as firmly wedded as they had been to the old "matric" it had been designed to replace. If a child "passed the Eleven Plus" a whole world of desirable careers thus opened before him; if he didn't, he often seemed cast out into the outer darkness.*

And thus the reign of equality in schools of England was inaugurated by the ceremonial immolation, each spring, of two-thirds of the eleven-year-olds of the nation.

* The bitterness of the occasion was intensified in that the odds in this Ordeal by the Eleven Plus varied enormously from place to place—so that a child's future depended no longer wholly on the accident of family, but also greatly on that of birth-place. The proportion of grammar school places available ranged, according to area, from 10·5 per cent to 45 per cent. The quality and number of other types of school also varied enormously from place to place at this period. One might with only average ability get a fine free secondary education—or a mockery of one.

IV

But the ironies of the Eleven Plus were multiple and complex. If it was an index of national inadequacies and a potent source of suburban neuroses it was also a powerful lever of change. As the arrival of the middle-class patient in the panel doctor's surgery had sealed the fate of the "two-nation" approach in medicine, so the middle-class experience of the full rigour of Britain's public educational system promised—ultimately—a similar result in education also.*

Nor, in an age when certificates were essential for almost everything (one no longer "ran away to sea": one took a course for Cabin Boys, Grade II) were these pressures confined to the middle class. Never before in British history had public education been so much and continuously in the centre of the national scene, so insistently demanded at all social levels. A social survey in 1952 showed that even in the unskilled working class the majority of parents now wanted their children to stay at school till sixteen, while a strong minority wanted them to stay till eighteen.** That this represented a real change of attitude could be seen from the figures for children in fact staying on at school, steadily rising, in all classes of secondary school, year by year, through the Fifties.

It was, in short, at last being discovered that education was too serious a matter to be left to educationists—and that, too, possibly marked a stage in the maturing of social democracy in England. Minister after Minister, Director after Director, was now obliged to spend a considerable part of his time making apologies for the Eleven Plus. Authority after authority precipitately announced changes, sometimes proudly claiming "abolition". More and more modern schools were acquiring "grammar school forms" or "extended courses to sixteen";†

* The limited yet formidable reservation in the matter of the public schools is dealt with in Chapter 16.
** "Social Class and Educational Opportunity", ed. J. E. Floud (1956).
† In 1958 the White Paper on Secondary Education officially approved this development, and the Government undertook to provide finance.

many were quietly dropping the "Modern" from their titles and becoming "High Schools" or simply leaving off invidious labels altogether. "Everywhere," reported an N.U.T. symposium,* "differences between types of school are breaking down. Outlines are becoming blurred and the degree of comprehensiveness of most secondary schools is increasing, year by year." Leicestershire introduced the experiment of a common school for all its children between eleven and fourteen, with transfer to a grammar school for all whose parents would guarantee continuing attendance to sixteen. Sheffield, Barrow and the North and East Ridings, built "bilateral" schools, combining "Grammar and Technical" or "Modern and Technical"; other authorities elected for "campus" schools, divided on traditional lines, but built on a common site, and sharing a common social life.

Thus though the Comprehensive School appeared to have been largely rejected formally,** its basic idea—so novel, so startling, so *shocking* in Britain when it was first mooted a few years earlier—was now stealthily re-entering by the back door.

In September, 1954, the first of the L.C.C.'s projected new "Comprehensives" was opened at Kidbrooke, an immense group of buildings, a blaze of crimson, yellow and blue, with 1,700 girls, 90 teachers, 5 gymnasia, a radio control room and an assembly hall like an aeroplane hangar.

"The First Palace of Learning!" enthused the *News Chronicle*. "Sausage Machine!" retorted the still unrepentant London *Evening Standard*.

But by now the heart appeared to be going from this particular battle. Or was it, perhaps, merely a pause to regroup? Whatever the answer the terrain had been illuminated as never before. The venerable religious dispute, with its endless sectarian claim-staking, which had bedevilled the development of English education right down to 1944, no longer obscured the view, and in the harsh light of the Eleven Plus the true issues for contemporary social democracy were beginning to stand out with scarifying visibility.

* "Inside the Comprehensive School", 1958.
** Particularly after the return of the Conservative Government which tended to discourage local authorities planning new Comprehensives.

15.   The Endless Middle

"We know that you, the organised
workers of the country are our friends
—indeed, it could not be otherwise.
As for the rest, they do not matter a
tinker's cuss (acclamation)"

—Emmanuel Shinwell, Minister of
Fuel and Power, to the E.T.U.
conference at Margate, May,
1947.

"The Middle Classes? Oh, yes, they
certainly are included among the
useful members of society. And the
Labour Government is vitally concerned about their welfare."

—Herbert Morrison, Lord President
of the Council, interviewed by
Picture Post, March, 1948.

ORDEAL BY the Eleven Plus was not the only tribulation of
the middle classes in these years. One morning in 1947
the *Daily Mail* leader page featured a piece by a staff
writer boldly headed FOUR JAM SANDWICHES. It told the story of a
certain middle-aged professional man who, clad in well-cut (if
faintly shiny) black suit, well-polished shoes, and impeccably
rolled umbrella, travelled daily on the 8.45 to the City. He had
an air of quiet authority and culture, and, inevitably (explained
the writer) his fellow-travellers found themselves respectfully
speculating about the contents of the important-looking brief-
case which he carried. Until, one never-to-be forgotten
morning, the brief-case fell open. And on to the floor of the
carriage were precipitated, neatly done up in brown paper, four
jam sandwiches—the distinguished man's lunch.

This was the "plight of the middle classes" and it was rarely
out of the newspapers in the postwar Forties. The plaints of the
"New Poor" of 1947 echoed those of the "New Poor" of 1921.

But inflation was much more sustained after World War II and Sir William Beveridge now pronounced it to be "as great a social evil as unemployment ever was". Not only had those living on pensions and fixed interest securities to watch them being steadily eroded by the slide, year after year, of the real value of the pound—vividly portrayed in charts in their newspapers—but the inflationary climate enabled the powerful trade unions of manual workers to establish wage levels which left the weakly organised white-collar man further and further behind.*

This discouraging experience was accompanied by others. While the middle-class man was unable to get a licence to build a house on mortgage (his traditional method), he saw the "workers"—often more highly paid than he—moving into well-equipped, newly constructed municipal flats and houses at low rents, subsidised out of *his* taxes. Denied the grammar school—which he regarded as peculiarly *his* school—he "scrimped and saved" to pay private school fees, while the working man—not having to "keep up appearances"—could let *his* son go to a secondary modern.** It scarcely needed Mr. Shinwell's much publicised assurance that the middle-class paterfamilias "didn't matter a tinker's cuss" to convince him that he and his kind were being cynically "levelled down".

At the merest mention of the rise of bus-fares or the depreciation of Gilt-Edged, the budgets flooded into the newspaper offices, filling their correspondence columns for days on end with searing details of genteel poverty behind trim suburban hedges.

There was a phrase with which these plaints began, a magic, nostalgia-laden phrase, "before the war". . . "Before the war we ran a small car, we lived in a modern flat, we threw occasional

* According to the Office Management Association survey the weekly earnings of manual workers passed those of experienced clerks for the first time in 1946, and by 1952 had reached those of senior clerks. At the other end of the scale, a Permanent Secretary of a Government Department, married with two children, received in 1956, after tax, only £225 more than in 1933, despite a 50 per cent rise in pay.

** Such middle-class "sacrifices" were sometimes pathetically ill-judged. In 1953 the Chief Education Officer for Surrey reported that 3,000 children attending private schools in the county were receiving education below the permissible standard.

parties, we danced regularly, we had all the cigarettes we wanted. . . . But now . . ."

But now, indeed! "We last went to the cinema in December, 1946 (Sorry, Mr. Rank!). We never enter pubs. . . . At lunch-time I have only Bovril and toast. We have had to give up out-ings and we cannot afford a holiday. . . . We are gradually getting down to bare existence."

As the months went by certain familiar figures began to emerge from these endless columns of relentless documentation: the doctor's wife who was being worn to a frazzle by inability to afford a maid,* the bank cashier's wife who might possibly manage to renew the loose covers on her twenty-year-old armchairs next year but one, the "struggling, middle-aged grammar school master with" (as one of them explained) "a tattered gown whose only value is the covering it affords to patched knees, threadbare elbows, and a bitter heart".

The grammar school master, indeed, typified, in almost classic form, the multiple bewilderments of this "old" middle class. His grammar school no longer held, unchallenged, its local monopoly position as the revered temple of Scholarship and Culture. He himself was valued, in money terms at considerably less than the working-class fathers of some of his new boys. And—"parity of esteem" indeed!—he was, despite his "Hons. (Oxon)", paid only a derisory sum more than non-graduate (perhaps even 'Emergency-trained'!) teachers in secondary moderns. As if to confirm T. S. Eliot's contention that egalitarianism was the enemy of culture he now found himself deprived of that modest comfort, the means to buy a book or go to a concert or otherwise partake of that intellectual refreshment necessary to his calling. Instead . . . "a thoughtful relative hands on the *Manchester Guardian* a day late".

With a sinking heart, such members of the "old" middle classes finally succumbed to the awful suspicion that somehow or other—though the metaphor was not one which would have naturally sprung to their minds—they had been "backing

* In 1951, only 1·2 per cent of private households in Great Britain had one or more domestic servants—compared with 4·8 per cent (England and Wales) in 1931. According to the Hunt-Regina servant's agency there were in the Fifties about 150 butlers still employed in private houses in London: a dying race.

the wrong horse" all these years; that, somehow or other, the working classes were having all the fun, and the middle classes all the "striving". And into their plaints there crept a new and querulous note, the whine of muted class war, class aggression directed not now from the bottom, upwards, but from the middle strata of society, sourly and ineffectually, downwards.

Alongside the "budget" letters pouring into the newspapers, there now flowed a second stream complaining of the turpitude, the indiscipline, the regrettable uppishness of Them, the British working classes. A foreigner visiting Britain might well have concluded that one of the main activities of the British middle classes was keeping account of the number of television aerials on council houses or clocking-on and off the "tea-breaks" and shovel-resting periods of the British Workman. With bright, bitter smiles, suburbanites endlessly exchanged British Working Man stories. A typical specimen in a large collection contributed to the *Sunday Express* told how a housewife who "had the decorators in" had returned home unexpectedly to find the men asleep on her twin beds. "On being aroused, one man asked: 'Is tea ready?'"

II

For all their protestations about "levelling down", the middle classes themselves were very substantial beneficiaries of 1945, particularly of the health service and the expansion of free higher education. If they were victims at all, they were the victims, not so much of "tinker's cuss" Shinwell or the "twisted-minded" Bevan—excellent whipping boys as these made—as of technological change. The grammar school master, aggrieved over the inadequate recognition of his superior status, might well have made common cause with the senior engine-driver, once Uncrowned King of the Iron Road, now mourning his vanishing "wage differential". The dignified book-keeper displaced by chattering girl comptometer-operators might, had he known it, have had a fellow feeling with the Black Country smith who watched semi-skilled "blue collar men" on bright and airy car assembly lines in Birmingham or Coventry taking home twice the pay earned by the time-honoured skills of eye and muscle it had taken him a lifetime to acquire.*

A hundred and fifty years ago, certain sorts of machines in certain sorts of workshops—or "mills"—had transformed English society, creating the urban proletariat and a particular sort of division within it, and, to some extent, outside it. Now different machines, in a very different sort of factory—or plant —were creating not only new divisions but a whole new world.

The pace of takeover and merger was to quicken notably in the Fifties. The small family firm which had supplied the economic foundation of the old middle class and much of its peculiar tone and ethic was less and less characteristic. Even in such traditional industries as cotton, pottery, brewing or baking, built up around family, the financiers, the accountants, the efficiency experts, were moving in. As mass production was complemented by mass distribution the small shopkeeper, too, secured a thinner and thinner slice of total trade or was obliged to join some large central buying organisation. Many fields were now dominated by large-scale impersonal organisations: a much-quoted study by the National Institute of Social and Economic Research showed that 512 of these large concerns accounted for almost half the total profits of private industry.

The first industrial revolution enveloped us in our urban desolation. The effects of the second were less visible but sometimes hardly less disturbing. And the fact that the two worlds, the world of the "first industrial revolution" and the world of the second, still existed side by side multiplied the confusion.

Yet transition from one to the other was now often mercifully swift. The plaints of the "old" middle classes in the Forties were to be swallowed up in the Fifties in the complacency of the rising new "middle income groups". Far from declining, the proportion of the population engaged in professional work, in

* This depreciation of the old traditional skills was a continuing but also an accelerating process. According to Zweig (*The British Worker*), in the building industry before the First World War the labourer had 64 per cent of the craftsman's rate; in 1922, 75 per cent; from 1945, 80 per cent. In engineering the premium for skill in 1900 was 50 per cent; in 1950 around 15 per cent. Many industries could furnish similar figures.

the Civil Service and in managerial and administrative jobs had in fact increased by 50 per cent between 1938 and 1951. It continued to grow. The expansion of "non-proletarian" or service occupations which is a well-established feature of advanced industrial societies was now reaching the point in England where even in an industrial town industrial workers might no longer preponderate.*

The effect of these developments on the whole tone and shape of English society was immense. The distinctive qualities of the old middle class had stemmed from a sharp consciousness of its middleness, an ever-present sense of position which involved both striving to avoid slipping back into the masses and a proper, sometimes Radical, pride in face of those Born to Rule. But there comes a point in the expansion of a middle when its true middleness, its finitude, is lost. As the Fifties progressed, it began to look as if for the English middle classes that Point of No Return had been passed.

Nor did it seem that any simple division into "upper-" and "lower-middle" and "lower-upper" and "upper-lower" such as had earlier saved the situation would avail. For many factors were now contributing to this disconcerting loss of definition. Hitherto, middle-class values had been buttressed by the old professions with their self-imposed codes. Not only were these professions themselves now often practised under radically changed conditions, but they were increasingly obscured in the proliferation of the crypto-professions and specialisms of the newer "middle-income-groups".

As the apparatus of mass-production grew in size and complexity, it required, on one side, whole armies of technologists and production men and accountants, on the other—to ensure effective meshing with the consuming masses—a great multiplication of publicity and advertising men, market research specialists and opinion pollsters, sales managers, agents, journalists, home experts, designers and commercial artists and publishers of many kinds.

* According to Professor K. C. Edwards, the proportion of people in towns engaged in service occupations (with the exception of a few special cases) now "invariably exceeds one-third of the total number employed and in the majority of cases exceeds one-half". In 1951 for England and Wales as a whole the proportion of directly "productive" workers to service occupations was 53 : 47.

16. *L. to r.*, Robert Boothby, Prof. Joad, Gilbert Harding, Dr. Bronowski.

What Happened to Harding: The Brains Trust (war-born, revived in 1948) belonged to radio and the serious-minded Forties. With television and the Fifties the arc-lit parlour game took over and the Television Personality was born. The Question Master moved into the place of the Prophet, Gilbert Harding took over from Bernard Shaw.

17. *Below*, Frances Day, Jerry Desmonde, Elizabeth Allen, Gilbert Harding.

"ALL I ASK IS THAT YOU GET IT PROPERLY BALANCED"

18. Low's cartoon shows the new Chancellor, Mr. Hugh Gaitskell, mounted, Service Ministers Shinwell and Strachey underneath.

1950: War in Korea imposed a crushing burden on a convalescent Britain, and further imperilled Anglo-American relations.

19. (*Below*) Mr. Attlee made a "dash" to Washington to save Britain and the world from the "hysterical" Americans and their Bomb.

Alongside, like an oil duct continuously lubricating the whole complex process, boomed the many-sided entertainment industry, also requiring a vast range of "specialists" and technicians.

Many of these people could not have done their jobs if their minds had remained fixed in the old middle-class focus. If they were prosperous—and they often were—their prosperity probably derived not from long-term application and the plodding observance of a professional code (though some showed a guilty tendency to prepare these) but from *flair*. Theirs was not the world of Thrift, Club Armchairs and Gilt-Edged but of the "economics of expansion" and the "cult of the Equity". They were more likely to think of themselves, in the advertising man's language, as an "income group"—A, B, or AB—than a class.

That other large body of middle income recruits—the scientists and the many new and rising varieties of engineers and technologists—was hardly more likely to fit the old middle-class niches. In the twenty years between 1931 and 1951 the number of scientific workers alone had multiplied more than three times and, as the *Situations Vacant* columns bore daily witness, the demand was still far from met. According to Sir Alexander Fleck, Chairman of the immensely diversified Imperial Chemical Industries, of I.C.I.'s 7,800 male managerial staff no less than 5,800 in the mid-Fifties were scientists and technical men. "Similar trends", he added "are observable in all branches of industry."

These were the men in grey pullovers and grey raincoats who now filled the First Class carriages en route to cities like Birmingham and Newcastle, shamelessly talking in highly miscellaneous accents their unintelligible shop. The odds would be rather more than even that their fathers had been manual workers. Their *alma mater* was more likely to be Redbrick than Oxbridge, and might well have been the "White Tile" of some large, bleak, provincial "Tech". They were as different from the old "professional man" as a Glasgow Scot from a Home Counties Englishman. Builders of a new world, they were not so foolish as to expect its divisions to coincide with those of the old one.

"I", Sir William Beveridge himself had written, "am a man

of the middle classes who, while having to work for a living, take their orders from no one." The new professional people— if they still merited that description—took their orders from a great many people. Indeed, they might not be so much individuals as specialist functions, fine cogs certainly, but cogs whose value depended on their close intermeshing.

Everywhere, in business and industry, in old arts like architecture and new ones like television—above all, in science —"the team" was the slogan and often also the reality of the times. Even the accountants who were now achieving control over vast commercial and industrial empires because only they could plumb their financial depths, even *they* could not function alone, needing to mesh with the complementing specialisms of production engineers, designers, personnel officers, marketing men. . . . Even the doctor, the very type of the old professional man, was now a cog in a complex machine; the once Godlike consultant, a State-salaried Civil Servant, his "merit awards" (from £500 to £2,500) determined by another of the now ubiquitous committees.*

III

English historians had long been accustomed to see in the steady expansion of the middle classes one of the principal sources of England's stability and growth. Ever since their great representative Defoe had catalogued their multiplying enterprises on his "Tour" the middle classes had left their mark on every age. They had bound the nation together, providing a ladder for ascent, yet preserving the social order. They had offered a lodging place to Dissent, so vital a principle in England's development; yet supplied the catalyst of peaceful change. In recent years, they had provided the pilots and planners of the rising Labour Movement. Beveridge was one of them as the Webbs had been and as, supremely, was Clement Attlee. The social revolution of 1945 bore their stamp.

* Of his medical peers, however. The consultants still managed to make the best of both worlds as few other professional men now could. By virtue of a hard bargain wrung out of Bevan they had been allowed to retain their private practices in addition to occupying State-salaried hospital posts.

If these values were exhausted, if this dynamic and central process of change had finally and irrevocably worked itself out, then this was indeed a turning-point in our island story.

What would—what *could*—replace these sustaining moral qualities, this inbuilt sense of purpose and direction?

The answers, so far, had failed to appear. What was offered was expansion, at such a rate and in so many ways that it seemed gratuitous to demand also an indication of direction.

As the middle bands of the social spectrum continued to broaden, so the edges of the lower bands continued to blur, and as mufflers gave place to blue collars and blue collars faded into white, there began to emerge that theme, the theme of the Endless Middle, which at so many points and so many levels was to be the theme of mid-century England.

F

16.   Free-for-All

"... . the nature of a child's education should be determined by his
capacity and promise and not by the
financial   circumstances   of   his
parent."
—White   Paper   on   Educational
Reconstruction, July, 1943.

"Moreover, a son at a well-known
public school is one of the success symbols of the self-made man. . . ."
—*Whose Public Schools?* by Robin
Williams (Bow Group), 1957.

SOCIOLOGISTS, whose terms were now beginning to percolate
into informed usage rather as those of the political economists had a century or so earlier, were beginning to write
a good deal about "social mobility". That good old barometer
of English social mobility, the free grammar school, was in
particular, providing some significant readings. Before the war
only 14 per cent of Britain's children had continued their
education beyond elementary school—and of these only a small
proportion had been children of the working classes. Yet by
the Fifties surveys* showed that the grammar schools were
beginning to present "a pretty fair cross-section" of the com-
munities of which they were a part. Taking England as a whole,
the children of manual workers now constituted about half the
grammar school population; the children of skilled workers
(around two-fifths) represented the grammar school's largest
single social element.

* *Social Class and Educational Opportunity*, ed. J. E. Floud (1956).
Social Mobility in Britain, ed. D. V. Glass. *Early Leaving*, H.M.S.O.,
15–18, Report of the Central Advisory Council for Education
(Crowther Report), Vol. II, 1960. *The Living Tradition* by Frances
Stevens (Hutchinson, 1960).

This was something new and clearly of great importance. It represented not only expanding opportunity for talented individuals, but also, in the once-for-all circumstances of the Forties and Fifties, the upward movement of a whole class.

And yet once again social democracy's growth had served to underline its continuing deficiencies. The children of semi- and un-skilled workers were still much under-represented (about one-tenth of the average grammar school) with consequent wastage of high ability.* The "social revolution" of the grammar schools owed as much to rising wages, better health and housing and the spread of education as to educational reform, and in these matters large sections of the population still had much leeway to make up.

There were other lags too. For it was not only at middle-class level that the schools were the arena for a long and confused battle—often invisible, but also often hand-to-hand—between old values and new. It was the schools in these years that had to absorb the first wave of social change. Two-thirds of the parents of postwar grammar school children had themselves not gone beyond elementary school. In some schools the proportion was much higher than this, in others much less. But whatever it was, teachers reported that it was easy to pick out the middle-class boys by their sense of purpose. For some working-class children and their families, on the other hand, the notion of steady self-directed application, of ambition to "get on in life", was alien. Teachers complained that the parents "hadn't a clue"; parents complained that the teachers were 'toffee-nosed'. There was the "Problem of the Early Leavers".

But if the values of the grammar school might challenge those of the home, the grammar school was itself changing as the post-war world pressed in upon it. And this went deeper than a mere broadening of tone and accent. The old grammar school ideal of gentility and cloistered scholarships, the ivy-clad tower of rustic brick, the stained-glass window, the Latinity, the clerical headmaster, had been in slow retreat for a long time. Now the process of secularisation took a leap forward.

Before the war the banks had been beseiged by grammar

* Demonstrated in the Crowther Report, 1959, by correlating school-leaving with the results of ability testing of National Service-men—a revealing exercise.

school applicants anxious to "secure a position". Now the banks had to advertise hard to get recruits. Something like a third of grammar school graduates (as against one-fifth pre-war) were going into industry; in 1947 only a quarter were entering clerical work and minor professions compared with half before the war. And science now claimed approximately 60 per cent of all Sixth Formers, though their schools were often still inadequately equipped to teach it.

Even more significant of radically changed attitudes—and of the big vulgar outside world breaking in both on scholastic calm and suburban refinement—was the fact that it had become the vogue for grammar school boys and girls of all social classes to take menial jobs at week-ends and in the holidays in chain stores and elsewhere. About a half of them did so.* Messrs. J. Lyons & Co., the caterers, were moved to insert in the personal column of *The Times* the following tribute to their schoolboy helpers: "Many of the lads are prefects, enjoying during term the dignity attaching to their seniority: yet with no sense of 'side'—too often a weakness of previous generations—they have scrubbed floors, poured tea, washed up, with a shoulder-to-the-wheel enthusiasm which, in the opinion of Lyons, augurs well for the future of Britain."

II

If their advantages were now accorded to intelligence rather than merely to money, the grammar schools continued to constitute a sector of educational privilege. The proportion of children remaining at school after the age of fifteen was in the first half of the Fifties still no greater than the proportion going beyond the elementary stage in 1939. Yet the extra year at school did represent for large numbers more than merely an extra year. Secondary education was not only a statutory right, but was becoming for more and more each year a significant reality.

By mid-1952, 2,000 new schools had been built or were building and the very buildings proclaimed the new age. There no longer hung about them the inescapable air of the second

* The motive, to earn their "independent" incomes, was not unconnected with the emergence of all the all-class Teenage Culture (Chapter 31).

class, of the "council school"—even though they were often constructed of standard prefabricated parts. The new primary schools were the first to appear—and nowhere was the revolution in attitude more strikingly declared. Their architects—or the best of them—had studied the ways and needs of children to some purpose. There was a feeling of space, of expanding horizons, even of adventure. Gay, often strongly contrasting, colours were now becoming almost as standard as the old dark green partitions and "institutional" brown glazed tiles had been formerly. In infant schools wash basins were scaled down to the Lilliputian world; cloakrooms were divided into small bays; each child had its own miniature locker.

In many places the change was obscured by the cluttered apparatus of the outgrown past, an appalling incubus. But in a few areas, like Hertfordshire, where there had been a large influx of population, the new world of the schools was fully realised. When parents could send their children to such a school as the new Barclay School at Stevenage, set in twenty acres of countryside, with a fully-equipped stage as big as the Haymarket Theatre's, with murals by leading artists, statuary by Henry Moore, as well as such now standard features as gymnasia and domestic science rooms, laboratories, craft shops and architect-designed animal hutches and potting sheds, they no longer worried unduly that it did not carry the time-honoured description, "grammar".

Though it had been advanced by Radicals and by the N.U.T. for half a century, the notion of secondary education not for a class or an élite, but for a whole nation, posed a number of tremendous questions which were still novel in England: we lacked both the agreed social philosophy and the experience confidently to deal with them. Yet the effort to do so set on foot a large and salutary process of discussion and of trial and error. And if the main focus of debate was the comprehensive school, the main laboratory of experiment was necessarily the "Secondary Modern".

Neither the school's name nor many of its methods were, in fact, new. But 1947's new start, the bold proclamations of intent, the new building, brought a fresh surge of creative enthusiasm. There emerged a theory and, sometimes, a practice, which looked to co-operation as well as competition, and had more of the stuff of true education in it than was to be found in many a grammar school.

It rested on a large democratic faith on the possibilities of the ordinary human individual. Since every child was unique, every child had something to contribute to the common stock. To enable him to do so, one must locate, stimulate and develop his "centre of interest" which—delivered from the straitjacket of external examinations—the Modern School would be free to achieve by a wide variety of non-academic methods.

Some Modern schools did indeed succeed in becoming a stimulating part of the community in which they were set.* They worked on "projects", reflecting local industry or perhaps housing; visited local factories and council meetings and were visited in return by local managers, postmen, mayors or M.P.s who explained their own jobs. Or they might "adopt" a farm, studying the farmer's cycle of work through the year. In London, and even across the Channel, parties of Modern school children on "school journeys" became a familiar sight.

Life, unfortunately, often failed to live up to school; the obstinate facts and prejudices of the outer world intruded destructively. Parents were apt to be anxiously utilitarian; teachers to miss the firm objective of external examinations; employers to demand the old paper warranties. Worst of all, there were all the uncomfortable questions underlined by the co-existence, under the tripartite system, of the "top-dog" grammar school.

And yet, beneath the confusions, the class conflicts, the frustration and the heartaches, the outlines of a national educational system, from primary school to university, were at last becoming vaguely discernible. Between 1947–48 and 1958 spending on public education, in real terms, doubled; expressed as a proportion of the national income it grew by 75 per cent.

And by the later Fifties some of the first-fruits of this educational revolution were discernible. (If many other factors were involved, the schools certainly played a substantial part in the change.) Hitherto the British working classes had been largely

* According to Professor H. C. Dent, *Secondary Modern Schools* (1957) this sort of thing could truthfully be said of about one-sixth of them while the rest were doing sound, but less original, work.

a "secret people", with their own language, ways of thinking, codes. Theirs was a world which remained—in the south at least—largely impenetrable by any person from the middle classes. In print and on the stage—since working-class writers were rare—representation of them was condescendingly "anthropological", from the outside looking in—the comic chars of *Punch*, Noël Coward's adenoidal naval ratings, the stoic, idealised workers of Orwell's *Wigan Pier*. As for the working classes themselves, there appeared to be only two alternatives to the traditional "not-for-the-likes-of-us" self-segregation: the political attitude of class-conscious challenge or the earnest, lonely, self-conscious, rather over-awed, attitude of the small body of working-class seekers after Knowledge and Culture.

Now it seemed that more normal two-way communication might at last be opening up. In many of the working-class children who left the new schools was to be noted a new sort of social assurance,* a new disposition to speak their minds—in accents and idiom of a new universality. Doors, which had been closed, were seen to be open. There were moments when it seemed that the Age of the Common Man—so long overdue in Britain—might yet be ushered in by the Age of the Common Boy.

III

In the universities, as in the secondary schools, new strata of the nation were being tapped.

For the boy without means before the war a university place —inevitably thought of as an Oxbridge place—had been held out as a rare and glittering prize for the brilliant. In the decade after the war, a university place was officially recognised as a normal right of all who possessed "good all-round ability".**

* Youth Employment Officers who recalled prewar days reported that young people for instance now had `a much clearer, more purposive idea of what they wanted to do after leaving school.

** Cf. Ministry of Education recommendation to local authorities making university grants: awards "should not be regarded as prizes to outstanding students but as a proper form of assistance for students of good all-round ability for whom it is in the public interest that a university education should be provided".

In fact, the proportion of young people going to university now doubled—one in thirty against one in sixty before the war. Public expenditure on university grants and scholarships had multiplied sevenfold. Yet, ironically—as at eleven plus—the effect was to extend competition rather than to reduce it. Again supply nourished demand, and in the postwar school-year the university place scrum or scramble—which spread confusion and anxiety over a large area—took the place of the prewar flying tackle which, successful or not, had had about it a certain epic quality. It was a very characteristic change.

There were, however, some signs of hope for the future. Despite the rich diversity of the English provinces the provincial universities had hitherto remained stunted and obscure, starved both of cash and of talent. Now "Redbrick" began to move strongly forward again. Indeed, it seemed not impossible that the social historian of the future might detect in the new assertiveness of these provincial intellectual centres—already a source of "new" novelists and prophets—a critical factor in the vast, still more than half-hidden, process of social evolution quickening in these years.

Five new universities had been created by development of university colleges. Several others, like those of West Sussex, (Brighton), York and East Anglia (Norwich), were being planned *ab initio* with an innovating enthusiasm which no longer touched a forelock to Oxbridge. At Nottingham, Birmingham, Southampton, millions were poured into the building of modern campuses and laboratories. Nor would provincial universities in future be so open to the reproach of being merely "suburban" establishments whose students went home after tea. Much attention was being given to the construction of what were rather forbiddingly called "Halls of Residence". In strategic places, large sums were being spent, too, in transforming the old "proletarian" white tile "Tech" into the new regional "College of Advanced Technology".

Students of technology, after three to five years' advanced work, were now to take the new (1957) Diploma of Technology, stated to be "the equivalent standard of a university honours degree" (though quite firmly NOT a university degree). English education was riddled with such odd, anachronistic caste distinctions, but it was increasingly evident that the whole structure and concept of university education was only at the beginning of a long course of change. Although so many felt the compulsion to "try for the university" not all were secure in the possession of the old middle-class sense of Election. As in the grammar schools, substantial numbers fell out under a mental or emotional burden that seemed beyond their present capacity to bear. And once again there came those vast questions that were so baffling because they challenged a system of assumptions which had not hitherto required to be stated because in England "these things" had always been "understood".

Who should university education really be for? Gentlemen? An élite, not of family but of intellect? Gentlemen *and* an intellectual élite, judiciously mixed?

Or was it the democratic right of all who wished for it?

Or merely of all who could benefit by it? (And just how *could* one select these?)

In the new climate the perpetual refrain of the prewar "Ratepayer" that public money was being "squandered" on "educational frills" had been abandoned. But there were signs that resistance to expansion was being transferred from the schools, where it would now have been immediately howled down, to the university level—with a curious and ironic change of stresses and sponsors. While some educationists were now reminding the nation almost daily that it was disgracefully behind other nations in its provision of university places, some university dons, fearing for "standards", were openly questioning whether expansion had not already gone too far.

But now Business, which had once been the expansionists' bitter enemy, was their self-interested ally. The pressures of science-technology, joining those of democracy and economics, were taking the situation beyond the control of the more jaundiced traditionalists and possibly beyond that of traditionalists of any sort.

The large modern industrial concern on which the national economic future now so clearly depended lived by the pre-emption of talent. In the perpetual talent-hunt which was the condition of its life, it was not only developing close links with universities and schools but was itself systematically seeking and training ability within its own ranks. Before the war, in the days of the "gentleman apprentice" who paid a substantial premium, training departments could have been counted on the fingers of one hand; now there were hundreds. Between 1938 and 1954 part-time day release from work for study increased eightfold; the number of technical National Certificates taken quadrupled. In the nationalised industries and the best private concerns much thought and money was spent in developing "ladder plans"—and from the mid-Fifties these were often being operated in conjunction with local colleges of technology and universities, through such devices as the new "sandwich courses" terminating in a degree or in the new Diploma of Technology.

Yet as the "university of industry" succeeded the "university of hard knocks", it was becoming evident that the "Age of Opportunity" carried its own peculiar frustrations. Regularised and canalised, the new "mobility" was without the romantic and buccaneering elements of the older "ambition". And if the success it accorded was thus apt to lack some of the old satisfactions, its failure could be more dispiriting, final, and deadly. For whether or not the Eleven Plus was "abolished", technological society had its own built-in Seventeen Plus. For those who could "pass" it, horizons opened widely; for those who could not, they visibly and relentlessly closed. Once again Science had given and once again Science had taken away. In a democracy which had so lately unfurled the brave new banner of Equality it was a result both ironic and intolerable. Significantly, there was already the beginning of a demand for "Training for All", even if the training course, as Lord McCorquodale, Chairman of the new Industrial Training Council observed, was only in "how to hump barrels".

IV

There were larger and more avoidable anomalies.

While the larger part of the educational system was being made over to ensure that, in the words of the White Paper, the nature of a child's education would be determined by "his capacity and promise and not by the financial circumstances of his parents", another part was being diligently directed towards ensuring the converse.

The Report of the Fleming Committee on the Future of the Public Schools, published in 1944, had inspired a successful play and film, *The Guinea Pig*, but very little else. Of all the social reforms conceived in the war years and earnestly canvassed in those old A.B.C.A. pamphlets, it was significant that this was now almost the only one which still remained conspicuously unimplemented.

Produced by a mixed bag of public school headmasters, trade unionists and industrialists, the Fleming Report had underlined the way in which "the social breach" in the nation was "aggravated" by this unique and central system of educational privilege. It had recommended that, for a start, a quarter of the public schools' places should be offered free to children from council schools.

The public schools had, in fact, offered, not a quarter of their places, but around 200. The county of Hertfordshire duly dispatched two "guinea-pigs" to Eton, two to Rugby and two to Winchester. But few places were taken up by local authorities, and of those that were, many were later abandoned.

The intellectual call for the "association" or "assimilation" of the public schools continued, but remained ineffective. Here it seemed was a task beyond even the British genius for compromise. It was not easy for a local authority to justify spending on a single "Fleming" bursar an annual sum that would almost pay a teacher's salary or provide a couple of much needed new placcs in a local sccondary school. Nor in industrial areas with a good grammar school tradition did normal parents have any great desire to dismiss their children to boarding schools in the south. "The public schools," wrote Sir John Wolfenden, former headmaster of Shrewsbury and Uppingham, "have always been schools for a minority. They are not in simple fact a digestible element in an egalitarian society".

This was obvious, but the complexity of English social attitudes and group loyalties was generally too much to permit intellectual honesty of this sort, even for many on the Left. Meanwhile, far from facing insolvency as had been feared in the war years, the public schools were booming. Fees, rising steeply, now reached up to £500 a year. Yet waiting lists stretched far into the future. The public schools in fact were making their own successful adaptation to postwar change. A working alliance with large-scale industry was being cemented. A growing number of concerns assisted their executives to send their children to public schools. An Industrial Fund of several million pounds was subscribed to give the public schools better science laboratories.

As more and more professional people of the "old" middle class were financially squeezed out (sending their children to local grammar schools) their places were being taken by the children of the rising class of industrial managers and of advertising-and-entertainment men for whom a son at a "public school" was the shining badge of their own success. In the Fifties, more than half the boys at public schools were "first generation".

In the Twenties the public school had been the much-battered target of "progressives", the subjects of "angry" exposures by novelists and playwrights. In the Thirties, the Old School Tie became faintly comic, focus for the derision of the Western Brothers. It had been left to the Egalitarian Forties to accord it both respect and power, tempered only by occasional embarrassed recollection of the resounding pledges of 1943.

Despite Labour's bold "democratising" intentions of 1945, nine out of every ten recruits to the Foreign Office even at the end of the Fifties—and in the world of Mr. Khrushchev—were still public school men. So was half the Higher Civil Service, the overwhelming majority of judges, bishops, bank directors and (in 1955) 80 per cent of the Conservative party in the House of Commons.

In 1924, the new Prime Minister, Stanley Baldwin, had boasted that he had formed a Cabinet "of which Harrow should not be ashamed". It included six members of the "Old School". Thirty-one years later, political reporters were noting that of the nineteen members of Anthony Eden's new Cabinet no less than ten were from his old school, Eton. More significantly, one in every three of Labour's postwar Cabinet Ministers had been a public school man. In 1950 Sir Stafford Cripps was able proudly to present the Headmaster of Winchester with a leather-bound copy of the Budget, put through by three Treasury Ministers (Messrs. Cripps, Jay and Gaitskell) all from the same Old School. Indeed the dominant tone of the Labour Government might be said to have derived from a mixture of Wykehamist intellectual austerity and the just, officerly leadership of Clement Attlee—in the best tradition of Haileybury.

The public schools, together with Oxford and Cambridge, had in recent years played a central part in that famous process by which the English Establishment consumed its "revolutions". Was that process effective—even now?

It often seemed so.

In the grammar schools, and other schools not so labelled, the old order was being effectively challenged. Grammar school sixth forms now spanned the social spectrum, were twice their prewar size, and still rapidly growing. The picture of 'social revolution' they formed was broadly continued in the provincial universities where by the mid-Fifties almost one-third of the undergraduates were now sons and daughters of manual workers. For London the proportion was 21 per cent.

In these universities two-thirds of the undergraduates came from local authority grammar schools. But when one moved on to Oxford and Cambridge, the whole picture suddenly changed. Now the majority of undergraduates (around 60 per cent) came from public schools, accessible only to the top 5 per cent of the nation's income-earners. In Cambridge the proportion of manual workers' children was 9 per cent; in Oxford, 13 per cent. The postwar social revolution appeared to have largely passed these famed foundations by.

And clearly, it was here, in their continuing "organic links"—or self-perpetuating co-optive arrangements*—with the two ancient universities that the true strength of the public school system as a social apparatus lay. For even in our changed world and changed society, Oxford and Cambridge retained their potent combination of social and academic prestige, their unique, commanding—and essentially aristocratic—position.

Yet, in England, with its devotion to the preservation of ancient monuments, there is always a danger of underestimating the

* Since not only Oxford and Cambridge but the constituent colleges are so largely laws unto themselves the selection criteria by which this remarkable preponderance of admissions from a relatively small number of schools was arrived at remained private and obscure. It was not disputed, however, that "family and social considerations" played their part.

extent and depth of the processes of change quietly continuing behind the facades.

The power of the old system of class assimilation had owed much to the comparative scarcity of the candidates: to the rarity of good free secondary education of any kind in Britain. That even now in the Fifties one-quarter of all the nation's sixth formers were public school boys was evidence not so much of the power, as of the fact, of privilege. As the educational revolution proceeded, as sixth forms yearly multiplied and the provincial universities developed and the slow, steady pressures of social democracy continued, the public schools' old semi-monopolistic position must be lost. The narrowness of social and cultural span which had been their unique practical strength might then work against them.

In any event, pressures more ruthless than those of social democracy were now at work. The old Oxbridge-Eton-Wigan Grammar School assimilative system had derived its vast assurance and prestige in large part from the classical tradition, the Platonic patina on the socio-cultural pyramid. But in a world whose pace was increasingly determined by the two crew-cut civilisations of the U.S.A. and the U.S.S.R. the easy assumption that four years of *Litterae Humaniores*, absorbed in suitable surroundings, automatically enabled our "rulers" to take in their effortless stride all the complex, crowding problems of the modern world became increasingly hard to maintain.

In the Fifties the arts still claimed nearly half the nation's undergraduates. But the drive for university expansion came from the side of science and technology: it was to them that the lion's share of the new funds was directed. The old mandarinate was increasingly out-flanked. The scientists, certainly, might not yet sit in the seats of power: but they could no longer be wholly confined to their dingy white-tiled quarters below stairs.

And even if the public schools did succeed in substituting the mystique of a managerial, for that of a pro-consular, élite, in this age of continuous technical change, it seemed probable that new men were now coming up too fast, too variously, to be contained within any neat small social power system.

In this longer perspective, scientific and social revolutions thus again appeared allies, although possibly only to the extent of substituting a competitively selected élite who managed for a hereditary class who ruled.

But the challenge to the old authoritarian régime came not merely from science, but from many directions, was made not only in the schools and universities, but in many settings and—like the theme of the endless middle (which was an aspect of it)—stood out increasingly as one of the central themes of these years.

The forces at work could be identified; the manner of their resolution remained, in the Fifties, uncertain. Meanwhile, whatever his private thoughts, no Conservative Prime Minister who wished his Party re-elected was likely to boast of forming a Cabinet of which Eton or Harrow could be proud.

17. Grass Roots

"The romanticist's description of Britain as one large well-tended park has never been more apt. The change since I was last in Britain in 1938 is incredible."
—Dr. C. P. McMeekan, director of Ruakura Animal Research Station, New Zealand.

"No other nation feather-beds its agriculture like Britain."
—Mr. Stanley Evans, Parliamentary Secretary to the Ministry of Food, 14th April, 1950.

BUT IN ENGLAND the hierarchical tradition had not originated, after all, with the public schools. It had deeper roots. From earliest days the land had been both the font and symbol of that quintessential Inequality which the English had so long taken for granted as a part of the order of Nature. And when City millions outbid and overwhelmed breadth of acres, the financial magnate had still sought the endorsement of the territorial magnate, the industrialist still needed his tweeds, dogs, prize cattle and rural weathering.

Even if it might have its elements of myth, the theme of the country gentleman, busy both on his estates and in his library, the Justice of the Peace, replenishing his fortunes by marrying into trade, while trade, simultaneously, gained dignity and acres, had formed one of the grand motifs of English history, a theme to which the rise of the independent, thrusting middle classes of the towns had formed the lively counterpoint.

It now seemed that one of these themes, that of the urban middle class, might, in its old dynamic form, be working itself out. What, then, of the other?

Both the pace and extent of war and postwar change had in

many ways been greater in the countryside than in the towns. Yet it had been absorbed with little of the heat generated there. For in the countryside the postwar redistribution of status and rewards had taken place within a larger redistribution of power and privilege between town and country.

The war had brought about an agrarian, as well as a social, revolution. After it, the continuing siege economy, the debility of Europe, had made the farmer as clearly a key figure in the battle for national solvency as the coal-miner or the engineering worker. A minor turning-point in our history, the Agriculture Act of 1947, had struck a new balance between town and country, farm and factory. It acknowledged that the era of dirt-cheap food from a colonialised world was at last over. In comparison with the *ad hoc* marketing boards, quotas and subsidies of the Thirties—which had the air of a succession of makeshift rafts belatedly flung out to keep the farmer afloat— the 1947 Act seemed to open the way to a new and permanent integration of the agricultural interest into the machinery of the State. The setting up of a nation-wide system of land-use planning under the new Town and Country Planning Act also testified to the change of heart, and to a decision to husband our island's natural resources as they had not been husbanded since the Industrial Revolution.

Together these two Acts of 1947 symbolised the newly established status of the farmer as the repeal of the Trade Dispute Act a year earlier had symbolised the establishment of the trade unionist. With his own secure place in the planned and managed economy, that sturdy individualist, the British farmer, now seemed, indeed, like so many of us, to be in some danger of becoming a sub-species of Organisation Man. His "targets" were allocated. The State was his effective paymaster. In the age-old farming calendar, the climax came now, not with the autumn harvest, but with the February Price Review, when support prices and deficiency payments, in one grand economists' haggle, were based on the total of all farmers' costs. The men who, in the Twenties, had watched their farm buildings crumbling, their land going sour, now strove to conceal their gratification as the warm rain of subsidies continued to shower upon them, grants for ploughing grassland, grants for draining fields or bringing in water supply, subsidies for fertiliser or lime, acreage payments for potatoes and rye, subsidies for calves and hill cattle and sheep, grants for improving farm cottages or marginal land. . . .

Between 1938 and 1949, according to the calculations of Mr. Colin Clark, the average farmer's real income doubled. From the dark slate villages of North-Wales to the mellow red brick ones of Worcestershire, from the lush pastures of Cheshire fertilised by the "milk-cheque", to the combes of Dartmoor and the fastnesses of the Fens (opened up during the war by concrete roads), the grass had never looked greener. Only fleetingly, in 1950, was there a slight rift in the blue skies, a brief flare-up of the bitter old town-country feud, when a new townee parliamentary secretary at the Ministry of Food named Stanley Evans, deploring the ever-rising price of foodstuffs, pointed out that the amounts now being paid out in subsidies to agriculture fell only slightly short of the farmers' aggregate net income of £284,000,000. No other country, remarked Mr. Stanley Evans, "feather-bedded" its agriculture as Britain now did.

It was possibly some evidence of the new status achieved by agriculture that Mr. Evans, who had arrived at the Ministry of Food in March, having delivered this *mot* departed, at the Prime Minister's request, in April.

II

If the system, geared as it was to the highest cost producers, was scarcely calculated to promote maximum efficiency, the British farmer nevertheless was now demonstrably far from being stuck in the mud. The 1947 Four Year Plan for raising agricultural net output by about 50 per cent above the 1938 level—and 20 per cent above that of 1946–47—was duly achieved on schedule. Between 1949 and 1955 no less than £300,000,000 of machinery was installed on British farms. The agricultural engineer, now as insistent a feature of the English rural scene as the farrier had once been, was devising a great variety of machines to carry out all manner of farming operations. "Farmyard manure handling," rhapsodised one farmer, Mr. Clyde Higgs, "is so fully mechanised that it has become almost a pleasure." Wandering down some high-banked lane in the depths of Hardy's Dorset one might come upon a farm-worker mounted on a roaring hedge-cutting machine, the clippings flying in his wake; or driving across East Anglia one would now find that vast flat landscape punctuated by the red-painted conveyors loading potatoes or sugar-beet into lorries. In 1939 there had been 55,000 tractors on the land; by 1954 there were 400,000.

The scientific revolution, which was transforming so many areas of life, was opening up new horizons on the farm also. Your three rustics, though still leaning as ever on their sticks outside the Red Lion, might be discussing not only the latest Price Review, but the need for "trace elements" on a certain pasture; they might be debating their choice of selective weed-killers or exchanging notes about early maturing achieved with chemically treated seed, or about the startlingly rapid growth secured in young pigs, calves or chickens by mixing in the latest antibiotic food supplements. Progress in such matters was often astonishingly swift. "A.I."—breeding by artificial insemination—had been experimentally introduced into agri-cultural practice only after the war; yet by the mid-Fifties one calf in every two born in England and Wales was being conceived, remotely and passionlessly, by semen from a few carefully selected bulls, at the official A.I. centres. In a single year one beef-type bull could pass on his superlative beef-producing qualities to 20,000 offspring; with the employment of frozen semen from 1951 onwards, he could continue to do so to thousands more long after he himself had been transmuted into steak.

And if now and again the voice of caution was raised against this massive interference with the age-old processes of Nature, it was speedily drowned by the compelling statistics of the agricultural economists. By 1957, the milk-yield of the average dairy cow was almost a third higher than prewar;* in ten years the yields of wheat and barley per acre had risen by over a third, that of sugar-beet by a quarter. The land had not known

* In one field at least the triumph of applied science would be questioned by no one: by an elaborate system of control and "attestation", county by county, the country was being cleared of bovine tuberculosis, so long a disgraceful menace to health. Eradication was completed in October, 1960.

such a stirring since the days of the great eighteenth-century "improvers", the Cokes and the Turnip Townsends.

From all directions the farmers' cars, trailers swinging behind them, converged on country towns that were sleepy no longer. On market days, towns like Shrewsbury, Hereford, Salisbury or King's Lynn had the pulse and throb of metropolitan centres. Around their fringes sprang up bright new packing and canning plants, booming agricultural engineering workshops, and even light industries.

For the effects of this rural renaissance extended far beyond the countryside itself. Displaced by machinery on the farm, villagers travelled into town to work. Farmers' wives, the new money burning holes in their purses, enthusiastically window-shopped in Birmingham, Bristol or Newcastle. The great gulf between industry and agriculture, town and country, which had divided English life with such unfortunate effects for over a century was narrowing at last, and on terms of co-operation and conscious balance rather than domination.

Admittedly, for many an "ex-urbanite" buying a house in a "much sought-after hamlet", as for many of the millions who swarmed out there in their cars every week-end, the country-side was often little more than a "picturesque" backdrop. But there were others. A sign of the times was the extraordinary success of the B.B.C.'s earthy radio serial, *The Archers*, which, set in the mythical (but authentic and up-to-date) village of Ambridge, gained ground steadily, after a modest start in 1951, until its daily instalments revolving around such matters as foot-and-mouth disease, mulch and the merits of second-hand tractors, held eight million listeners spellbound, finally surpassing the audience figures even of the "Diary" of "Mrs. Dale", the suburban doctor's wife.

III

Yet if diesel exhaust fumes now mingled with the traditional farmyard redolences and specialised branches of agriculture became industrialised, if the fragrant hay wain gave place to the stinking silage silo and, here and there, hedgerows were being grubbed up in the name of mechanical efficiency, over most of the island the fine-drawn pattern of field and lane, copse and common, remained reassuringly unchanged. To the disgust of the agricultural economists, something like two-thirds of Britain's farms still ranged between fifteen and a hundred acres, family affairs which for their owners represented a way of life rather than a means to fortune.*

But in the countryside, as elsewhere in England, it remained unwise to presume from unchanged externals that the social reality behind was also unchanged. However true blue its electoral map might still appear, rural England had not remained untouched by the tides of 1945. A county as remote and rural as Norfolk had returned Labour Members for all but one of its Parliamentary constituencies. Fewer and fewer villages now possessed a squire. The Agricultural Holdings Act of 1948 had guaranteed the tenant farmer against dispossession for anything but the most gross neglect. In any event, by 1950 well over one-third of the holdings in England and Wales were owned by the men who farmed them. This proportion increased as the big estates continued to be broken up. Death duties on estates of £100,000 which had been 20 per cent in 1938 were, in 1950, 50 per cent; on estates of £1,000,000 the confiscation of a half (1938) now became the confiscation of four-fifths. The landed proprietor increasingly embraced the device of the Estate Company to preserve the family fortune, but successive Chancellors made countering moves. In 1946 Dr. Dalton had extended the period in which gifts *inter vivos* were taxable from three years before death to five. In that same year the 10th Duke of Devonshire transferred to his family 97 per cent of his shares in the Chatsworth Estate Company (authorised capital: £5,000,000); in 1951 he decided to fell an oak-tree on his land and died two hours later of a strained heart—just four months short of the statutory tax-exempt period. The year before the *Daily Mail Year Book* had recorded that the Chancellor had taken his monumental cut of no less than fourteen millionaire

* Just as well!—for as the free market increasingly asserted itself and, from 1952, farm incomes fell, the problem of the uneconomic size of the small farm in modern mechanised conditions was increasingly brought home and many a small farmer found himself working long hours for a mere pittance. In 1958, the Government was obliged to come to the rescue with a special small farms aid programme.

estates since the previous issue. In 1937, it had been noted that one-third of the families in the current *Burke's Landed Gentry* no longer possessed any land; by the time the 1952 edition came out only about a half possessed land. Of the 500 peers listed in *Debrett* as having hereditary country seats, only 150 maintained them.

"Antique dealers from all over the world have been drawn to London by the wealth of material available," reported the *Financial Times*. "Tiaras and precious necklaces once worn at stately functions in great houses are no longer needed," an auctioneer was quoted as explaining, "and the owners are realising that they can turn these beautiful things into money."

But the euthanasia of the landed gentry was both prolonged and admirably arranged. Though the great house, which had once discreetly figured in the background of some family portrait by Gainsborough or Zoffany, might now be an agricultural college, a research headquarters, a school for handicapped children, congeries of flats, or a prison-without-bars, if one made one's way round to the back, one might come upon the lord and lady of the manor very comfortably ensconced in the old coach-house or "converted" stables with a few score pigs grunting profitably in hygienic modern styes, some hundreds of hens in the deep litter system, a washing machine in the kitchen, and a Jaguar parked under the barn.

With luck one might even donate one's family seat to the National Trust, and go on living there, rent and Schedule A and B tax free. Or one might participate more directly in the new society by joining what the newspapers were now calling "The Stately Homes League" jollily refloating one's fortunes on a flood of half-crowns, motor coach parties and "set teas". Like the grouse on its moors, the English aristocracy had developed over the years a remarkable capacity for protective mimicry, and postwar newspaper readers soon learned to accept as entirely normal an item such as that announcing that the Premier Earl of England, the 21st Earl of Shrewsbury and Waterford, had set up a roadside barrow outside the family seat, Ingestre Hall.

"Business is looking up", the 'titled barrow boy' was reported as saying. "We are changing the barrow for a caravan. It has to be on wheels, you know, to avoid development charges."

Deprived of the pivot of the big house, the "county" existed more and more in the strange vacuum of the glossy two shilling weeklies, still purchased, ritualistically, to lend tone to hotel lounges and the waiting-rooms of superior dentists. Since the war, reported Lord Winterton, fashionable hunting, with one or two exceptions, had "almost ceased to exist". The hunt was now likely to be a very local affair, mainly farmers having a day out, probably followed, on foot, bicycle and car by a motley collection of local people, sometimes regularised as a "supporters' club".

Rural like urban society, if perhaps at some little distance behind, was becoming less hierarchical, less family-run, more and more functional and complexly specialised. As the old landlord's historic functions were increasingly taken over by a diversity of agencies, the territorial magnate, the "Landed Interest", the squire and his relations, so long fixed in conventional but arthritic attitudes, were at last being firmly wheeled to the back of the stage by that typical mid-century mixture of big business cartel and propaganda and pressure group, the National Farmers' Union.

As the farmers, like the urban workers, consolidated their postwar gains, the N.F.U., like the T.U.C., gained enormously in status; it negotiated, with the Government (like the T.U.C.) over the division of the spoils—or the "cutting of the cake"; it constituted one more new "estate of the realm", or representative factor in the corporate state which Britain sometimes seemed on the verge of becoming. Pushing, heterogeneous, expert, its organisation expanded impressively. It had fully staffed offices in many market towns, a nation-wide network of committees, a public relations section, a powerful fatstock marketing organisation. When in the Fifties its headquarters were moved into an opulent new neo-Georgian building at Hyde Park Corner this seemed no more than fitting recognition of its position. Yet the N.F.U. was headed, and had been built up, not by a belted earl but by a skilful farmer-administrator, a graduate of the University of Leeds, James Turner, whose efforts, and again the parallel with the T.U.C. comes to mind, were duly rewarded by a knighthood.

As in urban England, Tripartitism appeared to have become, with extraordinary speed, a part of the established order of things. The N.F.U.—the Ministry of Agriculture intervening—

now found its complement in the National Union of Agricultural Workers, with 4,000 branches, in every county of England and Wales.* The "farm worker's"—ex-"farm labourer's"—change in status had indeed been hardly less dramatic than the miner's. An agricultural minimum wage had been instituted only in 1940, but in the immediate postwar years under the aegis of the new tripartite Agricultural Wages Board wage rates in farming advanced faster than in any other industry. Instead of touching his forelock for 30s. a week as in the Thirties,** the farm worker now filled in his time-sheets, got extra for overtime, and enjoyed twelve day's guaranteed holidays-with-pay. In Tolpuddle of the "Martyrs" fame, in 1953, the chairman of the local branch of the N.U.A.W. served with other union men on the County Agricultural Executive which could recommend the dispossession of an inefficient farmer; the union's district organiser was a former Mayor of Dorchester.

The "Drift from the Land" continued. Tolpuddle was less than half the size it had been in the Martyr's days; its school had been closed down, the children transferred to another in a neighbouring town. But in the Fifties, such changes were as often evidence of successful adaptation as of decay. A new rural life and society was shaping that was one of the notable, though least noted, phenomena of the times. As the farriers, saddlers and wheelwrights dwindled (in the first postwar decade the number of horses on the land fell by two-thirds), into their places flowed a stream of recruits to those elastic and versatile "middle income groups" which were developing in the countryside as in the towns—the agricultural officers, the engineers and the accountants, the marketing officials, the N.F.U. secretaries, the canning plant managers. . . .

The new rural society was knowledgeable, purposeful and often undogmatically democratic. Despite the advance of the Organisation, people—persons—were still visible in the village and the small market town. If the President of the village

* In some areas, like East Anglia, the N.U.A.W. claimed to have 80–90 per cent membership (of the possible total). Over England and Wales as a whole about one-third of the potential membership was organised: no mean figure in view of the obvious difficulties of communication and distance.
** In Dorset 33s. a week in 1939.

Women's Institute was perhaps the lady from the manor house, the secretary was quite likely to be the village help or tractor driver's wife. Addressing themselves with female practicality to the improvement of village amenities and the scarification of unhelpful officials, these W.I. village parliaments were now to be found in 8,000 of the 10,944 parishes of England and Wales.

And manifestly the new democracy of the villages worked. By 1955 piped water supplies had been carried to hundreds of villages; power lines had reached approaching 200,000 farms,* and bright new council houses were almost everywhere. The village school might still be a draughty pseudo-Gothic horror, but the school bus, the school meals van, and the travelling library were new and cheering sights in the winding English country lanes, reminders that rural England was now neither moribund nor forgotten.

Indeed it sometimes seemed that it was here, in this older England, so overwhelmingly associated with Tradition, that the vision of 1945, Mr. Attlee's society of a "new and challenging kind" that should "combine individual freedom and social justice", freedom and planning, had come nearest to realisation.

IV

Possibly this was because in a rural England so long formally dedicated to the inequality of man, the complexity and elusiveness and inwardness of the notion of equality was, paradoxically, better understood. In the hundred yards between the stately home's milk bar and cafeteria and estate office—as between factory floor and salesroom or the trade union branch office and disciplinary committee, or between National Health surgery and grammar school sixth form—it might change not once but a score of times. It was an ambiance, a part of the culture, a thing of the mind; while material and statistical changes might profoundly affect it, they could not determine it.

* A 1956 Women's Institute national survey covering almost 6,000 villages revealed only 500 as having no mains water; only 222 as having no mains electricity; a striking contrast with the results of a parallel survey a few years earlier. Rural electrification had been greatly assisted by the new national structure of electricity generation and distribution following nationalisation in 1947.

Socialists had long placed their principal stress on securing as a necessary foundation a greater *economic* equality. In terms of income redistribution they could claim some modest success, though, as usual, the war could claim more. The war had approximately doubled the standard rate of income tax—10*s*. in the pound (plus 100 p.c. Excess Profits Tax) against 4*s*. to 5*s*. between 1930 and 1938. This had been succeeded by peacetime income tax at 9*s*. (rising a further 6*d*. in 1951), with a 25 per cent tax on distributed profits since 1947. The result of these higher rates, and the accompanying shift away from the regressive indirect taxation more favoured before the war,* was a certain flattening of income peaks, and (thanks to surtax) a a spectacular lopping of the Matterhorns among them.**

This flattening of the peaks was accompanied by a certain infilling of the valleys. The effects of nation-wide full employment and rising wage levels—more particularly of unskilled workers—were complemented by the food and housing subsidies and family allowances which buttressed the lowest income groups. By 1949, according to Mr. Dudley Seers, there had been an effective transfer of 10 per cent of the nation's real produce from distributed property incomes to wages.

As a contribution towards "equality" the levelling up was vastly more important than the levelling down. As late as 1936 Seebohm Rowntree's second survey of York had shown almost a third of that city's population to be below the "poverty line". By the time Rowntree made his third York survey in 1950 the proportion under the poverty line had fallen to less than 3 per cent, ascribed almost wholly to old age and sickness and hardly at all to inadequate pay.† And if York was in some ways a

* In 1938 net indirect taxes formed 60 per cent of total taxes; in 1945, 40 per cent; and by 1950, 33 per cent. (I. M. D. Little, 'Fiscal Policy', *The British Economy 1945–50.*

** Thus, according to the Central Statistical Office figures the top 2,000 averaged £43,500 a year in 1938 and kept £15,000 of it; in 1956 the top 2,000 averaged £35,000 and kept only £6,000 of it. A £15,000 a year man with two children received net a little over £5,000 and from every subsequent £1,000 received a further £75.

† In 1936, 33 per cent of the poverty was found to be due to inadequate pay; in 1950—1 per cent. Furthermore, the less-well-off families were now found not just the other side of the poverty line, but well above it.

favourable case, broadly the same bold contrast between prewar and postwar would have shown up anywhere.

It was now, significantly, being pointed out that poverty is a relative thing. But not long ago it had been absolute enough, the bottomless sea that lapped threateningly at the feet of the greater part of working classes. In 1908, the cover of Leo Chiozza Money's *Riches and Poverty* had carried a graphic representation of the facts of life at that time. A large purple-coloured rectangle was divided into three parts. The first part, occupying almost all of the rectangle, was labelled POOR—38,000,000 Persons. In the upper right-hand corner was a small segment. This was labelled COMFORTABLE—3,750,000 Persons. In the left-hand upper corner was a tiny square labelled RICH: 1,250,000 Persons.

By the end of the Fifties it would, very roughly, have been necessary to exchange the "poor" and "comfortable" labels. This was a potent change. It enabled the validity of the claim of all to equality of consideration and treatment, as persons—human individuals—to become continuously visible—at a time when that claim was being freshly asserted by the shift towards the "one-nation" approach in the health services, education, social welfare and housing.

By strictly monetary or mathematical standards, progress towards equality remained minimal. The spread between highest and lowest incomes, after tax, was still of the order of 30 : 1. When the statisticians turned from income and focused on capital and property, it seemed that the Levellers of 1945 had small claim to that name. In his first Budget, in 1948, Sir Stafford Cripps, it was true, had introduced a very mild form of capital levy, assessed on the unearned incomes of those whose total income exceeded £2,000 a year. But this "Special Contribution" was apologetically described as "once-for-all" and was not again invited. Despite increased death duties—and in default of a capital gains tax—the power of money to breed money remained impressive. In 1936–38 about 2 per cent of all property-owners possessed £5,000 or over and owned two-thirds of all private property. By 1945–50, 1½ per cent of all property-owners held the equivalent sum or over, and, between them, 54 per cent of all private property. By contrast, over half the nation's households in the early Fifties had a "net worth" (excluding household goods, currency and insurance policies) of less than £100.*

And yet, in the light of the experience of these years, the precise consequences for social democracy of such glaring statistical inequalities was no longer so clear. Wealth was increasingly divorced from the hierarchial system and an identifiable "ruling class". The surviving landed magnate who wished to preserve the family fortunes against the Chancellor was obliged, to achieve adequate restoratory multiplication, to move out of agricultural land into finance, real estate or commerce.** True, the landed magnate on his way out might still meet the City man on his way in (the "tax losses" at least would be useful) and the two might occupy the same butts and blaze away at the same grouse on the Glorious Twelfth. But that famous English social sleight-of-hand no longer quite had the point it had. For one thing it required time—and time the world no longer had. Family remained a great but elusive force in Britain. But now its elusiveness was not only its strength but its weakness: it lacked the potent, the irresistible symbol.†

The characteristic accumulations of the time were the massive and wholly anonymous reserves of the great joint-stock corporations, owned by crowds of anonymous shareholders, disposed by scores of only slightly less anonymous managers. The main source of new money entering the market was now the insurance companies, the pension funds, the investment trusts and so on—again controlled largely impersonally, functionally, by many hands, "managerial" rather than proprietary. And though both might have their armies of servitors, the distance between Chatsworth or Hatfield and the glazed red brick fortresses of the Pearl and the "Pru" in Holborn or the Portland stone of Imperial Chemicals House, needed emphasis no more than did the difference between the Lord Derby who

* Savings survey by the Oxford Institute of Statistics.

** Emulating the acumen of his Grosvenor ancestors who acquired the farms which are now Belgravia, Chelsea and Mayfair, the Duke of Westminster spread his investments over the growing Commonwealth, from a variety of enterprises in South Africa earlier in the century to booming British Columbia in the Fifties.

† In the new mass society set-up, the Crown no longer provided it: see Chapter 25.

"owned Lancashire" and the Lord Derby who was a director of "Television of Wales and the West".

The City, certainly, remained the stronghold of the family-cash-school nexus and much was still heard of the dynasts of the Square Mile who so smoothly and discreetly, with a Livery-man's nod here and an Aldermanic or Bank of England frown there, kept the England That Mattered still safe from the merely vulgar and parvenu. Yet in the expanding consumer economy, which Keynes had delivered from the narrow vision of the orthodox banker, this was a feat yearly more difficult of accomplishment. The notion of the takeover bid as a force for social equality might seem ironic enough, yet in England where the egalitarian's toughest enemy was bred-in-the-bone hierarch-ical sentiment, it was not without point. These were the years in which—with a symbolism which might seem grossly over-done—Fortnum and Mason and the ABC Teashops (neatly spanning the social spectrum) were taken over by one Canadian, and a large part of the British Press (including *The Scotsman* and the *Sunday Times*) by another; in which that stately dowager of emporiums, Harrods, was carried off, in a blaze of publicity, by a go-getting Scots draper, and thrust into a takeover sack already bulging with a motley collection of mere departmental stores; in which, again in full public view, a former estate agent's clerk first almost "took over" the Savoy, the Berkeley (to convert into offices!) and Claridges, then graciously returned them to their owners on payment of substantial ransom; in which a former roller-skating rink proprietor, born in Whitechapel, appeared for a time to be "taking-over" almost everything in sight from shipyards to shoe-shops.

And as, in the next few years, the pressure of the great consumer market mounted and broke through all the old bounds, the complex highly capitalised machines of mass production, mass distribution and mass entertainment were soon engaged on levelling operations of a scope and penetrative power the merely political egalitarian could hardly have dreamed of.

Was this sort of "equality" wholly spurious—the false face of an exploitation which sought to reduce all to standard—and therefore processable—raw material? Or, whatever its ration-ale, was it, nevertheless, an effective reality?

Where did control lie in this vast, complex, ill-mapped

terrain of financiers and technologists, bankers and advertising men, insurance companies and trade unions, and the millions of consumers who turned thumbs up or down (or were deluded into believing that they did)?

Some certainly, were "more equal than others". But which?

The answer, which only a short while ago had seemed clear enough, was to become more obscure with each passing year.

PART THREE

STILL SHOOTING NIAGARA

"Democracy to complete itself; to go the full length of its course towards the Bottomless or into it . . . Complete "liberty" to all persons; Count-of-Heads to be the Divine Court of Appeal on every question and interest of mankind; Count-of-Heads to choose a Parliament according to its heart at last and sit with Penny Newspapers zealously watching the same . . . that, in a limited way, say fifty years hence, the Church, all Churches, and so-called religions shall have deliquesced into "Liberty of Conscience", Progress of Opinion, Progress of Intellect, Philanthropic Movement and other aqueous residues of a vapid badly-scented character."

—Thomas Carlyle, *Shooting Niagara—and After?*, 1867.

18.   Human After All

"So far as his amatory adventures are concerned the book does, with candour, or if you prefer it, crudity, deal with the realities of human love and intercourse. There is no getting away from that, and the Crown say: 'Well, that is sheer filth.' Is the act of sexual passion sheer filth? It may be an error of taste to write about it. It may be a matter in which some, perhaps old-fashioned, people would prefer that reticence continued to be observed as it was yesterday. But is it sheer filth? That is a matter which you have to consider and ultimately to decide."

—Mr. Justice Stable summing-up in the trial of the printers and publishers of *The Philanderer* at the Old Bailey, July, 1954.

"Is Chastity Outmoded?" . . .
"Marrying with a Baby on the Way"

—Titles of two chapters in the British Medical Association's popular booklet, *Getting Married*.

AN EVER-PRESENT difficulty of the student of contemporary social history lies in the fact that every generation, every decade almost, is fiercely convinced that its experiences are unique. In the field of morals, rarely capable of objective measurement, this difficulty is acute. But at least rapid if rough correction is available in a glance at the past. The decline of the family, the subject of so much urgent comment in the Forties and Fifties, was already being earnestly discussed in 1906; so was the decline of organised religion and the weakening of the old moral imperatives. After the First World War the divorce

G

rate doubled; after the second, it quadrupled. On both occasions, this—together with the accompanying emancipation of wives—was held to portend imminent and general moral collapse. The phenomenon of crime increasing with the rising standard of living and welfare greeted with such surprise in the Fifties was certainly not peculiar to them: crime had been rising all through the Thirties also. Nor was the juxtaposition "juvenile" and "delinquency" so startingly novel as we were now given to believe on almost every day of the week. On the contrary, whether by reason of their surplus energy, enterprise or perennial rebellion, the young had long contributed an impressive proportion of the nation's total crime.

Yet there were senses in which the postwar British might be justified in their belief that they lived in "new" times, with new moral problems. For one thing, those long-term changes which were mainly of scientific origin had now reached the stage where new social forms, a new frame of life, was beginning to consolidate. For another, some of the familiar factors of change seemed to be fusing into potent new compounds, setting up chain reactions whose ends could not be seen. The conjunction, for instance, of the psychologists, social anthropologists and statisticians and the now vastly efficient machinery of "mass-communications" was making it possible to hold up to humanity a magnifying mirror which presented an image that was larger-than-life, merciless in its precision, and very intimidating.

It had taken something like forty years for Havelock Ellis's pioneer studies of human sexual behaviour (earlier ruled to be "lewd, wicked, scandalous and obscene") to become available to the British public, and then only on a very limited scale. Dr. Kinsey, by contrast, became a household word almost overnight. In 1948, his 2¾ lb. *Report on the Sexual Behaviour of the Human Male*, was an instant best-seller on both sides of the Atlantic. Its remorseless statistics—that 86 per cent of 'human males' (i.e. Americans) had pre-marital intercourse; that nearly 70 per cent had had relations with prostitutes; that 45 per cent had been unfaithful to their wives and a similar proportion some homosexual experience between adolescence and old age—served as an effective trailer for the *Sexual Behaviour of the Human Female*, the second barrel which this industrious zoologist discharged in the face of the human race five years later.

For weeks before and after "K-Day", as publication day of the second Report was now whimsically named, acres of newsprint lying about the homes of Britain were filled with the new statistical revelation. British newspapers, among others, despatched correspondents to the Professor's headquarters in the little Indiana town of Bloomington, where, after signing an undertaking not to reveal more than a stipulated amount, they were admitted to a sound-proofed cellar for a preview. The more restrained employed suitable clergymen or doctors to review the report at length; the more popular (with the exception of the Presbyterian-controlled *Daily Express*) displayed no such inhibitions. The *Sunday Dispatch* illuminated successive Sundays with extensive selections of Kinsey research results such as that "23 per cent of unmarried girls were reaching orgasm through petting", that 40 per cent of males liked to make love with the light on while 81 per cent of females preferred to do so in the dark. The *Daily Mirror*, never one for beating about the bush, introduced the news with a front-page headline 3 inches high: "WOMEN", and carried on, inside, with double-page spreads accompanied by photographs designed to ensure that readers understood what was meant by "petting".

England's particular brand of Puritanism had depended on an insularity which was now becoming progressively more difficult to maintain. For the "K-bomb"—as the Press, fairly enough, called it—was not the only high explosive that winged across the Atlantic. The assault of the American theatre of Tennessee Williams and Arthur Miller was reinforced by a barrage of "mammoth" American war novels, like Norman Mailer's *The Naked and the Dead*, a best-seller in Britain in 1949, although the *Sunday Times* had characterised it as "an extreme case of obscenity" employing language "incredibly foul and beastly" and called for its withdrawal.

Back in those good old prewar days when the police carried away D. H. Lawrence's paintings, when Epstein's *Rima* was still regularly paint-daubed and Hemingway had not yet become a "tradition", the middle-class libido could be lodged at a safe distance in Paris or Cannes. But now its repatriation became inevitable. While the British Press was still spreading Dr. Kinsey across its pages, London errand boys were whistling (with more than the usual absence of proper feeling) "Love's

Roundabout", the dreamy theme-song of the French film, *La Ronde*, a witty and winking, sensual and musky, portrayal of the many moods of love. Opening at the Curzon in the West End in April 1951, *La Ronde*, directed by Max Ophuls, a French-naturalised German Jew, with music by the eighty-year-old Oscar Straus, pursued its bemused and amorous course for seventy-six weeks.

The influence of Continental films, increasingly in vogue through these years, portraying love and sex in all their graduations with an honesty and poetic realism that came as a revelation to many British cinemagoers brought up on the Hollywood formulae, was of a comparatively subtle yet pervasive kind. There were a good many such elusive influences.

Quite suddenly, it seemed, the old Puritan—or possibly merely the Victorian—crust began to crack. The unmentionable became, somehow, mentionable. Newspaper sub-editors for whom, only a year or two earlier, the blue-pencilling of a wide range of normal physiological and anatomical words would have been a mere reflex action, were now without a qualm exposing them to print. The whole complex and curious code of euphemism was indeed tending to be replaced by an embarrassing wealth of obstetrical detail. Some tabus, of course, remained, and sometimes there was a bizarre unevenness in the melting process: on one page the editorial department might be offering THE INTIMATE SECRETS OF 1,200 MARRIAGES while on another, the advertisement department was sternly instructing an advertiser to put chemises on his pixies. Yet a new climate was unmistakably setting in.

And "climate" was indeed now the right word—for unlike the "defiant" (*Private Lives*) or "daring" (*Point Counter Point*) frankness of the Twenties, the badge of an "intellectual set", this frankness, was unforced, matter-of-fact, and embraced, on some level at least, the larger part of society. In the interwar period a representative "sex" article in a popular woman's magazine or woman's page might have been: "Is Platonic Love Possible?" treated with an almost metaphysical vagueness; in a postwar woman's magazine, if the fiction pages maintained the same level of fantasy, "Aunt Margaret" in her advice to "Anxious" was likely to be briskly down-to-earth and diagram-

20. 1951, Festival Year, brought to London a "South Bank" and to Britain, renewal. Beneath the Dome of Discovery, seen rising above, the nation staked her claim on the future, offered a Whittle for a Stephenson, a Watson-Watt for a James Watt.

21. And (*below*) "Contemporary" was born. A sample room on the South Bank illustrates the bright clean "Festival style" that finally dethroned mock Tudor.

22. Uncertainly, the British sought a new, post-Imperial *persona*. In the Festival's Lion and Unicorn Pavilion the British Lion emerged as a whimsical "Ealing Studios" creature of plaited straw . . .

23. . . . but the new vistas opened up by the Festival were not all as scheduled. The ubiquitous "spiv" saw even a national occasion as an opportunity for a "fiddle". Cartoon by Grimes.

PSST! WANNA COUPLE OF TEN-BOB SHARES IN TH
FESTIVAL OF BRITAIN, GUVNOR?"

matic: medical writers now discussed such subjects as "Frigidity and How to avert It" in large circulation papers in considerable starkness of detail. Meanwhile, the B.B.C., which a few years ago might have been the headquarters of Dr. Thomas Bowdler himself, had taken to putting on "socially conscious" programmes which included, casually and without a blush, frank interviews with prostitutes, discussions of the merits of "Artificial Insemination by Donor" (starring wives who had tried it), and of the problems of sex offenders, alcoholism or abortion.

Nor was this new matter-of-factness confined to print or ether. More and more "unmarried mothers" were bringing up their children,* since parents, less worried about social ostracism, were allowing them to keep their babies at home. The term "unmarried wife" had become acceptable to certain Government departments, continuing the practice of the war years when "unmarried wives" had received Service marriage allowances.

Censorship was relaxed in the cinema—the "X-Certificate" came into force in 1951**—in the bookstore, and, finally, with the admission of homosexuality as a subject, in the theatre. The "banned" books of yesterday became the best-selling paperbacks of today. In 1954, Zola's *La Terre* was republished in English for the first time since its proscription in 1881; in the 1950's it was claimed that the works of Zola were selling many more copies in England than in France. Indeed the "troughs of Zola-ism"—as Tennyson had it—overflowed.

In the past in England the well-established pattern had been for such "thaws" to be succeeded by sharp "re-freezes". And for a while, in 1954, when five well-known publishing firms were prosecuted for having issued allegedly obscene novels, it seemed that this familiar cycle might be about to recur. In the event, the Stable judgment in the case of the American novel,

* Report, National Adoption Society. The Births and Deaths Registration Act, 1947, had already made provision for a birth certificate to be issued showing name, sex and date without reference to parentage.
** In fact the recommendation of a departmental committee on children and the cinema, appointed 1947. By its absolute exclusion of under-sixteens the X-Certificate opened the way for the liberalisation of film censorship which continued through the Fifties.

The Philanderer, was to mark not a turning-point in the old pattern but the beginning of a new one.* Quoting the celebrated "tendency to deprave and corrupt" judgment of Chief Justice Cockburn in 1868, which had hitherto provided the narrow criterion, Mr. Justice Stable pertinently inquired: "Corrupt whom?" Moral concepts, he pointed out, had changed since Victorian days. "You may think that if this (book) does reflect the approach on that side of the Atlantic towards this great question (of sex), it is just as well that we should know it and that we must not close our eyes or our minds to the truth because it might conceivably corrupt or deprave any somewhat puerile mind. . . ."

The decade which opened with the freeing of Zola was to close with the liberation of Lawrence.

II

Though it now came so rapidly, this notable change of tone had, of course, been long in preparation. It had taken fifty years to digest Darwin, another fifty to absorb Freud. In the First World War the psychiatrist had gained—with "shell shock" and "neurasthenia"—his first substantial employment. But "cowardice in the face of the enemy" was still possible; men were frequently shot for it.** In the Second World War the psychiatrist was in uniform from the outset, a routine figure, the familiar "trick cyclist" of the troops, the key specialist in the crucial field of "morale"—both our own, and (via "psychological warfare") the enemy's. And "cowardice" had a strangely old-fashioned sound.

By the time the war was over psychiatry had finally lost its

---

* The prosecutions and the Stable judgment were the genesis of a new Obscene Publications Bill, originated by the Society of Authors, widely approved by the Press, and finally taken over by the Government. This made it possible to take into account the "dominant effect" of a book, its literary quality or public interest and the manner of its distribution.

** Cf. Robert Graves, *Goodbye to All That:* "Cowardice was punishable only with death and no medical excuse could be accepted". . . . "Executions were frequent in France."

alien overtones; it was not only intellectually, but also popularly, accepted. The couch was the pivot of many films; in the newspapers, on the radio, and later on TV, a "psychologist" or psychiatrist was an "expert" only a shade less potent and omniscient than "an economist". His patient, disembodied voice permeated our society, the answer to Worried Wife's prayer, the relaxer of the Over-Tense husband, the key to the Problem Child.

A central figure of T. S. Eliot's much-discussed "problem play", of 1949, *The Cocktail Party*, was Sir Henry Harcourt-Reilly, a priest-psychiatrist, psychiatrist-priest—the symbolic hybrid of the age. Yet in any conflict of values between confessional and couch there now seemed little doubt which would prevail. Guilt was no longer the curse of Adam, to be borne with humility. It was a subject for therapy. There was a psychiatrist on every Church Moral Affairs committee, or waiting to give evidence in the anteroom. The modern church social worker, scientifically trained and certificated, detected not sin but maladjustment, sought a return, not so much to Grace, as to Normality, now comprehensively redefined by Dr. Kinsey and colleagues.*

Meanwhile, the analytical philosophers, drawing inspiration from the psychologists, industriously reduced metaphysics to the status of a sort of superior Grimm's *Fairy Tales* and ethics to a collection of prejudices, driving the theologians into apologetics of an intricacy defying the non-specialist's comprehension.

III

The majestic stucco façade of Victorian morality had, for a good many years, successfully withstood mounting structural strains. It had, after all, been designed to last. But the multiple shocks of this postwar world at last threw it over.

And as the dust cleared, it revealed the English embarking on a series of extensive surveys of the site, which ranged from

* There was in the Fifties strong support within the Church of England for a proposal (only narrowly defeated) to exclude the Devil from the revised Catechism.

the Royal Commission on Betting, Lotteries and Gaming, 1949–51 (finally ending the venerable street comedy of the bookies' runner and betting slips "seen to pass"), to the Wolfenden Committee on Homosexuality and Prostitution, which brought under close scrutiny between 1954 and 1957 other Victorian double standards. As the great Victorian Royal Commissions had been guided by public health doctors and sanitary engineers as they outlined a new structure for nineteenth-century towns collapsing under the industrial load, so the inquiries of the mid-twentieth century, confronted by different forms of obsolescence, relied heavily on social scientists and psychologists in their reassessment of the "facts of life" and their preliminary sketching of a new frame of social morals.

The foundation of this structure was still seen to be the family —though "family" now meant something very different from what it had in the past. The Royal Commission on Population showed that the small two-child family was now characteristic of all classes. If the professional classes were having slightly more children, the working classes were having fewer.* Large families had now become so rare as to be in danger of attention from the Sunday papers; they were, pronounced Professor Titmuss, "reproductive deviants" and might soon be "anthropological curiosities".

Postwar couples walked about, not arm in arm, but hand in hand. It was a habit picked up from the Americans during the war; that it continued afterwards suggests that it corresponded to the new situation. The war—in which nine million women had been mobilised—the acute labour shortage that followed, the extension of contraception (now become not merely mentionable, but respectable) had consolidated women's economic independence. In 1951 the Gallup Poll reported that when a couple went out together almost half the people now thought the girl should pay her whack; far more when the younger age groups only were consulted.

* The national average of postwar marriages appeared to be 2·2 children, half the family of the 1890's, one-third of the 1860's. The class range was now from 1·9 for clerks and shop assistants to 2·65 children for unskilled labourers. Regionally the only slightly deviant area was Liverpool, mustering an average family of 2·7 (Fertility Report 1951 Census). In 1951 around half the households with children had only one child.

In fact, most marriages were now founded—and often continued—on double savings and double incomes. In the early Fifties, something like 3,500,000 married women—almost half of all women at work—were taking their own pay-packets into the matrimonial home. Characteristic mid-century institutions like the B.B.C. granted maternity leave to their women employees and cheerfully expected to welcome them back again. And if wives now brought home at least part of the bacon, the middle-class male's habit of helping with the washing up and other household chores was now slowly spreading to other classes. Talking to 600 workers in several parts of England in the late Fifties, Ferdynand Zweig found that three-quarters now asserted the equality of man and wife in the home.

Clearly, such partnerships, in which collective decisions were continually having to be reached, were subject to risks unknown to the Victorian hearth-rug patriarchates, backed by the sanction of economic disaster for the disobedient wife. The old family, with the framed photographs of uncles and aunts, cousins, grandparents, ranged rank on rank across the mantelpiece, had been a miniature hierarchical society, sustaining a tradition and protectively (or stiflingly) enfolding its members, whose roles within it were well-defined and long established. In the new informal partnership family roles were multiple and overlapped in a way which might involve conflict between the claims of instinct and tradition and the demands of economics and ambition. For the children, too, admitted as junior partners at an early age, there were new possibilities of conflict. In the early Fifties the word "teenager" still carried an alien ring. But already the home had potential rivals in the State-backed youth club, the new school with all its after-hours activities and the street and café gang.

Such profound changes in society's fundamental unit necessarily set in train a complex of changes throughout it which were still far from completed. But at least the pretence that no change had in fact occurred had now been abandoned. The ground was not only being resurveyed; some tentative new foundations were also marked out. The Denning Committee on Matrimonial Procedure in 1948 noted the "need for a carefully graded system of general education for marriage, parenthood and family living". As a result, the Government gave its support to the National Marriage Guidance Council, which, by the mid-Fifties, had eighty local councils and 500 trained consultants, backed by panels of specialist advisers. The Royal Commission on Population, supporting this constructive approach, had recommended in 1949 that the giving of advice on contraception to the married be enjoined as a duty on the National Health Service. This did not happen; yet the Family Planning Association, its position now vastly enhanced, operated 300 clinics,* four in every five on Health Service premises. For the first time the Association could report that "voluntary parenthood, the freedom to decide deliberately when to conceive a child and how many children to bring into the world, has become part and parcel of our culture". Even the British Medical Association, infected by the new spirit, became socially minded enough to issue practical, frank (and best-selling) handbooks on "Getting Married".

Perhaps the most notable landmark of all was erected when, just eight weeks after the death of Marie Stopes—and something like four generations after the opening of this particular battle— the Lambeth Conference of Anglican Bishops went on record for the first time in a positive sense in favour of birth control. "The procreation of children," the Bishops ruled, "is not the only purpose of marriage. . . . Sexual intercourse is by no means the only language of earthly love, but it is, in its full and right use, the most intimate and most revealing. . . ."

In this large process of survey and reassessment in the light of scientific humanism, there remained, however, one failure of monumental proportions. After five years of wrestling with the established facts of Life and abstractions of Theology, the Royal Commission on Marriage and Divorce emerged from its ordeal largely preserving that nice balance of prejudice with which it had entered upon it. It failed to agree on a single major

* However, there were still many local authorities which continued to refuse facilities, and the Royal Commission on Population found that knowledge of effective contraception was still "very uneven". And a two-year survey by the Family Planning Association (report published 1962) suggested that among unskilled and semi-skilled manual workers married in the Fifties, one-third "never practise any form of birth control, however inefficient". For the population as a whole the proportion was one-quarter.

proposal, not excluding the one which had originally prompted its appointment*—the recognition of a marriage's death after seven years' living apart.

Immediate postwar experience had sharpened fears of "opening the flood-gates of easier divorce". In 1947, when County Court judges were brought in to help cope with the queues of petitioners, 60,000 marriages had been dissolved. This was compared with the annual average of around 6,000 in the last four prewar years, and the most dire conclusions drawn. But from 1954, as the effects of war died away, the rate fell below 30,000, which if high by comparison with prewar— and pre-Legal Aid—figures was less than 7 per cent of all marriages.

A larger proportion of the population was, in fact, now married than for many years past. In 1951, more than three in every four of those divorced remarried. But they did so— despite the defiance of the Bishops by a few Modernist clergy— without the blessing of the Church. The remarriage of divorced persons, the Archbishop of Canterbury carefully explained, even though totally unconnected with the breakdown of the first marriage, was clearly adulterous and deserving of reprobation, though it "often came as a real blessing to both the parties and the children".

Yet if the Church and the Law were still caught up in these well-nigh impenetrable thickets of doctrine, the nation as a whole had merely marched around and left them behind. The diversity and complexity of human beings and the necessity of a certain asymmetry were now freely acknowledged. Divorced actors—breaking with precedent—were now knighted; there were divorced Ministers in the Cabinet, even, for a while, a divorced Prime Minister. When the *Church Times* attacked Sir Anthony Eden for remarrying during the lifetime of his first wife the attack called forth a storm of protest in which probably most people now silently joined.

* Embodied in Mrs. Eirene White's (Private Member's) Bill to which the House of Commons gave a second Reading in March, 1951, by 131 votes to 60. The Bill was withdrawn when Mr. Attlee announced the appointment of a Royal Commission. Of the Commissioners' minor proposals, the most important aimed to secure the position of the children before allowing a divorce to be made absolute.

But perhaps the most conclusive evidence of the climato-logical change came with the debate that arose over the most fearsome of the Old Testament "abominables".

By 1952 the number of cases of "male perversion" "known to the police" (statistically) had reached five times the prewar level. In the next year or two prosecutions involving several well-known personalities made black and sinister headlines. In the past predictable reaction would have been a police "drive". But now there was also another response, increasingly characteristic of the times. In August, 1954, a departmental committee was appointed under the chairmanship of the Vice-Chancellor of Reading University, Sir John Wolfenden, to examine "the whole law and practice relating to homosexual offences and prostitution".

Moral indignation, it was now realised, was not enough. There was, indeed, surprisingly little of it. Canon Hugh C. Warner of the Church of England's Moral Welfare Council wrote to *The Times* welcoming the committee and stressing the "clear distinction" between the pervert and the "genuine invert who is psychologically a sick man".* So conservative an organ as the *Daily Telegraph* averred that it was an excellent thing to have a frank and responsible discussion of this "very difficult subject . . . which must have been a topic of more private discussion in recent months than for many years past". The discussion that followed was indeed far from private; the subject was debated at length and with few inhibitions in the Press, in Parliament, on the air and in the councils of the churches.

If, when it appeared in September, 1957, the Report exposed the vast ignorance and continuing confusion of psychologists in face of fundamentals of human behaviour, it equally demon-strated the completeness of their authority. Modern psychology resembled an endless maze, but it was a maze through which it was clearly now our duty to follow the experts unquestioningly to the end of time. Carefully excluding dogma and doctrine—how unlike the Divorce Report!—and such "coloured" terms as "natural" and "unnatural", insistently separating "sin", a personal matter, from "crime" and "law", a social one, the

---

* In fact, having studied all the medical evidence the Wolfenden Committee rejected this simplification.

tone of the Wolfenden Report was clinical and pragmatic. Yet it was, clearly, the tone of the times. The Committee's recommendation, made with one dissentient—a Scots lawyer— in favour of changing the tradition of years and making homosexual acts between "consenting adults (over 21) in private" no longer unlawful was greeted with a volume of approval that would have seemed impossible in England only a few years ago. "Don't be Shocked by This Report. It's the Truth. It's the Answer. IT'S LIFE", the *Daily Mirror* adjured its readers. And with less exuberance, and varying degrees of reservation, seven national dailies (including all the 'heavies'), the two Archbishops, the Free Churches, and, by a narrow majority after an all-day debate, the Church Assembly, shared this general attitude. No less than three national dailies ran public opinion polls on the Report. These revealed 40–50 per cent in favour of the radical change it proposed.*

It was in 1931 that Dr. G. J. Renier brought out that celebrated little book, *The English: Are They Human?*, particularly famed for its chapter on "Repressions". In the 1950's a new edition was called for. In his Preface to this Dr. Renier explained why he had decided to leave the text unchanged: to adjust it to the Postwar English he would need to rewrite the entire work.

The English had proved human, after all.

* On the other hand, the *Daily Express*, the *Daily Mail*, the *Sunday Times* and most of the leading provincial organs shared the fears of the dissentient member of the committee, Mr. James Adair, a former Procurator-Fiscal, that the proposed relaxation might be treated by homosexuals as a licence for proselytising activities, thus leading to a further undermining of basic moral standards.

19.   The Everlasting Maybe

"We are living nationally on what
might be called 'the moral capital
accumulated in the Past'."
—B. Seebohm Rowntree and G. R.
Lavers in their survey, *London
Life and Leisure*, 1951.

"In fact, I think we are a nicer people
than we were when I was young."
—Somerset Maugham, broadcasting
at eighty.

IF, AS IT SEEMED, there was now nothing to hide, there was,
equally, no place to hide it. In the pervasive climate of
social welfare, egalitarianism, and rising living standards,
the Submerged, formerly swallowed up in the vast sumps of the
great towns, tended to emerge—and even assert their rights.
Anonymous "ne'er do weels" became the "Problem Families"
The *demi-monde* which until 1916 could be discreetly accommodated in the Alhambra or Empire promenades and elsewhere, was a part of the whole world of the Forties, and was
judged as such.

When almost four years after the war ended, the lights of
Piccadilly Circus were switched full on again, 50,000 people,
the biggest crowd since V.E. Day, gathered to watch that
symbolic restoration. A blue spotlight cut through the half-
darkness to reveal on the Criterion balcony the figure of Zoë
Gail, the South African revue actress, singing the old wartime
hit, "I'm gonna get lit up when the lights go on . . ." (a
sentiment which, it may now seem odd to recall, evoked
considerable protest when relayed by the B.B.C.). Children
watched, goggle-eyed, from their father's shoulders, as the
crowd cheered each fresh spurt of incandescent colour.

In the middle-aged, the sight stirred a powerful nostalgia;
yet, for those who recalled earlier days, the scene at this "heart

of Empire" already seemed alien and strangely tawdry. It would be a year yet before the Edwardian-opulent halls of the Criterion Restaurant would be turned into a popular cafeteria. But already the classic façade of the London Pavilion was half hidden by vast cut-outs of curiously over-developed women, sprawling in varying degrees of proneness and dishevelment. Two years earlier the London Pavilion had established a tradition (in the curious way in which traditions were now being established) by presenting the "shocking" American movie, *The Outlaw*, starring Jane Russell, hitherto little known but now, as a result of a vast publicity campaign—the proto-type of how many others!—well understood to be Mean! Moody! and Magnificent! The magnificence was clearly somewhat specialised—and thus had been set in motion the cyclical process, more complexly organised now than formerly, which drew eyes upwards from women's legs, the centre of interest through the interwar years, to alternative foci of attraction.

Commercialised sex was, however, by no means confined to the hoardings. London, it was said, now shocked its foreign visitors; it had become "the worst city in Europe". Whether there were more prostitutes than before the war could not be determined, although there were probably more "semi-amateurs", and, with increasing matter-of-factness and out-standing visibility, they had extended their operations from the traditional beats to the respectable residential streets of Bays-water, Mayfair, Stepney, and of some provincial cities.

There were other causes for concern. Crime ('indictable offences') after having risen by a half during the war years, had not only failed to recede but had, in several years, touched new peaks. It was noticed with horror that more than half the convictions for "breaking and entering" were of young people under seventeen, often still at school. (In 1951, a peak year, one in fifty of the 14–17 age group was convicted of an indictable offence, compared with one in a hundred in 1938.)

More disquieting than the actual amount of crime, which was, after all, still comparatively modest, was the undertone of senseless violence. The newspapers were full of the terror imposed by juvenile gangs—the "Elephant Boys", etc.—whose moronic depredations and "smash-ups" seemed to be plunging us back into the dangerous street life of the early eighteenth century.

Once, magistrates observed, to use a knife in a fight had been considered shameful and un-British; now it seemed to have become the badge of manhood. Once there had been such a thing as a "fair fight". Now a fight had become a demonstration of gang brute force, of Fascist-style power. An ugly little word moved into the headlines: COSH BOY, often accompanied by photographs of the armoury now favoured: the bicycle chains, the broken milk bottles, flick knives, knuckledusters, home-made coshes. . . .

Like everything else, crime had been depersonalized, mechanised, complicated. Stealing from old Mr. Jones, the corner grocer, was one thing; helping oneself in a help-yourself chain store another. The thief—and the young delinquent— had been raised to a higher power by the motor-car. Sometimes, as the total of systematic big money "raids" grew, he appeared to be acquiring like his American confrère an almost entre-preneural status.

These were unlooked-for phenomena of the "New Britain" and their appearance gave rise to much anxiety. Some blamed the "coddling" of the "Welfare State"; others found both quality and quantity of "welfare" still deficient. The King George's Jubilee Trust pointed to the two-year military call-up which erected a "high hurdle", concealing from the young the "need to plan and work for the future". What was needed, insisted writers of half a million firm letters to the Editor, was more discipline, the "good larruping" confidently recommended by Lord Chief Justice Goddard. Others, with even greater confidence, laid the blame on "Dick Barton, Special Agent", the ex-Commando hero of the B.B.C.'s punch-drunk serial, which from 1946–51 held an audience of 15 millions glued to their loudspeakers nightly.

The rumble of moral doubt continued to form a sort of ground-bass in the orchestration of the times. There had, many complained, been a general falling away of standards: there was "a general impression that there are no particular rules in the game of life". Lying, announced Dr. Garbett, Archbishop of York, enlarging on "our moral chaos", was now looked on as "a legitimate means to escape from detection and punishment": the "only commandment was 'Thou Shalt Not Be Found Out'". The brittle phrase of the Twenties—"I couldn't care less"— was in currency again. (And even if one *did* care in this complex postwar world, bleakly locked in its barren ideological struggle, it was not easy to see what one could actually *do*.)

As ever when the nation's moral health was in issue, there were the darkest allegations about sexual morality. Chastity, observed the Bishop of Exeter, had never been held in lower public esteem since the reign of Charles II. However, Mr. Geoffrey Gorer, the sociologist, having meticulously examined 10,000 detailed answers to a questionnaire designed to reveal current (1951) English attitudes to sex, love and marriage, concluded: "There seems every reason to believe that the sexual morals of the English have changed very little in the present century."*

Possibly the verdicts of the Bishop and the sociologist were not quite so far apart as might appear. For not until 1938–39 had the Registrar-General inaugurated that devastating progression from the statistically general to the statistically particular, which Dr. Kinsey was so enthusiastically to continue, by including in his returns a small item showing that of all first-born children in Britain nearly one-third were conceived outside marriage.**

In so far as sexual morality is statistically measurable what mainly emerges is a monotonous constancy. War years apart, the illegitimacy rate has remained around 4–5 per cent for the last three-quarters of a century—although it could be argued that with the advance of contraception it ought to have tended to fall instead of—in the later Fifties—tending to rise.

What had changed was not so much behaviour—or the real code—as what was admitted, the expressed code. But without

* *Exploring the English Character.* Half the married population— male and female alike—stated that they had had no sexual relation- ship whether before or after marriage with any other than their spouse.

** Of these "irregularly conceived maternities", 70 per cent, he added, were "regularized by marriage of parents before birth of child" (a figure with which service postings were to play havoc in the war years).

the Victorian draperies, there were still many who felt indecently exposed; the discovery that the English were "human after all" might reasonably take the English a few more years to get used to.

II

Moreover, the other side of the medal of Victorian "hypocrisy" had been a series of standards which, however unrealistic and distorting, were at least visible. If any standards were offered by the approach via the social sciences rather than by law, dogma, and tradition, they were elusive and—so far— had had to be sought, gropingly, by the individual for him or herself.

As the prosecuting counsel was to cry in the *Lady Chatterley* trial: "There must be standards, must there not?" Many, through these years, echoed that baffled cry. In every sphere, the absolute was failing; the "full life" was what people sought now, not the "good life". Authority seemed to face its final declension. The old middle class, which had given England its particular moral tone, was swallowed up. The social hierarchy which had given the Established Church its rationale was crumbling. The secularisation of English life was at last all but complete. Almost down to 1938 the B.B.C. Sunday had been given over to Bach cantatas, church services, and sober talks. Now—though the shed skin of Sabbatarianism was not yet wholly cleared away—Sunday was the peak day for comedy series, dance music and panel games. Only about one in seven people,* predominantly women, went to church. "The average Anglican vicar," reported Canon Mervyn Stockwood, "is the warden of a very small hen roost." "Many people", wrote another cleric, the Rev. Daniel Jenkin, "appear to cherish their churches precisely on account of their archaicism. Within them they can evoke the memory of a vanished social order more readily than in almost any other place."

In particular, vast industrial and working-class areas had absolutely minimal contact with organised religion, Roman Catholicism excepted. Somewhat earlier than the Labour Party,

* But almost twice the proportion if one took only Scotland.

Dissent had become the victim of its own success. Middle-aged and now cosily "established", the Nonconformist Conscience slumbered on, turning only lightly in its sleep from time to time.*

Some claimed, it was true, to detect at last the turn of the tide. Here and there in prosperous suburbs churches were beginning to fill again. At Oxford and Cambridge, elderly dons were heard to say that they could not recall so much undergraduate interest in religion since before the First World War. But however "due", a national religious revival still seemed improbable, short of some catastrophic flight from Reason. If people had become too sophisticated for a Fundamentalist heaven-and-hell** equally they were not sophisticated enough to grapple with the intricacies of a theism that had made its peace with Darwin and Freud. The clerics who, nevertheless, drew adherents *en masse* were those who—like Drs. Billy Graham and Frank Buchman—succeeded in papering over this gap by the use of sophisticated techniques of publicity and persuasion. They "sold" God in slick packaging. But what the 1,300,000 people who bought the Billy Graham packet at those astonishing crammed meetings in the vast Harringay Stadium in 1954 really got out of it remained a matter of doubt.

Most people continued to inhabit the modern limbo vaguely located between science and religion, fully entering into or understanding neither. If challenged they would have cited Christianity as the authority for such moral code as they had. But it was a residual Christianity, whose adherents now apparently felt no more need of a physical church than did Buddhists. Numerous anxious surveys showed that though a large majority of Britons continued to affirm a belief in God and more than half taught their children to pray (possibly on the general principle that it was "good for them"), fewer and fewer believed in a personal God. Half (including many churchgoers) no longer believed in the after-life; and of those that still

* As, for instance, in 1956, when the new State Lottery, the Premium Bond scheme, was inaugurated.

** The survival and growth of an apocalyptic sect like Jehovah's Witnesses suggested the continuance of social and cultural deprivation in our society, and also, as with the Mormons, a highly efficient American-designed proselytising organisation, but was otherwise insignificant. Total British Isles membership, 1960—44,000.

did, fewer and fewer had much idea what form this might take.*

But if this was "residual Christianity", the residue was by no means the dross. Nor was the picture by any means wholly one of apathy. There was not the appetite for spiritual panaceas, for mystical cults like Yoga or pseudo-religions like Couéism, or for single truths like Social Credit that there had been in the interwar years. But though more detached and critical, interest in the transcendental was real enough. Clear, modern-minded books on religion sold in large quantities. There was a strong interest in cosmogony: the works and radio talks of Fred Hoyle, the Cambridge mathematician and astronomer, attracted for his "continuously created" universe the same large fascinated audience that Jeans and Eddington had for their "mysterious" and "expanding" universe of the Thirties.

Certainly neither these mild speculative exercises nor this continuing underwriting of the golden rule (if not possibly of the whole Sermon on the Mount) added up to a faith that would inspire life and action. And bodies such as "Christian Action", formed in 1946 by a group of ex-Service undergraduates at Oxford, under the leadership of the Rev. John Collins, then Dean of Oriel, with the support of Sir Stafford Cripps "to make a dynamic Christian gospel operative in everyday affairs" remained peripheral and somehow lacking in conviction. The postwar church had no "Dick" Sheppard and no Archbishop Temple.

Perhaps what the Church needed was a few good old-fashioned Rationalists, with the light of battle in their eyes. But that species, too, appeared all but extinct.** With the death, in 1953, of Bishop Barnes, of Birmingham, still stoutly questioning the Miracles, the old science *versus* "religion" (i.e. dogma) battle receded finally into history. The Fifties could not enjoy even the exhilaration of debunking; only the

* An interesting pointer here to a more sophisticated approach was the rapidly increasing popularity of cremation: in 1940 less than 4 per cent of those who died were cremated; by the end of the Fifties, the proportion had reached a third.

** Oddly enough, or not so oddly, the few survivors appeared to be mainly women, like Professor Barbara Wootton, or Mrs. Margaret Knight, of Aberdeen University, whose radio talks in 1954 on the moral training of children without religion aroused a national rumpus of a strangely "dated" kind.

bleakness of having been debunked. The romantic idealism of a Marie Stopes gave place to a Kinsey's relentless recording of "coital activities"; for the philosophical resonances of a Havelock Ellis was substituted the plodding clinicism of the Wolfenden Report; and the perfervid vision of a Wells with his supreme faith in the omnipotence of human reason was lost in the arid formulae of nuclear nihilism.

III

For a people in whom the moralistic urge was ingrained this could be an uncomfortable situation. The desire to fight the good fight could not be adequately met by employment as a psychiatric social worker. If the intellect perforce accepted science's many shades of grey, the emotions still craved the blacks and whites of the old morality, the reassuring immutability of some massive simplification identifiable with Natural Law.

The dilemma was lived out in the long and impassioned debate that arose out of the attempt to abolish the death penalty for murder. The Criminal Justice Act of 1948 was worthy of the place accorded it among the foundation documents of "the New Britain", even though its subsequent translation into practice was largely blocked by lack of funds. It eclipsed the idea of simple retribution, advanced a stage further the principle that the punishment should fit the criminal rather than the crime. Introducing the sentence of corrective training, it promoted the approach that prison "treatment" was something to be flexibly assessed by the appropriate social scientists and Prison Commission experts, rather than a penalty to be rigidly imposed by lawyers. It formally abolished 'hard labour' and 'penal servitude' and—in the face of the protests of the Lord Chief Justice—it put an end to flogging.*

So much might have been conceded. But in the Bill's passage through the House a Private Member attached a logical conclusion in the form of an amendment abolishing the death penalty for an experimental five years (as recommended by the Parliamentary Select Commmittee of 1930).

That sounded the tocsin.

* Save as a disciplinary weapon of last resort in penal institutions.

For though the number of executions was small and declining, "capital punishment" had a powerful emotive and symbolic value which extended over the whole culture. It stood for inevitable retribution against the evildoer; it provided the illusion of a strong morality. When, after vigorous debate, the House of Commons passed the Abolition amendment by twenty-three votes, the Lords, rallying from the backwoods, threw the Bill out. They were sonorously supported in this attitude by the Judges. It was the lawyers, not the clerics, who really manned the last ditch against Science.

When the Lords also rejected a compromise "degrees-of-murder" Bill, the Government fell back on yet another Royal Commission, charged this time to consider not the merits of capital punishment but the manner of its application. If executions could somehow be made humane and even attractive the demands of "humanists" and "moralists" could be reconciled.

However, after endless examination of hangmen, prison governors, police officials, doctors, and conscientious study of lethal methods employed elsewhere—gas, guillotine, electric chair, hypodermic—the Royal Commission neatly pitched the ball back into the Government's court. The "real question now," it concluded, "is whether capital punishment should be abolished or retained".

The hangman, whose operations had for a time been suspended, resumed his place among us. He had, for all that, an increasingly anachronistic air. For the climate of humanism was pervasive. Whether or not, as some alleged, the individual sense of responsibility had diminished, a *social* concern was increasingly evident. The old might sometimes be neglected by their children, children by parents; yet it is doubtful whether there can ever have been so much practical unsentimental consideration of the lot either of the old or of the young, or so much done or planned for them. There was also a growing appreciation that mental disturbance was a form of ill-health like any other. And murder was evidently often the outcome of mental disturbance.

Uneasiness grew with an incident which occurred in the winter of 1952.

It was trivial enough in its beginnings. A little girl, going to bed in her home in Croydon, looking out of her bedroom window, saw two figures climbing into a confectionery warehouse across the street. Her father, whom she called, dialled 999. Within a few minutes the police had the building surrounded.

Figures appeared on the warehouse roof. The police climbed after them. A shot echoed in the narrow street. A struggle seemed to be going on around a lift-stack.

There were shouts and more shots.

Then the crowd saw the gunman run to the corner of the roof. He hesitated on the edge. Then he dived.

His fall was broken by soft earth. It was a sixteen-year-old boy named Christopher Craig.

A few moments later, Craig's accomplice was brought down the stairs by the police, the nineteen-year-old Derek Bentley. Also brought down was the body of a policeman, shot between the eyes.

The Craig-Bentley case sent a shock of horror through the nation, tearing brutally through all the vague, well-meaning discussion about "juvenile delinquency". Craig's father was a bank official. His home was in a "respectable" suburb. But what really burned the case into the public mind was a legal "accident". Being under eighteen, the killer Craig escaped the death penalty. His dupe, so clearly a dupe, Derek Bentley, being nineteen, was hanged, though he had been recommended to mercy by the jury. He was a Grade IV mental defective. He had been armed with nothing more than a knife and a knuckle-duster. He had, in fact, been held by the police when, just before the fatal shot was fired on the roof, he had given the shout— "Give it to them, Chris!"—that was to echo through the long, painful trial.

This result, while in accordance with the Law, affronted both normal instincts of humanity and the national sense of fair play. Not since the Thompson-Bywaters case in 1922, said the *Daily Express*, had an execution aroused such controversy. "In every pub and every club, in every home in the land, the question is being discussed: 'Should Bentley hang?'" Telegrams of protest poured in from all over Britain. In the House, the night before the execution, there was a painful, emotion-charged scene which ended with the Speaker's refusal to allow the matter to be debated. After that, in a last desperate effort, an all-Party deputation of M.P.s waited upon Sir David Maxwell Fyfe, the Home Secretary. At 1 a.m. a crowd of demonstrators marched to Maxwell Fyfe's chambers in the Temple.

Next day, the horror continued with the morning papers' streamer headlines: "BENTLEY WILL HANG TODAY." And with them, on the front pages, a harrowing picture of the boy's shattered family at the gates of Wandsworth Jail.

There was something like a crisis of conscience. Perhaps we were less tough than we were. Or was it that we had momentarily glimpsed a forgotten truth—that in a society, as in an individual, poverty has its non-material forms?

The officers of the Law could not concern themselves with such imponderables. They continued to cling to the reassuring blacks-and-whites of the M'Naghten Rules on insanity, which predated modern psychology, as firmly as did the Bishops to the hardly more realistic doctrine of marital "guilt" established by the single act of adultery. Though the psychiatrists were beginning to work in increasing numbers *behind* the judicial bench, in front of it they were still made to conform to the categories of the lawyers and thus rendered ridiculous.

In 1955 a new motion to suspend hanging, in the names of three Tory and three Socialist Members, was lost in the Commons by thirty-one votes. On both sides views were strongly, even passionately, held. Although it crossed party lines, this was, in reality, one of the central issues debated in these years.

Opinion polls continued to show considerable majorities for retaining the gallows. In the contemporary chaos many drew grim assurance from the thought of the ultimate penalty. The wages of sin is death.

Yet disquiet grew. There was the hanging, attracting immense publicity, of the twenty-eight-year-old mother of two children, Mrs. Ruth Ellis, for a crime of passion, the shooting of a faithless lover; there was the execution of the half-witted, doubtfully guilty Evans for killing his baby, coupled, bizarrely, with the reprieve by the Home Office (after sentence of death in face of psychiatric evidence) of the mentally defective Straffen who strangled little girls.

It was all getting a little out of hand; too much for modern stomachs anyway. The legalistic categories were all too clearly hopelessly inadequate to the complexities of the human behaviour as now understood. The abolitionists began to gain distinguished adherents of many occupations and persuasions. Packed meetings up and down the country generated the sort of intense moral fervour that had scarcely been seen in Britain since the great days of Free Trade.

The long battle—which, in a sense had begun a century and a half earlier when Romilly embarked on his civilising mission —was almost won. In February, 1955, the House of Commons, on a free vote, recorded its belief that "the death penalty for murder no longer accords with the needs or true interests of a civilised society". Four months later, Sidney Silverman's Abolition Bill was given its Third Reading.

The Homicide Act, which the Government was now forced to bring in, offered a patched-up and obviously unsatisfactory compromise. But it did, nevertheless, implicitly apologise for the death penalty, at the same time reducing the number of hangings to around four a year. And if the new Act still incorporated the M'Naghten Rules, it also provided a way around them in the defence of "diminished responsibility", even seeming to admit what a Lord Chief Justice had but lately called "the fantastic theory of irresistible impulse".* (Since "diminished responsibility" carried a reduction of the charge to manslaughter, it opened the way to complete discretion in sentencing.)

Very cautiously, the psychiatrists were being brought out from behind the Bench to the front of it. With equal caution it was at last being conceded that criminology was not necessarily an oddity of foreigners: a research unit was set up within the Home Office, official support given to the establishment (in 1959) of an Institute of Criminology at Cambridge.

IV

It had been a slow, quiet, very English victory. But it had also been a critical one. For now not only the churchmen, but the lawyers, too, were in retreat. Science, once more allied with

* As determined 1960 by the Court of Criminal Appeal, P. *v.* Byrne, Byrne being a sexual psychopath who had strangled and mutilated a girl.

developing social democracy and human compassion, had elevated Original Virtue above Original Sin. But, as ever where science was concerned, there remained a doubt about the precise quality of the emancipation conferred. If the "everlasting nay" was rejected, for the ordinary man the "everlasting yea" remained heavily obscured. If the "democratic" jury was, in some degree, freed from the rigidities of the hierarchs of the Law, it was submitted to other Experts, whose disciplines might be more supple, but were hardly less esoteric. It was a characteristic mid-century evolution almost caricatured at the end of the decade when, in the *Lady Chatterley* prosecution scores of experts were marshalled in the witness-box to establish "literary quality" and "public good" which, under the new Obscene Publications Act,* qualified the old "tendency to deprave and corrupt".

The lawyers did at least consider it their duty to attempt, however ineffectively, to clarify the principles and processes of the Law for the people who had to live by it. So much could not always be said for the newer "experts". Yet as experts multiplied, so did the belief that the experts were the custodians of the facts. And the facts—so far had the message of scientific positivism now penetrated—were now beginning to acquire at large the appearance of absolute values in themselves, the only affirmation possible.

In the circumstances of the 1950's this was a particularly dangerous error. For however salutary their uncovering and revealing their light, the facts remained merely means, not ends; the ends to which they could be turned, in a society organised as ours now was, were remarkably various and might not always be announced.

"When the rigid secrecy is swept away, a sane and natural reticence becomes for the first time possible", Havelock Ellis had written in the Preface to his *Studies in the Psychology of Sex*. It became possible. So, also, did the process by which the "X-Certificate", introduced to protect children while liberalising film censorship,—became that supposedly irresistible

---

* "For the public good on the grounds that it is in the interests of science, literature, art or learning or of other objects of concern." The Act, which had originated as a Private Member's Bill, made it possible to hear expert testimony of these points.

commercial invitation, "the X-iest of Films"; so also did the powerful attraction between the statistics of Dr. Kinsey and those in the circulation manager's office. If, in the triangle of forces shaping this society, science-technology exerted its pull on one corner, and one-man one-vote democracy on another, the third corner was occupied by a force which, for all its old-fashioned sound, still exerted a pull powerful enough to distort the whole "factual" structure—the drive to maximise private and corporate profit.

Skilfully worked out, the contemporary equation, science-technology plus social democracy, could produce an answer which sanctified and rendered immensely potent the Iron Law —the institutionalised, deodorised and semi-automated greed— of the corporation accountant.

20.   Vital Statistics

"A newspaper may successfully accelerate but never reverse the popular attitude. . . ."

—Hugh Cudlipp, *Publish and Be Damned! The Astonishing Story of the Daily Mirror.*

"THE BIGGEST DAILY SALE ON EARTH"

—claim on *Daily Mirror* masthead.

"NEWSPAPERS VINDICATED!" the *Daily Mail* crowed across its front page on the June morning in 1949 when the Report of the Royal Commission on the Press came out. "Read It!" adjured its leader-writer, underlining the awe-struck admiration with which the Commissioners had beheld that daily technological miracle, "the penny newspaper", such "remarkable value for money", "a brightly coloured kaleidoscope of the world day-by-day".

Though further reading of the Commissioners' observations would in fact have disclosed that their admiration was far from unalloyed (and this treatment of their Report might seem remarkably prompt confirmation of that "undue complacency" and "deficiency in self-criticism" of which they complained), the jubilation displayed by the 'Tory Opposition' Press, was from their point of view amply justified. For despite their strictures on the "triviality and sensationalism" of much of the popular Press, their recognition of the compulsion to maximise circulation, and their deploring of the consequent pursuit of the "lowest common denominator of taste and interest", the Commissioners appointed by the Labour Government had to admit that two years of earnest inquiry had quite failed to disclose a satisfactory alternative. If the British Press was, as the Minister of Health, Mr. Aneurin Bevan, complained, "the most prostituted in the world", this form of prostitution appeared to be no less inevitable than that shortly to receive the attention of the Wolfenden Committee.

This conclusion, thus bleakly committed to print, may in restrospect be seen as a critical defeat for the aspirations of the Left, one more point of departure for the long dispirited withdrawal from that Promised Land which had seemed so close at hand in 1945.

To have reported adequately on the Press at this time, the Royal Commission would, in fact, have had to remain in continuous session. For when the clamps of wartime newsprint control were loosened in the autumn of 1946 circulations had leaped forward in an extraordinary fashion. By 1949 total sales of national and provincial dailies was 50 per cent higher than prewar and those of the Sundays *twice* the prewar level. With a total consumption of 60,000,000 papers a week, the British had become the greatest newspaper-reading nation on earth (disposing of twice as many per head as, for instance, the Press-conscious Americans).

More important than this extraordinary boom in total sales was the even more extraordinary hypertrophy—again peculiarly British—of individual circulations. We could now claim "the world's biggest-selling newspaper", the *News of the World*, whose sales, at their peak, exceeded eight million copies weekly, the "world's biggest daily", the *Daily Mirror*, with around 4¾ millions, and the "world's biggest women's magazine", *Woman*, with a sale of over three millions. These were peaks, but gigantic circulations were now becoming normal.

Newspaper sales had been expanding, with the spread of literacy and with technical progress, for more than a century. But now a new stage in this long process had been reached which was as significant, structurally, as had been Northcliffe's anchoring of sales to the net sales certificate and the advertiser at the turn of the century. The market was at last approaching saturation. And, as it did so, the harsher laws of the big business world were brought for the first time into full operation. The financially strong gained strength, the weak grew weaker. The war had already quadrupled the price of newsprint. Now costs and advertising rates became geared to the mammoth postwar circulations. Whereas a sale of two millions had seemed fabulous when the *Daily Herald* attained it in 1935, it was now becoming the economic minimum for a popular daily in Britain.

Those merely middle-sized, middlebrow journals which the Royal Commission had so lately wished to encourage and whose social value it had underlined, now inevitably came under heavier pressure than ever. In the fight for the remainder of the market, the advantages of the giants were great, and became yearly greater. By 1950, the *Daily Mirror* and the *Daily Express* were between them selling over a million copies a day more than all the seven other national "mornings" put together; half Britain's families read one or the other; amongst the nation's young, something like one in two read the *Mirror*.

The characteristic feature of the Press scene was no longer the "gramophone chain" of the "Press Lord" which had given rise to the call for the Royal Commission, but the blanket-sale newspaper (which, so to speak, abandoned mere gramophones in favour of wiring the entire nation for "stereophonic sound").

The position of such a newspaper imposed upon it a process and a logic of great sociological importance. "Mirror" was, indeed, a suggestive description of this new social institution —yet a mirror of a peculiar kind, which refracted as well as reflected, a mirror whose first necessity was to reflect not the outer world (although it *might* do that also), but a collective image or *persona* of its readers. Into this mirror, from one side, flowed all the half-formed ambitions, the emotions, the social trends and vague aspirations; within the mirror, these were examined, confirmed or rejected, transmuted with that intuitive sociological sense that is good popular journalism; and out again was projected a bright, sharp, larger-than-life image which had a considerable, if elusive, effect on the evolution of postwar society.

If both the *Express* and the *Mirror* inevitably inhabited the endless middle, the commercial need for sharply distinguished brand styles enabled them to project strongly contrasting images, as the position of our society, suspended, rather uneasily, between class and mass, still allowed them to do. The *Express* inhabited the semi-detached, semi-sophisticated world of Suburbia; the *Mirror* lived in class-conscious solidarity—despite the garages—on a vast postwar council housing estate. Both papers proclaimed Success. But the *Mirror* represented the up-and-comingness not so much of individuals, as of a class, or a mass, the civilian successors of those endless Other Ranks it had championed and put "in the picture" in the war.

On their behalf—but since 1945 with a new assurance and therefore somewhat reduced stridency—it continued to cock a snook, to pride itself on its proletarian honesty in calling a spade a spade and, more often than not, a bloody shovel. The voice of the *Express*, by contrast, was pitched in the ever-bright, ever-smart key of the rising middle-income people, vibrant with money talk and "in" names and vogueish catch-words, while still perennially saluting the return of the spring to the trim back gardens of Britain. Yet, different as were their faces, both papers were subversive of the old English social order and convention, the one working the native vein of working-class Radicalism, the other in the American republican tradition of rags-to-riches capitalism.

These twin projections proved so nearly on target that the *Mirror* and *Express* gained between them more than 90 per cent of the new millions who had acquired the newspaper habit since 1939. But they had more in common than ambition and a taste for subversion. Beneath the "brand" styles and packaging, a readership of class-spanning millions narrowly dictated the same basic ingredients: the extra-human "human story", Gossip, Crime, Royalty, Sex, Money. Here the two papers were pace-setters, and were rarely without their serial drama of film-star love life, against a backdrop of luxury hotels and Mediterranean skies. Whole forests of newsprint were felled to chronicle the minutiae of Rita Hayworth's marriage to, and later, estrangement from, Aly Khan; and when the fabulous Ingrid Bergman, so long the embodiment of healthy virtue, announced that something was dead inside her and left her American doctor husband for Roberto Rossellini, the Italian film director, there could be no room for doubt that this was the News, the Whole News and nothing but the News.

Though the *Express* maintained a costly foreign news service, whereas the *Mirror* tended to carry its discoveries about "reader-interest" to their logical conclusion, both clearly accepted the daily necessity to entertain, excite or perish. This was the first law of their being. And the well-trained mid-century reader co-operated with the necessary (possibly very temporary) suspension of disbelief. Once, the dead weeks of summer had been celebrated as the newspaper 'silly season'; it seemed doubtful whether this distinction was any longer useful: by the Fifties the silly season was twelve months long.

The logic of the new situation was inexorable. Enormous amounts of capital, the incomes of great numbers of people, were at stake. The vast new circulations *had* to be held, and held against incessant competition. Fortunately, in case of need, there remained one "Lowest Common Denominator", one circulation stimulant, apparently endlessly potent and highly reliable: Sex.

This, certainly, was a fact of which the English Sunday newspapers had long been aware. Yet in certain important respects what was happening was new. The technical virtuosity, the thoroughness and volume of the exploitation, the spread-over into other media, sometimes seemed to suggest that Capitalism had developed its equivalent of "Pornosec", that division of the Ministry of Truth which in Orwell's *1984* was charged with the supply of cheap pornography for the Proles.

The *Sunday Dispatch*, booming after serialising *Forever Amber*, a feast spread out over thirty-seven weeks from 1946 to 1947, continued methodically to lay history under tribute, with a rich diet of serials detailing the Life and (more particularly) Loves of Lucrezia Borgia, Catherine the Great and Liana, the Blonde from the Jungle. The new post-Kinsey "thaw" had profitably opened up the medical field, and when a former British fighter pilot and father of two announced that henceforth he would be known not as "Robert" but as "Roberta", the "family weekly", *Picture Post*, ran his/her account of this intriguing transformation for some weeks, with numerous "before" and "after" photographs. A thwarted Sunday paper thereupon announced that after weeks of patient investigation it had established that the necessary organic changes had not, in fact, taken place. Another cashed in with an article by a personal friend of the ex-fighter pilot, speculating on the prospects of his becoming a wife and mother. Meanwhile, "Roberta's" father, a General in the Army

24. 7th February, 1952: The new Queen comes home from Kenya after the death of her father, King George VI. At the foot of the aircraft steps, her Ministers —Mr. Churchill, Mr. Attlee, Mr. Eden—await her.

25. New Towns, New Art—and, for millions, a new way of life. Public patrons like the New Town Development Corporations gave support to a vigorous new generation of British sculptors. *Above*, Franta Belsky's "Joy Ride" finds its ideal setting in Stevenage Town Centre—for the New Towns belonged to the young.

Medical services, was holding a Press conference to clarify the position.

And whereas the old *News of the World* had presented—and at this stage still did present—its police court dredgings in time-honoured style as the personification of the world's bottomless evil, the rising new school of the *Sunday Pictorial* struck the note of man-of-the-world sophistication, put its sex in spangles rather than handcuffs, and rejected the old vocabulary of euphemism ("clothing disarranged", etc.) for the new one that evoked the wink rather than the moralistic shudder. A pioneer in this more subtle ambivalence, it was rewarded by seeing its sales soar to the remarkable figure of 5,600,000.

Nor was the preparation of the next generation of readers neglected. In 1947, the *Daily Mirror* took over a semi-derelict weekly called *Reveille*. Across the front page each week it spread a "Luscious Lovely", posed "provocatively", cut out and blown up a foot high. The inside pages it filled with a black headlined hodge-podge of extraordinary juvenilia: GREW TALL DRINKING BLOOD . . . SULTAN HAS 2,038 WIVES IN FOUR COLOURS . . . FACE PANTIES . . . SECRETS OF THE PENNY ROOM: DEBS AND THEIR BRUISES . . . MAGIC NUMBER BRINGS QUADS . . . and in a quite short space of time watched the circulation soar from below 100,000 to 3¾ millions. Lord Rothermere, duly impressed, similarly transformed his hitherto staid and obscure *Overseas Daily Mail*, and saw its sales, too, duly shoot ahead to the plus two million mark.

Henceforth, the schoolboy snigger would carry its note of sophistication and authority; hardly indeed a snigger any longer, more like a junior leer.

The Press Council, which was almost the only result of the Royal Commission's years of labour, was not set up until July 1953. But by October of that year it had found it necessary to record—as its members moved from Bench to Dock and back to Bench again—* that it was "deeply concerned about

* Since the Press had rejected the Royal Commission's recommendation that 20 per cent of the Council, including the Chairman, should be lay members it was, like the medical profession, judge of its own conduct, and had on occasion round its table of judgment representatives of the very "sinners" whom it was instructing to go and sin no more.

H

the unwholesome exploitation of sex by certain newspapers and periodicals. . . ."

But though appearances might at times seem to suggest some sort of Bacchanalia, much streamed by in the realms of subconscious fantasy—public now as well as private. All in all the erosion of the intellect still appeared a somewhat more likely result than the stimulation of the passions.

II

The Popular Press, in the postwar mammoth sale form, was the result of the contemporary equation: 'count heads' democracy plus technology plus the economic logic and dynamic of capitalism—with the latter the critical factor. Popular radio, which also arrived in these years, was the result of a somewhat more complex equation: technology plus war plus "count-heads" democracy plus social science—with the profit drive at this stage coming into the picture only indirectly through the patterns it had created, ready-to-use, across the Atlantic.

In the annals of the British Broadcasting Corporation the story unfolds in these years like a parable of the times.

The B.B.C. of the interwar years had been an almost perfect embodiment of the old authoritarian culture: truth and beauty handed down, with due care and befitting gravity, from the Portland Place Olympus. For the B.B.C.'s first great Director-General, Sir John Reith, had, as he himself explained with admirable lucidity in his autobiography in 1949, set out to use "the brute force of monopoly" to give the public "everything that was best in every department of human knowledge, endeavour and achievement"; to give it what it *ought* to want since "few knew what they wanted and fewer knew what they needed".

Reith was fortunate in the moment of his resignation, in 1938—when a dictator even more powerful than he was about to take over. The war beat much of the starch out of the B.B.C.'s perpetual dress-shirt front.* It was vital now to make genuine

---

* In 1925 it had been decided that announcers should wear dinner-jackets at the microphone to establish the proper tone. It took a war to remove them.

contact with the mass of ordinary people; to lighten the boredom of the soldiers and war workers; to bind home and war
fronts in a common camaraderie. This was radio's obvious
role. In 1941, the first British "soap opera", "Front Line
Family", went on the air. So, too, did the Brains Trust, where
the listener was no longer merely lectured, *de haut en bas*, but
was admitted by proxy to the forum, and allowed to heckle a
little. With entertainers like Tommy Handley, news-readers
who were at last permitted names and personalities, with war
reporters of a vastly expanded news-service like Chester Wilmot,
or Wynford Vaughan Thomas, voluble in a bomber over
Berlin, the B.B.C. was becoming for the first time really
absorbed into the national life, every man's third ear.

When peace came, "Front Line Family"—now demobilised
as "The Robinson Family"—soldiered on; "Music While
You Work" still poured from the loudspeakers. It was clearly
impossible to return at once to the old régime of Olympian
detachment. Equally impossible for the B.B.C. to abandon the
Reithian mission.

Fortunately, in its new Director-General, Mr. W. J. Haley,
former editor of the *Manchester Guardian*'s profit-providing
companion, the *Manchester Evening News*, the Corporation had a
man who was no stranger to the art of straddling cultural
worlds. The Haley compromise was ingenious, if scarcely
unprecedented. Henceforth, there would be three programmes,
stratified by brow. Lowbrow, Middlebrow and Highbrow,
C-stream, B-stream and A-stream—those now well-recognised
gradations in which the human intellect was divided—would be
neatly accommodated by "the Light", by "the Home", and by
—with what exquisite tact the name was chosen!—"the Third".

Instead of being viewed as charges to be roped, willy-nilly,
up the peaks of Mount Olympus, the public would henceforth
be seen, through the Haley-modified viewing apparatus, as
"a broadly based cultural pyramid, slowly aspiring upwards".
"The listener," ruled the new D.-G., "must be led from the
good to the better by curiosity, liking and growth of understanding." Meanwhile, to spur him with a glimpse of the shining
peaks ahead, the Third Programme had been inaugurated with
an address by Field-Marshal Smuts in September, 1946.

So much for the contribution of democracy born of war. The

part played by social science in the postwar seduction of the B.B.C. was less visible, but hardly less effective.

A few years before the war the B.B.C. had acquired a small sub-section named "Listener Research", then generally regarded as the harmless eccentricity of a certain Mr. Robert Silvey, who was for ever producing graphs and devising what he called "sampling techniques". It is ironic that Reith's B.B.C. should have been a pioneer of scientific day-to-day audience-polling in Britain—although it seems probable that Reith himself recognised the dangers from the start. Listener Research, he told the Beveridge Committee on Broadcasting in 1949, was "inevitably a drag-down, subversive, a menace".

Subversive or not, the war gave Listener Research its head. Through its interviews and listening panels the ordinary listener was able for the first time to talk back. It is true that the verdicts of the plebs were not published, but were locked away in the Corporation's filing cabinets like guilty secrets. Listener Research, it was laid down, was to be the "servant, not the master, of programme-planning". But, as Mr. Maurice Gorham, head of the Light Programme, observed: "it was a servant nobody could afford to displease".

Particularly not the planners of the Light Programme, who with the aid of this remarkable "servant", had by 1949 captured almost two-thirds of all the B.B.C.'s listeners, thus establishing in Britain a new force of peculiar pervasiveness—popular radio.

Devoted to "entertainment in the widest sense", the "Light" swept along on a tide of undemanding music and bonhomie, filling the aching void of every minute with warranted consumable sound. Its staples, the panel game, the request programme, the quiz, the fifteen-minute "real life" serial, the thirty-minute comedy show, with ready-to-use laughter, appeared capable of infinite repetition. And though, at first, there were still the R.A.F. echoes, the source of most of this was obvious enough. B.B.C. NOW A YANKEE BABY IN CARBON COPY OF U.S. PRO-GRAMMING, ran a headline in *Variety* in 1948.

"Twenty Questions" even had a transatlantic "Question-master", Stewart MacPherson, whose folksy, fast-talking, classless North American radio style rapidly made him a household word through postwar Britain.

III

It was, significantly, the rise of the Light Programme that made possible that outstanding mid-century accession to the British way of life, the electronic personality. For, hitherto, the B.B.C., because of its monopoly position and "Establishment" psychology, had been extremely wary of permitting the build-up of strong nation-wide radio personalities. The Light, since it was so clearly labelled "For Amusement Only", removed this difficulty.

In 1946 a Northern newsreader named Wilfred Pickles, who had gained some slight fame in the war years by reading "bath" and similar words in the national news-bulletins with a short "a", was made chairman-interviewer of an American-style "audience-participation" show, with small money prizes, handed out on the spot. With his Yorkshire warmth and directness, Pickles succeeded in further enlarging the hole which the war had blown in the class-based pomposity of the B.B.C. He revealed the decency, humour, and idiosyncrasies of ordinary British people with a sureness of touch that won the gratitude of some millions of them.

But, as the successful formula of "Have a Go" was relentlessly exploited, as the laughter-signals, 'Are you courting?' and 'Give 'er the money, Barney!' rolled from the loudspeakers of the land, week after week, month after month, and year after year, as the Press (and everybody else) cashed in on this apparently inexhaustible new source of "reader-interest", "yer old friend, Wilfred Pickles", for all his gritty reality, inevitably acquired that larger than life quality which, joined as it was to the "common man touch", clearly belonged in the new magic mirror already demonstrated by the multi-million-sale Press.

Although "Have a Go" rattled on into the Sixties, Wilfred Pickles, with his regional, "working-class", "the-people-to-the-people" note, was essentially a figure of the Forties, of wartime camaraderie, sound radio, and the Beveridge revelation. The Fifties, of the Endless Middle, were the terrain of Gilbert Harding, ex-schoolmaster, ex-police constable, ex-crammer, ex-law student, a rolling stone who in middle life had found lodgment in the wartime monitoring service of the B.B.C. In 1947 Harding became quiz-master of "Round Britain Quiz", in 1948 he chaired the revived Brains Trust and in 1950 took over Twenty Questions. In the following year, in "What's My Line?", his personality acquired an extra dimension through the television camera's lens. His resonant, instantly recognisable voice, his rather brooding presence, his ready flow of words made him the supreme practitioner of a new profession—master of the national panel or parlour games. But it was not merely to professional competence that Harding owed his immense fame. Like Pickles he tended to behave on the B.B.C.'s perfected air like a normal human being. He would permit himself from time to time to betray a mild irritation with the fatuities to which he was solemnly committed.

Not long ago these so-called "outbursts" would have ensured Harding's instant banishment. But now Audience Research showed that they merely guaranteed the greatest happiness of the greatest number. And again as the mass-sale Press seized on so reliable and made-to-measure a running story, Harding's "rudeness" like Pickles' "sincerity" took on Jehovah-like dimensions. The front pages were full of him. His face gazed "belligerently" out of the advertising columns, "glared" down from the hoardings, looked "outspoken" over untold thousands of ghosted "What-I-Say-Is" articles in magazines and news-papers. That instantly recognisable gravelly voice seemed to echo out of the void, everywhere.

All this was a far cry indeed from the drawing-room radio personalities—A. J. Alan, Sir Walford Davies, Vernon Bartlett, etc.—of prewar days. Yet although they loomed larger than life, the new electronic Personalities still somehow became invisible members of the family circle, a part of the furniture of the home, in a way that film stars had never been. They were the universal comforters and compensators; they filled, as they say, a "long-felt need". In an England where the individual was increasingly isolated and alone Wilfred Pickles was every-body's friend; in an England where the individual felt increasingly powerless Gilbert Harding cocked a snook at authority, told *Them*. (All the more deliciously for having a touch of "gentlemanly" authority himself.)

Yet "Gilbert"—as the common man with proud (and rightful) proprietorship called him—was, like the multi-million-sale Press, close-pinioned by his own vast success. He was a function, another specialist, the visible part of an enormously complex machine, which was now fitted with a monitor to ensure that day by day, almost hour by hour, the profile it presented was being cut to the current market requirement.

Once the worth of performer or book or play had been a matter of qualitative judgment, with many intangibles and qualifications. Now the verdict was issued in *figures* with the precision of science and the authority of democracy. There it was, the personality's audience rating, the paper's net sales certificate, the market research report, the box office takings, the bestseller list, the top ten, the 40 per cent of British married women and the 25 per cent of single women who had experienced premarital intercourse. . . .

If, as some said, contemporary man was groping for standards —for the authority gone from life—standards, authority—of a sort—was becoming available.

IV

With "pop radio" going full blast, the B.B.C. (its staff five times prewar size) now heavily involved in Britain's fastest-growing industry, the industry of public diversion, with the "mass mirror" Press in being, and the opinion-polling mechanism in gear, the conditions were present for the arrival in Britain of that complex and pervasive phenomenon to which J. B. Priestley, returning in 1954 from a visit to the United States (its place of origin), affixed, by a happy stroke, the name of "Admass".

The advent of "Admass", carried a stage further that erosion of old frontiers that was so much a part of the times. As "news" became inextricably blended with "features" (like "sin" with "maladjustment")—more subjective than objective, but subjectivity of a peculiar kind—the newspaper world melted into the world of electronic personalities, into the film world, into the world of bestseller publishing, into the world of advertising and packaging and printing and salesmanship and market research and the ever-expanding realm of Public Relations (into which more and more journalists now went every year) to form a vast ectoplasmic envelope enclosing the Western way of life.

Vital to the process was the capacity to generate that atmosphere of pseudo-sophistication already noted in a large section of the postwar mass-sale Press, obscuring motivations and inducing in the consumer a profitable bemusement. The cult of "Vital Statistics", for instance, was not in itself new; but its systematic, mechanical, pseudo-statistical, calculatingly whimsical, silly-serious, multi-media-ed, multi-motivated, global exploitation was. Whereas the Victorian cult of the bustle had affected few but the dressmakers and, presumably, the wire-workers, the postwar cult of the bosom underpinned the film business, nourished a large branch of popular journalism, caused the expenditure of millions in advertising, and brought a fantastic boom* to the "foundation garment" industry whose ingenious structures were hymned by poetic yet practical copywriters on the posters ("HIDDEN TREASURE . . . Adds Fullness *Confidentially*") that now greeted the commuter as he rose or descended on the escalators of London's Underground.

Thus, almost before the ink was dry on the report of the Royal Commission on the Press, it was depressingly evident that the indictment had been framed by the National Union of Journalists in terms that belonged to a vanished world of simplicity and innocence.

For it was, after all, superfluous for the sinister advertising hand to slip its *douceurs* into the reluctant editorial hand, or for the Press baron tyrannically to impose his views, if all shared the same nervous system, if all were servants of the same machine-and-market. Lord Beaverbrook might assure the Royal Commission that he ran his newspapers to propagate his ideas, but he, no less than the journalists he employed, was a prisoner of the machine he had helped to build. The age of the Press Lords

---

* The results were spectacular in more senses than one. In 1954 total production in Britain was 4·2 million brassières and 5·6 million foundation garments. The comparative figures for 1959 were 20 millions and 35 millions respectively—and the boom continued.

was over. This was the age of the managers, the financiers, the technicians, the accountants.*

Particularly the accountants.

* It was significant, for instance, that Mr. Roy Thomson, the newest Titan of the British newspaper scene, was, on his own admission, primarily a businessman, disavowing all missionary intentions, while—also on his own admission—the same was broadly true of the hereditary heir of Northcliffe, Mr. Cecil King, postwar constructor of the fantastic Odhams-Newnes-Amalgamated Press-Mirror-Pictorial Empire, whose chief lieutenant, Mr. Hugh Cudlipp, was first and foremost an editorial technician—with a Welsh imagination.

21.   Culture and Anarchy

"Why do I spend half of Sunday
reading the papers? . . . The dirty
ones get more and more wet about
the mouth, and the posh ones are
more pompous than ever."
—Jimmy Porter in *Look Back in Anger,*
    Act III, Scene 1.

"The penguin figure had the right
note of dignified flippancy, we
thought."
—Sir Allen Lane, of Penguin Books,
    in an interview, *World Digest.*

GEORGE BERNARD SHAW died at his home at Ayot St. Lawrence in November, 1950. He was ninety-four and had begun to seem immortal. It was hard to believe that the last Shavian quip had been delivered, the last Shavian headline made, the last postcard written. Shaw was the last of the long line of the literary prophets who even in the Thirties had still seemed to bestride the public scene. Wells had gone in 1946; Chesterton ten years earlier; Belloc was eighty, ailing and silent. The men who could stand forth in that way before the whole nation now were no longer the great figures of the Pen but the electronic personalities, or the scarcely less Admass-made adolescents who might soar into the headlines for a few weeks before giving way to newer sensations. It was no longer G.B.S. and G.K.C. embodying and dramatising the power and clash of great ideas, but Gilbert Harding and Eamonn Andrews coruscating in "What's My Line?" over the proper definition of a saggar-maker's bottom-knocker.

The "polarisation of culture" produced, or at least intensified and underlined, by the advent of Admass was becoming one of the central intellectual topics of the day. From the blank and apparently unappealable verdict of the Audience Rating and the Net Sales Certificate the guardians of the "old" culture retreated in alarm, ruling verbal lines and throwing up fortifications to give at least some momentary illusion of the familiar order and authority, before withdrawing into that series of intellectual pillboxes and aesthetic redoubts neatly symbolised by the Third Programme.

Meanwhile—so much for the "pyramid, slowly aspiring upwards"—the Third's share of total listeners fell from 4 per cent in 1946 to 1 per cent in 1949 and then dwindled to a number too small (below 36,000) to be assessed by the sampling techniques of Audience Research. For the dangers of the process of polarisation were by no means confined to its effects at one pole. As a technical innovation, the Third Programme, with its freedom from fixed time-points and its liberal patronage of composers and writers (it was the Third which commissioned Dylan Thomas's *Under Milk Wood*) had much to be said for it. Its champions were fond of remarking that it was "the envy of Europe". But in the current situation its basic premise that the good might not be popular was all too easily extended to read that the unpopular and totally ineffective was bound to be good. The Third/Light dichotomy, at a critical point in Britain's cultural development, facilitated the contracting-out of those who were much needed on the wider stage, promoted the "Professional Intellectual" or "Third Programme Type" and encouraged an untimely revival of the tired and tiresome old Aesthetes *versus* Phillistines theme.

Outside the Victoria Palace, currently presenting the 'Crazy Gang', a new poster went up: "NERVO AND KNOX: NEVER HEARD ON THE THIRD." The Third was always good for a laugh. It had become a sort of shibboleth in an incipient *Kulturkampf* which, to the intelligentsia, was more real than the class war, although of course far from unconnected with it. The genesis of this was complex, owing something to each of the three main factors of the postwar equation: expanding democracy, science-technology, the economic logic of big business. As it proceeded, there seemed less and less room for occupants of the old middle ground; it was "for us or against us" now, "minority" or "mass", "serious" or "pop".

By the time (1956) the P.E.N. Congress met in London to face the question: "How should writers reach the new readers of the present-day world?" the answer seemed to come smartly enough: they ought not to dream of trying. J. B. Priestley stoutly advised writers to seek their audience wherever they might find it, and departed. But Priestley belonged to the comfortable old world of the prewar middle ground. More typical was Marghanita Laski's shuddering verdict: "What writers are concerned with using mass communication media is commercial writing at its very lowest . . . I feel sure that this commercial writing is degrading and abominable; it is writing of which one feels thoroughly ashamed. This is in the nature of things."

There was much talk about the existence of a sort of cultural Gresham's Law by which the counterfeit and trashy was driving out the true and honest coin.

II

None of this, certainly, was new. Carlyle, with the Niagara roar of 1867 in his ears, Matthew Arnold, confronting the rampant plebs whose "revolution against taste, once begun, will end in irreparable chaos", Dr. Thomas Arnold deploring ("all rabble-scrabble") *The Penny Magazine*, established in 1825 to fill the gap between (as it explained) "those dull and moody publications that are not read through" and "those that are greedily bought up because they inflame the imagination, flatter the passions, corrupt the morals, and lull the mental energies", had said most of it before and better. Nor probably was it altogether unique that the pessimists were shrillest when the expansion of culture, in their sense of the word, was proceeding most rapidly.

Radio and the gramophone, those instruments of much maligned "mass communication", had proved vastly more effective instruments of musical education than the parlour piano. In "unmusical" London alone four million seats were now sold each year for concerts, opera, and ballet. In 1949–50, too, lively young audiences, extending more widely across the social spectrum than before the war, were bringing a "commercial" boom to verse-drama and acclaim to a new and prolific verse-dramatist, Christopher Fry, whose *The Lady's Not for*

Burning, despite a medieval setting, ran for nine months at the Globe.

Never within the memory of theatre people had Shakespeare been so popular: in a single month in the Fifties no less than five different Othellos were to be seen—one, an imaginative interpretation on film by Orson Welles, one on the radio, a third in the West End, a fourth at the Old Vic, where Richard Burton and John Neville alternated in the part. Even that old theatrical hand Terence Rattigan, excellent barometer of popular taste in the theatre, was now alternating his offerings to "Aunt Edna" with plays apparently designed for a more serious and discerning uncle.*

The wider awareness of the graphic arts which had developed in the war years had persisted into the peace, spectacularly declaring itself in 1947 when the queues winding around the Tate Gallery, waiting to enter the Van Gogh Exhibition, were so long that police were needed to marshal them. The turnstiles at the public art galleries now clicked away at twice their prewar rate; special exhibitions were crowded like bargain sales. In London private galleries proliferated. Despite the efforts of Sir Alfred Munnings and a few fellow last-ditchers, "Modern Art" was no longer considered either uproarious or outrageous. Rarely now did a public authority have to cover up or take away. On the contrary, it was to the Moderns in the Tate rather than to the Old Masters in the National Gallery that the public flocked, able now to feel the sharp immediacy, the edge of excitement in pictures which were clearly comments on our day, even if baffling comments. In such comment anyone could join and a good many did. Admissions to the Tate more than trebled in the Fifties.

Art was now more than ever in the headlines and the gossip columns. Inevitably these concentrated on the more sensational developments and multiplied them. Yet behind the furore, much quiet, solid work was going on, drawing support now from a public interest livelier and more genuine than for

---

* Thus *The Browning Version* (1948) was followed by *Who Is Sylvia?* (1952); the *Deep Blue Sea* (1952) by the *Sleeping Princess* (1953); followed—Uncle now again clearly in the ascendent—by *Separate Tables* (1954), sensitively exploring the problem of loneliness in modern life.

many years. One sign of this underlying vitality was an improvement in the design of ordinary objects. Another was the welcome accorded to the enterprising and adventurous new generation of British sculptors whose work first began to thrust itself upon public attention at the first open-air exhibition staged by the L.C.C. in a green grove in Battersea Park in 1948.

The open-air exhibition became a postwar institution, helping to free sculpture in the public mind from the convention-bound associations of museum and town hall. It did much in particular for the work of Henry Moore. Often savagely ridiculed before the war, the massive genius of Moore was now very widely recognised. But "modern sculpture" no longer meant merely one or two "notorieties". Quite a number of younger postwar sculptors had quickly achieved world reputations; and, even more remarkably, their work was being bought for New Towns, for the new schools, and, by a few progressive local authorities, for their parks and estates.

III

All this seemed at least as suggestive of renaissance as of a return to the Dark Ages. But the pessimists were unmoved. Such interest, they alleged, was merely shallow and peripheral compared with that of the more fortunate folk of earlier times for whom art and culture had been an integral part of life. Earlier critics had been in the habit of locating this Golden Age, at a prudent distance, in the great days of Athens; later ones, somewhat less securely, had discovered it in medieval Merrie England—before the machine's arrival. The newest critics, like Richard Hoggart, won acclaim by placing it firmly among the Victorian working classes in the days of the good honest music hall and the earnest artisan, grubbing in the "penny box" for the "precious volume"—before, that is, the advent of mass communications.

In any strict sense most of these confident verdicts were unprovable either way. But probably the most significant test area now lay in the world of books. For not only were books still supreme in their capacity for developing and transmitting ideas, but this was a tradition-ruled world which was now coming under some of the strongest contemporary pressures.

For many years, for the mass of people, books had seemed to form the high walls of a sort of inner fortress of culture, accessible only to those who had been, at least, to the grammar school, and thus possessed themselves of "book learning". These postwar years were the years in which it became inescapably evident that not only had this fortress been breached, but that over considerable lengths its walls had been flattened.

Great rivers of books flowed in and out of the public libraries: in the decade after the war issues doubled in many places and continued to rise.* In 1950, a survey by the International Gallup Poll showed Britain as the "best-read" of six leading democracies—over half of our population were now book-readers.** British adults in the Fifties were *averaging* twenty books a year—a remarkable enough figure.

Again the initial stimulus had come from the war. And now, after it, new techniques of marketing and production were brought into play. At their peak in the mid-Fifties, the four or five major book clubs had, between them, 350,000 purchasing members to whom they delivered nine million volumes a year. About the same time a new word was coming into common currency, the word "paperback". Cheap reprints were well over a century old. Paperbacked books were not new. But now in their universality and casual egalitarianism paperbacks seemed somehow to match the times. From ten millions a year (home and export) before the war sales had reached sixty millions by 1958, and continued to rise steeply. The 'paperback revolution' put books in profusion on to the streets of towns that had never owned a bookshop. It put books into hands of vast numbers, particularly of the young, who would have felt self-consciously "out of their class" with a traditional,

* Public Library issues totalled 392 millions in 1958.
** When asked whether they were just then reading any books, 55 per cent of the British replied that they were, compared with Norway (43 per cent), Canada (40 per cent), Australia (35 per cent), U.S.A. (21 per cent), Sweden (33 per cent). A similar survey in the town of Derby arrived at one-third of the population reading a book: still a remarkable enough figure. Yet the amount spent on actually buying books in Britain, though much greater than prewar, was still less than £1 a head per annum.

expensive hard-cover volume. To these "books" in the past had meant magazines. Now books also meant books.

With print orders running to 250,000, and best-sellers in hard covers now reaching 100,000 against less than half that prewar, publishing, in the wake of journalism, was becoming more and more of an industry, less and less the dust-laden, earnestly aspiring or gentlemanly vocation of tradition. There were the usual amalgamations into larger groups, the usual appearance of City finance. Most books—with varying degrees of calculation—had always been produced for the market. But now, as output rose steeply, the assembly lines, the standard products, became more visible—sometimes devastatingly so.

And what was the product which producers could most reliably produce and the consumers could be relied upon steadily to consume? Sociologically, it was an interesting question, and there seemed little doubt, at this time, of the answer. The favoured commodity was fact, assorted fact, authentic, yet "stranger than fiction", exotic, yet blended with the pedestrian for piquancy and conviction. Reconstructions of bygone disasters, documented to the last sigh as the great ship went down; episodes of history unrolled in cinematic detail; the jungle, with head-shrinkers, red-tailed pygmies, giraffe-necked women, compèred by travelling anthropologists, missionaries and white hunters. . . .

As it happened, an almost inexhaustible reservoir of fact of the required quality lay at hand. One day in 1948 a London departmental store buyer named Eric Williams received a letter from his literary agent. It informed him that his account of his escape from Stalag Luft III, through a tunnel camouflaged with a vaulting horse, had now been rejected by four or five publishers. "Really," the letter concluded, "there is just no market for war books."

In 1949, however, *The Wooden Horse* was at last published by Collins, discovering a public so large and eager that Williams made £20,000 out of book rights alone, and sent scores of other ex-P.o.W.s rummaging in their drawers for old war letters and diaries. The escape stories opened the flood-gates. Now from every section of every Service, from every front and every "back room", the "war books" came tumbling to fill the void of peace. For the best part of a decade it appeared that

i

one could read three new "war books" every week, and that, indeed, many did.

But for all the range and depth of experience of the war years there was little in this immense output that struck deep, or seriously sought to reflect the psychological realities of war. The preoccupations of Richard Hillary, in *The Last Enemy*, best-selling war book of the war years themselves, had not survived the peace. In extraordinary contrast with the books that came out of the First World War—but did not appear for the most part until ten years after it—there was little disillusion (admittedly there had been less illusion), little self-examination, few poetic undertones, or indeed undertones of any sort. There was neither Romanticism nor Realism; just, for the most part, matter-of-fact details, marshalled in the sort of brisk, breezy narrative that would have commended itself to the old *Boy's Own Paper*.

Boys, in fact, were enthusiastic supporters of the great war book boom; it is interesting to speculate on the picture of the war which, relying wholly on such sources, they must have conjured up.

If in the world of popular newspapers, the old hard lines between news, comment and features tended to be eroded in the ruling interest of entertainment and salesmanship, so in the field of popular book-publishing, the traditional frontier between non-fiction and fiction was losing some of its clarity. If the best-selling non-fiction authors "fictionalised" (i.e. subordinated to simple narrative form) their fact, best-selling fiction authors were apt to be those who offered a high degree of factual documentation. Where the difference was least, the sales were often highest. Commander Nicholas Monsarrat's novel of the war at sea *The Cruel Sea*—whose sales reached the phenomenal figure of over 400,000 in a little over a year after publication in 1953—was a notable case in point.

But the appetite for the thickly documented background— which reached its highest pitch of mechanical efficiency in popular American writers (and was also an important feature of successful electronic serials)—was by no means confined to war novels. The most successful writer of postwar adventure stories, Hammond Innes, an ex-journalist, moved his readers about the world from the wilds of Labrador to the Anti-Atlas or to an Antarctic whaling station, each setting presented in careful detail observed on the spot. In the "crime" field, the naturalistic novel—Agatha Christie notwithstanding—was slowly driving out the conventional whodunit; on the oceans, C. S. Forester tied his reef-knots and lowered his top-gallants with much-appreciated expertise; while science-fiction animated the facts of the nuclear age.

And there was Nevil Shute.

For the contemporary student the sociological significance of individual "serious" writers, painters and other artists must inevitably be obscure. Genius may transcend its times as well as reflect them. Short of genius, intellectual vogues, however "important" at the time, may—today especially—be of no more significance than changes in fashions in women's hats.

But the steady best-sellers of a period are more reliable indicators—especially if, like Shute, they owe nothing to the exploitation of violence or sex. And Nevil Shute, the most consistently and vastly read novelist of the period, does, in fact, have an air of belonging to the Forties and Fifties as firmly as Trollope to mid-Victorian times or Maugham to the Edwardian years.

To begin with, he was that very unliterary, but very mid-twentieth century, thing, an engineer—and an engineer in one of engineering's newest and most scientific branches, an aeronautical designer. An engineer's grip on detail, harnessed to a gift for narration, enabled Shute in *No Highway*, published in 1948, to dramatise a highly technical problem of aeronautical research with such conviction and urgency that its equations and processes acquired a life of their own, transcending that of the individuals who worked with them. It was indeed the vitality of the contemporary technological landscape in which they were set, the author's sober—almost do-it-yourself—practicality that breathed into Shute's characters such life as they had.

And however exotic the setting, whether Shute's story dealt with running an airline in the Persian Gulf or fighting forest fires in Australia, the voice—the "I" of the books with which the reader could so easily identify—was quiet English suburban. But engineers' suburban now, flat, functional, and relatively

classless—or at least "endless middle"—very close to the true
centre of postwar Britain.

Shute, furthermore, answered people's need for moral
reassurance. His characters—as in a distant nuclear-age echo
from Bunyan—were nearly always "fundamentally decent"
people, making mistakes perhaps, but earnestly doing their
duty as they saw it, and somehow coming through in the end.

Little of this popular documentary fiction began to have—or
indeed sought to have—the moral and imaginative depths of
a Defoe or even of Graham Greene (who was also unique in the
ease with which he bridged pre- and postwar worlds and the
"pop" and "non-pop" gulf).

But then, neither did most so-called "serious" novels.
"Are there," inquired *The Times* editorial, one day in the
Fifties, "half a dozen men or women in the fiction written since
the war whose names and fortunes are generally familiar?
Is there a novel of which the prophecy could confidently be
made that it will be read and re-read?"

The Times answered itself in the negative. Yet—though the
"polarisation of culture" did not help—such deficiencies
clearly could not be laid wholly at the door of the "democratisation" of books. The cataclysmic violence of the times, the
collapsing of the old class system within which English novelists
had lived and written, the post-Freudian disruption of techniques, the lack of any firm place to stand in a moral sense,
were all obvious factors.

The novel as a form no longer held the powerful central
position it once had; the proportion of novels to other new
books, both as published and as issued from libraries, was
significantly falling.* The novel no longer seemed the inevitable
vehicle for the great theme or message or even for literary
experiment. In the "serious" novel, the note of affirmation,
which the millions sought in Shute, was largely absent. From
this machine-dominated society in flux the inclination of the
"serious" novelist often appeared to be to retreat into the

* The proportion of novels had fallen from nearly a third prewar
to around one-fifth, though this was not an absolute fall, since more
new titles were being published than before the war. In 1950 there
were 3,700 new works of fiction, an average of over seventy a week.

private world of childhood, or into the "sordid bed-sitter", incubating neurosis, variegated aberrations and fantasy. If any attitude could be said to emerge as characteristic of the "serious" novel-writing of these years, it appeared to be that of social satire, moving through a wide range of tones from the feline precision of Angus Wilson to the enthusiastic debunking and nose-thumbing of Kingsley Amis.

Looking further afield, at books as a whole, there was little evidence that the postwar proliferation had lessened the number of good things available: rather the contrary. For industrialisation in such a field can provide a strength and breadth of base and a ramification of structure which—as the latter-day reappearance of half-forgotten classics as well-printed, "egghead" paperbacks has hinted—*can* support a wide variety of work if the will to do so exists. Nor was it really any longer possible—uncomfortable as some apparently felt without it—to draw any firm line between the "serious" and the "popular". From the documentary war novel or fictionalised fragment of war the reader might easily pass, for instance, to Winston Churchill's majestic history of the war, launched in 1948 with *The Gathering Storm* or to Chester Wilmot's *The Struggle for Europe*, a massive one-volume account published in 1952 which quickly sold over 100,000 copies.

History, biography, memoirs, were among the strongest forms of the postwar years and those which most often succeeded in combining commercial success with quality. A great deal of good vigorous historical writing found eager readers, and came in all shapes and sizes from Mrs. Cecil Woodham-Smith's piquant examination of the Crimean fiasco, *The Reason Why* to Arnold Toynbee's apparently endless philosophical safari through Time and Space, in fact completed in the Fifties. Skilful and industrious "popularisers" like C. V. Wedgwood, Sir Arthur Bryant, A. L. Rowse, combined scholarship and literary quality in the tradition of G. M. Trevelyan (whose *Social History* published in Britain in 1944 was a solid best-seller) and were making history—Elizabethan, Cromwellian, Regency or Victorian—enjoyable and alive to millions. Meanwhile a new school of historical novelists, widely read and some of the best of them women, were rescuing the form from the "gadzookery" that had long beset it.

IV

The alarm of the intelligentsia had much the same source as the disquiets of the old middle class—or the distress of the grammar school mind in face of the Comprehensive School. They felt lost in a world whose "recognised" landmarks were swept away, whose processes no longer conformed to those in which they had been educated and with which they were at home.

But the old cultural geometry just would not work any longer. In the early Fifties the People's Palace in the Mile End Road, established in 1888 to "bring the best in music and drama to the working classes" of the East End, was obliged to close its doors. Only one-tenth of its seats were being filled. Its public, no longer content with the role assigned to them, were streaming "up West" where, among the cinemas, thronged concert halls, the theatres, the bars, the overflowing bookstalls, the bright lights, they were offered not merely "the best in music and drama", but an "up-to-the-minute" menu that was apparently endless in its diversity and also completely "à la carte". It offered the possibilities of cynical exploitation, continuous distraction, acute indigestion, emotional or intellectual nourishment or a comfortably comatosed bewilderment. But, whatever the result, there was no escaping the "democratic" necessity of picking one's own meal.

This was something else the war had completed: the disestablishment of culture. People had the five-day week, the facilities, the money. "Culture", no longer the prerogative of a leisure class, had lost its scarcity value, the compulsive lure of the all but unattainable. (And was not necessarily the worse for that!)

Nor between the strenuously aspiring artisan and his Good Book ("the precious Life Blood of a Master Spirit", as the old Everyman endpapers had it, amidst Morrisian foliage) and the shining Ruskinian (or Haley-ian) pinnacle, was there any longer that comfortable old *John O'London's Weekly*-Robert Lynd-J. B. Priestley middle ground, relaxed and pipe-puffing, yet easily confident in its possession of cultural title-deeds. Instead, there were the curious, extraordinarily assorted crowds pushing around some *al fresco* art exhibition, where one might, according to taste and without prejudice, purchase an "appealing" dog study or some student's latest *tachiste* essay. Self-education, no longer confined to the rigours of the W.E.A., overlapped with hobby-ism; an authority like the L.C.C. now offered an astonishing diversity of leisure courses, and evening institutes were crowded every winter with people of all ages,* studying everything from pottery to Russian, from ju-jitsu to Greek drama.

In the traditionally educated these bizarre juxtapositions tended to give rise to the sort of dismay such American departures as the consumption of cheese with marmalade occasioned in the European gastronome. Yet this was the catholicity which could stimulate as well as bewilder. The outlining and enlarging—with the aid of Press, radio, cinema, television, the book publishing "industry" and so on—of a highest common factor in our population was at least as significant as the Admassian formulation of its lowest common denominator.

And such an extending highest common factor was very much of a reality. Instead of being left with nothing but the *Sunday Pictorial*, the *News of the World* and *Reveille* as the efficient operation of Gresham's Law would seem to require, the greatest *rate* of circulation growth in newspapers and journals had been in the "quality" field where, significantly, there was none of the "writing-down" or condescension that had characterised some old "middle-ground" organs. In the decade after the war, both the *Sunday Times* and the *Observer* had doubled their sales and continued to forge ahead; the *Manchester Guardian* had trebled its sales in fifteen years, and the *Daily Telegraph*, after a long steady climb through the years, had in 1952 passed the million mark. Most other serious journals could show similar records of growth.

The leaven of public secondary education, now in its second generation, was at work in peace as in war. Even in the mass-directed Light Programme, serious programmes, such as the daily half-hour of foreign and domestic reportage, Radio

* According to G. A. N. Lowndes, in London, in the age-group 30–40 something like one in seven were in 1955–6 attending such "further education" classes. On a more severe definition of adult education, in liberal, non-vocational subjects and probably under university auspices, the 1954 national enrolment was two-and-a-half times that of the last full year prewar.

News-reel, had been able to hold audiences running into millions, and the astonishing proliferation of Penguin and Pelican Books in these years, placing specialists in all fields under contribution in an immense—yet casual and informal—library of contemporary knowledge offered further striking evidence of cultural expansion.

Sir William Emrys Williams, Penguin director and, appropriately, creator of the Army Bureau of Current Affairs—that act of hope and faith of the war years—estimated the "Penguin public" in Britain in 1956 at around 10 per cent of the population. To those dealing principally in unverifiable Golden Ages, this might not seem a large figure. Yet it was drawn from all classes now, and self-recruiting. Its very eclecticism and casual approach to scholarship facilitated its fertilising social influence and its growth from the edges, outwards. It might carry the Pelican *Roman Britain* in one hand and the *Daily Express* and the latest "escape" story in the other. It was not self-consciously or guiltily aware of any laws of intellectual miscegenation. Being a fan of "The Archers" on the "Light" did not exclude a taste for Ibsen on television or prove any impediment to the enjoyment of the incisiveness of a radio talk by Bertrand Russell.

If therefore—as the Light-Third polarisation seemed to suggest—the old middle ground had fallen out of our society, it was in fact being replaced by a base wider, more diversified, possibly less secure, and so changed in character as to be hardly detectable by the old charts. More and more people were, in fact, making their own unique choices, and in doing so were emerging from "the mass" while still, in the conditions of the new society, necessarily belonging to it, and finding no shame in that.

There are few words more equivocal than the word "sophisticated", so much a word of the times, and, in some measure also, a diagnosis of them. Yet the new sophistication was real as well as sham—as any brief course of prewar films, or comparison of say, Tommy Handley, first radio comedian of the Forties, with Tony Hancock (or of ITMA with "Take It from Here") would quickly show. If the old tight little community of allusion, ultimately based on classicism, was breaking down, there was another, vastly wider, possibly shallower, freely recruiting, and rapidly changing.

It was indeed in this rapidity of change, the mechanically powered proliferation, that the greatest dangers lay—the danger that eclecticism would widen into total lack of discrimination, that stimulation would reach the point of delirium, that sophistication, in its ambivalence, would open the way to exploitation.

For it was not only that the time-warranted certitudes of Everyman had been overtaken by the "up-to-the-minute" diversity of Penguin and Pelican. Those jolly birds themselves were now afloat on an endless sea of print. Paperbacks of innumerable and ever-multiplying breeds, with eye-assaulting covers—"YZ the novel that makes XY look like a vicarage tea-party"—clamoured for attention as vociferously as bookies at a race-meeting. And behind there was the sense of the assembly-line and the conveyor belt, for ever bringing up more, to feed the new great market of the Fifties.

For the first time in her history Britain now had a majority of book-readers in her population. As if to symbolise the passing of this major mile-stone, the old "Everyman Library" itself was now bringing out volumes in paperback form. Yet the new readers confronted difficulties hardly less, though very different from, those of the small band of Victorian working men earnestly seeking "self-improvement" from the classics. How to navigate this new Niagara of print? If standards were no longer handed down, values no longer "received", how were they formed and known? Somewhere, it seemed, there must be an answer. Possibly the young had it; at any rate they seemed singularly unalarmed. But for many of their elders the spread of culture still appeared to march hand in hand with the extension of anarchy. It still seemed a question which would prevail.

V

And if, seeking guidance, people turned to the practitioners and critics of the arts themselves, they were likely to receive even less help than seekers after moral standards gained from the scientists.

For the contemporary eclecticism was not merely the result of the untutored appetites of the plebs. It arose out of the contraction of the world. The contemporary distraction, the unceasing pursuit of novelty, was caused not only by the manipulations of Admass, but also by the pervasion of the experimental method—the continuous recession of "reality" in art as well as in science, as science continually exposed new psychological, mathematical, nuclear or cellular depths.

In music, the death of Vaughan Williams in 1958—the year of his Ninth Symphony—broke the last link with the assured Edwardian and Elgarian world. Sectarianism and fragmentation were now such that, in the words of one musician, "Many a name [of a modern English composer] whose mention seems indispensable to one observer is practically unknown to another."* Most music-lovers, it is true, were able to avoid these confusions by the simple expedient of ignoring the moderns with the exception of a few, like Britten, Arnold or Walton, and continuing to live in the warm familiar world of the classics. But if that was possible—at a price—in the concert hall, no such "solution" now availed in the art gallery. Modern art was all-enveloping. The wartime "truce" in which English Neo-Romanticism had flourished was long over, and artists once again lived in a welter of words, of complex, hugely question-begging theories which often enough appeared to bear only marginal relation to their actual practice.

There was a rapidly growing absorption in abstraction of all kinds, and though some artists still permitted the inspiration of nature to be visible, an increasing number excluded it as sternly and guiltily as many composers now suppressed any hint of melody. Various sorts and degrees of "automatism" were in vogue, the brush-strokes welling from the unconscious, or the painting which accommodated itself, in the words of Victor Pasmore—a former "realist" now converted to abstraction and "constructivism"—to "the fluid four-dimensional space-time concept of modern thought".

The artist lived in the consciousness of half a century of unending development behind him, in the wash of spent enthusiasms and collapsed causes. If the world of art still seemed to be furnishing a last ditch for ideology and metaphysics, the desperation of that position was now evident. What

* Hugh Wood: "English Contemporary Music", in *European Music in the 20th Century*, ed. Howard Hartog. Pelican, 1961.

was "urgent", what was "vital" now? In art, as in music, as in "serious" writing, it had never seemed more necessary to know—or more difficult to be sure.

But the young kept their ears pressed to the ground, listened to the buzz of names, and put a bold face on it. And in the mid-Fifties the answer they had been waiting for came from America—henceforth to be influential in artistic, as in other, modes. The theory of "action painting" had a beguiling simplicity which not only swept away a number of perplexing aesthetic problems, but had a convincing air of being the logical destination to which modern art had all this time been travelling. The young espoused it with enthusiasm. By 1958, the Young Contemporaries Exhibition, in which the work of students from all over Britain was collected, was dominated by two large rooms lined from floor to ceiling with vast canvases over which gallons of paint had been spilled and sploshed and dragged in "accidents" of glorious but anonymous abandon.

But painting, after all, had long been in flux. When people thought of the absolute in art they had in recent times probably tended—with the Greeks somewhere in the subconscious—to think of sculpture. And although, before the war, Epstein and Henry Moore might have qualified that feeling for some, they had nevertheless left sculpture representative of the stable and unchanging, centrally concerned with man, woman, and Eternity.

These certitudes, too, were now dissolved as the new generation of sculptors made over their ancient art to reflect the restlessness, the ceaseless flux of the nuclear age. For them, Moore's carving from stone, his respect for the shapes and textures of Nature, were too limiting. They preferred that new sculptural tool, the welding arc, textures, compounded of gypsum and iron-filings, rough, jagged or incised. Reg Butler, who found fame in 1953 by winning the first prize in the international competition for a memorial to the Unknown Political Prisoner, "drew in space" with welded iron rods; Lynn Chadwick, trained like Butler as an architect, produced sinister metal constructions on thin legs which he called "balanced structures"; Kenneth Armitage, while remaining principally concerned with the human body, saw it (he explained) "like an engineering structure", seeking to bring out its underlying patterns of tensions and stresses.

The new sculpture claimed to have reconciled and reunited art and science, to have set man back in his true place in the universe as rediscovered by modern science and technology.

But there were those to whom it once again seemed—as they looked at these bleak cage-like structures or at, say, the cog-encrusted robots of Eduardo Paolozzi—that what was happening might be better described as abdication. What meaning, what standards, were possible to Man who rediscovered himself as a bombinating particle in a ceaseless and unpredictable flux? There were moments in these years when art seemed to be foreshadowing a disintegration, a breakdown in significance and communication as complete as that symbolised in *Waiting for Godot*, the extraordinary Beckett play which in 1955 was filling the Criterion Theatre week after week with audiences at once enervated and fascinated by its inarticulate despair.

In such a world, numbers seemed to offer the only firm point to cling to. If art had no net sales certificates, as yet no viewer statistics, it had prices paid, inches of gossip column space devoted. As in action painting, manipulation was permissible in the aftermath of the "accident". The final triumph of Admass, if it came, would come not from its power to corrupt, but from the fact that the accountants' standards appeared the only ones now both visible and durable.

PART FOUR

BETWEEN PAST AND FUTURE

". . . in this Festival, we look
backward with pride and forward
with resolution."

—King George VI, opening the
Festival of Britain, 3 May,
1951.

"Like the basic personality of the
individual, the nuclear or central
area of the culture is resistant to
change. . . if a particular piece of
the (jig-saw) puzzle is removed,
we can only replace it with a
similarly shaped piece."

—J. A. C. Brown, *Freud and the
Post-Freudians.*

22.　The Shadow of the Bomb

". . . a world in which nations set
themselves to co-operate for peace
rather than to plotting for mutual
destruction by war, open or concealed."
—First Condition, Beveridge Report.

"We consider Formosa to be a valuable irritant against the Communist-
held mainland . . ."
—U.S. Joint Chiefs of Staff.

B^{Y THE} spring of 1950, the "bonfire of controls" kindled by
Harold Wilson at the Board of Trade the year before was
spreading fast; people could sniff the ozone of returning
freedom. What was left of the wartime Control of Engagement
Order had gone in March; points rationing and the five
shilling restaurant meal limit in May. Fish was freed and so
was steel. There was more foreign currency for holidays, more
licences for private building. One by one, the half-forgotten
things of prewar life made their reappearance—wrapped and
cut bread, humbugs, Devonshire cream. . . .

That Whitsun, long queues of cars, some wonderful ancients
among them, formed at the petrol pumps ("Pool" still) as their
owners, a little self-consciously—for in nearly eleven years one
lost the habit—ordered the attendants to "Fill her up!" "Many
motorists," reported *The Times*, "staged little demonstrations of
tearing up coupons while standing by the petrol pumps."

At the end of February in the highest polling yet probably
also the quietest election in British history—"positively
demure" was Winston Churchill's deprecating description—
the Labour Government had been returned with its majority
reduced to eight. "WELL, THEY'RE IN—BUT FOR HOW LONG?"
the *Daily Mail* conceded, unkindly, across its front page. For
the first time since 1935 the House of Commons contained no

Communist Member. As it never had before,* the Communist Party had fought the election on a national scale, putting up a hundred candidates. All but three had lost their deposits. But though the Communists had bitterly assailed their "brothers-in-arms" of 1945 as "the Tory Fifth Column", Labour could take little satisfaction in their annihilation. The "two camp" world, forcing the Labour Government into a close alliance with "capitalist" America which did violence to the Party traditions, was not favourable to Labour either.

Yet even for Labour's chastened M.P.s, chained now to their benches, with "Major Attlee" scanning his "sick returns" as anxiously as he once did before a "big push" on the Western Front, even for them, the future that summer appeared not without promise. The medicine of devaluation appeared to be working. Exports were rising. In the March quarter of 1950 the Sterling Area had achieved its first gold and dollar surplus for many years. British production, reported the Economic Co-operation Administration in Washington, was running 52 per cent above prewar levels. "The Economic Survey", by this time as firmly established a harbinger of spring as the primrose, relaxed a little, abandoning its precise "targets" for each industry (the problem of reconciling full planning with "freedom" having anyhow so far eluded solution). The formidable eyebrows of Sir Stafford Cripps no longer seemed set in quite so stern a line; and, two years earlier than expected, Britain threw away the crutches of Marshall Aid.

Housing queues were as long as ever. But new housing estates were beginning to make an impact on the landscape in many parts of Britain. In the West Country, a new Plymouth arose, white and shining, from the blitzed ruins of the old. Everywhere the pavements were crowded with window-shoppers preparing to renew their tattered household goods. The B.B.C.'s first regional television transmitter had opened at Sutton Coldfield in December, setting off a wave of television buying in the Midlands. At the London Zoo, Brumas, the baby bear, was drawing phenomenal crowds.

Could it be, Labour's sleep-starved M.P.s asked each other,

* In 1945 they had put up 22 candidates, lost 12 deposits, and got in—for the first time—two members (for West Fife and Mile End).

26 and 27. "Juvenile delinquency" was a topic of the times, but the Craig-Bentley case touched the national conscience more deeply. Despite a storm of protest, the Home Secretary, Sir David Maxwell Fife, refused to reprieve the nineteen-year-old, mentally subnormal Derek Bentley, and harrowing pictures of the condemned youth's family visiting him on execution eve appeared in the papers. Revulsion at this and other cases lead to the historic free vote in the Commons in February, 1956, in favour of abolishing the death penalty.

28. The New Commonwealth was now coming home to the British in more senses than one. Shipload after shipload, year after year, the West Indians arrived like this at Victoria Station, eager to seek their fortunes in "the Mother Country". In hospitals, on the railways, and elsewhere, they became indispensable. But there were complications.

hopes rising, that the long-delayed fruits of Socialist "Planning with Freedom" were really about to ripen at last? Had that glorious summer of 1949—despite the devaluation that had gone with it—really thawed out the last of the ice of 1947? There was some talk about the British climate becoming permanently warmer—a movement of the Gulf Stream, perhaps, or the retreating of the Polar Ice-cap.

II

It was only when the British, reluctantly disengaging themselves from these pleasant domestic preoccupations, took a look across the Channel that they experienced a sudden, sharp spasm of doubt.

Yet even here it had, until very recently, been possible to hope that things were improving. In May, 1949, a Soviet locomotive, bearing a white Picasso peace dove on its boiler, had puffed its way into Western Berlin. After 321 days, the siege was over, the blockade lifted. In the struggle for the soul of Europe, Communism had met its first real defeat.

That victory had been quickly consolidated. In mid-August, elections were held in the new West German Federal Republic —the first since Hitler. The High Commissioners, (who under the new Occupation Statute had now superseded the Allied Commanders-in-Chief) were empowered to readmit Germany into the community of nations in proportion as the new Federal Republic inspired "confidence that it was proceeding towards the establishment of a free, democratic and peaceful" régime.

"German Militarism" was still sternly deplored. Despite the protests of Dr. Adenauer—whose Christian Democrats had secured an electoral majority of eight votes over Schumacher's Social Democrats—dismantling of German "war" industry went ahead.

But the pace was slowed and soon dismantling halted. Under American leadership, and with continual assistance from our late "great Russian Ally", the requisite confidence in German intentions appeared to be returning with quite remarkable rapidity. The Federal Republic was admitted first to O.E.E.C., then to the new Council of Europe at Strasbourg. The developing

I

economic and cultural integration of Western Europe was now powerfully promoted by the decision of the Americans to stay in Europe, deploying their vast resources through the new North Atlantic Treaty Organisation.

This, admittedly, was still largely on paper: Germany was still weak, animated by the rueful spirit of *ohne mich*, and burdened by millions of destitute refugees. Yet, behind the shield of Churchill's "supreme deterrent", the Bomb, it nevertheless seemed possible that Western Europe's military reorganisation and integration could proceed steadily in reasonable security.

And then, late in the evening of 24 September 1949 there came into British newspaper offices a duplicated handout. It was short and to the point. *His Majesty's Government has evidence that within recent weeks an atomic explosion has occurred in the U.S.S.R.*

In a moment the world was changed.

An early result, reported a diplomatic correspondent, "was expected to be the storing of a number of atom bombs in Britain, under American control". A U.S. Air Force spokesman added that the American B29's, the familiar "Flying Fortresses" based in Britain, would probably now be replaced by long-distance A-bomb-carrying B50's. From Washington President Truman announced that the United States would go ahead with the manufacture of the Hydrogen Bomb—the "H-Bomb", the "Super-Bomb", the "Horror-Bomb", the Bomb with the mushroom cloud "100 miles wide".

Professor Einstein commented briefly: "General annihilation beckons".

Soviet divisions, Soviet tanks in Berlin or behind the Elbe— that at least had been a tangible peril. Now the threat was invisible, unpredictable, ever-present and cataclysmic.

How came it that Russia had the Bomb three or four years before she had been expected to get it? In America that February a Senator Joseph McCarthy of Northern Wisconsin had an answer. The State Department was "thoroughly infested with Communists". And not only the State Department. There were others, many others, subtly undermining the country from within. He had a list of names. . . .

As if in confirmation, in Britain that same month Klaus Fuchs, a Harwell physicist, was charged at Bow-street Magistrates' Court with having passed secret information to the Russians between the years 1943 and 1947.

At the Old Bailey trial there was the same strange, inconsequent mixture of the pedestrian and the fantastic, the trivial and the shattering, that had run through the Alger Hiss trial a few weeks earlier on the other side of the Atlantic.

The silent assignations in bar parlours . . . the secret recognition codes . . . the copy of *Tribune*, five books, held by two fingers . . . the scraps of information passing, fleetingly, on the streets. . . .

Behind the mild, bespectacled features of this young and brilliant physicist there now appeared the fantastic image of global conspiracy, of a sort of fanaticism, compulsive, all-devouring, which the world had not known since the wars of religion.

There were no protests against the sentence on Fuchs as there had been against that on Nunn May, four years earlier. "Fuchs", wrote Alan Moorehead, "had committed the crime which society is least able to forgive: he had made society distrust itself."

And that, in England in recent times, was something new and strange.

III

By the end of 1949 the Chinese Red Armies, the demoralised forces of Chiang Kai-shek melting away before them, had gained possession of the whole of China. But the importance of this massive event—the most potent symbol yet of Asia's resurgence—was only dimly appreciated in a Western world which preferred to interpret history in terms of the machinations of an omniscient "international Communism". Checked before Berlin, Communism, it was explained, was now switching its "drive" to the Far East. In accordance with the Truman doctrine of "containment", the Americans promptly interposed their

Fleet between the Mainland and Chiang's refuge on Formosa.

But there appeared to be an alarming number of directions in which a Communist drive might be directed. In Indo-China, "gateway to South-East Asia", Red China now possessed a common frontier with the veteran Vietnamese revolutionary, Ho-Chi Minh and his Viet-Minh armies pressing down on the Red River Delta; in Malaya the Communist guerillas who had long been disrupting the economy of "Britain's dollar arsenal" could take heart; Burma still ravaged by "White Flag" and "Red Flag" Communist bands lay wide open to Chinese infiltration.

But the most immediate threat lay further to the east, in a peninsula of scrubby hills and marshes, 150 miles wide and 600 miles long, where the charade of the Occupation division of Germany was reproduced with depressing faithfulness. At the end of July, 1949, the last of the American Occupation troops had left South Korea. Less than two months later, an exhausted United Nations Commission reported that owing, in part, to the "world-wide antagonism between the U.S.S.R. and the U.S.A." any prospect of an accommodation between the "People's Democratic Republic" in the North and the "democratic" Republic of Korea under the American-educated Syngman Rhee in the South was "more and more remote". The country faced the prospect of "a most barbarous civil war".

As at the other side of the world, the British went on joy-rides with their first unrationed petrol, in this remote peninsula of whose people they knew nothing, "frontier incidents" grew more uncontrolled, taunts and threats flew through the air, and the wizened goblin face of Syngman Rhee grinned out of the pages of the newspapers as he hurled defiance at "the Reds", involving wherever possible his American sponsors.

Those Korean "Reds" who now had the support not only of Communist Russia, but of a great Asian nation, a new Communist power, confident of the rightness of its cause, and flushed with victory.

The stage was set. The world, the audience, waited.

On 25th June, 1950, North Korean forces moved across the 38th Parallel in strength. Five days later they were in Seoul.

Within twenty-four hours, President Truman had authorised American air and sea support of South Korea. Four days later he threw in the U.S. ground forces.

The black headlines tumbled over one another. u.s. BOMBERS ROAR INTO ACTION . . . BRITISH NAVY JOINS IN . . . maCA. BLASTS NORTH BASES . . .

So there it was. Prague. . . Berlin . . . and, now, over the brink at last—Korea.

Thousands of Britons had arranged, that summer, to spend their holidays in Austria, a country enjoying an increasing vogue because of its cheapness. Now many had qualms about travelling so far East and cancelled their bookings. For no one really believed this was a Korean—or even an Asian—affair. The tanks driving southwards from fallen Seoul, hemming the defenders in the Pusan bridgehead, were Russian tanks. The fighters in the air above were first Yaks and later MIGS. The image that looked out from the screaming headlines was not the chubby face of "Chairman Mao" but the implacable mask of Josef Stalin.

It was as if the dire prophecies of Sir Halford Mackinder, a generation earlier, were coming to pass at last: "Who rules East Europe commands the Heartland; who rules the Heartland commands the World-Island; who rules the World-Island commands the World."

The Russians had since January been boycotting the Security Council because of its refusal to seat Red China. This enabled the Council to condemn the Korean "act of aggression". But it also made the Communist threat appear more alarming and intangible.

In Europe the picture was hardly less menacing. Our triumph in Berlin had proved brief and bitter; our acceptance of the division of Germany could now be seen for what it was, a counsel of despair. The blue-shirted People's Police in East Germany appeared every day to be more like an army. In the gravest speech he had addressed to the Commons since the war, Winston Churchill drew a grim picture of the Russian armoured columns behind the Elbe, the 25,000 tanks, the eighty divisions, starting to roll across Europe, reaching the Atlantic, and subjecting our island to "a bombardment by rocket-propelled and guided missiles incomparably more severe than anything we have endured or imagined".

A Civil Defence recruiting drive was launched. OVER 40? THEN YOU CAN VOLUNTEER. Ten hours' training in decontamination drill, the use of Geiger-counters and similar subjects would qualify for "the neat navy blue uniform" which would be ready in the autumn. Meanwhile, the newspapers were full of stories of "The Big Switch", the formidable diversion of peacetime industrial production to meet the doubled, £3,400,000,000, rearmament programme. In a broadcast to the nation Mr. Attlee warned his hearers that the promised rise in the standard of living, the "relief we had all been waiting for", might not now appear.

The first two British battalions seconded to the "U.N. Forces", pledged to "resist aggression", reached Pusan at the end of August. But as people listened to the news on the radio with all those all-too-familiar phrases about "strategic withdrawals" to "prepared positions", as they went to the cinema and saw on the news-reel British naval vessels being—as the Gaumont-British commentator put it in his hearty games-master voice—"taken out of moth balls after the long years of peace", their hearts sank.

In the blank despair of that summer, in all political parties and at almost all social levels, resentment turned against our "American allies". The guns that flashed in Korea illuminated not only the scrubby Korean hillsides but differences between the thought-processes of the Americans and ourselves so profound that at times we appeared to be inhabitants not only of different continents, but of different planets.

Five months before the Korean War began, Britain had officially recognised the new régime in China, seeing nothing to gain and much to lose in refusing to acknowledge so huge and unchangeable a fact. Many believed that Mao's Communism, unlike the Russian variety, was primarily agrarian and reformist; while to the Old China Hands in Hongkong this was only one more of the many Chinese revolutions through which British trade had continued to grow and flourish.

But while the British, old and wise in *realpolitik* as they believed themselves to be, saw the picture in shades of indeterminate grey, the Americans, still moved by that Wilsonian-type

idealism which had long found an outlet in China, still youth-
fully confident of their power to remake the world according to those democratic truths that had been revealed to them,
saw it in sharp blacks and whites. Revolution challenged
revolution. In American eyes the island of Formosa quickly
acquired something of the sanctity of an eastern Plymouth Rock;
the weak and ageing Chiang Kai-shek appeared en-haloed,
the George Washington of Asia.

It was one of history's grimmer jokes that at this moment
command of the United Nations Forces in Korea went to a
soldier who combined in his person just those aspects of the
American character that had both repelled and fascinated the
British since the days of Dickens's Hannibal Chollop. Flamboy-
ant, brash, larger-than-life, 110 per cent American, General
Douglas MacArthur made no secret of his conviction that he
was the God-given leader of a holy war or of his urgent desire
to carry his avenging fire across the frontier into "Red" Chinese
Manchuria. His frequent, highly coloured declarations of this
high purpose were echoed from across the Atlantic by American
politicians now vying with each other—the elections being on
the way—in the manly vigour with which they flourished the
"Ultimate Weapon".

On their "sceptred isle" which, according to the new scheme
of things, now became an "unsinkable aircraft carrier off the
coast of Europe", the British listened to these orotund utterances
with mounting distaste, and finally with despair.

Yet there it was. For all its narrowness of scale, this was world
war and we were in it. Below the stark headlines "MACA. BLASTS
THAT", "MACA. DECLARES THIS", the maps of the Korean peninsula
with the thick arrows indicating "two-pronged advances" or
"pincer-movements" studded the front pages of the newspapers.

In a world balanced on the edge of cataclysm, truth and
falsehood, fact and fiction, were daily more indistinguishable.
"Macarthy-ism" and "MacArthur-ism" began to seem equally
a part of the normal course of things. The "Red Dean" of
Canterbury was no longer even mildly amusing. The *Daily
Mail* appealed to business firms to withdraw their advertising
from the *Daily Worker*, and the Middlesex County Council
proceeded to smell out and "ban" the Communist headmasters
in its schools.

As it never had in the worst months of the war, M.I.5 and all it stood for now came into its own. It was, oddly enough, the year of that cinematic *tour-de-force, The Third Man*. Before the year was out the insinuations of that haunting zither theme seemed real enough. While in London Dr. Fuchs had been undergoing patient interrogation by British security officers, in Budapest a British businessman named Edgar Sanders had been making abject confessions of sabotage and spying through the phantasmagoria of a People's Court trial. In the French Chamber of Deputies, Communist delegates staged fights to obstruct an Anti-Sabotage Bill. And by October the newspapers were full of the mysterious disappearance from Helsinki of yet another Harwell scientist, a Dr. Bruno Pontecorvo.

Pontecorvo's black Standard saloon, left unclaimed in a Rome garage, was much featured by Press investigators who claimed to be hot on the trail. But the trail vanished. Where was Pontecorvo? No one knew, but few found it hard to guess.

Yet the word "treason", for all that, had an oddly old-fashioned sound. Was it really still definable in those old terms of betrayal of country, of "adhering to the King's enemies"?— in this nuclear age where the simple old patriotisms and loyalties were overlain and challenged by the internationalism of science and technology and where these, in their turn, were cut about by the two warring, mutually exclusive, world churches of Washington and Moscow?

Again there was the feeling of helplessness, of long-familiar foundations slipping and sliding beneath the feet—never more so than when nine months after the Pontecorvo disappearance, the newspapers were ablaze again with the "Case of the Missing Diplomats", Guy Burgess and Donald Maclean. Not even the heart of the so-called Establishment, that fortress of the ruling few, the British Foreign Office, was proof against these complex and disturbing treacheries.

In face of these cumulative confusions even the British sense of humour succumbed. Newspapers published long stories about the "loyalty" of schoolgirls,* and from the Midlands it

* E.g.—from threequarter column report in *Daily Mail:* "A mother called her three pretty daughters together in a North London flat last night. She accused dark-haired 18-year-old Brenda, her eldest, of luring 15-year-old Geraldine, her youngest, into

was reported that the Alan Turner Opera Company had purged their membership of Communists for their March production of *Chu Chin Chow*.

IV

By the end of September, General MacArthur was back in Seoul. Instructed by the U.N. General Assembly to "secure stability throughout Korea", he now moved across the 38th Parallel in pursuit of the fleeing North Koreans.

India and other Powers had warned the Americans that China would intervene directly if her border were threatened; that what had begun as a "police action" might then become world war. Nevertheless, on 24th November MacArthur proclaimed an "end-the-war" push to the frontier. The troops, he announced, would be "home by Christmas".

In Britain and in Europe people looked on helplessly with a sort of numbed horror.

Events soon showed their emotion to be justified. On Tuesday, 28th November, the evening papers reported that the "Chinese hordes" were pouring into Korea. Two hundred thousand had been thrown into the battle; half a million more were massing. And behind lay millions of others, a human avalanche that was starting to move. . . .

For two days a stunned House of Commons debated the situation—the "entirely new war" as the ever-ebullient MacArthur called it. Halfway through the second day the tape machine in the corridor began to stutter out the report of President Truman's Press conference. The use of the atom bomb, the President said, was under "active consideration", though he hoped, of course, it would not be necessary.

The formal words sped through the lobbies and into the Chamber. Members were staggered. The Americans were plainly mad, dangerously, disastrously, mad. Members' relief when the Prime Minister announced at the end of his speech that he was flying at once to see President Truman was patent.

Communism. 'You and your Communism will break up the family,' she said. Geraldine, in tartan skirt and grey jumper, lay across the tiled hearth, whistling."

ATTLEE WILL FLY SUNDAY, revealed Saturday's evening papers. TRUMAN WILL BE AT AIRPORT, promised Monday's *Express* across its front page.

A photograph of the Prime Minister, about to take off, a sprig of white heather in his button-hole, reassured breakfasting Britons.

ATTLEE ON LAST LAP, announced the early editions of the evenings. TRUMAN GREETS ATTLEE, triumphantly concluded the Late Night Final.

The sigh of relief that went up was almost audible. Good old Clem Attlee, so sensible, so reliable, so *English*. He carried with him, wrote Tom Driberg, M.P., "a new declaration of independence on behalf of the overwhelming majority of the British people of all parties".

Mr. Attlee returned from his mission. "MacA" pulled back from the frontier and was in due course sacked by President Truman. Then, "PEACE MOVES"—announced almost daily—"SEND HOPES SOARING."

Yet somehow, as the weeks went by, it became apparent that the new "declaration of independence", if delivered, was proving no more effective than its predecessors. Involvement in Korea seemed deep and endless. Army Reservists, the "Z-Men", were called up in January. War correspondents still filled miles of newsprint—the Chinese bugles in the dawn, the pathos of the refugees, the onrushing Red hordes. . . . And, in April for a while, Korea really did come home to the British: the Gloucesters lost 600 men killed and missing in their four-day stand on the Imjin River.

Yet, as the war dragged on, the whistles and whooshes on the news-reels, the shots of napalm bombs raining down on "enemy" villages and the rest began to seem merely one more endlessly monotonous element in the background of the times. Though the headlines were still urgent with attacks and counter-attacks, then with "peace-talks", pending, started, deadlocked, broken off, then with the interminable attitudinizings, bickerings, and "walk-outs" at Panmunjon, the British public gave only fitful attention. It did not seem to have a great deal to do with us.

For was it not more than ever clear that for "U.N." one should read "U.S."? Dismay deepened—and there was an outcry in Parliament—when in February the news leaked out, via Denmark, that an American Admiral had been appointed, under NATO, supreme Commander, North Atlantic, with control of the British Home Fleet.

"For the first time in history," protested the *Daily Express*, "the Royal Navy is put under foreign command." "I do not think," Churchill told the Commons, "that our country ought to have fallen so low in the walks of humility." "A slap in the face," summed up Admiral of the Fleet Lord Tovey.

For those who still failed to grasp the point, it was explained that the Americans had the ships, the planes, the military and economic power: we hadn't. Until the autumn of 1952 we had not even exploded our own atom bomb. The *Pax Americana* might be nerve-wracking, but it was one of the "facts of life". We might not like it, but we must learn to live with it.

23.   "Contemporary"

"1951 should be a year of fun,
fantasy and colour, a year in which
we can, while soberly surveying our
great past and our promising future,
for once let ourselves go. . . ."
—Gerald Barry, Director-General
   of the Festival of Britain, Press
   Conference, 14th October, 1948.

"It *was* nice, wasn't it, last year,
Festival Year? It was the nicest thing
that happened in England in the
whole of my life."
—Marghanita Laski in the *Observer*,
   1952.

CLEARLY THE bill for Korea was going to be crippling. The
price of everything from men's suits to galvanised buckets
was rising; the meat ration had fallen to eightpennyworth,
its lowest yet; and those dreary power-cuts were back again.
The massive expenditure on rearmament, again stepped up at
America's insistence, had quickly forced economies, including
a 50 per cent charge for National Health spectacles and
dentures which brought one more "Keep Left" revolt and the
resignation of the Minister of Health, Mr. Aneurin Bevan. As
the Americans continued to stockpile, prices continued to
spiral, and with the balance of trade again in peril, the new
Chancellor, the hitherto little-known Mr. Hugh Gaitskell,
appointed after Cripps's breakdown in health, was forced to
inaugurate his period of office by increasing the income tax and
surtax, the profits tax, the entertainment and petrol duties, and
many other taxes.

But in spite of these further "sacrifices", despite Korea and
the "hysterical" Americans, Macarthy-ism and MacArthur-ism,
Dr. Pontecorvo, M.I.5, and the butchers' almost metaphysical
problems in cutting eightpennyworth of meat, the British were

stolidly determined not to be put off their stride. Like a convalescent who at last begins to feel his strength returning, they were determined that, this time, being "up", they were staying "up".

Grey, battered old London was beginning to preen herself again. In St. James's Park, the newly painted stucco of Nash's Carlton House Terrace shone white through the trees. And office workers, pouring each morning over Waterloo Bridge, paused—as they had from time to time since the new river wall was started in 1949—to watch, rising on the South Bank, the curious skeletal shapes of what, it was explained, was to be a national gesture of faith in the future, a 'Festival of Britain'.

Whether that gesture ought, in fact, to be made had been a subject of controversy from the start. It was, some protested, an ill-timed frivolity. A monstrous waste of scarce raw materials. A political stunt by Herbert Morrison—"Lord Festival" as the papers called him. As the warehouses and mean streets which had so long disgraced the south bank of the Thames were torn down in preparation, a process begun by Goering's bombers, the storm grew. The site, announced Professor A. E. Richardson would give rise to the most dangerous congestion. Chelsea borough councillors voted to boycott the whole affair.

But as time went on, and from the grandstand of the Victoria Embankment Londoners looked across the river to watch the rubble mountains giving way to vague, mysterious shapes, the mood imperceptibly changed. All through the summer of 1950, visitors enjoyed the free show of spidermen crawling about the complicated steel latticework of a sprawling structure which those in-the-know said was to be "The Dome of Discovery". By the end of November, when the all-metal roof was in position, the thing looked like some squat, gigantic mushroom. By March of the following year, when the famous "Vertical Feature"—now officially named the Skylon—floated upon its cradle of cables, people were beginning to experience the first obscure stirrings of the "Festival spirit". There was a growing sense that something unusual and somehow significant was afoot.

On 3rd May, the King, speaking into a microphone set up on the west steps of St. Paul's, declared the Festival of Britain open. His voice, relayed by radio all over the world, was firm. Standing there on the steps of St. Paul's with his family around him, he appeared to the watching crowds on Ludgate Hill his usual modest, conscientious self, fully recovered, it seemed, from the serious arterial ailment in the legs that had laid him low two years before. But many, when they examined the close-up photographs in the papers afterwards, were shocked to see how drawn and tired his face looked.

That first Friday was a grey, drizzling London day, turning to heavy rain in the afternoon. The gay umbrellas of the Festival's many open-air cafés were sodden and there were pools of water on the paths. Even so, it was soon evident to the eager ticket-holders who streamed across the Bailey bridge—its coloured spinners rattling their invitations from sixty-foot masts —that if the weather was traditional English, the show was not.

In the memories of many on the South Bank that afternoon still stirred memories of the Imperial pomps of the Wembley Empire Exhibition of 1922. This, it was immediately clear, was a thousand miles from all that. Here was no Elgarian evocation of our mighty past, but a whole, crisp new world, a clean break.

Making a virtue of necessity, the Festival's designers had taken the available materials, wood, plastics, glass, fabrics, asbestos, and combined them with imagination and skill. Aluminium brought lightness and sparkle; wood, showing its natural grain, contributed mellowness; great walls of glass, and light, unsupported ramps of concrete, gave a wondrous illusion of space. Even so ephemeral a material as canvas or perforated hardboard was used with highly civilised effect. Chairs, made from wire or bonded sheet-wood, would have baffled Chippendale, yet were strangely comfortable and, if some thought them precious, others found them elegant. Everything, the litter baskets, the signboards, the plant pots, the conical metal lampshades, seemed fresh and new. People soon began to sense that a common approach, a recognisable style, ran through them. It came, to some, as a revelation.

The site proved to have been an inspired choice. The Thames, London's true heart, came into its own again, united old and new worlds across its grey waters, lending an almost mystical extra dimension to the tiny, twenty-seven acre, area.

From this "South Bank" Londoners discovered a new magic in their city, an aspect familiar, rich, yet hitherto rarely seen— the historic skyline of the Victoria Embankment sweeping down in its stately curve from Wren's dome to the towers of Westminster.

II

The Great Exhibition of 1851 had been outward-looking; the Festival of 1951 was addressed primarily to the British people themselves. It was not exultant, but psychotherapeutic.

The strength of the English had long lain in a quiet conviction of their own innate superiority, a firm idea of themselves which was all the more potent for lacking the articulateness of the French, or the vehemence of young nations like the Americans or Australians. Down the years the idea had modified: a capacity for adjustment without apparent change was part of its strength. Then, somewhere in the interwar years, between the brittle Twenties and the sleep-walking, finally nightmarish, Thirties, the capacity for adjustment had at last been outrun.

The impact of war, like electric convulsion therapy for the mentally confused, had wiped the slate, provided a new start. Tentatively remodelled, the idea had begun to re-form. But, in the confusions of the war's aftermath, somewhere between the terrifying Continental precision of United Europe, the nebulosity of the "Third Force", and the multiple images of the the new multi-racial Commonwealth, it had been lost again.

Festival Year resumed the search—and resumed it with a new deliberation. In this new phase of life, the nation groped towards a new balance between its past, its present and its future. Churchillian historical rhetoric had resounded well enough from the sounding board of war; in the age of the *Pax Americana*, it rang a little hollow. So the "Festival style" was clean, bright, and new. It looked neither to classical Athens, nor Imperial New Delhi, nor to chromium-plated skyscraping New York, but to the modest, model social democracies of Scandinavia. It caught hold quickly and spread first across London and then across England. And the name it acquired in doing so was significant, too: "Contemporary."

In an island hitherto largely given up to gravy browns and

dull greens, "Contemporary" boldly espoused strong primary colours. "After that long grey winter," wrote a woman reporter, visiting the Festival, "this galaxy of colour was like a glass of champagne. Everywhere I looked brought fresh impact—vivid reds, blues, greens, lemon yellows—bubbles pricking my nose."

Everywhere, pervading the Festival grounds, was this strange "un-English" atmosphere of space and light and sparkle. And when night fell, the whole Festival acquired a new magic, with the Skylon shining mysteriously in the sky, the diners in the new Festival Hall's restaurants gazing out through that huge glass wall over the dark glistening waters, and down below the river boats coming and going, carrying visitors to the rococo delights of the Festival Pleasure Gardens—opposite the long-vanished Cremorne—and located, improbably, in Battersea.

It was a premeditated departure, all this—the colour, the striped umbrellas, the open-air cafés and the rest, a deliberate disowning of the old Puritan "taking-our-pleasures-sadly" tradition, a ceremonial re-erection of the maypole. It was a throwing off of the stifling weight of Victorian grandeur, a clearing out of the last of the Wolseley helmets, Zulu assegais, and the faded Edwardian red plush from the national attic.

The famous old English Philistinism was likewise being ritually discarded. With its emphasis on design, its many murals, sculptures, reliefs, and "mobiles", commissioned from old and new British artists, the Festival—in a manner quite unlike any earlier one in Britain—was suffused, almost dominated, by the arts.

Tentatively but hopefully, like a woman in a hat shop, torn between a desire to be smart and show *flair* and a sneaking fear of appearing merely freakish, the British were trying on a range of new *personae*, studying the effect in the mirror, to see which one was really and truly "us".

The Scandinavian fashion accorded well enough with the Beveridge-A.B.C.A. idealism that had come out of the war years; its "civilised" values set us off nicely from the power- and dollar-lusting primitives across the Atlantic.

But was it not, perhaps, a trifle austere?

There were other approaches.

In the Lion and Unicorn Pavilion, designed to present "The

British Character", the visitor, entering, was confronted by a lion and unicorn in plaited straw, tugging on a rope which opened a wickerwork cage from which streamed white plaster doves. At the end of the floor, Tenniel's White Knight—a disembodied purple-gloved hand patting him on the back—presided on a prancing steed over an area devoted to British "Eccentricity and Humour".

Other purveyors of seasonable new *personae* had already been thinking on similar lines. By 1951, the "Ealing Comedy" was well on the way to establishment among postwar traditions. The first of them, *Hue and Cry*, had been put on at the Tivoli in the Strand in that appalling February of 1947, while, at the Odeon, Carol Reed's *Odd Man Out* was still suffusing Leicester Square with its Fenian (and Masonic) gloom. *Hue and Cry* was a light-hearted trifle (starring Alastair Sim) about a young boy and his pals who in the course of reading a 'penny blood' had stumbled upon the code-messages by which a gang of London thieves concerted their jobs. It was grotesque; but it was also distinguished by a wonderful freshness of vision and humour, and a clear, vivid impression of London—as the critic C. A. Lejeune wrote at the time—"as a great city of buildings and wharves, skylines and pavements, roar and silence, and change of light".

In the years that followed these two apparently incompatible elements—the "Alice-in-Wonderland" grotesqueries and the sharp photographic vision that derived from the school of wartime documentary—were effectively blended in a long succession of films—in 1949 alone we had *Kind Hearts and Coronets*, *Passport to Pimlico* and *Whisky Galore*—that not only lightened these grey years but were doubly welcome as a quiet, "characteristically British", reminder to All Whom It Might Concern that though the Yanks might now rule the waves and the Russians produce their own atom bombs, the British still possessed that unique and priceless gift, the "British Sense of Humour", which, of course, notably included the ability to laugh at themselves.

But as Ealing's apparently endless flow continued, the proportions of the two basic elements, the whimsical and the documentary, shifted. By Festival Year, with *The Lavender Hill Mob* (in which Alec Guinness, an actor now becoming increasingly known, played an amiable middle-aged bank clerk who diverts his bank's bullion shipments), there were signs that whimsy—always liable in England to go to the head—was gaining the upper hand. It continued to grow until Ealing's preoccupation with semi-derelict branch lines, venerable "puffers" in the Western Isles, "veteran" motor-cars,* and eccentric old ladies verged on the pathological.

Meanwhile, out at Festival Gardens, Nellie, the wayward locomotive of the Far Twittering and Oyster Perch Railway, lovingly constructed with preposterous funnels, weather-cock, frying-pans and cobwebs to the design of Emmett, of *Punch*, was drawing crowded trains through Tottering Woods!

Yet—though it owed too much to that English cult of amateurism which was proving so ill-suited to this postwar world—as a sketch for a new *persona* Ealing's Alec Guinness, amiable, diffident, but nobody's fool, was at least home-made, and preferable to the prewar made-in-Hollywood model represented by George Arliss or Aubrey C. Smith, of the whisky red visage, gruff manner and Empire-building upper lip.

Not that there were not,—both in public cinemas and in the private cinemas of the mind—moments of reversion to the prewar programmes. A notable one occurred at the end of 1949 when the British frigate H.M.S. *Amethyst* broke out of the Yangtse River where she had been trapped three months earlier by the advance of the Chinese Red armies.

Against the background of world conflict, the "Yangtse Incident"—as it was carefully named to convey proud "British-style" understatement—was indeed an incident, and a very minor one. But the Royal Navy—how evocative that name still was!—had been in action again, and all Britain went wild as if at the news of some famous victory.

The *Amethyst*'s officers and men were subjected to series of triumphal parades and receptions. Simon, the ship's cat—wounded in the dash down the river—was awarded the "Cat's V. C." and, draped in the White Ensign, was buried with honours in an animals' cemetery.

---

* *Genevieve* was in fact made by an Ealing Studios director, Henry Cornelius, though not under Ealing Studios' auspices, but independently.

Less obtrusive forms of escape were available to ease the pains of *persona*-change. Mr. John Betjeman gained many new recruits for the cult of Victoriana. There was a persistent demand for books about antique dealers, about the "Gay" Twenties, about governesses and life in the great houses in those spacious days when—as one title put it—there were still "Twenty Shillings in the Pound". And even the cool clarity of the Festival's Scandinavian décor was, after all, relieved by a "Regency" stripe.

III

In this groping search for a *persona* that would be both durable and fitting there was, however, an area that offered a firmer point of departure.

When in 1851 Prince Albert had solemnised the marriage of art and science, there had been few who had not been thrilled by a sense of that union's fabulous fertility—the roaring factories, the opening continents, the floods of deep-mined coal, the iron roads knitting together Europe under the master hand of the British engineer.

A hundred years later, in 1951, the frontiers of the possible were hardly less sensationally extending. And again—though the other circumstances were very different—we British could reasonably claim to be bold pioneers.

We did so. The Americans, admittedly, now far outstripped us in productive power and in the multiplication of research. But in science what mattered was quality, not quantity. That we had. Our role henceforth must be that of suppliers of the "back-room" genius of the Second Industrial Revolution; in technological as well as in political matters we must be the Greece to America's Rome.

It was a pleasant idea, and, by 1951, we were able to include under the vast metal canopy of the Dome of Discovery much that lent it colour. There were those two key, war-forced inventions, Watson-Watt's radar and "W.U."—Whittle's—and the world's—first turbo-jet engine. There was the medical revolution in which Fleming's discovery of penicillin at St. Mary's had been central. On display under the Dome, too, was a model of the atomic pile which that winter was to warm the buildings at Harwell—though the Advisory Committee on Scientific Policy gave warning that to develop nuclear energy to the point where it could contribute to the nation's power resources was likely to take a generation at least.

For years now Britain's historic staple industries—cotton, coal, shipbuilding, parts of the iron and steel industry—had seemed enveloped in gloom as well as grime, weighed down by the burden of advanced old age. By 1951, however, thanks to our scientists, a whole range of bright mid-century industries, oil refining and petrochemicals, synthetic fibres, pharmaceuticals, plastics, electronics, aircraft, had declared themselves. The engineering industry—with its high content of capital and skill and its proliferation of new products—had expanded vastly during the war and had since maintained a rate of growth for which, wrote Professor G. C. Allen, "it would be difficult to find a parallel in history". By 1957 it had reached double its prewar output (by volume)* and was able to take up much of the slack in Lancashire where old King Cotton was at last irrevocably toppled from his throne.

The gnarled old industrial body was renewing itself at last. If the "New Britain" of the politicians had seemed a doubtful quantity, the technologists' "New Britain" was a brilliant and ever-present reality.

The crowds, milling on the South Bank, craned their necks to exclaim at the vast wing-span of the Brabazon airliner as it flew over the Festival grounds, a 130-ton, 100-seater giant, designed—as they had so often read in the papers over the past few years—to beat the Atlantic head-winds and fly to New York non-stop. That same year the de Havilland Comet, the world's first and only jet airliner, was demonstrating our "long lead" in jet aircraft design as, under the much-publicised test pilot, John Cunningham, it drew its vapour trails about the world. Equally without precedent, the turbo-jet Vickers Viscount was just about to come on to the market, and was arousing world-wide interest.

* Between 1939 and 1956 numbers employed in electronics more than trebled, output multiplied by ten. In petrochemicals output was 10,000 tons (1945), 634,000 tons (1958); in plastics, 28,000 tons (1938), 500,000 tons (1959); in pharmaceuticals, £19m. (1935), £143m. (1955).

For British metallurgists and designers the jet engine had set unprecedented problems. To develop a single new aero-engine could now cost £20 million. Yet the challenge was being met. Rolls-Royce jet engines were to become as world-famous as Rolls-Royce cars, and the exports of British aero-engines spiralled through the Fifties.

It was not, in fact, until 1951 that the "marriage of art and science" so prematurely announced by Prince Albert in 1851 really began to find its feet. It proclaimed itself, for instance, in the beauty of the Comet, dictated by aerodynamics, yet achieving perfection of form. It announced itself, more controversially, in the Festival Hall, the first modern postwar building in London, a scientifically designed concert hall with seats for 3,000, insulated and suspended like an egg on a cradle, a place of space and light and simple gaiety totally unlike anything the capital had known before. It showed itself at a thousand points in the Festival, where a large number of young architects and designers had been given the chance of their lives and had seized it with both hands.

The time had been ripe. For these young men "modernism" was no longer the unsure and brittle affair of chromium-plate and "streamlining" it had all too often been in the interwar years: it was the air they breathed. So the young, for once, built their world—and the young acclaimed it. When 1950 ended Britain had stood poised between the old world and the new. The Festival of 1951 gave her a playful push, over the threshold, into the Future.

IV

Thus the Festival's therapy was effective therapy. The Korean War might drag miserably on. Prices might spiral. But Mr. and Mrs. Ordinary Citizen and their children, as they trudged around the bright pavilions, ate ice-cream under the striped umbrellas, put on their "3-D" polaroid spectacles in the "Telecinema", watched the "water mobile" splashing away outside Basil Spence's Ships and Sea Pavilion, or took a river-boat down to Battersea, were conscious not only of aching feet but of widening horizons.

While they remained within the Festival's twenty-seven-acre

"New Britain", euphoria continued. But the moment they stepped beyond the bright coloured screen, and picked up a newspaper, the dream dissolved abruptly.

To assume a new *persona* in a new world is one thing: to do so with the old world still tumbling about one's ears is another. After the débâcle of 1945 the shining new "multi-racial Commonwealth" had been hopefully unveiled in 1946–47. Yet five years later the collapse of the old structure was still noisily and confusingly forcing itself upon the attention.

All that summer the headlines had been full of the words "ABADAN" and "OIL". As the Festival authorities tried out its turnstiles in April, Dr. Mohammed Mossadiq's Bill to nationalise the Anglo-Iranian Oil Company, representing several hundred millions of British capital, had passed the Persian Majlis.

It had long been a tacit assumption of the British system of geography—hitherto rarely questioned even in the Middle East itself—that the oil which so abundantly flowed from the desert sands was a tribute predestined by Nature for the West which could employ it. The Persian Prime Minister's dissenting opinion was deeply disturbing.

A succession of British—then American—negotiators flew out to Teheran. Large concessions were made. As they were made, Persian demands were stepped up. "British Imperialism", Dr. Mossadiq explained to the world, had been "enslaving" his poor country for fifty years past.

"PAY UP—OR WE CUT OFF OIL", a British headline grimly summed up the Persian approach in mid-June. In August, evacuation of the oil families began. Britain—the Government asserted—had every intention of standing by her rights. Warships were being despatched. Troops might be landed.

The case was referred to the Hague Court (which ordered arbitration), finally, at the eleventh hour, to the Security Council.

Against a background of hysterical mobs, attempted assassinations, threats to the British oilmen and—this at least was a novel note—the tears and fainting fits of the Persian Prime Minister himself, the tragi-comedy moved inexorably towards its predestined close.

On 3rd October, three days before the Festival ended,

the remaining 330 British oilmen, under Persian expulsion orders, were evacuated on the cruiser *Mauritius*—ignominiously leaving behind them a great unmanned refinery, a British-built and run town, and the rich oilfields which had been a vital part of the British economy since the First World War.

For a variety of reasons, the Labour Government had been unable or unwilling to apply in the Middle East the method of boldly cutting loose from the embittered past which had proved so effective in South and South-East Asia. Despite the collapse of Britain's Palestine mandate, despite all that had happened in India and elsewhere, there were still many Britons who thought of the Middle East, subconsciously at least, as they had since the days of Allenby and Lawrence, as a rather colourful and romantic British parish. The shock they were to experience in these months of 1951 was thus all the greater.

In mid-July King Abdullah, of Transjordan, Britain's favourite Arab son, was assassinated. In October, four days after the evacuation of Abadan, the Egyptians broke off the long-drawn negotiations for the revision of the Anglo-Egyptian Treaty (expiring in 1968) under which our Canal Zone base was held. The dismal course of events in Persia was now repeated in Egypt. Farouk proclaimed King of the Sudan . . . blockade and counter-blockade, with our men shut up in the Canal Zone . . . the shoot-and-run raids by the Egyptian "Liberation Militia" . . . Egyptian threats against "collaborators" . . . British demolition of Egyptian houses . . . atrocity stories swelling the rising chorus of hate. . . .

Once again, the British newspapers carried pictures of British women and children being evacuated from territory long tacitly considered virtually British. Once again, there was the ritual announcement that Britain would stand firm. And, once again, the mounting, dervish frenzy of the street mobs. . . .

On Saturday, 26th January, the explosion came.

For nine hours, between 9 a.m. and 6 p.m.—when the Egyptian Army cleared the streets—mobs ran amok through the western quarter of Cairo, murdering and looting. Seven hundred banks, hundreds of shops, the great Western-owned departmental stores, were torn apart and fired. In the wrecked

Turf Club, ten British nationals were done to death. Shepheard's Hotel was gutted.

In Britain, the man-in-the-street was both angry and baffled. How did it come about that one fainting, weeping, clownish old Mohammedan in Teheran—or a fat and feeble young one in Cairo—could thus kick Great Britain with impunity? How could a nation which had so lately welcomed home the heroic *Amethyst* submit to such humiliating indignities—from mere wogs!

A large part of the Press was ready with the answer. It was, the *Daily Mail* still insisted, the fault of the Socialist Government which "threw away India", and in particular "our greatest instrument in that vast region, the magnificent Indian Army". "They have surrendered position after position," agreed the *Daily Telegraph*. "When the lion falters," explained *Time and Tide*, "the jackals gather." "An impression prevails in the Middle East," said the *Spectator*, "that any kind of insolence can be directed against Britain with impunity. This must be stopped without further delay. . . ."

These time-honoured sentiments were echoed by a large number of politicians, including some on the Left.* For if in matters of "morals" insularism was weakening, political insularism remained largely unimpaired. Few in Britain even now had any inkling of the volcanic force of Asian and Arab nationalism; few appreciated that between the small peninsula of Europe and the vastness of Asia, the centre of gravity had permanently shifted; or that in the drama now reaching a climax in the cataclysmic scenes at Abadan and Cairo, the curtain had risen with the fall of Singapore.

Thus while the notion of Britain as "centre of the multiracial Commonwealth of six hundred million citizens" provided a *persona* which was at once flattering, contemporary, and had

---

* Some members of the Labour Cabinet, including the Foreign Secretary, Herbert Morrison, were in favour of sending a military expedition against Persia's oil-nationalising régime. The Prime Minister, Mr. Attlee, however, has since declared that he would have considered such a course "quite wrong morally and politically". The issue was never, in fact, fully tested because the Service departments advised that the necessary resources were not available.

certain elements of truth, both the march of events and old habits of mind continued to render its future precarious. The special kind of nationalism which had called the New Commonwealth into being now seemed to threaten its continuance. To the British, to the West, the struggle in Korea was a struggle against world Communism; to Asian members of the Commonwealth it was apt to appear most strongly as merely a chapter—or a paragraph—in the epic of Asia's resurgence. Under the leadership of India, perpetual, self-appointed "Third Force" mediator—in Korea and elsewhere—the "ex-Colonial" areas of the Commonwealth were already developing with other "ex-Colonial" areas of the world those sharply felt if oddly compounded sympathies which five years later were to find expression in the "Afro-Asian" idea proclaimed at Bandung.

It was also becoming clearer every year that the development of Africa—West, Central and Southern—would in fact be critical for the New Commonwealth's future. The education of the British newspaper reader in these matters was now proceeding at a quickened pace. If in the first phase of African rediscovery it had been carried forward by the Great Groundnut Story, in the second it was as effectively advanced by another, hardly less illuminating modern parable—the story of "Ruth and Seretse".

Grandson of the Great Khama, last of the kaffir kings, and chief designate of the Bamangwato tribe who inhabit the arid Bechuanaland protectorate, Seretse Khama was a law student of the Inner Temple when at a party at a colonial students' hostel he met Ruth Williams, a Notting Hill typist. The two continued to meet and presently announced their intention of marrying.

A simple enough happening, it might have been thought. Yet this simple happening was to become the centre of a storm that echoed around the world, the foundation of a drama in which white racialism and African nationalism, black tribalism and white liberalism, parochial intrigue and global mass communications came together in a bizarre rehearsal of larger and more tragic conflicts to come.

Under Commonwealth Relations Office pressures, the clergyman who had read the banns of the couple's marriage refused to proceed with the ceremony. Undismayed, "Ruth and

Seretse"—as they soon became to every newspaper reader in Britain—went to a registry office and were married. Vastly photographed, endlessly interviewed, they came through their ordeal with dignity, and captured the sympathy of a large part of the British public. The Scottish Nationalists made Seretse a vice-president.

To the satisfaction of the Press—for this was a "human story" to end human stories—the affair ran on for many months, culminating in a solemn Judicial Inquiry, sitting at Serowe, "the straw hut capital" of Bechuanaland, and followed by the exile of Seretse, whose marriage was stated to have rendered him "unsuitable" to the chieftainship.

The reasons for this "unsuitability" were unspecified, but not difficult to connect with the propinquity of the white populations of Southern Rhodesia and that fellow member of the Commonwealth, South Africa.

Africa, it was becoming clear, was going to prove a continent even more troublesome and baffling than India in the interwar years. And it was altogether characteristic that while at one end of it, in Bechuanaland, the British Government still acted out its old paternal role, exiling the disobedient chief, at the other side, it was releasing Kwame Nkrumah from jail to contest the Gold Coast's first General Election. Meanwhile, in Kenya, six million land-hungry Africans were protesting with mounting bitterness the domination of 50,000 Whites. Not until the autumn of 1952 would the strange words MAU MAU appear in the headlines; but already the Kikuyu revolt was in the making.

Nevertheless, for the British in the world of the *Pax Americana* the notion of the Commonwealth remained peculiarly comforting. Still, in Rosebery's phrase, "creating its own precedents", it remained the widest, most variegated, area of free, workaday, co-operation in the world. It furnished, in these critical, explosive, years, a unique and indispensable bridge between the fanatical, wilful, impoverished young nationalisms of Asia and the disillusioned, wealthy, old ones of Europe. However elusively, it did indeed provide some sort of Third Force, without which the world would have been an even more perilous place than it was.

V

And so, as the sixth decade of the twentieth century got under way, the British, living still on the verge of financial catastrophe, trapped between the rival fanaticisms of East and West, exposed, as ex-Imperialists, to the adolescent rages of the new nationalism, lived manfully through their "year of fun, fantasy, and colour" and sought, with an unwonted self-consciousness, the critical new balance between their past, their present and their future.

And then, in the new year, came an event which, in an instant, somehow transformed the whole quality of the situation, seemed for a moment to sweep away the last remaining certitude—and then to restore them all.

At 11.15 a.m. on Wednesday, 6th February, 1952, a special edition of the London newspapers came on the streets. It was black-bordered. Its news was stark and simple. "It was announced from Sandringham at 10.45 a.m. today that the King, who retired to rest last night in his usual health, passed peacefully away in his sleep early this morning."

The shock was the greater in that the news was totally un-expected. Only the day before the King had been out shooting hares at Sandringham. There had, certainly, been anxiety about him in September after his operation for lung resection. Crowds had gathered outside the Palace then, filing past the bulletins hung from the railings. But before long their tone had been re-assuring. Recovery had seemed confirmed when at the begin-ning of February Princess Elizabeth and Prince Philip had set out for Kenya on the first leg of a five-month Commonwealth tour.

And now the King was dead.

The news spread swiftly from mouth to mouth in unbelieving whispers. The muffled bells began to toll. "A great hush, a Sabbath stillness", wrote a witness, "descended on the City."

And, in a moment, by this strange and ancient magic of monarchy, the thing the Festival had failed to achieve in months was achieved. The British people were one and knew who they were. There were no more doubts, no hesitancies. This was no Fourth Reich or Fifth Republic; this was England.

Equally remarkable was the effect beyond the seas. What the world saw now was not merely a small, half-bankrupt island in the North Atlantic, but a great and historic nation, rich in its living tradition and the continuity of its growth. In the new Republic of India, the newspapers appeared with black borders. Thousands of Indians queued to pay their tribute, signing books opened for that purpose. In South Africa, people knelt and prayed in crowded departmental stores. In the United States the "anti-British" *Chicago Tribune* came out with the single headline: THE KING IS DEAD.

It no longer seemed so urgent to throw off the burden of the past, to be "contemporary". Through the complex, ancient, ritual that followed, the sense of rootedness, of the nation's great reserves of strength, grew and deepened. It grew through the meetings of the Accession Council . . . through the mournful progress of the King's body from Sandringham to Westminster . . . through the proclamations of Queen Elizabeth II to fanfares from the tabarded trumpeters . . . at St. James's Palace, at Charing Cross, at the Royal Exchange. . . .

From 8 a.m. to the early hours the people filed, two deep, past the catafalque at the lying-in-state in Westminster Hall— an endless queue of men and women, standing patiently waiting their turn in the February rain and snow, a queue sometimes four miles long winding along the Embankment, and over the Thames bridges, and down the opposite bank, moving very slowly forward, taking hours to reach the Hall, all sorts and conditions of people who had made their way here from all over Britain.

It was sometimes said that the true religion of the British was patriotism. Perhaps that was still true. Though the motives which drew people to Westminster Hall were certainly mixed, there could be little doubt that many had a deep and solemn sense of participation in an historic moment in our island story, or that some, the older ones among them, felt that what they were here witnessing was the end of an era.

For in that grave conscientiousness, that obvious sense of duty that was his clearest characteristic, George VI seemed a last, strong link with the Victorian Age.

Now he was dead, and a girl of twenty-five reigned in his stead. If, in May, 1951, a new age was proclaimed and ushered in by artifice, in February, 1952, an old one, by nature and by history, was ended.

24.   New Elizabethans?

"The Coronation of the young
Elizabeth II has filled not only the
British, but rather strangely, the
French, too, and much of Europe with
renewed optimism and faith in the
future. . ."

—M. Christian Dior, in the *Daily
Mail*, March, 1953.

"The Queen Mother, the Duke of
Edinburgh, Nanny Lightbody, Group
Captain Townsend—the whole show
is utterly out of hand . . . the Royal
Family ought to be properly advised
on how to prevent themselves and
their lives becoming a sort of royal
soap opera."

—Malcolm Muggeridge in the *New
Statesman and Nation*, 1955.

IN 1952 the British found themselves not only entering
upon a new reign, but under a new political régime also.
The Radical wave of 1945 had retreated; the familiar
pattern of English politics had reasserted itself. In six years
Labour had pushed through a series of reforms which had been
building up behind the log-jam of British conservatism for a
quarter of a century. Having at last nerved itself to carrying
through its most unequivocally Socialist measure, the nationalisation of the iron and steel industry, the Labour Government
had exhausted both the ideas and the impetus of 1945. The
vague and emasculated programme with which in 1951 it
confronted the electors suggested that it had lost the courage of
its convictions also. The continual crises, domestic and external,
had taken their toll. Bevin was dead, Cripps was a sick man,
Bevan in the wilderness. With the electoral verdict of 1950 to
serve as object lesson, the Party's "consolidators" had triumphed.

But consolidation is not, traditionally, the function of the party of the Left. As the Festival of Britain ended, the new political equilibrium was neatly recognised by a continuance of 1950's swing of the electoral pendulum just sufficient to replace an overall Labour majority of six by an overall Conservative majority of seventeen.*

Observing that she would miss the old place, Mrs. Attlee moved out of Chequers and Mrs. Churchill moved back in. And that note of quiet domesticity more or less reflected the reaction of the nation at large. It was the Americans, not the British, who, once again, got excited. WINNIE IS BACK! THE LION LIFTS HIS HEAD, exulted their newspapers. But in England at least the war was over. The organ tones which had exhorted the nation to "blood, sweat and tears" could not compass percentage rises in productivity or the all-important statistics of trade balance and dollar gap. That required voices in a different key: and the thin dry voice of Mr. R. A. Butler did not differ notably from the thin dry voice of Mr. Gaitskell, his predecessor at the Exchequer, as, in mid-November, he announced that the sterling area was now in deficit all around the world and that as Britain was "in danger of being bankrupt, idle and hungry" further import cuts, reductions in rations, and an excess profits tax had unfortunately become imperative.

There was a rueful joke in "Take It From Here", the radio comedy serial—"Have you seen Jimmy's new suit? It's a conservative cut." "What's a conservative cut?" "It's the same as a Socialist cut—only they're more polite about it." For the Conservatives, as for the Socialists, practice was still being dictated by the hard facts of the war's apparently interminable aftermath, now further prolonged by Korea. As the much-heralded Tory "dash for freedom" appeared to be terminating in the cutting of the travel allowance—twice in three months— to £25, Swiss hoteliers were reported to be finally writing off the British.

* Yet the Labour Party achieved the highest total vote in its history, still somewhat higher than the total Conservative vote, and larger, as percentage of total votes cast (Lab. 48·8 per cent, Cons. 48 per cent) than the Labour vote of 1945. The fact that, despite all this, the final result probably summed up well enough the national state of mind is not the least of the mysteries of the British electoral system.

The new Government did, however, possess one powerful advantage (in addition to being "more polite about it"). It had someone to blame. With an assurance that all would work out now that matters were once again in the proper hands, it proceeded to set right Labour's "doctrinaire" nationalisation of road haulage and the steel industry—the latter only concluded in February 1951—by their "doctrinaire" de-nationalisation. This ritualistic "unscrambling" of the "Socialist omelette" was, however, to prove hardly less difficult an operation than that famous metaphor suggested, and, spread over the years,* took on the air of an academic exercise. For the rest, the Keynes-Beveridge basis of postwar society had by now come to seem almost as much a part of the natural order of things as the weather. Even Winston Churchill, now aged seventy-seven, no longer joked about the "full employment" to be obtained at Wormwood Scrubs. Any suggestion of a challenge to organised labour was scrupulously avoided; the Tory Industrial Charter's reiterated pledge to reverse, in part, Labour's repeal of the Trades Dispute Act was quietly forgotten.** Under Sir Walter Monckton, the carefully selected Labour Minister, the trade unions retained "estate of the realm" status and Lincoln Evans, the iron and steel workers' leader, found it possible to accept both a knighthood and the vice-chairmanship of the supervisory Iron and Steel Board established to co-ordinate the planning of the de-nationalised industry.

If in 1952 the "transformation" theme of Festival Year was sustained, that plainly was due less to a new Government at Westminster than to a Queen upon the throne.

Elizabeth's youth and radiance had been heightened and even lent a certain pathos by the circumstances of her accession. That February picture was still fresh in people's minds: the young Queen, in her black coat, alone, halfway down the steps

* The refloating of the steel companies was still not completed when the Fifties ended. Road haulage's "unscrambling" proved even more difficult. Since there were no takers for a large number of long-distance lorries, they were simply left in their unregenerate nationalised state under British Road Services. "Unscrambling" had, however, gone far enough here to prevent any attempt at road-rail co-ordination in the national transport system.

** The 1950 Manifesto had proposed to restore 'contracting-in'.

of the airliner that had brought her back to Britain; the four grave Ministers, Attlee next to Churchill, waiting, bareheaded, on the tarmac. Comparisons with the young Victoria were inevitable. Even more compulsive, at least to newspaper editors, was a somewhat forced harking-back to a much earlier queenly golden age. Learned historians were recruited to illuminate the theme under such headlines as "The Signs are Bright for a Great Revival". The *Daily Express* got its staff artist—"as a stimulant to your understanding of history"—to "recreate the Elizabethan scene" in a large tableau of "modern Elizabethans", including Margot Fonteyn in a farthingale, Sir Frank Whittle in doublet and hose, and Mr. T. S. Eliot in a ruff. Five faces were left blank, and for these, readers were invited to submit nominations.

As, over the months, the changes made necessary by the Accession came one by one into effect, as "King's Counsel" became "Queen's Counsel", as the Royal couple moved from Clarence House to Buckingham Palace, as the new stamps came out or the new "silver" coins appeared with their delicate un-crowned profile of the girl Queen (by a woman artist, Mrs. Mary Gillick), there was again the sense of new beginnings, and the nation felt itself renewed in the youth of its Queen.

II

Quite early in the postwar period editors of popular news-papers and magazines became aware of the phenomenal pulling power now generated by a good Royal story. A Princess on the cover, a "free-pull-out" Royal portrait group in "full colour", a Royal serial, became the recognised pick-me-ups for flagging circulations.

These were, indeed, heartbreaking days for the conscientious Republican. That same Stafford Cripps who had once darkly warned that it might be necessary to "overcome resistance from Buckingham Palace" when Labour came to power, was to be found, when Labour had, fervently defending his Govern-ment's decision to increase Princess Elizabeth's allowance on the occasion of her marriage. The heir-presumptive, insisted the Labour veteran Arthur Greenwood, must get "the rate for the job". And those few Socialists who still felt it necessary to

29. CORONATION NIGHT IN THE MALL

30 and 31. Through the dark days, Britain's hopes for the Future were sustained by the shining success of "the Comet". And in May, 1952, the Comet, "the world's first jet airliner", triumphantly went into B.O.A.C.'s regular South African service. But first Prince Philip, here accompanied by Sir Geoffrey de Havilland, took a ride in her. The record was brilliant—but bitter disappointment lay two years ahead. (*Below*)

DAILY EXPRESS

No. 16,706   MONDAY, JANUARY 11 1954   CONTROLLING SHAREHOLDER LORD BEAVERBROOK   Weather: Dry, with bright spells   Price 1

The last hours of G-ALYP ● Arrives Rome 95 mins. late ● Leaves Rome ● Contact lost ● Due in London ● Wreckage sighted ● Boats at scene ● Dead brought to Elba

COMET CRASH: 35 LOST

Burst into flames, then dive in sea

This is the lost Comet G-ALYP in flight

GIRL WHO MISSED THE PLANE

REBELS SAY: 'STRIKES DON'T PAY'
They face guerrilla boss today

Express Staff Reporter

MEN working on a £15,000,000 iron plant, believed to be one of the key targets of the guerrilla-strike electricians, yesterday repudiated the leaders of their Communist dominated union.

Of 290 members of the Electrical Trades Union engaged on the new iron-works at Scunthorpe, Lincs., only 37 raised a hand for a strike in support of the national claim for 3d. an hour more.

News of the vote sent "General" Frank Foulkes, leader of the E.T.U. hurrying from his London headquarters to Scunthorpe last night.

Australi cuts mo import control

SYDNEY, Sunday

Australia will give Br exporters a big boost April by taking off of her remaining im controls.

Only imports of t goods will still be cont

Mr. Butler, the British sellor, believes that v for £40,000,000 of sp —mainly machinery, tractors, and chemical by £40,000,000 . . .

LATEST

Daily Mail

NO. 18,056   THREE HALFPENCE   FOR QUEEN AND COMMONWEALTH   SATURDAY, APRIL 10, 1954

GOVERNMENT BANS ALL COME

irworthiness Certificate taken away until crash faults are discovered

Two surprises in East v W

DULLES | BRITA

omment | IN CRASH | Strike at the

indicate that they considered the rate somewhat high were nevertheless at pains to make it clear that they did so not from any lingering Republican sentiments but merely in order, as Mr. Emrys Hughes explained, to liberate the Royal couple from their "gilded cage". Even the Scottish Nationalists, so busy burning out or blowing up those pillar boxes in their northern cities on which the mongram "E.R.II" now appeared, merely wished, in an excess of ardour, to claim the Queen ("E.R.I") for their own.*

We were, it seemed, all Royalists now. In an age more consciously egalitarian, more utilitarian, than ever before, Monarchy, the quintessential inequality, the supreme extravagance, had never appeared more popular, more pervasive or more firmly based. In part, this was no doubt that process of psychological action and reaction long ago demonstrated in the United States where universal egalitarianism notoriously lent a compulsive fascination to the rare, licensed, exception. The growing impersonality and 'bureaucratisation' of life, the increasingly 'managerial' nature of politics, inevitably drove people to seek their more public emotional satisfactions in the small area that still retained the recognisable old "human" forms. In the new line-up, Ministers, politicians of all parties, trade union chiefs, were increasingly apt to appear as "They"; by contrast Queen, Consort, Princes and Princesses were tending to come out more as "We". Moreover, as the sole surviving monarchy among the major Western Powers, the British Royal House possessed a unique global glamour that could provide a flattering enhancement of that "We"—as was now about to be demonstrated.**

* A similar point had been made one blustery Christmas afternoon in 1950, when the Coronation Stone, "the stone of Scone", had been spirited away from the Abbey to its "rightful home" in the north by a party of Scottish students. But though the Scottish Covenant Association claimed to have secured two million signatures to its petition for Scottish Home Rule, no Scottish Nationalist candidate could secure election in any postwar General Election (and Scotland already, of course, enjoyed a large measure of devolution).

** The Coronation telecast was relayed by twelve Continental transmitters in over thirty languages. The Rank Technicolor film, *A Queen is Crowned* was rapturously received in over fifty countries, breaking house records in New York, Boston and Detroit. In

K

"A family on the Throne," Walter Bagehot had written in a famous passage, "brings down the pride of sovereignty to the level of petty life . . . sweetens politics by the seasonable addition of nice and pretty events. . . ." The point can never have been more powerfully demonstrated than by the British Royal Family in the Forties and Fifties. Spanning four generations, each representative of its time yet contained within the larger harmony, the single family frame, it had 'something for everyone'; "gay" members for the gay, serious for the serious, old-fashioned for the old-fashioned. In a febrile world of apparently collapsing moral values, the unselfconscious picture of domestic normality it presented was inevitably reassuring.

And now by the multiplying power of "mass-communications", the life of this Royal Family had become a part of everyone's life. All could feel involved in the making of the Queen. All could recall the small girls, heads just above the balcony, at George VI's Coronation . . . the pudgy, giggling Brownies . . . the leggy girls with scarves over their heads, riding in Windsor Great Park . . . the self-conscious Girl Guides, on the Palace balcony again . . . the young woman in A.T.S. uniform . . . the dancing partners . . . all leading up to the great romantic questionmark, so compulsive in the headlines.

In this great Royal serial there was it seemed in these years always a "continued in our next". The bleak November days of 1947 had been enlivened by the display of wedding gifts at St. James's Palace. Would, or would she not, promise to honour and *obey*? At the Suffragette Prisoners' dinner that year Miss Marion Reeves, a veteran of the cause, publicly hoped that she wouldn't. Princess Elizabeth, *The People* was shortly confiding, would not get the £4 Free "Beveridge" Maternity Grant because "Prince Philip has not paid enough contributions on his National Health Service card". It was endless, immensely photogenic, irresistible. Princess Anne, the second baby, caught by a telephoto lens over the Palace garden wall . . . Elizabeth, the radiant young wife and mother, in the uniform of a colonel of the Grenadier Guards, mounted on the police horse, "Winston", deputising for her father at the Trooping

Germany—a not untypical reaction to the hypnotic power of this thing—a critic wrote: "I wanted to throw up my hat and shout, 'God Save the Queen!'"

of the Colour. . . . And then, the Canada tour, a wonderful transcontinental scenic adventure in which all Britain shared through the medium of a fine colour film which drew crowds everywhere.

And, through it all, lending continuity and depth, the majestic figure of old Queen Mary, now in her middle eighties, yet unchanged, and, it almost seemed, unchangeable, bringing to this crisis-battered workaday England a fascinatingly anachronistic courtliness, the almost extinct air of *noblesse oblige*.

It was indeed a "human story", larger than life, packed with incident, replete with historic and other overtones, such as might have been made for the requirements of the mass-circulation Press. And in these postwar years material and media came together with remarkable results. Early setting the pace, the magazine, *Woman's Own*, gained 600,000 new readers overnight by capturing the nursery reminiscences of the Princesses' former governess, Miss Marion Crawford, better known to them—and now to the world—as 'Crawfie'. In a single August week in 1950, *Picture Post* was running "A Month in the Life of Princess Elizabeth", *Everybody's* was offering "The Life of George VI" by Hector Bolitho, and the *Sunday Dispatch* was publicising "Princess Margaret" by Godfrey Winn ("An intimate picture of the routine and highlights of Palace life . . . you will realise that it is, in fact, the story of *every* younger sister").

To this extraordinary all-pervasive enlargement of the Royal image, the newest mass medium, television, now brought an edge of particularity, a note of immediacy, that just prevented the whole thing from floating right away into the realms of pure Hans Andersen. The television cameras were at the funeral of George VI, and few would forget the sombre picture of the three black-veiled Queens at the door of Westminster Hall, or the sudden glimpse of the Royal dukes, side by side, in the procession, Windsor, briefly back from exile, looking curiously about him, the schoolboy Duke of Kent, locks of hair protruding from beneath his top hat, while the crowds waited, silent, in the grey streets at Paddington, and, on their screens, the viewers watched the birds wheeling over Windsor's Round Tower as the flag came fluttering down.

III

And the drama of the Accession was followed by the ritual of the Coronation in which the old magic of religion and the newer magic of science were potently blended. The Coronation occupied a single day. But it projected a broad, bright, anticipatory beam through the months before and left a warm, pink glow over the months behind. In one way or another its repercussions were felt at every level of the nation's life.

Already, in March, 1952, well over a year before the appointed date, orders were pouring into Birmingham, the heart of the souvenir industry. A Central Souvenirs Committee critically examined a swelling torrent of objects—the scarlet pennant with the Royal cipher for cyclists, the home-safe hopefully gilt-lettered 'Savings in the New Reign', the crown-embroidered panties (disapproved) and, from Staffordshire, the first coloured and decorated pottery released on the home market since the war. In July, the London County Council became fiercely divided over whether its half million schoolchildren should be presented with a "modernist" propelling pencil in blue plastic or a "traditionalist" inscribed beaker. In October the Earl Marshal, the Duke of Norfolk, set up his Coronation Headquarters in Berkeley Square, and the columns of the newspapers, heavy with the endless comings and goings at Lake Success and Panmunjon, were bejewelled with the names of Rouge Dragon, Portcullis Pursuivant and Bluemantle Pursuivant (in charge of 'Dress, Press and Ceremonial').

As the weeks went by, there began to filter from these gorgeous heraldic figures a stream of rulings and snippets of information which rejoiced the hearts of the Commonalty. Sandwiches, it was intimated, might be carried in coronets. Ermine trimming on peers' robes would not be insisted upon: rabbit skins might be used instead. Henry, sixth Marquis of Bath, got into the headlines early by insisting on travelling to the Abbey in his family coach-and-six, despite the Earl Marshal's repeated warnings that, if he did so, he would have nowhere to park it.

Other, humbler, preparations were under way. Seedsmen reported a threatening shortage of plants producing red, white and blue flowers. With large sums of money at stake, some commercial concerns now drew a veil of strict secrecy over their plans. In late December, a "spy" was unmasked in Fry's chocolate factory at Bristol, and prosecuted for handing over details of the firm's Coronation box designs "in an unlit doorway". The tempo was quickening. Plans of the processional route appeared and the papers began to print a flow of informative articles: how to distinguish a duke's coronet from a viscount's; the significance of the various articles of the regalia—and what happens "If Someone in the Abbey shouts 'No!'"

Crowds began to gather, mysteriously and suddenly, outside Buckingham Palace; the police had to clear a path for the sentries to walk. The papers were full of enormous pictures of the young Queen and her sister, incessantly coming and going, radiant and rather larger than life.

In March, President Tito of Yugoslavia paid a visit to Britain as a guest of the Government, lunching with the Queen at Buckingham Palace (Mr. Evelyn Waugh dissenting). Elsewhere the portents were not good. In Egypt the hopes raised by General Neguib's apparent reasonableness after the Officers' Revolt and Farouk's deposition had not been fulfilled. And although the prospects of peace in Korea looked a little brighter, America was edgy and suspicious, as McCarthy smelled out new victims, and Taft demanded that the United States, deserted by faint-hearted allies, should "Go it Alone!"

And in London, at the end of March, the old Queen, Queen Mary, died—two months before her eighty-sixth birthday and ten weeks before her granddaughter's Coronation.

That grand event continued to unfold with the inevitability of a process of nature. Over the grey tarmac of London Airport there now erupted a wonderful stream of colour—tribal chieftains from Nigeria and Tanganyika in their brilliant robes and crimson tarbushes, sultans from the Malay Peninsula, sheiks from the Persian Gulf, Queen Salote from the Tonga Islands, stately and maternal.

In Kensington Gardens, a tented town for 17,000 Commonwealth troops was building. . . . There was the noise of sawing everywhere. Carpenters planed planks on the pavements of Whitehall. Giant cranes stalked the Mall. The West End disappeared beneath the scaffolding.

London was in the grips of Coronation fever. By 8.30 a.m. on Whit Sunday a queue of 300 was waiting for the first of London Transport's "Round the Coronation Route" coaches. Others did the sights by car, bumper to bumper, all through the West End. Parties on foot munched their sandwiches sitting in the tiered stands, imagined what it would all look like from these seats of wealth and privilege, and issued their verdicts on the decorators' efforts. Mum, perhaps, had lost her heart to the traditional criss-cross festoons and banners of the City; Maureen, who had a modern-minded art mistress, boldly supported the strange scythe-and-fishnet trappings of Oxford Street; but Dad, a reactionary in these matters, found the turquoise lamp-standards a little hard to take, and had stood in frank bafflement before Eros's gilded cage. Since Sir Hugh Casson's declared aim was to achieve "a harmonious diversity" as of " a series of differently furnished rooms" such amateur critics had no lack of scope. But, in the end, most familes were drawn back to the Mall, with those huge glittering crowns, suspended in the sky beneath the gold-and-azure arches, and the Palace closing the vista in a shimmer of blue exhaust smoke as the cars crept forward, eight abreast, an endless band.

No professional publicity expert would have dared so long, sustained and intensive a "build-up". After a whole year, it did indeed begin to seem that the event itself must come as an anticlimax.

It did not.

By Coronation Eve 30,000 people were bedded down, twelve deep, on both sides of the Mall. Twenty thousand others were trying to find places to join them. The rain lashed them, and as night fell the thermometer plummeted. People wrapped old newspapers round their legs to keep warm. But these discomforts merely served to underline the epic quality to the occasion. "C-Day", one reporter observed, seemed to have been planned almost as carefully as "D-Day": the crowds had come armed with stools, spirit-stoves, blankets, gramophones, radios, tinned food, even tarpaulins and rubber dinghies.

"It's waterproof if you don't want to read it!" the news vendors quipped next morning, as they picked their way between the rows of stiff and steaming bodies. But people did want to read it. For across the front pages was blazoned the story of the conquest of Everest—after thirty years of repeated attempts and bitter defeats—by a lanky young New Zealand bee-farmer named Edmund Hillary and his Sherpa guide, Tensing.

"New Elizabethans" if ever there were any!

That was how it was with this extraordinary business; at one moment, it was as full of the trivialities and banalities of life as Mrs. Dale's Diary; at the next it soared to heroic heights or touched some chord of poetry.

The crowds could not see within the Abbey; yet millions did. In pubs, in clubs, in village halls and private homes, chairs were set out for Coronation "viewing parties". Later, the B.B.C. released the figures: 20,400,000 people, almost half the nation, had watched the ceremony on 2,700,000 television receivers. And they saw what few in the Abbey could. In contrast to the greyness of the morning, the pictures were almost startlingly clear: the details of robes, regalia and jewels came through in brilliant relief, and when the Queen's face was seen in close-up her emotions almost seemed to communicate themselves to the watchers in their homes.

Elizabeth II it was justly said was the first British monarch really crowned—as the rubric requires—"in sight of all the people". For two-and-a-half hours the millions sat, entranced before their screens, as they watched the chief actors in this rich and complex rite slowly moving through its prescribed parts. Noted one of the "viewers" that day: "It left me and others in a mood of reverent astonishment such as is evoked by a great work of art."

There had been grave doubts among the eminent about the wisdom of allowing this thing, television, into the Abbey. Now there were public recantations. Television in England came of age with the Coronation much as radio had with the General Strike.

IV

Nor in the days that followed was there any abrupt let-down, any disconcerting anti-climax. There were the Queen's drives through London, the Thanksgiving at St. Paul's, the glittering gala performance of Britten's new opera, *Gloriana*, at Covent Garden. There was the Derby, where the Queen and 750,000 of her subjects saw the newly knighted Gordon Richards win his first Derby, at his twenty-eighth attempt. There was the Trooping ceremony, with the Duke carrying his Field-Marshal's baton now, the Guildhall lunch, the visits to Wales and to Windsor, the naval review at Spithead to which even the Russians sent a cruiser, the *Sverdlov*.

And still the crowds swarmed into London, paying their half-crowns to tread the Queen's way in the Abbey, milling in the Mall. . . . But enough is enough. "Many of us—but hardly all," wrote the *Manchester Guardian* at last, "have had a deep spiritual experience. Now we have to settle down."

It no longer seemed so impossible a feat. Emotion which since the "great days" of 1945 had vainly sought expression had found it. Whether in street parties, village celebrations, or on the pavements of the cities, the wartime sense of community and nationhood had been briefly reborn. As in war, it was a feeling that transcended class. Through the extraordinary alchemy of Monarchy, the new egalitarianism had somehow accommodated the old inequality, the old magic, the new.

But as the Coronation receded, earlier doubts returned. Was it not rather true that the unique nature and power of the occasion had concealed the fact that the two magics were not only not of a kind, but—as the Townsend-Margaret Affair was soon to suggest—profoundly anti-pathetic; and that the new magic, parasitic in the first instance, might be finally disruptive, all-devouring?

The old magic of monarchy had depended upon Position, remote, dignified, immutable, at the apex of the social pyramid.

On such a rare occasion as the Coronation, the nobility might still flank the throne, the peers fill the Abbey, the Church brilliantly fulfil its role, the monarchy shine forth in all its traditional pomp and majesty. But the everyday scene was very different. The Church of England evoked neither awe nor obedience. This was the age of the "Reluctant Peer" (for whom ennoblement spelled political suicide) and of that guilty contradiction, the Life Peer—a device resorted to in a desperate attempt to rouse the House of Lords from the coma into which it now appeared to be rapidly sinking.* When, in 1949, preparing the way for steel nationalisation, the Labour Government had cut the Lords' delaying power from two years to one, their action had seemed almost academic. For on any serious issue it had now come to seem impossible that the will of the elected House should not prevail. In 1957, it was true, a Cecil, still at the elbow of the Sovereign, might well have determined which of two men should be Britain's Prime Minister; but such influence, though impressive in its longevity, was plainly residual. Even a Cecil could not control the machine or the market whose world this now was,** a world in which England's nobility, old and new, were engaged in debating the Government's new scheme for peers' expenses allowances, calculated at a rate which, according to one noble lord, implied that a "bed-sitting room or cheap lodging house was good enough for a member of the House of Lords when a business executive stayed at the best hotels".

As for that other natural support of the old hierarchical structure, the Army, the dissolution of Empire was now rapidly completing that process of erosion which the First World War had launched and the Second rushed forward. Young Guards

* The first list of life peers under the new Life Peerages Act was announced in mid-1958. Although Lloyd George's Parliament Acts of 1911 had a Preamble expressing an intention to reform the Upper House at an early date, and, although, in 1955, that intention was still being expressed, notably by Lord Salisbury (who favoured some tempering of the hereditary element with life peers), successive plans had failed to find the necessary inter-party agreement. In six years, Mr. Attlee had created 100 peers; but by 1956 only fifty-five remained. Many had to work for a living, and couldn't afford to attend the House of Lords very often.

** An interesting sign of the times appeared in the 1959 election when in a Tory television broadcast the 14th Earl of Home was prudently and unceremoniously removed from the programme in favour of a television technician and TV personality, Chris Chataway.

officers, with their bowlers, immaculately furled umbrellas and faintly supercilious air, might still uniquely decorate the vicinity of St. James's, but whatever their military worth, the last war had been the war of "putting you in the picture", of the National Serviceman, the R.A.F. and the G.I. and it was yearly becoming more evident that the next war, if there was one, would be the war of the scientists.

The pageantry remained an asset of immense value to the British tourist trade. Yet the hollowness of much of it was every year more visible. Grey toppers went by bus to the Eton-and-Harrow match—and everybody knew about Moss Bros. "It would be a fair guess to say that three-quarters of the men who wore morning dress at Ascot this week were not wearing their own clothes," reported the *Economist* in 1955, and added, "It is difficult to believe in the permanence of a social convention that requires people to wear clothes that hardly anyone nowadays even pretends to own." And not only, perhaps, of a social convention. For most of the two million people, trudging each year round the stately homes, the noble occupants, though personally on duty at the souvenir counter, had little more real significance than the Czars for Russian workers trooping round the Hermitage or Winter Palace. "International café society"— money-based—was the target of the gossip-columns, snob or non-snob, such great London houses as still stood were business or Government offices, and the Duke of Bedford, with the long-famed enterprise and progressiveness of the Russells, was reported to be in conference with Mr. Billy Butlin about future arrangements at Woburn.

Even Buckingham Palace was now unionised. Thus, if the social routine of the Queen's year still largely followed the pattern established in Victorian and Edwardian times when society could still carry its capital S, the anachronistic nature, and general tattiness of much of it, the need for modernisation, was becoming—under the continuous arclight glare of modern publicity—increasingly evident. In 1957 it was announced that Court Presentation Parties, involving the whole curious, absurd and commercialised business of "debutantes", were now to be abolished. "Natural regret at the change," observed *The Times* cryptically, "would not be widely felt."

In the year 1864, the future Edward VII wrote to his mother,

Queen Victoria: "We have always been an Aristocratic Country and I hope we shall always remain so, as they ["the High Classes"] are the mainstay of the country unless we become so Americanised that they are swept away and then the state of things will be quite according to Mr. Bright's views who wishes only for the Sovereign and the People and no class between."

In the Fifties, with the assistance of the processes Edward himself had done much to set in motion, it began to look as if the situation he feared might—in essentials—be on the way to realisation. There was a call for the shaping of a "modern, democratic monarchy", freed from the obfuscations of "stuffy" courtiers and—in the famous phrase of Lord Altrincham, Tory editor of the *National Review*—"the tweedy set". "Court circles" should be widened; the door opened on the "gilded cage" deplored by Mr. Emrys Hughes in 1947; and by such modern devices as the much commended "new style" Palace lunches attended by eminent footballers, actors, novelists, racing motorists, film producers and so on the Queen must be brought into touch with "the real people".

In so complex an age, the inherent contradictions of "democratic monarchy" were not, however—as was now to be demonstrated—to be quite so easily resolved. For if not a "class" in Edward VII's sense, something did necessarily stand between "the Sovereign and the People", something Mr. Bright could scarcely have foreseen; the complex, high-powered, semi-automated machine of "Admass". And despite TV at the Coronation, this machine was, as we have seen, no mere neutral transmitter. It had its necessities.

If the old magic had depended on continuity and remoteness, the new fed on "intimacy" and change. And was projected by profit—Coronation month had brought the biggest newspaper sales boom of all time.* The vast mid-century "Court" so created was very different from that of the *Court Circular*. That "divinity that doth hedge a king" was not so much reduced "democratic" reality as—in the immortal phrase of Mr.

* The *Daily Mirror* circulation had exceeded 7,000,000, more than 50 per cent above normal.

Arthur Christiansen, editor of the *Daily Express**—"sprinkled with stardust"; the monarch was processed into a super personality in whom—as in all Admassian personalities—the consumer or the audience naturally possessed proprietary rights.

"Who on earth advised the Queen to wear the outfit she had for the Somerset-Thynne wedding?" demanded a woman reporter of her 14 million readers. Newspaper public opinion polls to determine what members of the Royal Family should or should not do were now a regular institution, accompanied by the cosy American style of first-name headline address. "HOW CAN YOU TELL THE KIDS?" headlined the *Sunday Pictorial*, when "red tape" was allegedly delaying the Duke of Edinburgh at Gibraltar on his way home from his world tour. "What of Prince Charles and Princess Anne? They haven't seen their father for 118 days. How can anyone explain to them: DADDY COULD BE HOME FOR TEA, BUT . . ." Next day, revealing American rumours—in the best Hollywood tradition—of a "Royal split", the *Mirror* proffered further advice in letters four inches high: FLY HOME PHILIP. After that, it was left to the *Sunday Express* to brighten the week-end by saluting the SMILING DAY when the Royal couple finally met in Lisbon, an eagle-eyed sub-editor happily noting, across two columns, A TINY SMEAR OF LIPSTICK ON HIS FACE.

In its long history, the British Monarchy had worn many faces: but never one quite like this. For this mass-produced "intimacy" was vastly different from that of the old Cockney crowds who had shouted and sung about "Good Old Teddy", or from that of the scribblers who had lampooned the earlier Hanoverians. It was machine-made, formula-packaged for market, continuous—and overwhelming.

Princess Margaret, in particular, all Europe and America over, was "always news". A newspaperman calculated that in the first twenty-nine weeks of 1954, 214 articles and reports about her had appeared in London newspapers alone. And when in the course of their industrious chronicling of Princess Margaret's escorts, the newspapers detected an increasing incidence of a certain Group-Captain Peter Townsend, a former

* "Our feature pages should be sprinkled with stardust or whatever it is that women wear that catches the light at first nights"— Bulletin for guidance of *Daily Express* staff.

fighter-pilot who had served as Deputy Master of the Royal Household, the gossip-columnists redoubled their efforts. "The Romance of the Century" was soon occupying vast acreages of newsprint.

In the Townsend-Margaret affair the two worlds of Monarchy, the old and the new, met and clashed—with obvious echoes of the clash, almost two decades before, that had ended in the Abdication. For Group-Captain Townsend was divorced, and the Church with its ruling on divorce was, however anachronistically, still the *Established* Church with the monarch at its head.

By the winter of 1955, when Group-Captain Townsend returned from Brussels whither he had been tactfully posted, the *Manchester Guardian* was reporting that "nothing much else but Princess Margaret's affairs is being talked about in this country". The arclights were full on now, creating a whole garish, harshly lit world of their own—a striking demonstration of the advance of the publicity machine since the Abdication (with its initial, long-maintained Press conspiracy of silence).

The affair was potently dramatised as a battle not only of eager youth against crabbed old age, but of aristocracy *versus* democracy, of "the stuffed shirts" against the non-stuffed shirts. The *Daily Express* assailed the Archbishops and even hinted at Disestablishment. The *Mirror* discovered a "Wicked Plot" against a young girl's happiness in which the editor of *The Times* was deeply implicated. The *Pictorial* offered its usual non-stuffy encouragement: COME ALONG, MARGARET, PLEASE MAKE UP YOUR MIND!"*

Yet despite these vociferously expressed sentiments, despite the "verdicts" of newspaper polls, here at least it was the old hierarchic world that prevailed. Princess Margaret duly issued a statement of renunciation from Clarence House, "mindful of the Church's teaching that Christian marriage is indissoluble and conscious of my duty to the Commonwealth". If there was, as the Duchess of Windsor complained in her memoirs, "something steely and unhuman in the monarchical principle", it was, it seemed, "steely and inhuman" still.

Several million Britons were left with a vague feeling of

* And was duly reproved by the "stuffed shirts" of the Press Council for "coarse impertinence".

bewilderment and even of revulsion. "New Look" and "Old Look" continued, here as elsewhere, to alternate and overlap, and it began to seem that the task of harmonising them, of accommodating the continuity of tradition to the weekly verdict of poll and rating (and accounts' office)—or of reconciling the English "organic" habit of growth to "American Way"—might prove more complex and troublesome than we yet guessed.

V

Nor was the Scandinavian model, the King-on-a-bicycle, really very relevant. The Queen, certainly, was no longer 'Elizabeth R.I.' George VI had dropped the 'Imperator'; his daughter had been enthroned as 'Head of the Commonwealth and other Realms and Territories'. But this, implying seven crowns instead of one, increased rather than decreased her ceremonial duties.

By air (though not by bicycle), Queen Elizabeth II was nearer to Canberra or to Ottawa than Queen Victoria had been to Balmoral. And if in obedience to their natal 'anti-Imperialism' new Asian Dominions like India, Pakistan and Ceylon lost no time in declaring themselves republics, the monarchy, given the change of title, remained an institution in whose refulgence they were not unwilling, from time to time, to bask. As the various tours of the Fifties—to Jamaica, to Ceylon, to New Zealand, to Nigeria—showed, the glamour of one of the world's last great monarchies—at least with a young woman on the throne—was something that could transcend race, religion, colour and political prejudice. The Crown remained one of the few visible, tangible symbols linking this vast world-wide association.

Overseas as well as at home, the monarchy thus still had a central—potentially critical—role. And whatever dangers the Fifties might hint for the future, in these years at least that role was fulfilled with extraordinary success. The parallel with the 1850's, with Victoria and Albert, was not perhaps so inapt after all. Once again there had been a royal marriage which seemed well adapted both to enabling the age to define itself and to acting as a catalyst of profound change. As Victoria's marriage had provided the stereotype for the new prosperous middle-class society of her day, it seemed possible that Elizabeth's might ease the way for the very different society of the Endless Middle. It was a marriage which in some way represented an alliance of the old society and the new. Elizabeth was a child of the postwar world, but her Englishness remained a narrow, class, Englishness, apparent in speech and deportment. Her consort, on the other hand, was 'international', apparently classless, informal, totally unpompous. Into a Royal Family which had hitherto tended to confine itself to the traditional healthy but monotonous pursuits of the English landed gentry, he imported a cheerful contemporary and even "technological" note. In an age of the machine he was on terms with machines. Lecturing the British Association on the significance of the electronic brain, taking off in a helicopter from the back lawns of Buckingham Palace, presenting his own programme on television, or scudding through the waves in a small boat in a manner that had little to do with the Imperial Cowes of Edward VII and the Kaiser, "the Duke" hit the headlines in a way that accorded well with the image of both the 'New Britain' of 1945 and the 'New Britain' of 1951.*

To those who could see little future in either the "Court Circular" or the *Sunday Pictorial* approaches to monarchy, the Mountbatten interpretation seemed to offer the best hope as British society—with the small 's'—began to move rapidly towards that state of affluence where it resembled less and less a hierarchical pyramid and more and more an endless, bright curtained suburb—where every man—and more particularly, every woman—was sovereign in his—or her—semi-detached castle.

* A piquant footnote to this process of "democratisation" was provided by the *Sunday Times*, commenting on the Queen's attack of sinus trouble in 1958. Having abandoned their sheltered lives in a closed community, the paper explained, the Royal Family was "now coming into daily contact with members of the public—and their coughs and sneezes. . . . In medical circles it is thought that the Queen will continue to be vulnerable to nasal infections until her natural immunity rises to common level."

PART FIVE

THE NEW LOOK

"The cure of poverty is not in
personal economy but in better
production. . . . Economy is the
rule of half-alive minds."
—Henry Ford, Chapter 'Why be
    Poor?' *My Life and Work*,
    1922.

"The expense that is laid out in
durable commodities gives maintenance, commonly, to a greater
number of people than that which
is employed in the most profuse
hospitality."
—Adam Smith, *The Wealth of
    Nations*, 1776.

25. Not Marx, but Marks

"The abolition of poverty depends
more on the rapid circulation of
capital than the redistribution of
wealth. . . ."

—*Memoirs of the Earl of Woolton*, 1959.

"Right now the basic insecurity the
workers feel is this: they are haunted
by the spectre of the van driving up to
the door to take away the TV set."

—Mrs. Elizabeth Braddock, Labour
M.P.

W HEN THE Russian sailors from the *Sverdlov*, at the Coronation naval review, came ashore at Portsmouth they
were much photographed "strolling" with their British
or American "comrades" or lighting cigarettes for members of
the W.R.N.S. When these pictures appeared in the papers,
readers examined them with particular care, searching those
amiable if stolid features for some hint of what went on behind
them. For the seemingly impossible had happened: on 6th
March Stalin had died.

"The mind boggles . . ." the *Observer* had written in an
editorial headed "New World". And that, certainly, had been
no over-statement. In February, the Iron Curtain had still
seemed as blank and impermeable as ever, the Cold War
stretched away endlessly into the future, and one had resigned
oneself to a lifetime enmeshed in those interminable speculations
which the "analysts of Soviet Affairs", sitting at their desks in
London, and gazing, metaphorically, across the steppes,
distilled from a couple of down-page lines in *Red Star* or *Pravda*.

And then, overnight, all this was changed. News came
pouring out of Russia with telegraphic immediacy. Malenkov,
Beria and Molotov, we learned, had delivered the funeral

orations. "Collective leadership" was to be the order of the new day, with Malenkov, *primus inter pares*, as Chairman of the Council of Ministers. "Peaceful co-existence" had been proclaimed. There were to be more consumer goods for the Russian people. Many categories of prisoners were amnestied. Molotov, astonishingly, had agreed to use his good offices to bring about the release of nine British civilians long interned in North Korea, and several American journalists had received visas for Moscow.

But before long the old doubts reasserted themselves.

Was this perhaps—in the obscene jargon of these years—just one more "peace offensive"? A stratagem to lull the West while the Kremlin recovered and reorganised?

The flabby features of Malenkov staring blankly out of the British newspapers offered little reassurance. In June the Workers' Rising in East Berlin was suppressed by the Red Army troops and armoured cars. But conciliation followed. In July, as London prepared for its Coronation Year river pageant, Beria was arrested. At Panmunjon an armistice was signed at last; after months of recrimination the exchange of prisoners got under way. And another name, that of a miner's son from the Donbass, was moving into the headlines. In September, Khrushchev was formally elected First Secretary of the Central Committee of the Communist Party—a position Prime Minister Malenkov had relinquished in the interests, it was explained, of the new principle of "collective leadership".

We should not, after all, be able to dispense yet awhile with the Kremlinologists and their complex deductions from the position of Commissar X on the group photograph in Red Square. The "enigma" remained. For all that, the change was immense. Hope was reborn. The Russians were beginning to look differentiated and vaguely human. The world, it almost seemed, might be beginning to open up again.

II

The climatic change at home was hardly less dramatic.

Not until July, 1954—more than nine years after V.E. Day— was the last of the wartime rationing restrictions—that on meat—finally abolished. But then, almost at once, affluence came hurrying on the heels of penury. Suddenly, the shops were piled high with all sorts of goods. Boom was in the air. Balance of payments crises were now, apparently, something one took in one's stride. In the middle of the 1955 crisis, with its severe credit cut-backs and increased taxes, Birmingham traders reported that there was now "so much money about" that there were three-months delays in supplying many items of home electrical equipment, four months for the better furniture and up to a year for most cars. One firm, certainly, was said to be in difficulties. It had stocked up with the 14-inch table television receivers when "everybody" was demanding "17-inch consoles with doors".

In the six years following 1950 the money passing across British shop counters increased by almost 50 per cent. But more important than either the amount or the improved quality of the merchandise was the appearance of a "new" class of goods of American origin, now for the first time produced for a British mass market.

Major E. Beddington Behrens has told how, in 1947, he imported an American automatic washing machine into Britain and invited "many leading industrialists" to join him in its manufacture. The response was disappointing. "I could not persuade them that there was a market for more than a few thousand a year." Ten years later, one in every three middle-class and one in every five working-class homes in Britain had an electric washing machine. Often enough, it was flanked by a refrigerator, by a new model "eye-level" or "automatic" cooker, a TV set, a "gleaming" power mixer, or some other of the newly established "necessities of life". Spending on electrical, electronic and durable goods now rose nearly six times as fast as other consumer outlays.

These were the years in which the "consumer-durables" became pivotal in our economy, their production indices the subject of almost daily anxious comment by economists charting the national future. Social and psychological effects promised to be no less far-reaching. Here was a complex of goods, "contemporary", smart, complicated and/or substantial, costing tens of pounds rather than shillings, which not only provided the nucleus of a new style of life but—especially when fitted into the new house they seemed to demand—had the power to turn millions of people, with remarkable speed, into "property-owners".

At an earlier stage in the diffusion of industrial wealth social historians had gauged the rising standard of life by the growth in the consumption of sugar; at a later stage, they measured by tea. The historian of the 1950's will have no such simple measuring rod. In 1956 after a long inquiry into actual household expenditures, the basis of the official cost-of-living (retail prices) index was changed. The weighting given to food was reduced; candles, lump sugar, rabbits, turnips and similar items were thrown out of the basket, and into it was poured the brimming cornucopia of the mid-twentieth-century industrial civilisation—soda water and dog food, nylons and washing machines, apples and pears and camera films, telephone rentals and school ties, dance-hall tickets and second-hand cars. . . .

III

More than a generation after Henry Ford had laid down his first assembly line and begun to expound his High Wage philosophy, the British were, at last, beginning fully to enjoy the fruits. Britain, in the Fifties, was experiencing the sudden, proliferating abundance—and a little of the attendant dazzle— of the America in the Twenties.

Governmental propagandists were not slow to point to the tonic properties of "Tory freedom", and to Mr. Butler's "Incentive", "New Look", "Boost" or "Bumper" Budget (*vide* Press) of 1953 which—taking sixpence off the income-tax and a quarter off purchase tax—had at long last opened the flood-gates of demand. And perhaps it might be claimed that in this postwar period the two political parties had been employed by an electorate with an instinctive sense of role and timing: the Tories to dismantle the wartime machinery of control when much of it was no longer necessary,* the Socialists to keep it going while it clearly was.

* E.g. their demolition of the Utility scheme, discontinuing of bulk purchase, restoration of the Liverpool Cotton Exchange (instead of the Raw Cotton Commission).

But one does not credit the lock-keeper who opens the sluice with producing the water. The long delay in the "Ford-isation" of Britain (and Western Europe with her) had been due partly to the world trade slump of the Twenties, and the stunting economic nationalism that went with it, in part to the lack of adequate economic knowledge, and in part to a ruling class of politicians, bankers and businessmen who looked at our society through either semi-feudal or Ricardo-Marxian spectacles.

By 1945 most of these obstructive influences had been either removed or modified. The Labour Government had decisively changed the priorities and balance in British society. The "spirit of Beveridgism and Fair Shares" had silenced the bankers at a critical juncture. The nationalisation of the Bank of England, if largely a formal act, had nevertheless symbolised an intention to govern economically as well as in other ways. We had had Dr. Dalton's inflation instead of Mr. Montagu Norman's deflation. The economy had been kept at full stretch through seven years of arming against Germany, followed by another seven arming against Russia. However much or little could be credited to the new levers of control, continuing full employment had forced the British employer out of his ancient Ricardian preoccupation with wage-cutting. It had compelled him to bid for labour and organise to make high wages economic.

The control of investment and consumption in the interests of rebuilding exports had meant that though since 1948 industrial production had increased (by volume) at an average annual rate of just over 4 per cent, little of that impressive growth had been reflected in the standard of living at home. But the capacity—war-supercharged—was now there. And after Korea, when the terms of trade turned in our favour and exports to the U.S.A. went ahead, some of it could at last be released to serve the home market. Between 1951 and 1959 average consumption per head was to rise by 20 per cent—as large a gain in nine years as in all the twenty-six years between 1913 and 1939.

This forward surge depended on new consumers as well as on new techniques. It required a steady, nation-wide demand from masses of open-minded, eagerly acquisitive customers. In prewar days, despite the continuing long-term rise in real wages, the creation of any such climate would have been prevented by the existence of the vast Depressed Areas of the north, cluttered with the wreckage, mechanical and human, of the first industrial revolution, and with endemic unemployment, which even in 1937, was running at a rate between 20 and 30 per cent. Only after the war was legislation enacted* requiring the siting of new factories to comply with social needs. Between 1945 and 1947, under the Labour Government's licensing pressures, one-third of all new industrial building had been in the "Development Areas". By the Fifties, the new light industries deployed along the "coaly Tyne" were employing more people than the traditional shipbuilding and ship-repairing together. Millions were being poured into the modernisation and reorganisation of the coal mines. In South Wales, nylon spinning, watchmaking, the great new steel and tinplate installations and hundreds of new factories brought new life and hope to once despairing valleys. For every seven people who left Wales to find work in the Thirties—as for every three who left the North-East—only one left in the Fifties.

This was one of the major—if still only partial—successes of postwar planning. It was greatly assisted by the extra-ordinary dynamism of some of the "new" industries, most notably perhaps on Tees-side where I.C.I. poured millions into its vast and ever-expanding petro-chemical and synthetic fibre kingdom.

The Beveridge Plan had assumed an average unemployment level of 8 per cent. But now for fifteen years unemployment had remained under 2 per cent. Many areas had experienced sustained labour famine. Households with two, three or even more wage-earners were common,** and overtime, at high rates, tended to be the rule rather than the exception. When

* Made possible by the Distribution of Industry Acts, 1945 and 1950, and the Town Planning Act, 1947, under which central planning permission was required for the erection of new factories in the interests of proper industrial balance through the country. The Local Government Act, 1948, by equalising local authority resources, removed one of the most persistent handicaps of the Depressed Area local authorities.

** In 1954 there were 3,807,700 households with two earners; 1,857,300 with three or more earners. This out of a total of 10 million households.

rent-controlled or subsidised housing and the continuing fall in the working-class birth-rate were taken into account, it became clear that the cumulative effect in terms of household spending power ought to be impressive. It was. By 1955 the *average* expenditure of the British household had reached £19 a week.*

The light engineering towns of the Midlands and south-east now began to acquire an almost New World gloss. In Coventry council houses with £60 a week coming in were not uncommon. For the prosperity of the booming industries could not be confined, spilling over, locally and regionally, to many occupations, from the dustcarts to "the buses".**

Here was a new social fact whose social, economic and political repercussions would take some years to absorb. But at least a start had been made. Newspapers, addressing advertisers, now ceased to conceal and began instead to boast of their working-class readership. "Who's Buying the New Consumer Goods?" inquired the *Daily Herald* ("the acknowledged newspaper of the wage-earning class"), going on to offer "statistical proof" that "in the last five years or so the skilled and unskilled manual workers have emerged as the biggest spenders on a whole range of goods traditionally regarded as 'middle-class products'."

IV

From the austere but substantial foundation of Socialist Egalitarianism the gleaming structure of the People's Capitalism now rose bizarrely. Its core was provided by the rapid development of an "American-style" mass market —i.e. a mass market no longer confined to a comparatively narrow range of "cheap" articles, but covering a wide diversity of goods, prices, designs and qualities.

Inevitably this had an accumulating effect on many of the nation's familiar economic institutions whose patterns had been

* Blue Book on National Income and Expenditure, 1956. By 1959 the figure had reached £25 10s.

** In Britain as a whole the income group receiving £500–£750 after tax rose from 1·9 millions in 1949 to 5·8 millions in 1954. Comparable change in the value of money £100 (1949) equalled £125 (1954).

established since the Twenties or earlier. These, remodelled, speeded in their turn the process of change.

Before the war, the symbol of widening prosperity had been the great departmental store. A grandiose structure, offering a glimpse of opulence for the little woman up from the suburbs, it had by the Thirties reached all the main provincial centres. Now came a significant change. Relatively, the departmental store fell back, and the pace was made by the chain stores which had branches, not only in the city centres, but in every substantial High Street.

They were, however, chain stores transformed. The model was not now the palatial, the pseudo-aristocratic. Nor was it the 'refined' lower middle-class Booterie of the Thirties. The chain store organisation which most successfully adapted to the new climate was a firm of "working-class" origins which had itself slowly ascended with its customers the long road to affluence. As the "Original Penny Bazaar", Marks and Spencer had been founded in 1884 by a Polish refugee named Michael Marks and a Yorkshireman, Tom Spencer. Through the interwar years the firm had developed, steadily improving its merchandise, acquiring some, but not too much, "respectability". But it was not till after the Second World War that it finally burst from its somewhat dull chrysalis to emerge as the classless, efficient, decently functional, distributive model of the new age, a place where doctor's wife and docker's wife could, impartially and without fuss, avail themselves of the growing range and quality of mass-produced goods the new market made available.

At the cost of many millions, the firm's stores were made over to provide a sense of spaciousness, of order, of democratic good manners. Though the widest market was aimed at, the emphasis was no longer on price, but on quality control and precise and accurate specifications. In co-operation with their manufacturers, the firm maintained a large technical research and development staff at an annual cost exceeding £500,000. "Their task", Sir Simon Marks told his shareholders in 1956, "is to study ways and means of upgrading our goods, always bearing in mind value and price. Their duties are to keep abreast of any interesting developments in the textile field which can be speedily incorporated in our goods."

It was an ideal statement of the services afforded by the new People's Capitalism, and, as long as one stuck to articles as easy to check and as unquestionably desirable as clothing, it was hard even for a fanatic anti-Capitalist to withhold admiration. In the decade after 1948 Marks and Spencer's profits more than quadrupled. But the service rendered was manifest and great. There were few families in Britain which did not wear some of the firm's garments, and many that were largely clothed by them. Clothes for children, in particular, under such influences, showed a notable improvement in colour, fabric and design in these years.

Thus the economic mechanism which had showed its potentialities in the lightning spread of the "New Look" across the pavements of Britain in 1947 was now built into the national structure. And this, perhaps, was the essential revolution of the Fifties—the revolution according to Marks, not Marx, which yet echoed uncannily, if in a somewhat different key, the universality and the practical humanism of the "Beveridge-Attlee" revolution of the Forties.

Other major national distribution chains, building their strength by amalgamations and 'take-overs', were now transforming themselves on broadly similar lines. The bold black-and-white signboards of the "Fifty Shilling Tailors" changed discreetly, first to a non-committal "F.S.T.", then, with much internal and external restyling, to "John Collier" shops, with a facsimile signature as their "personalising" emblem. For here, too, one could now dispense with both the image of "cheapness" and the mock Savile Row touch. With one in every two suits worn made by the three great multiple tailoring groups, it was no longer necessary to be on the defensive. Nor were any apologies, in fact, due. Three-quarters of the suits sold by the multiples were made-to-measure by a method which combined individual cutting with the economies of factory production. The old "navy blue serge" and brown "reach-me-downs" largely disappeared. The "grey flannel bags" of Old England were replaced by "slacks" of many weaves, fabrics and hues. Lightweight summer suits and jackets made their appearance on the mass market. In the Fifties, as the Marksian revolution gathered pace, the British male as well as female was restyled from top to toe.

"Half our trouble in England," Ernest Bevin once told an American audience, "is that we suffer from a poverty of desire."

From darkest Durham to the blackest Black Country this particular form of "poverty" now came under attack. Millions were being poured out in redesigning shops and shopfronts to extend, Cinerama-like, shining new horizons of possession before the stick-in-the-mud Englishman and his once dowdy wife. In five years there were more changes in the shopping scene than in the previous fifty. Shoe stores became glittering glass avenues, cunningly lighted to lure the passer-by from the pavement into their own particular never-never land of continuous consumption. Every substantial High Street in the Kingdom was a-boom with radio-and-electrical chain stores, their windows gleaming with all the proliferating apparatus of the complicated life. "Trading up" became the successful retailers' watchword. An immense amount of research, thought and money was devoted to the packaging of all manner of articles. No longer was it enough to cry heartily, "Friday Night is Amami Night!" Shampoos might be presented under such names as "White Rain", and packed in plastic sachets with pictorial evocation of hibiscus and southern skies. Englishmen, who might have been dimly aware that they needed a new suit sooner or later, were now made aware that this year "charcoals" were imperative, or that next year would be the year for "lovats". As for our "old mac complex", this, an advertiser now informed us, was "a blot on our national character".

From 1950 on, advertising expenditure grew at an average rate of 13 per cent a year, and by the second half of the Fifties had reached over a million pounds a day—the second highest total in the world. Advertising agents are paid on the basis of the cost of the advertising placed, so that when postwar newspaper circulations soared, and advertising rates followed them, the whole structure inflated like a balloon. The advertising industry became yearly more pivotal, prestigeful, ramified, "scientific". It found eager new entrants in Oxford and Cambridge. Statisticians, social scientists and psychologists were enlisted. Public Relations divisions proliferated. The market-research lady, armed with samples and clip-board, was now rarely off the British family's doorstep. ("Snooper" no longer!)

These were the years in which advertising men finally succeeded in shaking off that old barker's straw hat and assuming the black homberg to which their central position was now seen to entitle them. They no longer merely sold an article, but generated an atmosphere, propagated a philosophy and projected a vision of the good life.

At this stage, the electronic salesman had not yet been invited inside the house. But, already, a place was being laid for him at the table.

V

If the basic fuel of the boom was supplied by full employment, if its accelerator was pushed down by Admass, the flywheel, sustaining and building up the revs., was hire purchase. So much the more modern-minded economists, Socialist and Tory alike, now hastened to explain to the few remaining "moralists" still dragging their feet before the dawning age of plenty. The "plain van" required before the war even of the impeccable "Mr. Drage" now passed into the limbo of social history. Far from being shame-faced, housewives in the New Towns were reported to like the Hire Purchase firm's vehicles stopping outside their homes: it showed all and sundry that their credit was good!

In one of his Oxford Street furnishing stores, Mr. Isaac Wolfson, Chairman of Great Universal Stores, a leading exponent of the hire purchase method, opened a special lounge where H.P. customers, seated on "contemporary settees", could view large-screen television while waiting for their hire purchase contracts to be made out and signed. "The whole nation," Mr. Wolfson happily told his stockholders in 1958, "has taken to buying nearly everything on the instalment plan."* In the preceding five years, total instalment credit

---

* A pardonable exaggeration, but in 1953 a survey by the Oxford Institute of Statistics showed that no less than 35 per cent of the better-paid working and less-well-paid lower middle class was buying goods on hire purchase. 13% of households headed by "managers and technical workers"' also had some H.P. debt. A 1956 survey showed half the television sets and one-third of vacuum cleaners being bought on H.P.

debt had doubled. Spreading through all classes and over an ever-wider range of goods, from refrigerators to perambulators, airline tickets to holidays, hire purchase was, indeed, soon to be described as a "Britain's second banking system".

Under this fertilising rain of consumer credit, Mr. Wolfson had watched his organisation's profits spiral from around £1,500,000 in 1945 to £21,500,000 in 1957. Even so, he told his stockholders in 1958, hire purchase sales in Britain still only represented £10 per head of population against £70 a head in the United States.

"You will, therefore, see what the potentialities are . . ."

About half the total of hire purchase debt was incurred in the purchase of cars—around half of all second-hand ones were bought that way. Thus two of the most potent mechanisms in the shaping of the new way of life were geared together—with impressive effect.

When the New Town of Harlow was on the drawing board, one garage was planned for every ten dwellings. By the time Harlow was half built demand had forced up the ratio to one garage to every two homes. The number of cars in use was to double in the Fifties, reaching the socially critical point where travel by private car began to imperil the viability of public transport.*

But as significant as the growth from one car to every seven families at the beginning of the decade to one car in every three-and-a-half families at the end of it, was the fact that the greatest part of this expansion of car ownership was accounted for by new owners among skilled manual and lower-paid white collar workers.**

Social historians writing of an earlier period have often noted the effects of the "safety bicycle" in widening the horizons of the masses. But if the bicycle was a means to an end, the car was

* According to Sir John Elliot, Chairman of London Transport, about half London's bus routes were by 1956 unprofitable "because of the enormous growth of private car and motor-cycle travel". Provincial transport undertakings and the railways reported a similar trend.

** Survey, growth of car ownership 1957–60 by social grade of household, quoted *Financial Times*, 20th October, 1960.

both means and end. Its very possession conferred on its owner an extra dimension, a psycho-social, as well as a physical, mobility.

The social and economic development of the Fifties was indeed paced by the motor-car. A machine of some 20,000 component parts, symbol of the multitudinous skills of advanced industrial civilisation, it was a central generator of industrial activity, the spinning gyroscope of Continuous Consumption, worked for, work-providing, pivotal in an immense complex of industries.

Physically, it was the machine whose challenge was most visible, as it choked the circulation of our towns, and, with each passing year, set its mark more firmly on our landscape. But its less visible effects were more far-reaching. As the Common Man climbed into his new—or more probably second-hand—car, touched the starter, and depressed the accelerator, he rode off not merely from town to suburb or country, but also from one way of life to another. As the cars rolled off the assembly lines and into the new garages they released latent acquisitive instincts, stirred dormant ambitions, and acted like magnets, drawing towards themselves all the newly necessary "consumer durables", the "target goods", "prestige goods", "emulation goods" which were now appearing on the British Common Man's horizon.

Already the "problem of incentives" which had so worried poor Sir Stafford Cripps seemed to belong to some distant, half-forgotten world.

As for our lamentable "poverty of desire", it afflicted us no longer.

26. "Housewives' Choice"

"In her function as a consumer an immense amount of a woman's personality is engaged. Success here is as vitalising to her as success in his chosen sphere to a man."

—Mary Grieve, Editor of *Woman*, addressing the Advertising Conference, 1957.

"Lord Teynsham asked the Government whether it was true that a window displaying a Nativity Scene in the Warrington showrooms of the Electricity Board depicted the Three Wise Men proffering a washing machine, an electric cooker, and a refrigerator. . . ."

—House of Lords debates, 20th December, 1955.

IN THE old battle of "Women's Rights" little remained but mopping-up operations. For thirty years Governments had saluted the principle of equal pay for equal work while protesting that, unfortunately, the financial position made this quite, quite impossible. Then, suddenly, in 1955, in the civil service and in teaching the thing was done.* The long-standing civil service rule barring the employment of women after marriage had been dropped a little earlier. Almost without a fight, the last male strongholds were falling. In 1946 even the Foreign Office had opened its doors to women. In the Fifties, Oxford (and later Cambridge) overcame its traditional monasticism at least to the point of removing the historic quota limitation on women undergraduates, which the Warden of Wadham now

---

* This concession, to be realised in stages over seven years, did not extend to the industrial employees of the Government, much less to industry itself.

boldly declared to have been "most foolish, out-of-date, finicky". Women's "societies" were at last admitted to be "colleges" with full status, opening up—theoretically!—the possibility of a woman Vice-Chancellor and women proctors. And if the Oxford Union still wavered,* the House of Lords in January, 1959, grasped the nettle and resolved on a motion of Lord Reading to do what it had hitherto repeatedly refused to do—admit hereditary peeresses in their own right. A powder room was already installed—the first four women life peers had been introduced the previous October. By the end of the Fifties, only the Church,** the London Stock Exchange, the Jockey Club and a few Pall Mall clubs continued to hold out.

Yet to the veterans of the Cause, the victory seemed somehow strangely hollow. The younger generation, they complained, when they met to pay annual tribute to the memory of Mrs. Pankhurst, had let them down. Over a quarter of a century after women gained the vote, their representation had reached its all-time peak in the "revolutionary" Parliament of 1945— 24 members out of 625. The House, lamented a woman M.P., was still "a masculine citadel". Things were somewhat more encouraging in local government,† but it had to be admitted that however "valuable on committees" women might be, as public figures their impact was minimal. It would have been difficult to point to a single female figure in the emancipated Fifties who could command a quarter of the authority of a Florence Nightingale, a Josephine Butler, an Annie Besant, a Mary Kingsley, a Beatrice Webb or any of the remarkable Victorian women who left so powerful an impress on that age when the mere thought of votes for women was blasphemy.

* The Oxford Union capitulated in February, 1962, by a two-thirds majority vote admitting women to debating membership.
** In the Convocation of Canterbury of 1956, the Archbishop of Canterbury spoke in favour of a "speaking ministry" for women as opposed to a "ministry of the sacraments". But even this was rejected. The R.C., Methodist and Presbyterian churches likewise barred women from their priesthood. A few provincial stock exchanges theoretically admitted women.
† Outstandingly so in the County of London, where the L.C.C. had around one-third women members. In the Fifties, the L.C.C. had two women chairmen of the whole Council, and a deputy chairman.

L

"Most women," summed up the former suffragette, Vera Brittain, in 1953, "still occupy positions as substitute-delegates, vice-chairmen, sub-editors, and assistant-secretaries." If a quarter of the nation's doctors were now women, these were, in practice, mainly concerned with women's and children's diseases. If thousands of women worked in banks, the first woman bank manager (i.e. of a branch of a clearing bank) was appointed only in 1958. If there were 400 women in the Administrative Class of the Civil Service, they could claim only one Permanent Secretary and a couple of Deputy Secretaries.* Despite the example of such pioneers as Dame Caroline Haslett, only about fifty women engineers of all types were training each year. In industry, indeed, England—in this respect behind France—was still far from realising "equal pay for equal work". Anyhow, in practice, work relatively rarely was "equal". The traditional division of labour between men and women, broken by the urgencies of war, had quickly reasserted itself and women in industry once again did the dull repetitive jobs, "a position"—as Ferdynand Zweig defined it— "somewhere in the middle between the adolescent and the mature male". Their national average wage was about half that of men's.

The New Woman, in short, had turned out to be remarkably similar to the old woman after all. She was better as a social worker or as a novelist than as an engineer; as a personnel officer or B.B.C. producer—"helping other people to create things" as Mary Adam, assistant to the Controller of Television put it—than as a politician or trade union leader (even in unions where women predominated).** A striking postwar success was in police work, again dealing principally (but by no means wholly) with women and girls. By 1956 there were only four police forces in the British Isles without their complement of women officers.

* Women solicitors numbered 300, or 2·5 per cent of the profession; there were 1,000 architects (5 per cent), 1,100 accountants (3 per cent) and about 100 women members of all the professional engineering institutions. There were 1,000 dentists (out of 12,600) and 10,000 doctors.
** E.g. in the weavers' unions there was only one woman secretary among seventy officials. Of 7,250,000 women at work, only 1,700,000 were members of trade unions.

' . . . . And now the B.B.C. takes great pleasure in presenting ' Hamlet,' by W. Shakespeare—as it would be produced by sponsored T.V.'

" Granpa, that's the washer, not the telly."

32 and 33. The spectre of "Americanisation" haunted the debates 1952–54 on the future of Television. The news that a chimpanzee named Fred J. Muggs had appeared in the commercials interrupting the Coronation film on U.S. television seemed to confirm the worst fears—illustrated by *Cummings* in the *Daily Express* in June, 1953. But pure B.B.C. or impure Commercial, television was now getting a real grip on the nation. The Box became the centre-piece of a new way of life at a speed that was bewildering for the older generation—as a *Sunday Dispatch* pocket cartoon (*left*) makes clear.

Television, with its voracious appetite for novelty
completed the machinery
of Admass and ushered in
the reign of the Gimmick.
34 and 35. A butcher's
apron and a beard made
Philip Harben (*above*) a
household word, while
Miss Norma Sykes, a
Blackpool landlady's
daughter, was trans-
formed into the "fabu-
lous" Sabrina by the
simple device of remain-
ing mute. Insistently promoted, the cult of "Vital
Statistics" brought a
boom to the foundation
garment industry.

Galling as it might be to the old-time feminist, women appeared reasonably content with this state of affairs. Fewer and fewer women in all classes now felt it worth while to try to disguise the "dominant interest". At Wallasey, a survey of high school girls showed that 74 per cent were so anxious to get on with their husband-hunting that they left school without completing their courses. Much the same was true of Manchester, headmistresses of that sober city agreed. Women now made up about a quarter of the nation's university students. But "the chances of a girl coming down heart-free are growing less", reported a *Times* correspondent. "Her length of service to an employer is dwindling. It can be as low as eighteen months, and a working life of more than five years for a woman graduate is becoming a rarity." At Oxford itself, the women's secretary of the University Appointments Committee publicly regretted that she had not studied geography—"since so much of her time is spent in considering which places are within reach of towns where her candidates' fiancés have their jobs."

One of the first uses to which women had, in fact, turned their enhanced economic independence had been to provide, so to speak, their own dowries. Financed by joint earnings, marriages of brides under twenty-one had reached double the 1938 level by the first half of the Fifties and now constituted three out of every ten marriages. By the age of twenty-five more than half the women of England were lawfully wedded wives. For the remainder the risk of being "left on the shelf" had rarely been less. Marriage rates, reported the Registrar-General in 1955, were being continuously "maintained above the highest level ever reached in the nineteenth century, even for a single year".

The ever-willing regiment of spinsters upon whom Governments had long relied for the cut-rate staffing of their schools and hospitals was rapidly melting away. The maiden aunt would soon have vanished from the scene she had these many years adorned.

II

If, to the ex-suffragettes, the young women of the Fifties might seem shamelessly to hug their chains, they were enabled to do so by the knowledge that the shackles were now more decorative than effective. The melodramatic, once-for-all choice, 'career or marriage?', was largely obsolete. Jobs were now taken up or laid down as convenient. And even if careers were not pursued, the women of the Fifties were not unaware that at this juncture in the nation's social and economic evolution history had allotted to woman in her traditional place a central and dynamic role—an influence and power greater than was to be gained by emulation of the male.

Year by year, since the war, through all the economic crises, the war scares, the changes of government, the tremendous process of rehousing the people had gone quietly ahead. By 1958 10 million people—one in every five in Britain—were living in new, postwar, homes.

Again this was a process which had been going on in the interwar years, but which had now accelerated, broadened and reached the point of accumulation where it emerged as a nation-wide social transformation. With the new factories, the New Towns, all the new estates, a new environment declared itself.

A new environment that clearly called for a new way of life.

In the shaping of this way of life—or the much canvassed new "standard of living"—the role of woman, the homemaker, would at any time have been important. But now it was crucial. For, liberated at an early date from cradle-watching, spending not only the household's money but "her own" (one-third of wives, twice the 1939 proportion, having jobs), fashion's eager slave, the woman of the Fifties possessed at once the time, the resources and the inclination to bring to perfection the new arts of continuous consumption. She was the essential pivot of the People's Capitalism, and its natural heroine.

Nor did she have to go far to get on to terms with the scientific revolution. It came to her. Even if her home itself was not new, a substantial part of the materials entering it were. In the late Forties, the first nylon shirts had been displayed in solitary splendour in the more exclusive outfitter's windows, priced at six or seven guineas. We shall never know how many wives watched their husband's precious nylon shirt disappearing as they boiled it in an effort to restore its whiteness. But they learned. Coached by the manufacturers, they were soon expert in the precise water temperature, the appropriate washing technique, the correct dial setting on the new thermostatically controlled irons, for each new fabric. And new fabrics—their chain molecules fixed under a variety of spells—seemed to be emerging from the laboratories almost every week.

For with the full development of nylon the chemist had really come into his social kingdom. A flavour of the *Ersatz* and "lower class" had lingered about prewar rayon, ex-"art. silk". But nylon, the first true synthetic, enjoyed its glamour in its own right and had enough of it to shed some over all women. Nylon and the British-invented terylene not only broke down the venerable textile traditionalism of wool, silk, mohair and cotton, but dissolved class lines also. Since both attracted dirt and could be so easily washed they also launched another minor revolution—in personal hygiene.

As the chemist extended his operations the simple old snobberies of "costly materials" lost much of their edge. He waved his wand over once-prosaic plastics, and the familiar world was transformed. Suddenly buckets were flexible and a deep translucent red. Buying a table, the housewife sought the new heat-resistant finishes. Polishing it, she invoked the aid of "dirt-repelling silicones". The benefits could be real even when the "science" offered was pseudo. In 1951 the detergents —developed during the war as soap substitutes—were reincarnated under brand names, and commercially marketed. Washing-day, once a steamy affair of rubbing-boards, coppers and elbow-grease, now became a semi-mystical process involving possibly "the miracle double-action Bluinite". Here as in so many other ways in these postwar years the saving in physical wear-and-tear for the average woman was immense.

The kitchen, not long ago synonymous with woman's subjugation, now became the shining badge of her triumph. The temple of those twin symbols of the new life, the refrigerator and the washing machine, it was, as speculative builders knew, "the most important room in the house" which—to judge from much that was written in these years—often appeared to have been constructed principally in order to accommodate it. Here—and this was certainly a comment on our age—rather than in boudoir or drawing-room, was the heart of the feminine dream. Warming to their new role, British manufacturers of pots and pans who had hitherto confined themselves to staid creams and greens now burst into a profusion of colours and finishes. "Science" crowned their tribute with "gleaming" gadgetry, whirring and wires.

People were eating better—more milk, cheese, eggs and poultry, rather more fruit and vegetables, more biscuits, less bread and less jam. Nevertheless, the conservative British male, particularly the proletarian male, continued to be dedicated to the "stodge of life" until mid-decade—when "science" launched another attack on tradition. Between 1955 and 1957 sales of the new deep-frozen foods doubled, and in the following three years doubled again. The frozen food cabinet appeared even in the little corner shop and the prewar "canning" revolution with its menu of tinned salmon, baked beans and pineapple was overtaken by the postwar "deep-freeze" revolution of frozen chicken or fish fingers, frozen chips, frozen peas and frozen strawberry mousse.

But the invisible effects of science's domestic inroads were perhaps more important than the visible. Historically, anthropologically, women have generally been seen as society's traditionalists, handing down through the years its lore, customs and complex of tribal prejudice. In England this would seem to have been broadly true at least of women of the largest social class down to the war.

It was a view, it began to seem, which might yet need to be drastically revised. The New Woman of the Fifties might not conform to the vision of H. G. Wells or Mrs. Pankhurst, but on "the new frontiers of living"—as the admen put it—she blazed the trail.

III

Every week in the Forties and Fifties scores of families pulled up roots in towns and streets where they and theirs had lived for generations. For the collier's family leaving some dark and huddled Durham pit-row for Berthold Lubetkin's bright New Town of Peterlee, for the Cockneys from "the Buildings" making the twenty-five mile trek to the wide open spaces of Frederick Gibberd's Harlow, emigration to Canada could hardly have brought a change more radical. A lifetime of "slipping around the corner" to pub or club was abruptly broken off. Mum—miles away now—couldn't "pop in" for a cup of tea and a natter.* Sitting on the doorstep to watch the world go by was "not done". In any case, all one would have seen would have been a row of front doors, brightly painted, neat—and closed. In those first few weeks after moving in, New Town doctors learned to expect many calls in the middle of the night, arising, they explained with admirable tolerance, from "feelings of insecurity".

It was, perhaps, in an extreme and simplified form, the characteristic insecurity of the Age. Yet as the weeks went by and grew into months, the night calls first tapered away, then ceased. The wife had seen behind the neighbour's lemon-coloured front door; her husband had, by invitation, surveyed the neighbour's back garden. With a two-year start, the Joneses were already enviably ahead: they had a "console" TV, a new "Princess" pram, a "Hotpoint" washing machine, an "automatic" cooker, "Prestcold" fridge and a budgerigar in a bright blue cage. There was no time to lose. The hire purchase contracts were signed; overtime was located; the wife got a job. By the old working-class standards the rent was already sky-high. But the rent was only the beginning. By comparison with the old easy-going, hand-to-mouth way of life, what was being embarked upon now was high finance. (If the night calls on the doctor ceased, the day calls didn't!**)

This immense change from the old "face-to-face" living of the street to the new "window-to-window" living of the "avenue" was not, of course, an experience peculiar to the postwar years; but it had never affected so many people in so few years.

In the mid-nineteenth century the noviciate middle classes, proudly packing their new homes with the products of the new

* In their Bethnal Green survey (*Family and Kinship in East London*, 1957) Young and Wilmot found that one-half of the married women had seen their mothers in the previous 24 hours.

** A postwar survey by a team from the London School of Hygiene of the large Oxhey Housing Estate near Watford—to which Londoners were moved—showed anxiety neuroses running at twice the national figure. Cases of sleep disturbances and undue tiredness were four times, headaches three times, and duodenal ulcers 2½ times, more frequent than the number expected from national experience.

industrial machine, had turned for guidance to the indefatigable Mrs. Beeton, whose, 1,172-page *Book of Household Management* sold no less than two million copies in the nine years between 1861 and 1870. A hundred years later the new transients-en-masse turned to the colour-gravure women's magazines. The circulation graphs of two of these, 4½d. weeklies broadly aimed at the "endless middle", were among the most astonishing cultural phenomena of the time. From a base of 75,000 in 1938, the sales of *Woman* reached 2,225,000 by 1952 and 3,500,000 five years later, when the magazine was being read by one in every two women in the country between the ages of sixteen and forty-four. By the mid-Fifties 12 million women were reading two women's magazines a week from a field of fifty—and new ones were still being launched, quickly attaining sales running into millions.

For the old-time feminists—and indeed for new ones, if there were any—the women's magazines must have been the bitterest pill of all. The world they offered their readers was exclusively female; they enclosed them in a sort of portable purdah. Their fiction, though more sophisticated both in setting and manner than formerly, was inspired, according to Miss Mary Grieve, Editor of *Woman*, by "a unanimous acceptance that to be loved and loving is better than to be brainy, rich, or nobly born". Yet the most important business of the women's magazines now lay not with dreams, but with their realisation—at least in token form. The pages that mattered were the practical pages that overflowed with colourfully illustrated information on how to entertain, how to dress, how to be well groomed on a typist's pay, how to cook beef strogonoff, make a lampshade, knit a two-piece, have a baby, tell a child about sex, keep a boy-friend in hand and a husband uxorious. If sometimes conveyed with a spurious gaiety, the advice was for the most part sound, carefully considered and attuned to the *Zeitgeist*. Five-and-a-half million women wrote off trustingly to *Woman* in a single twelvemonth much as they might once have gone to Mum (who probably now also had an anxious letter of inquiry in the magazine's mail).

The transition which the women's weeklies smoothed was one not merely from class to class, but from one form of society to another; from one national period—on the far side of the gulf of the war—to another, very different. They were themselves very characteristic products of the time. Since costly colour-gravure presses made possible lavish presentation at very low unit cost, they were no longer required to make a choice between the "conspicuous consumption" of *Vogue*, the lower middle-class cosiness of *Home Chat*, or the warm naïveté of such old "only-a-working-girl" favourites as *Red Letter*. They were, like the Health Service, truly national.

Under their guidance the message of the Festival was translated into domestic, more absorbable, terms. The past was past. Out with the leaded lights and mock Tudor rafters! An England which had discarded Empire needed a clean sweep and a new start inside the home also. The materials were at hand. The three-piece suite in uncut moquette, with the "Jacobean" sideboard, set out geometrically as if to establish the stable order of society, was no longer obligatory. On the contrary, a studied informality and flexibility were to be the new "keynotes".

But if Olde Worlde "dark oak" was out, the austere distempered walls of the "Modern" of the Thirties were likewise rejected. Walls were clothed in wallpapers of much improved design—and, possibly, if the occupants were in the "Contemporary" vanguard, the fourth wall might be done in different style or boldly contrasting colour. On the carpets and elsewhere bold single colours were being used with a new and notable lack of inhibition. Bloated armchairs which had once blocked rooms like overfed Edwardian clubmen were now increasingly replaced by lightweight affairs whose structure—now visible— paid at least some minimal regard to the human frame and whose foam-rubber seats were detachable.

Before the war there had been little to bridge the gap between cabinet-makers' furniture and the mass-produced gimcrack of mock-Grand. "Contemporary", with its cleaner lines, more visible structure and use of "natural" woods, was well suited to machine production. In these years several large manufacturers like Mr. Lucian Ercolani and Messrs. Gomme, of the "G-Plan", began quantity production and publicising of a wide range of well-designed and inexpensive furniture, acceptable alike in home of banker or vanman.

Here again were signs that we were at last ceasing to be

embarrassed by the machine and were now learning to use it. The prevailing note of the "new home" was of a certain quiet functionalism, not the "Functionalism" of the Thirties, but a common-sense assimilated functionalism that came from a growing appreciation of the way in which science could offer efficiency and comfort at minimum cost and fuss.

Another thing that suggested that in this respect some sort of turning-point might have been reached was the fact that a serious assault had at last been mounted on the Olde English Draught. The long sacrosanct open coal fire was now challenged by a wide range of heating systems from slow-combustion stoves to infra-red fitments. And not, probably, since the invention of the electric lamp, had so much detailed practical attention been given to room lighting.

Yet there was no longer the bigoted insistence on functionalism as the only path to salvation and it was characteristic that— possibly to soften the often rather surgical note introduced by "contemporary" direct and multi-point lighting—there was a surge of enthusiasm for indoor vegetation. Many a woman of the Fifties nourished her *Tradescantia* or *Philodendron* with all the devotion her grandmother had bestowed upon the maiden-hair fern in the old art pot.

Even materially these were large changes; when their psychological implications were considered they became much greater. Naturally they were not immediately and universally accepted. But the remarkable thing in a people so deeply traditionalist as the English was the extent to which they were. In 1953 an exhibition at Charing Cross Underground Station placed rooms furnished "old style" and "new style" side by side. Voting revealed an almost equal division between those who found the new "deficient in comfort and cosiness" and those who found the old "dark and depressing". But when the under-thirty-five's only were taken, the informality and "open-ness" of the "contemporary" room won hands down.

IV

Traditionalist resistance was made more difficult because not only were so many agents of social change at work, but some of the most potent were at work within the home itself. Not the least of these was TV.

In the intimate history of most British families in the Fifties the Day the Television Came forms a sort of postwar watershed. For many thousands the very act of acquisition, a financial transaction practically obligatory yet larger than had ever before been undertaken, acted as a kind of initiation into the new consumers' society.

Deriving prestige from its costliness and "scientific" mystery, the set moved at once into the centre of the family circle, displaced the fire over which the British had huddled for generations and proceeded to reorganise the household's life around itself.

In those first few "post-Television" weeks many a long-cherished custom was quite casually shattered. In Northumberland a miners' lodge appealed to the Coal Board to speed the fitting of bathrooms in the pit-rows. Miners' daughters, it explained, were objecting to Dad lingering to watch TV while he swilled away the coal dust in his tin bath before the fire. The sacrosanct ritual of meals was broken. Gathered before the hypnotic screen on the low "television chairs" that now made their appearance in the shops, families took their food from large "television plates", gropingly, in the half-darkness. The pubs and the Dogs languished. The sales of draught beer, so long the sustainer of the Broad Masses, slumped. The sales of bottled, and, later, canned, beer soared: it could be consumed *en famille* in front of the set.

In these years television worked in potent symbiosis with rehousing and the woman-centred "consumer revolution" to bring about a return to the home and a preoccupation with the home such as had hardly been seen since mid-Victorian times. Even football, "the Match", so long the heart of the Saturday ritual for millions, began from 1950 onwards to shed some of its crowds. At the cinema, where only a year or two ago patient queues had endlessly waited, the gaps in the stalls yawned wider each year. Between 1954 and 1959 more than 800 cinemas were obliged to shut down. Admissions halved. As the neon died and the glittering chandeliers in the foyer gathered dust, the "Super Cinema", domed and gilded, or chromiumed and tiled, lush carpeted and enveloped in the scented ooze of the Mighty

Wurlitzer, joined its predecessor, the Gin Palace, in the vast and curious lumber room of Britain's social history. The Common Man had no longer an acute need of one-and-nine-penceworth of vicarious luxury. With the aid of his new house, his car, the H.P., his wife's magazines, and his do-it-yourself kit, he could build an only slightly less colourful—and much more satisfying—world for himself at home.

For the new domesticity—unlike the Victorian version—was very much a joint, bi-sexual creation, a characteristic product of the "partnership marriage". If the Little Woman was busy applying one of the new quick-drying "wonder paints" with one of the new sheepskin paint rollers, her husband might very well be sawing hardboard, lagging the cistern or poring over some blueprint from one of the "do-it-yourself" periodicals which had attained immense sales at record speeds.

Arriving from America in the second half of the Fifties, the "do-it-yourself" movement greatly eased the financial strains of changing patterns of living. Almost three-quarters of all wallpapers sold were now being sold directly over the counter to the public. The sales of portable electric drills zoomed. Wood shops were besieged. Some alert furniture manufacturers now took to marketing their products in pieces. "All you need," they advertised, "is a screwdriver." By this time there appeared to be many Englishmen who found this appeal irresistible.

As pride of proprietorship grew, periods of immurement lengthened, and "the local" grew emptier. But when paint brush and putty knife were laid aside for a moment, and the pub revisited, it was now increasingly likely—in all classes— that husband and wife would go there together. The old sexual segregation—so long a mark of working-class culture—was, —like so much else in it,—progressively breaking down.

But the new homes, if better equipped and designed, were still often stunted. Perhaps that was why—much as the lifer in his cell makes a friend of a mouse—the families of the Fifties so frequently kept tropical fish in aquaria, or budgerigars in nickel-plated "palaces", furnished with tilting ladders, mirrors, "bobbing-willies" and bells. The cage-bird population of Britain had multiplied by ten since the war, reaching six million by 1956. But even the keeping of budgerigars had its anxieties. "Lost" notices, rainstreaked, pinned to garden gate or tree, and appealing for news of the errant family virtuoso—"blue and yellow, answering to the name of Jimmie"—became a poignant feature of the suburbs.

There were, in fact, now more budgerigars in Britain than dogs, one of the odder sidelights on the social history of the Fifties. Yet despite all that tiny rooms and municipal housing committees could do, the doggieness of the British remained unabated. The Tailwagger's Club reached a new peak of one million members, all duly issued with badges of rank as Staff Sergeant, Corporal or Private, dogs. For the Dog World, too, reflected the new standard of living. Not only had the number of pedigree dogs doubled since the war but if your cat or dog could read, he or she was now in the enviable position of being able to order from appetising advertisements a fine range of canned goods—Kit-e-Kat, Purr or Pussikin, Wow, Woof, or Meet ("Chunks of Rich Meat in Nourishing Jelly"), Winalot ("PROTEIN to repair tissues, MINERALS to build bones") or the "multi-vitaminised" Tibs. By the mid-Fifties the dogs' and cats' dinner industry had reached an annual turnover of £10 millions, and was marching triumphantly on towards new heights.*

Nor could anything shake the devotion of the British to their gardens (which indeed had often preceded and fed the new devotion to the house). "Mr. Middleton", the much-loved sage of the B.B.C.'s compost heap, died, and Fred Streeter reigned in his stead. And as his and other earthy voices rumbled from the radios of the land a legion of new gardeners who had moved out of the town streets hung on to their wise words and learned to eye the few square yards of clayey earth behind their new homes with possessive peasant pride. Earlier and earlier each year Woolworth's counters overflowed with brilliant-hued seed packets, compact with promise, and as every Swiss had his rifle, so now almost every Englishman had his rake and hoe, determined—as Giles indicated in an effective cartoon—to "get his plants in", whether or not the Americans exploded the BIGGEST EVER H-BOMB.

* 1962—£23 m.

V

The Victorians would have had no doubt about what their
attitude should be to all this home-centred activity. Their great
grandchildren were not so fortunate. As the Fifties proceeded,
the rumble of perplexed debate about "crime-in-prosperity"
and alleged moral laxity was deepened—often from the direction of the intellectual Left—by much bemoaning of the "New
Materialism". The women's magazines, it was pointed out,
virtually ignored the outer world. Abandoning the community
concern that developed in the war years, people were selfishly
shutting themselves up in their private houses, or in that small
house on wheels, the motor-car. They were polishing their cars
or hanging wallpaper while—so to speak—Rome burned.

Less harsh interpretations seemed possible. The connection
between the ideas of William Morris and the portable electric
drill was not, certainly, immediately obvious, yet nothing was
more reasonable than that the ordinary man, deprived of the
opportunity of expressing his individuality in his working hours
should increasingly seek to do so in his leisure. And these were
the years in which millions gained for the first time the means to
do so—the leisure, the working materials, the living space and
—not least—the privacy.

The new proprietary pride was, after all, a very modest
pride. If the made-over homes were expressions of status, it
was not necessarily of *class* status, but of human—or individual
—status. In these matters in England there was so much leeway
to make up. When the new base had been built, then forays into
the outer world could be undertaken with new energy, curiosity
and assurance.

The great home-building period of Victorian times, the
spread of bourgeois comfort then, had provided the base for
the great Victorian novelists; it had produced smugness, but
it had also produced the prophets of Socialism, and how much
else besides.

Thus the precedents were not altogether discouraging.
But now not only was the base vastly greater in size, and hence
morally and socially inchoate, but the machinery of the market

was infinitely more complex. Cool, clear choices became difficult. The packages were all so distractingly attractive that
it seemed almost superfluous to inquire about the contents.

It was at this point that the concentration of economic
power in women, as consumers, caused a quiver of doubt.

When Gordon Selfridge opened his opulent new American-
style store in Oxford Street in 1909, and declared it "Dedicated
to the Service of Women", the notion had seemed novel—even
quaint. But now, fifty years later, many powerful commercial
and industrial organisations had discovered a similar dedication.

If to the English husband his spouse was still very apt to be
"the old girl" or "the wife", to the English advertising man she
had become an intensely desirable creature to be wooed with
Transatlantic ardour. In the once sternly masculine domain of
automobile engineering, torque and gear-ratios surrendered
to styling and colour—which was now said to follow, with rather
less than a year's lag, the changes in dress colour fashions.
In its new advertising the staid Westminster Bank pictured the
manager, sitting behind his desk, chatting with a smart young
woman, while the Midland put out a gaily illustrated new
client's guide which referred to "accidental" overdrafts as
"very naughty". Even the author of the slogan BASS FOR MEN
now felt it necessary to accompany this with a large female
head, and the legend, "The Kind of Man I Like Drinks Bass!"

It was not necessary to maintain that this exaltation of the
Female Principle—however novel in England—was wholly
unfortunate in its effects. It was something, after all, to have
broken down the large British motor manufacturers who had
stuck to their Wellingtonian "straight-up-and-down" approach
right until 1948, when the "revolutionary" Morris Minor
appeared at the Motor Show like a dapper—and profoundly
un-English—ladybird with a grin.

"Not for a generation," said the Council for Industrial
Design, "have so many people been interested in better design."

Yet, to the male at least, it sometimes seemed that this new
New Woman played her role of heroine of the People's Capitalism with a dangerous facility. Long conditioned to the pursuit
of fashion, notoriously given to "impulse-buying", naturally
attracted by bright packaging, with emotive keys well established

and standard, she seemed in her new economic power to open up in our society a large and possibly critical area to Admassian manipulation.

For all their practical editorial content the women's magazines were vast compendiums of advertising. The editorial content meshed with the advertising content—closely, though not usually directly. "Advertisers who want a better motivated women's magazine for family selling should look at this week's issue of *Woman's Realm*," proudly claimed an Advertisement Director, above the heading 'Greater Editorial Insight'.

Thus intensively rehearsed in their role as pace-setters of the consumer democracy, the women of the Fifties sometimes seemed to be about to realise the worst fears of all those males who had fought so long and so strenuously against "Votes for Women". As the beauty editors issued their *Diktats*, the slimming cult held the nation in its fanatic grip, and as each new system of starving without malnutrition succeeded its predecessor—the bananas-and-milk diet, the all-protein-and-fat-diet, the Swedish milk diet, the Gayelord Hauser diet— austerity descended on a million dinner tables, the Little Woman rotated her calorie counter (supplied by *Woman*), and thousands of men, succumbing, were to be heard exchanging notes on pounds lost and gained in a manner which would certainly have baffled their Edwardian fathers.*

Newspapers—the popular ones at least—were now largely edited for women; female journalists overflowed from the Fashion and Home pages where they had once been confined to fill large areas of newsprint, notably increasing the level of brittleness, malice and discernment. Editors, with well-developed instincts of self-preservation, sought the "woman's angle" on almost every subject from finance to pig-iron production. Even *The Times* now acquired a Women's Page. Meanwhile, the women's magazines, monstrously bloated with the offers of competing manufacturers, bled the general magazines of both advertising revenue and family pence, so that, one by one, they gave up the unequal struggle and perished.

* "Scientific medicine" added its contribution: In 1959, 5·6 million National Health prescriptions were issued for drugs intended to suppress appetite in the control of obesity.

For many years the dog that symbolised and represented Britain had been the bulldog. In the Fifties, necessarily, symbols changed. But the results were sometimes a little odd. In terms of popularity, the Top Dog, now lolloping far ahead of all other breeds, was the miniature poodle, a sagacious animal, and unrivalled, as the fashion photographers knew, for setting off a dress.

27.   Semi-detached, Open Plan

[The 'classless society' is one in which] "while the occupations and the incomes of individuals varied, they would nevertheless live in much the same environment, would enjoy similar standards of health and education, would find different positions accessible to varying abilities equally accessible to all of them, would intermarry freely with each other, would be equally immune from the more degrading forms of poverty and equally secure against economic oppression."

—R. H. Tawney, *Equality*, 1931.

"It is not possible to construct for Banbury and district a simple *n*-fold class system. . . ."

—Margaret Stacey, *Tradition and Change: A Study of Banbury*, 1960.

"We have to wipe the ice-cream off the window almost every day now."

—Officials of Mappin and Webb, the jewellers, explaining "sadly" the closure of their Oxford Street store, 1955.

THE BRITISH PROLETARIAT, though the original modern proletariat and the inspiration of Marx, had notably failed fully to live up to the Marxist specifications. The British "working classes", nevertheless, had possessed a distinctive and well-established philosophy and value-system which had coloured a very large area of the national life. Based on mutual aid, on standing together with one's mates, it had underlined, for instance, the virtues of not being a "boss's man", of not trying to get "above oneself" but rather of maintaining with dignity and pride one's proper place and function, "knowing the job", but not "spoiling the job". It had offered, in some ways, the freedom of the private soldier in the vast anonymity of the ranks—with similar severe limitations and similar large opportunities for irreverence and for the enjoyment of day-to-day living. And if this position was at some points modified by Nonconformist chapel or political conventicle, the ambitions these nourished had in the circumstances of the time transcended individualism to become class—and hence human—aspirations.

But now some of these long sacrosanct attitudes were beginning to weaken. Strange things were happening to the British Working Man. Trade unions were reporting difficulties in restraining members from "persistent hogging of overtime"; in some areas, workers were said to be "following overtime around the district". Many travelled long distances to secure a high pay packet. Others were taking on a second, "independent", job after regular working hours.

A new sort of working class was coming into being. How it would go forward, what values it would develop, only the future could tell. The one thing certain was that it could not go back. For the old qualities, the old attitudes, had derived their strength and consistency from the way in which they had corresponded to the needs of the old situation—first among which was the need to survive. They were further preserved by the segregation of the vast working-class industrial ghettoes with their distinctive dress, food, furniture, manners and language.

Now, not only was the threat of disaster for the most part removed, but there had come into being a universal, all-class environment, a largely common apparatus of life. At the same time, the physical stigmata by which the working class was recognised and recognised itself were vanishing. If death rates of adults and infants—vastly reduced as the latter were—still showed some surviving class bias, when one came to the children and young persons a new equality was manifest. In 1954 the L.C.C.'s Principal School Medical Officer reported that "marked differences between the measurements of children from different parts of London had now largely disappeared".*

Technology, continuing the levelling process, was taking much of the dirt and sweat out of work. In the shipyards, prefabrication and welding broke up the clangorous old partnership of riveter, heater and holder-on; in the Potteries, the old fireman, king of the ovens, tending his smoking kilns day and night, was giving place to a button-pusher, setting in motion the mechanism of clean, silent, electric tunnel ovens; on the building sites, the former hod-carrier was attendant upon hoists, bulldozers, trench-cutting machines; on the railways the sweaty, gritty struggle of man *versus* boiler on the open footplate was being exchanged for an upholstered seat in an electric or diesel locomotive with windscreen wipers and demisters and the neat hot-plate for the making of tea. Even the docker drove a fork-lifter now, while, at sea, the shipowner who wished to remain in business took care to provide even the crews of "dirty British coasters" with cabins, showers, laundries and common rooms.

In the bright new factory—or the refitted old one—the driving "get-on-or-get-out" foreman was now almost as great a rarity as the beer-swilling worker or the brawny man-in-a-muffler of the old-fashioned cartoonists. The very word "labourer" had come to seem a little shocking and where the reality itself was unavoidable personnel departments were sometimes at pains to devise attractive euphemisms.** But in fact the old army of "labourers" was now giving way to the new army of the "semi-skilled", the blue-collared attendants upon machine processes who occupied a much more indeterminate place in the scheme of things. As the new industries and techniques grew and multiplied, as mass-production increasingly replaced "jobbing", the time-honoured hierarchic world of crafts and skills was enfiladed and outflanked.

* *Report on the Heights and Weights of School Pupils in the County of London in 1954.* Also Dr. J. N. Morris, Social Medicine Unit, M.R.C., in address to British Sociological Association, 1959. In some northern towns where the first industrial revolution had left deeper scars, differences still lingered.

** The jobs which still required brawn or remained tough and dirty increasingly—unless highly paid—failed to find takers. There was now a chronic shortage of boatmen for the canals, of quarrymen, of blacksmiths and, in many places, of roadsweepers.

New supervisory tasks multiplied, too, and here the blue collar world merged into the white, the "new" working class and the "new" middle class from the technical colleges and universities touched hands in a widening No Man's Land.

Anglo-American Productivity reports were still apt to stress the gulf to be found in Britain between "staff" and "men", "office" and "shopfloor". Yet the character of this, too, was changing. That large system of privileges which had once distinguished those in receipt of "salaries" (however puny) from those paid "wages" no longer appeared quite so inevitable and preordained. By 1957 nearly half the nation's male workers were in line for "private" occupational pensions.* Sick pay and "guaranteed" pay were common; "severance" pay—if still comparatively rarely realised—was widely recognised to be a justifiable demand.

In the matter of holidays,—perhaps the most obvious source of violent class contrasts in the past,—levelling-up had been both swift and cumulative. When in 1937 the Holidays-with-Pay Committee began its inquiries, only 1½ million workers were receiving paid holidays under collective agreements. By the end of the war, the number entitled to one week's paid holiday under collective agreement or statutory order had reached 14,000,000. Six years later, the campaign for *two* weeks' paid holiday (in addition to six paid public holidays) was in full swing, and one-third of all workers were estimated to have achieved that goal. In the second half of the decade the fortnight's paid holiday became all but universal.

This (particularly when linked to higher wages and the five-day week) amounted to a minor social revolution in itself. The old "'appy 'ampstead" character of the plebeian "day out" was at last disappearing; it was no longer an explosion or sort of bacchanalia; the "chara" for the "beano" became the luxury motor-coach for the Grand Tour. More than half of the adult population was now going away from home for their holidays, spending an average of £20–25 a head. And though Bournemouth still required more First Class coaches on its trains than any other town in the country, solid Mums and

* Significantly, a scheme was in preparation by which even agricultural workers, a class traditionally underprivileged, would draw an occupational pension of £4 a week at sixty-five.

Dads were now to be observed in large numbers sniffing the ozone of the rich with the proprietary air they would earlier have felt appropriate to Blackpool or Southend. The furthermost reaches of Devon and Cornwall quickly fell before the new invasion, and as Lancashire accents rang out in some once "select" Devon combe or Cornish cove, the "upper middles" who were determined to remain "upper middles" without defilement or dilution, gathered up their dogs, lavender water and nannies and began the long retreat to the recesses of Skye or Connemara.

II

The day came when David Low was moved to produce a cartoon which featured, suitably equipped, "Lower-class Workers", "Middle-class workers" and "Upper-class Workers" —the last seen in fur-coats and top-hats, questioning a policeman.

Low's comprehensiveness was well advised—for if, as so many politicians and others claimed, the working class was "becoming middle class now" it was a sort of middle-classness which lacked the essential spirit, the competitive "onwards-and-upwards" striving of the old one.

In August, 1955, a youth who had turned in a progressive job to earn £14 a week on piecework expounded the new philosophy to a *Manchester Guardian* reporter: "You could never get married on a bare 44-hour week. If you get the opportunity to work, you can get everything in ten years—television, washer, everything. Otherwise you might be banging away all your life!"

As a statement of aims it was mainly interesting for its sublime limitation. If "keeping down with the Atkinsons" was being abandoned in favour of keeping up with them, there was certainly no desire to overtake them. For if aims were now orientated less to self-preservation and more to enjoyment (or "relaxation"), the new attitudes, like the old ones, were formed by circumstances. Although large opportunities of advancement now lay open to working-class youths, only a minority would in fact be able to make use of them. Most would attain their maximum pay level in their twenties, and would be doing the same, or a similar, job when they were sixty. Nor, probably, would they have any say in how the work should be done. On this important level acceptance would be a necessary condition of life; ambition a vain fret. And the real life would be lived, even more than in the past, outside working hours—with the difference that the means to expand and develop in that time-out-of-work now existed.

Yet in this postwar world of large impersonal organisations there were now many members of the so-called middle classes willing to admit that their own occupational vistas were hardly less limited. The "machine revolution" in the office, gaining pace rapidly in the Fifties, dethroned the dignified old senior clerk, the secretary, the book-keeper and ushered in the "factory-office" of operators and "data-processors". Personnel departments, busily grading and labelling, importing "management trainees", possibly from the universities, confined and damped the once diffused fires of ambition.

At the same time the proportion of clerks of working-class origin had now reached one in two. For these at least the idea of organising for collective advance was not wholly foreign. Thus while part of the "working classes" were exploring the possibilities of individualism in the suburbs, part of the "middle classes" were discovering the value of solidarity at the office. In 1946, the Bank Officers' Guild, renamed itself, after a merger, the National *Union* of Bank Employees. An official explained: "Much of the social and economic doctrine that commanded the support of that middle class society to which bank men and women belong is now regarded as effete." In the ten years following this brisk shedding of inhibitions, the union's membership almost doubled until it exceeded the total of the more genteel internal staff "associations".*

The main growth in the trade union movement was indeed now taking place within the "white collar" unions whose organisers reported a widespread change of attitude.**

* It still failed, however to win recognition from the Big Five banks with the exception of Barclays. It had affiliated to the T.U.C. in 1940.
** There were, of course, still enormous gaps—in the insurance offices, for instance. But by 1955 there were thirty-five white collar unions with a total membership of around 1½ million.

N.A.L.G.O., the National and Local Government Officers' Association, a trade union since 1920, grew by 80 per cent in the fifteen years after the war, becoming the seventh largest union in Britain and the largest white collar union in the world; the N.U.T. enlisted over 75 per cent of teachers qualified; and the civil service was now highly organised from top to bottom. In the managerial society, trade union representation, far from being "disloyal", could appear merely neat and proper. And while it was true that most white collar unionists saw their unions as strictly "non-political" negotiating agents, that went for an increasing proportion of manual unionists, too.

Journalists, musicians, actors, ciné-technicians, had for some considerable time been convinced and effective trade unionists. But there were dubious, indeterminate types. The doctors and the teachers, by contrast, were, at their different ends of the scale, exemplars and guardians of the middle-class ethos—and it was the doctors and teachers who were now to display a "militancy" and "solidarity" which many a manual workers' union might have envied. It kept them mutinously in the head-lines for months.

For many years "elementary" school teaching had provided the classic avenue of ascent—or the escape-route—for the working-class boy or girl. For about as many years such teachers had been both patronised and sweated. Their active union, the N.U.T., had been regarded by their grammar school colleagues much as a Brahmin regards a *sudra*. The 1944 Act, however, had changed much of that. The profession was unified, pay and conditions brought under a common code and Burnham Committee. The N.U.T. now had vastly more grad-uate—and three times more grammar school—members than prewar.

Yet it no longer seemed vital to establish the attainment of middle-class status by clinging to middle-class respectability. All through the winter of 1955 the papers were full of the stormy meetings of the teachers in towns all over Britain. The addition of 1 per cent to the teachers' contribution to their pension scheme had proved the last straw. The worm had turned. In Glasgow the teachers called a protest rally in school hours and 170,000 children had to be given half-holidays. In Sheffield, a teacher of twenty-seven years' standing, jumping the gun on the unions' "No-dinner-money-collection" programme, was suspended by the local education committee. He promptly took a job as a lorry-driver.

"A poor example," frowned *The Times*, still safe in Mrs. Miniver's England, ". . . a course any self-respecting professional person should be ashamed of." But in these vulgar times, alas, the proof of the pudding is in the eating—and both doctors and teachers shortly found the pudding notably improved.

In the late Thirties, George Orwell had recommended the lower middle classes to "start sinking into the working-class" ("After all," he wrote, "we have nothing to lose but our aitches"). By the late Fifties it began to look as if many were taking his advice—although "sink", at least if it implied material descent, no longer seemed quite the word.

Not long ago, wives working had been—with a few professional exceptions—very much of a "working-class" thing. Now it was precisely in the better-off middle class that wives most tended to go out to work—and the motives—among them escape from boredom, the desire for independence and the need to provide the wherewithal for the made-over home—were much the same as in the so-called working-classes. As private school fees soared, more and more "old" professional families were turning to the public system; just as middle-class wives, thinking twice about £200–300 nursing-home fees, were having their babies "on the N.H.S.", a piece of social exploration which in the case of one Cambridge don's daughter also brought forth a book, entitled *National Baby*.

In the second half of the Fifties that time-honoured institution of proletarian life, the pawnshop, went into a decline.* The pawnshops that managed to survive were reported to be doing so, not in the traditional manner, taking Dad's best suit from Monday to payday, but by pledging more durable and costly articles for the convenience of the middle classes!

Meanwhile, new and old classes and categories—worker, bourgeois, life-peer alike—met, mingled, washed their cars and signed their hire purchase contracts in the capacious comfort of the Endless Middle. From the loudspeakers rolled the oleaginous but inescapable strains of "Oh, mein papa", from the

* From around 3,000 in 1931, the number of pawnbrokers had dwindled to 1,500 by 1950 and to a mere 1,000 five or six years later.

Golden Trumpet of Mr. Eddie Calvert. And the latest Gallup Poll showed once again that about half the British people now considered themselves middle class.

By which, of course, they meant NOT "working-class". What else they meant was not yet very clear—to them or anybody else. They were simply rejecting the old stereos, simply making the half-instinctive recognition that in this England of the Fifties it had finally become impossible to describe the social present in terms of the social past—even though these were only terms that currently existed.

III

These changes had been eased—and given their necessary frame—by the "Beveridge revolution" which, as it pervaded the national life, increasingly caused the old class colorations to be shed in favour of the neutral tones of all-embracing social service. The 1949 Housing Act, for instance, had no longer enjoined local authorities to provide housing specifically for "the working classes", as earlier Acts had. It left them free to provide for all.

And housing did in these years in fact come to be regarded as a largely classless public service like municipal transport or water supply. By the mid-Fifties, after a decade in which 75 per cent of all new home-building had been by local authorities, no less than one-quarter of the British nation—a wide social cross-section with a wide range of incomes—lived in publicly-owned flats or houses.

The expression "council house"—with its lingering odour of charity and the second-rate—was now coming to seem as dated as "council school"—particularly in those many areas where progressive authorities had moved decisively away from the old barrack-lines approach to provide estates with landscaping and pleasantly varied site-planning. The Ministry of Housing now suggested to local authorities that not only had all the old paternalistic regulations become inappropriate, but the growing practice of rent-payment by cheque was one to be encouraged.

The mixing together of high- and low-rent houses, in deliberate reversal of the old practice of class segregation, was official policy in the New Towns and on many postwar public estates. For a variety of reasons, it did not always work out as well as had been hoped, but in the wider perspective the desegregationists had some powerful forces working on their side. Bomb devastation, the immense upheavals of the war years, the movements of people since then in search of work and into the new industries*—and, a little later, the large programmes of slum clearance—had, in effect, set up in Britain a vast social mixing trough. Great gaps had been, and were being, torn in the fabric of the old working-class England. From over 200,000 in 1939 the population of Stepney was by 1951 down to 99,000; in the East End only a quarter of the population had been "born within the sound of Bow Bells".** The long, slow, retreat of the Cockney which had been going on, little observed, for most of the century, was culminating—the East End was "East London" now. In Manchester and Salford, the Lancashire of L. S. Lowry was visibly disappearing; in Birmingham the sledge-hammers of the demolition squads cut a swathe through the honeycomb of slums that constricted the city; in Glasgow—though here as elsewhere years of work remained—the old Gorbals too was going.

Since sites for rehousing were in acutely short supply, the "tone" of many a "select residential area" was hopelessly fractured and prewar "luxury flats" were challenged by the—often superior—municipal flat-blocks rising around them. At the same time middle-class frontiersmen were pushing out into working-class areas, painting the front doors of their workmen's cottages pink or yellow, and hoping to compensate for a "poor address" with a well-burnished coach-lamp.

Notwithstanding all this, one of the broad socio-political divisions of the Fifties lay—as every Parliamentary candidate who went out canvassing was acutely aware—between the great army of local authority tenants and the great—and growing—

* Between 1951–58 more than one million men and women moved their homes to find jobs, according to the Government's *Bulletin for Industry*.
** More in some areas, e.g. one-half of Bethnal Green's inhabitants had been born there.

army of those who either owned their own houses or were buying them on mortgage.

As the Fifties proceeded, and private and speculative house-building, freed from licensing, accelerated, this division became more emphatic. Yet it was by no means a class stratification of the old simple, solid, immutable sort. It was, in part, the result of postwar accidents of location and 'points score'. But since at postwar wage levels it was possible for a wide cross-section* of the population to purchase houses on mortgage, it was also often enough class by choice, "political" or "psychological", rather than economic, class (although, obviously, the choice was conditioned by occupational and family tradition also). Such self-election was certainly not new. But when so many people could elect themselves with comparative ease the nature and significance of Elect-ness inevitably underwent drastic change.

The picture, already highly complex, was further confused by large regional—even local—differences in the rate of social change. The contrast in England between the North and the South was—as any traveller from, say, Luton or Reading to Blackburn or Gateshead would agree—still a pretty startling one. But now the old roles were reversed. It was the South and the Midlands that made the pace, the North that maintained the traditional strands in the pattern, the North where the old working-class society held out against the society of the Endless Middle. Up there in the North were the endless miles of workers' barracks, not technically "slums"—indeed all too durable—yet firmly set in the working-class mould of the nineteenth century.

* According to a survey, 1960, by the Co-operative Permanent Building Society of mortgage purchasers of new houses 37·7 per cent were wage-earners (as distinct from salary-earners) and 40·4 per cent had incomes below £750 a year. For existing (i.e. not new) houses, the corresponding figures were 55·7 per cent wage-earners: 58·7 per cent with incomes below £750. Dr. F. Zweig's survey in the mid-Fifties of workers in four large plants showed home-ownership increasing: 30 per cent of Mullard's Mitcham workers owned their own homes; 31 per cent of Dunlops at Birmingham; 37 per cent at the Workington Iron & Steel Co.; 47 per cent of Vauxhall workers at Luton.

Here was the land of our "great industrial heritage", the land of The Vaults and the corner fish-and-chip shop, the land which still housed our basic industries, the greater part of our people, and did much to account for that shaming statistic in the 1951 Census—that one-third of the dwellings in England had no fixed bath.

Thus, if there were no longer "two nations" in the full Disraelian sense, there were still "two Englands". If there was no longer "The Poor", there were still many who happened to be poor because of personal misfortunes such as desertion, widowhood, or persistent ill-health. With a chronic housing shortage and 850,000 (1955) existing houses officially "condemned" as unfit for habitation, bad luck in the housing stakes was also a fertile source of misfortune. Old Age was another, and Lord Beveridge himself in 1953 sadly pointed out that one in every four people on "Beveridge" retirement benefit or widows' pension was having to go to the National Assistance authorities for help.

In the dazzle of new prosperity there was perhaps a greater danger than before that such "anomalies"—extensive as they were—might go unnoticed. Yet once exposed to view, their anomalous nature was now glaring. Despite the persistence of the old forms, the anomalies and the time-lags, the new affluence and the forces released since 1945 could not be confined, but were working powerfully through at many levels whether in South Wales pit village, "traditional" Dorsetshire countryside or "proletarian" Southend.

No conservatism could be more profound or instinctive than that of the old British working-class. Yet though the assimilation of the still unassimilated might take time—for they were many—it would surely come. Woodbines were still Britain's largest selling cigarette, but very, very gingerly, line by line, month by month, and year by year, the makers were "smartening up" the long-familiar but antiquated packet; the dog tracks were zealously refurbishing to shake off their old "cloth cap" image; and the directors of Rowton Houses ("800 BEDS AT SIXPENCE A NIGHT") were busy developing their old cubicles, first into "Semi-Specials" and "Specials", and then into "Super Specials"—separate wings of 30s. a-week bedrooms with hot and cold water, built-in wardrobes, curtains and rugs.

"In the extension of this scheme," wrote their official historian in 1954, "lies Rowton Houses' richest promise for the future."

IV

The peculiar condition of Britain in the Fifties often seemed to be that of a technological society inside a traditional society, an "endless middle" pushing out vigorously against the enclosing ends—top and bottom—of the old class structure.

Firm as the traditional Eton-Oxbridge-Establishment area might still appear, the dynamic of the new society was great. While to older people, the so-called class "sound barrier", educationally buttressed, might appear an invincible bar to social intermixing, the young, born into the polyglot clamour of the TV and do-it-yourself age, were notably unembarrassed by it. Many were now bilingual or even trilingual: one idiom and accent for the home, another for street-corner or club, yet another for office or beauty parlour. The class system no longer totally enclosed them; they could step outside and walk around it. The local aristocracy were serviceable for opening the Flower Show—if no TV Personality was obtainable.

And, increasingly, the dominant logic of full-scale mass-production dictated the Endless Middle's expansion. Rich and poor were both now minorities, and to the mass-producer and mass-distributor minorities were a nuisance. Their effective weight, both economic and social, was thus further diminished, and the image of the classless middle shone brighter. At one end of the social scale, the Co-ops, so long a power in the industrial North, watched their share of retail trade rapidly shrinking; at the other, the stately Debenham and Freebody's was by 1955 planning to enter the chain-store field "owing"— as the chairman delicately explained to shareholders—"to the shifting pattern of income groups".

The characteristic new products of the assembly line, the washing machines, the electric mixers, the "sink units" and so forth, were as frankly classless as the equipment of an operating theatre. And not only was the conveyer-belt now levelling up rather than down, but—in the home, as on the air, as on the bookstall—it predicated patterns different from the traditional slow percolation of new goods and styles from the Top downwards. Unlike the piano which had also in its time rearranged the drawing-room, the "Telly" was never a symbol of middle-class status. As early as 1951 sets were owned in the ratio 40 middle class to 60 working class, and from the middle Fifties (according to B.B.C. Audience Research) ownership reflected an accurate cross-section of the nation.

The motor-car was now showing signs of following the same pattern. By the late Fifties, throughout the length and breadth of Britain, on council estates as in Acacia Avenue, Sunday morning was devoted to the ritual laving of the car, just as Wednesday evening in three families in every four was devoted to the filling-in of football coupons.*

Class Distinctions and the Advertiser: Has Socio-Economic Grading Outlived its Usefulness? 'Media-Planner' asked in *World's Press News* in 1960.

By then the point required no underlining.

The car receiving the Sunday libations might, it is true, be a Hillman Minx or a Ford Popular or a Jaguar; it might be new or second-hand, last year's or prewar. But as income levels rose and the assembly lines poured out an ever-widening range of goods, these differences could appear as a matter of personal taste or order of priority rather than, simply, of class.

The eclecticism already noted on the bookstalls was experienced over a wider and wider area of life. The pattern established, for instance, by Mr. Charles Forte, the most notably successful caterer of the period, was very different from that either of the old ABCs or of the gilt-and-marble halls of the old Corner Houses** of the earlier popular eating-out revolution. Within a stone's throw of Piccadilly Circus, Mr. Forte offered a kaleidescopic range of colourful establishments,

---

* Six in every ten postal orders sold in Britain were now sold for enclosing with football pool coupons. By 1955 the total annual stake had reached £74,000,000, by 1960 £111,000,000 compared with a prewar peak (1938-39) of £22,500,000.

** The Corner Houses were now also made over to provide less "splendour" and more variously packaged specialisation, a costly transformation whose inspiration was now American-technological rather than, as earlier Baronial-Hall-French-Viennese.

ranging from the Café Royal to a milk-bar, and including a
brasserie, an "Italian" restaurant, "speciality" fish, steak
and chicken restaurants, a coffee house, a quick lunch counter
and so on. Specialisation brought the "economies of scale".
Presentation multiplied variety. All were clearly open to all.
You paid your money and you took your choice. It was the
motto of the age.

One result of this "democratic" diversity and continuous
consumption was that true conspicuous consumption in the
Edwardian manner became not only technically difficult of
effective achievement, but also "undemocratic" or "in bad
taste". So the contemporary millionaire either withdrew with
his fellow millionaires to remote Scottish grouse moors, or
settled for the discreet Renoir or Monet. When Sir Bernard
Docker, assisted by Lady Docker, sought with their silver-
plated Daimler, the steam-yacht *Shemara* and a general air of
uninhibited pleasure-chasing to revive the grand style, they
made the headlines and filled columns of news-space, but the
emotion aroused was amusement rather than awe or envy, and,
in the fullness of time, as Sir Bernard was ousted from the board
of his father's company, B.S.A., the "Gay Dockers" disappeared from the papers.*

The potency and the accumulating effect of these factors
making for classlessness were now confirmed by the speed and
ease with which two very American institutions, imported in
the Fifties, were assimilated into English life.

To have taken the washing of one's dirty linen in public as
the launderettes did and to have made it in England—the

* The period was notable for the final closure of many of the
restaurants of the Edwardian period: Frascati's, Oddenino's, the
Carlton (with Hitler's assistance), the Holborn Restaurant, all of
which were demolished, with the odd tear. Pinoli's was turned into
a Services' Club.

The standard managing director's Rolls or Bentley was psychologically a quite different matter. It was a badge of rank in corporation society, a matter of being "properly dressed". It is significant
that despite this, the Conservative Government clapped a £2,000
price ceiling on these company cars in its 1961 Budget (for tax
allowance purposes), thereby threatening the car side of Rolls-
Royce with ruin.

36. Young Man-about-Town, 1954 Model—a revealing moment at the Mecca Dance Hall, Tottenham. The *avant-garde* "New Edwardians" became the conventional uniformed "Teddy Boys" and finally petered out in the—no longer "with it"—"Teds". The older generation looked on with varying degrees of astonishment, amusement, resentment and alarm.

37 and 38. The "American Invasion" of the Forties, with musicals like *Oklahoma!* and plays like *A Streetcar Named Desire*—seen above at the Aldwych in 1949—revealed the moribundity of much of our theatre. But from the mid-Fifties a new generation of British dramatists spoke with a contemporary accent and idiom, discovered a new sort of hero—and the Provinces. John Osborne's *Look Back in Anger* (*below*) which opened at the Royal Court in May, 1956, seemed some sort of turning-point.

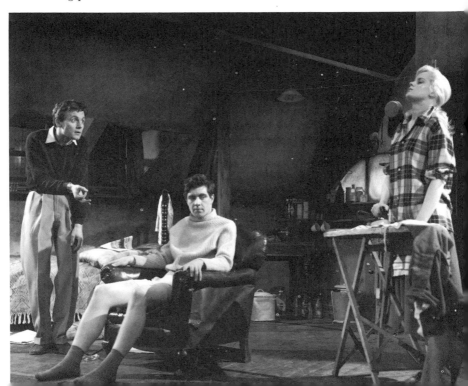

England of the Municipal Wash-House—something of a classless or all-class social occasion was a triumph of the contemporary functional approach (a salute to "know-how" rather than to *savoir-faire*) and of the allied art-sciences of "packaging" and design.

To have brought the big brash supermarket to the sedate English High-Street, with its High-Class Family Grocers, its dignified banks, and Tudor (baked jam roll) cafés, and to have made such a roaring and rapid success of it, was a development hardly less startling. According to the available figures in 1947 there were exactly ten self-service stores in Britain. Nine years later they were being opened at the rate of fifty or sixty a month, one in every six pounds spent on groceries and provisions was being spent in them—and the supermarkets were upon us.

Here again was the classless, mechanical, servant. Here again the bright, clean-cut functionalism, the carefully planned layout, often coping with 20,000 customers a week, the "prepackaging", the "oven-ready" meat in its papier-mâché tray, the cleaned and cellophane-bagged potatoes or carrots, the "know-how", the automatic, all-embracing, "technological classlessness" of the times, the classlessness of the Vespa or the Diesel railcar.

And here again was the New Abundance, the inconspicuous conspicuous consumption, the *embarras de richesse*, the tinned lychees from Hongkong or steak-and-kidney pudding from Hoxton, Imperial Tokay or canned beer, champignons or slab cake, piled high on shelves that seemed endless, all clearly ticketed, all freely accessible, pouring down into the capacious wire-baskets of the circulating, goggle-eyed, itchy-handed populace. In the supermarket—which might cost £100,000 to equip—the "high consumption economy" seemed to come to full flower, and the cash registers at the barriers, spilling out their rolls of figures, rang out the popular salute.

V

This emergent society was thus in many ways very different from the "New Britain" envisioned in the war years and

M

sketched by the Labour Levellers of 1945. Yet it still reflected some of that New Britain's aims—as glimpsed, perhaps, in a whimsically distorting mirror. On a good many counts we had come nearer to the classless society as defined by R. H. Tawney, although we had approached that classic Socialist end by some notably unclassic means.

But if Robinson's Barley Water now found it politic to dispense with the courtly Old Heathers, and Rose's Lime Juice banished the ever-attentive Hawkins, a powerful nostalgia remained. The delicious old English game of "placing" people à la Jane Austen was not easily abandoned. On the contrary, it had now become so complex and difficult as to acquire a certain morbid fascination. Hence the astonishing stir caused in 1956 by the publication of a "guide" to the speech usages by which members of the Upper Class (or "U-people") could be infallibly distinguished from the Rest. Founded on a philological dissertation, "Linguistic Class Indicators in Present-day English", compiled by a Birmingham Professor for the edification of the Finns, the book—as its title *Noblesse Oblige* suggested—was presented by its editor, Nancy Mitford, as a sort of sophisticated joke. People, however, exhibited such an extraordinarily avidity for the information that, for instance, the Upper Class possessed "false teeth", whereas the Rest had "dentures", that the book rapidly became a best-seller and the expressions "U" and "non-U" went into the language. Soon "U" was calling to "U" in the Personal Column of *The Times*.

Lady (and dog) would like to stay as paying guests with pleasant, informal country family during July; English, Protestant, "U".

Yet if this was a sign of the times it was necessary to make sure in which direction it was pointing. In England, class—whether reflected in Austen-ian innuendo or Left-wing sneer—had always been implicit, "understood" rather than stated (rather as sex had once been). That it should now be exposed to full view, examined, dissected, and put under the sociological microscope was almost as radical a departure as the intrusion of Freudian psychology in the Twenties. And on some, the first effects appeared to be hardly less disturbing.

But a self-consciousness of this sort—and indeed any widely

diffused sociological awareness—in fact drove one more nail into the coffin of the old English class system. Of course, snobbism might continue to flourish; there would still be "good addresses" and "bad addresses" (although these were now apt to change with baffling rapidity); rugger-playing schools which felt entitled to patronise soccer-playing schools; culture-vultures who, talking Bratby and Elba, pitied others who had only just arrived at Van Gogh and the Costa Brava. It was also true that the dissolution of the old class lines, ennoblement by the Gossip Column (ranging from smarter Islington to St. Tropez) might open the way to an American-style traffic in "status-symbols", just as the large-scale industrial organisation might make for the multiplication of distinctions of rank, and hence for the establishment of social "pecking orders".

Yet the new question: "What does he *do*?" was totally different from the old question—with its sublime and sublimely unconscious arrogance, "Who *is* he?" Moreover, even when the new question could be accurately answered, it was far from offering a definitive "placing". A sociologist questioning a large group of students in Banbury in the Fifties found that "at first students produced as many class systems as there were students". Sociologists for whom "class" was basic grammar, a necessary frame for their studies, were now being obliged to devote whole books to agonised—and generally vain—attempts to uncover some definition and arrangement that would hold water for more than a week. One, Dr. Michael Young, boldly summoning the Future to his aid, visualised a class structure remodelled on simpler, grander lines into those who could pass examinations and those who could not. But, alas for sociologists' yearning for security, it was obvious that even in a "Meritocracy" in the conceivable future "getting-on" would, as ever, depend on many factors besides intellectual merit.

As old and new societies still intermeshed and interacted, the outcome remained unpredictable. Yet some interesting pointers were visible.

For all the talk about "sound barriers" there had, in fact, been much progress towards a national norm of common speech, comprehending, with relative ease, a fair range of regional variations, and certainly far from prewar "B.B.C." It owed something to the width of "mass communications"; and as television added its contribution, the more extreme and arrogant forms of public school or "U" speech began to appear almost as quaint at home as they long had across the Atlantic.

There were other signs of a growing social cohesion: the emergence, for instance, of a new generation of playwrights who, though otherwise differing widely, shared an ability to handle, on level terms, the idiom and speech nuances of all classes. The rough-hewn "slice of life" drama which came to power and influence in the latter half of the Fifties was a thousand miles away from the elegant, verbal contrivance of Fry or the precision and detachment of T. S. Eliot which had held the centre of the stage when the decade opened. But it is possible that it gave some hint of social evolution also. The young writers discovered by the English Stage Company, founded at the Royal Court Theatre in 1956, presented working-class or lower middle-class life from the inside, looking out, not from the outside, looking in.

A parallel trend was visible even in farce. The famed Aldwych farces of prewar days had dealt with "U-Types" at the Old Hall; the Whitehall farces dealt with R.A.F. Other Ranks, landladies, sailors, seaside boarding houses, policemen at home. . . .

At the same time there were hints of a movement of the novel back into the mainstream, setting aside "literary" experiment and bridging the Third-Light gulf to deal, not wholly with cliques and neurotics, but with ordinary people who might actually live in the provinces.

As the eighty-three-year-old Somerset Maugham, invited to comment on these developments sagely observed: "You see, you have never before had a literature from the under-privileged. But now they are going to these secondary schools and grammar schools and they are becoming articulate. . . ."

If this were true, "they" were of course becoming articulate at the very moment when they were ceasing to be under-privileged. For all that, the extension of social range was made; and might now prove too large to be smoothly absorbed by the old class-cultural apparatus.

There were many small signs, clues, straws in the wind pointing in a similar direction. Cowes, once an elaborate set-piece in class distinction, was now casual, relaxed and full of small sailing dinghies; Cheltenham had become a brisk town of light industries; *Punch*, so long an inexhaustible fount of jokes about the oddity of the lower orders, had undergone in 1953–57 its Muggeridge-*New Yorker* revolution; and if the postwar transformation of the "rat-catcher" into the "rodent-operative" might seem a regrettable pomposity, it did nevertheless hint at something which was real enough in these years, a groping towards a decent human norm of behaviour and language, the seeking of a comfortably classless haven somewhere between the obsequious 'Sirs' and 'Ma'ams' of the prewar order and the "mates" and "ducks" of the Forties.

One day in 1957, a survivor of the aristocratic age, apparently still imperfectly adjusted to the new one, addressed the Editor of *The Times* on the subject of the failure of an omnibus to halt when he wagged his umbrella at its driver. He was solemnly rebuked for this improper, undemocratic gesture, not only by the conductor of the vehicle, but—in another letter to *The Times*—by a peer of the realm.

28.   The Subtle Terrorism of Words

"The Labour Party is a Socialist
Party and proud of it."
—*Let Us Face the Future*, 1945.

". . . the vulgar fallacy that some
ideal society can be said to exist of
which blueprints can be drawn and
which will be ushered in as soon as
certain specific reforms have been
achieved."
—C. A. R. Crosland in *The Future
of Socialism*, 1956.

FEW PEOPLE, in the Fifties, were likely to have much
difficulty in according adequate recognition to the
economic sources of politics. As the mid-decade boom
raised levels of consumption, and in "council house" and
home-on-mortgage alike people began to acquire durable
property in unprecedented numbers, the notion of *"Fair
Shares for All"* began to appear pedantic beside the delicious
and ever-present prospect of "Shares for All". Despite the
time-honoured phrases of trade union militants and 1955's rash
of strikes—dockers, bus drivers, locomen, miners, newspaper
engineers—the "class conflict" which had put the hard,
cutting edge on the Labour Party vote was progressively
losing definition. In this bright new world, the larger cake had,
as Sir Stafford Cripps had foretold, duly produced the larger
slice, leaving people freer than ever before to opt out of the
"working class".

Bandying millions with the nonchalance of conjurers
keeping a dozen balls in the air, the "take-over" financiers as
dramatised by the Press—and the names of Messrs. Clore,

Wolfson, Fraser and Samuel were now rarely out of the headlines—were apt to appear boldly modernising, Napoleonic,
rather than predatory. Between mid-1952 and 1955 ordinary
shares prices on the average doubled; in the summer of 1954
the Stock Exchange settlement staff was reported working
till 4.30 a.m. "to cope with the rush". Meanwhile, the ding-
dong battle for the control of the Savoy Hotel group ushered in
the great real estate and property development boom which,
spreading outwards from the Metropolis, was to become a
major motif of the next five years.

Already, in late 1953, the ever-sensitive—if still determinedly
cauliflower—ear of the *Daily Mirror* had registered the change
of key. "The *Mirror* is Leftish, of course," its controller, Mr.
Cecil King, observed to an interviewer in 1955, "but we've
been moving right for the past two years. That's because the
country has been moving right."

In May, 1955, in what the newspapers called "The First
TV Election"*, this judgment was confirmed by the return
of the Conservative Government with a trebled (if still fairly
modest) majority. There had been much speculation about
the effects this potent new force, television, might have on
British political life. In the event, it seemed to have remarkably
little and the election was duly pronounced by an expert
observer** "the most apathetic yet seen in the twentieth century". Mr. Harold Macmillan, the Foreign Minister, just back
from talks in Paris, rather nervously introduced a film of Tory
Achievement, including a bonfire of ration books. Mr. and
Mrs. Attlee were seen beside their chintzy fireplace at "Cherry
Cottage", Clem driving home his points with waves of his pipe.

The chintz seemed entirely appropriate. This time the
Labour Party did not even bother—as it had earlier—to invite
the complacent Welfare-State-nurtured young to "ASK YOUR
DAD". Even in the minds of many "Dads", the memory of the
Depression, the Dole Years, the Hunger Marchers and the rest
was now fast receding. From the eminence of the mid-Fifties
the Thirties began to seem as remote as they had from the
parallel position in the nineteenth century: the swelling tide of

* There had been a limited experiment with a single fifteen-
minute telecast for each party in 1951.
** D. E. Butler, *The British General Election of 1955.*

machine-generated production had once again absorbed and carried away the surge and surf of Radicalism.

II

The remarkable speed and completeness of the Conservative recovery from the "historic" débâcle of 1945 owed something, of course, to the British ruling class's justly famed skill in strategic withdrawal and to that ease in the theft of "the Whigs' clothing" which came from long practice. It owed more to social, economic and geopolitical forces of a size and strength unforeseen in 1945.

"Clean break" as it had appeared after the war, 1945's "New Britain" had been essentially linked to the interwar years, both as a reaction from them, and, in the longer perspective, as a resumption and acceleration of those processes of social evolution released, politically, in 1867 and 1906. The 1955 Newer New Britain—with the full-width mass-market "consumer democracy" in being—was, by contrast, something, psychologically at least, really new. Once set up, its machinery appeared to gather momentum, make its own pace as powerfully as had the very different machinery of the nineteenth century. But now the patterns being established were Transatlantic rather than native.

In 1955, the full emergence of the "New Look" and the supersession of the Old were marked and symbolised by the retirement from the leadership of their parties and from active political life of Mr. Churchill, in his eightieth year, in April, and of Mr. Attlee, in December.

There was a good deal in the "New Conservatism" which both these veterans might have been excused for failing to recognise as bearing much relation to the familiar Toryism they had known all their lives. It was only a little over ten years since Churchill, at the Mansion House, had made his famous declaration that he had "not become the King's First Minister to preside over the liquidation of the British Empire". Now, Conservative Ministers—almost as a matter of routine—found themselves doing exactly that. "Scuttle" or no, it was a Conservative, not a Labour, Administration which in 1954 made the agreement with Egypt for the rapid evacuation of our troops from the Canal Zone; it was the Conservatives who, following the postwar pattern established by Labour, rushed Malaya, Ghana, the Sudan and Nigeria* along the road to self-government. And if, in the old conflict of interest between Settlers and Natives in central Africa, the Settlers had felt their supremacy assured with the Tories in office, they, too, were soon to learn their error.

But the abandonment of time-honoured positions under the pressure of world change was by no means confined to one end of the political spectrum. After a long-drawn struggle within its ranks, the Labour Party had in 1954 accepted German re-armament—by nine votes in the Parliamentary Party and almost equally narrow majorities in Party Conference and Trade Union Congress. The wan ghosts of Internationalism and Anti-Militarism ("The Prussian Jackboot") stirred in the Party's cellars. But they remained there. The Party's cellars, by now, were full of just such ghosts.

In a world dominated by the U.S.A.–U.S.S.R. confront-ation, and living under the long shadow of the Bomb, the scope for the striking of traditional party attitudes was severely limited. A deterioration in the situation, a new slogan—like "massive retaliation"—on the lips of American senators was enough to bring all parties hurriedly together in the "bi-partisan" cause of "British common sense". As in the winter of 1950 all England had stood behind Mr. Attlee, speeding across the Atlantic to save the world from President Truman, casually flourishing the Bomb at the Chinese invading Korea, so in April, 1954, all England anxiously followed Mr. Eden, the Prime Minister Designate, as at the Geneva Confer-ence of nineteen nations he strove to pull back the West from that "brink" which held so fatal a fascination for America's Foreign Secretary, Mr. John Foster Dulles.

Dulles was calling for direct military intervention in Indo-China to "save the Free World in Asia". The situation was indeed desperate. Viet-Minh troops, aided by Chinese "volunteers", were thrusting down from the Red River delta,

* Attained in the case of the Gold Coast in March 1957, of Malaya, August 1957, of the Sudan, in January 1956, of Nigeria in 1960.

sweeping the French before them, and, in President Eisenhower's words—pushing the "cork out of the bottle".

As the Americans renewed their warnings to China, exploded
their new hydrogen bomb in the Pacific—and in Australia Mrs.
Petrov noisily "chose Freedom"—American Globemasters
shuttled French reinforcements into the beleaguered fortress of
Dien Bien Phu.

At Geneva, Red China—still excluded at American insistence
from the United Nations—made her debut on the world diplomatic stage. A photograph of a smiling Chou En-lai, "a trim
figure in his navy blue tunic", duly appeared in the *Daily
Mirror* over the caption, "The Man from China".

But the Conference had only been in session ten days when
Dien Bien Phu, with its 12,000 defenders, fell. On 3rd June, the
British at their breakfast tables were confronted by the sombre
headline: DULLES GIVES GENEVA SEVEN DAYS.

It took considerably more than seven days. But thanks to the
devoted work of Eden and Mendes-France a peace pact based
on the partition of Indochina on the Seventeenth Parallel was
concluded.

It had been a critical moment in the long and complex
relationship of East and West. And—with Dulles growling
from the wings like a Covenanting Elder denouncing heresy
in the Non-Elect—the British role had been central. By a
happy stroke Eden had called in the Asian Commonwealth
countries, then meeting at Colombo, to guarantee the cease-
fire arrangements. The Third Force, which six years ago had
appeared extinguished in the Prague *putsch*, was now seen to be
a reality after all.

In yet another way events at this time forced a significant
departure from traditional positions. The French rejection of
the European Defence Community, which now became final,
had been in large part due to Britain's refusal to enter into
military commitments firm enough to counter-balance the
weight of the Germans. E.D.C. having failed, Eden made a
round of European capitals, rapidly improvising from Bevin's
old Brussels Treaty Organisation, a new structure, "Western
European Union". He won France's agreement with a pledge
to maintain four British Divisions and a Tactical Air Force in
Europe. And he undertook that Britain would not withdraw

these forces against the wishes of the majority of the W.E.U. members except in event of acute overseas emergency.

Permanent military commitments on the continent of Europe were against the most profound British instincts. That they could now be accepted and, even more, that they could be committed to writing, was one more measure of the distance which the tide of events had brought us.

III

At home, the smooth realignment of the Conservative Party was greatly facilitated by the graduation of Keynesianism into full economic orthodoxy. By concentrating attention on the technicalities of production, investment and growth, Keynesianism diverted it from the ethics and equity of distribution, which was the Labour Party's classic territory. In the Crippsian years it had been the social control and social purpose implicit in Keynesianism that Governmental propaganda had stressed. The Conservatives were able to inherit this accumulation of moral capital and have private enterprise too.

It was true that, especially at first, there was a determined change of slogan and accent designed to demonstrate in the most bracing possible way the profound contrast between the new Keynesian Conservatism and the late detestable Keynesian "Socialism". But however much lip-service might be paid to the beneficent effect of the play of the market, the Tory "dash for freedom" was inevitably brought up short by two effective and continuous restraints.

The first was the precarious electoral balance in Britain throughout these years. The second—made more insistent because the first narrowly limited possible action—was the no less precarious balance of trade in a crowded island compelled to import half its food and to divert a vast part of its resources to defence production.

Together these factors exercised a sterner discipline than ever Whips could have commanded, and sufficed to keep the Conservative Party treading that "Middle Way" charted for it by Mr. Butler's official policy reshaping committees, and spotlighted by the "new Conservatives" of the "One Nation" group.

Thus while much was heard of the salutary effects of a modicum of unemployment, minor unemployment occurring in 1958 found the Government taking prompt action to remove it, providing aid for local developments and virtually directing (with *douceurs* to industrialists in the form of large subsidies) the siting of new large plants. In the same way, a great deal was heard of the need to free rents. In the event, decontrol was applied to only a relatively small proportion of housing, although the abandonment of 'development charges' and building licenses in 1953–54 unleashed a land boom. Food subsidies were trimmed; minor tax changes tended to favour the higher income groups. According to the calculations of Mr. Dudley Seers, the redistribution of the Forties was now put into reverse. The earnings gap between the "tycoons" and the Rest, of whose narrowing Cripps had boasted, was opening up again.* Yet, by former standards in these matters (except for the property bonanza) the changes were undramatic.

In 1945 "Planning" was a Socialist slogan carrying overtones of revolution. Yet by the end of the Fifties—however sketchy the performance—planning was tacitly accepted as a routine task of government. The vast investment programmes in "the public sector", the postwar régime of inter-Governmental loans, the mechanisms of European co-operation—in defence, rehabilitation, currency management—demanded it. So did much else. British agriculture remained directed, subsidised and its price administered. The Conservative Government intervened to force the reorganisation of the aircraft industry, to concentrate the cotton industry. There was the interesting spectacle of a Conservative Minister of Labour publicly rebuking a great Midland motor firm for its failure to co-operate adequately with the trade unions.

From time to time, it is true, there was a brief return to the old *laisser-faire*, Sound Finance/Stern Banker stance of prewar days. But the satisfactions this yielded were short-lived. For most of the time "Butskellism"—a word the *Economist* had coined by telescoping the names of the Tory and Socialist

---

* Incomes of £6,000 after tax, one in 10,000 in 1949 were thirty in 10,000 by 1959, seven in 10,000 in 1956. In 1949 there had been just over 5,000 earning after tax between £4,000 and £6,000. In 1956 there were 14,000, in 1959, 25,000.

Chancellors—remained a necessary addition to the language, indicating the triumph of the Economic Manager over Old Cause in both parties.

"When my new theory has been assimilated and mixed with politics and passions," John Maynard Keynes had written to George Bernard Shaw in the Thirties, "I cannot predict what the final outcome will be in its effect on action and affairs. But there will be great change. . . ."

The prophecy was sound. And perhaps the most immediate and important change was the deflation of politics and the neutralisation of "passions". For whereas the classical economists, outlining their symmetric and Euclidian structures, had merely provided a frame for the political great debate, the new economists, operating in realms of higher mathematical abstraction where few could follow them, had blueprinted complex machinery of control, which they themselves would operate.

Though such devices and techniques might mark a new stage in man's control over his material environment, they inevitably delimited the political drama. As the psychologists and social scientists had dethroned the old moralists, so now the "scientific" economists were similarly serving the politicians.

The political parties certainly could, and did, package and market fragments of economic jargon under their own labels. Labour might accuse Conservatism of infatuation with "restrictionism" or "monetary controls". Labour's opponents might taunt them, not now with being in receipt of Russian Gold, but with causing "distortion" in the economic mechanism.

But this was a poor exchange for the old rhetoric of politics, for the sombre grandeur of a Churchill, the intuitive appeal of a Baldwin or a Bevin, the Celtic flights of a Lloyd George or a Bevan, or the simple Sermon-on-the-Mount emotionalism of a Lansbury.

But there it was: the central debate now was an economists' debate. Could price stability be combined with expansion? Were monetary and fiscal regulators adequate—or were physical controls needed as well? Was the Sterling Area a tremendous asset as some claimed—or a disastrous delusion of grandeur as others insisted? Was the flexibility brought by decentralisation more valuable than the economies that came from centralisation? And so on.

Almost inevitably, Ministers began to look more and more like public relations officers for economists, passing down their verdicts translated into suitable baby-talk. Sir Stafford Cripps and Mr. Gaitskell cut away at "slices of the National Cake"; Mr. Butler "pruned the roses"; Mr. Harold Macmillan, Chancellor in his turn (1955–57), publicly worried about the danger of "blowing the fuses".

The fact that the economists rarely appeared to agree on the moment or variety of doom in store for us merely added to the hypnotic attraction of their pronouncements and contributed to the Fifties much of their characteristic bemusement.

Was the nation facing disastrous inflation? Threatened by incipient deflation? Over-extended? Not extended enough? Mr. Roy Harrod issued his verdict on Monday, Sir Oscar Hobson contradicted it on Tuesday, and on Wednesday the Prophet Colin Clark pointed a lean, statistically incontrovertible finger.

And yet it was something perhaps that, unlike the Sound Bankers of the Thirties, the economists *did* disagree; that, unlike the bankers, they frequently conducted their debates in public, looked some way at least beyond the money market, and appeared to hold each other accountable to society at large.

IV

Thus, although the reconstructed House of Commons chamber into which members moved in 1950 scrupulously reproduced the features of the old one, destroyed by a bomb in 1941, it could not reproduce the old political drama. It was not only that the harsh colours—the mass poverty and unemployment, the ravening advance of Fascism in Europe—were absent. In the managerial society of mammoth organisations, many decisions crucial for the nation were made by them in private, between each other, or in conjunction with Government departments. In a world increasingly ruled by the equilibria established by pressure groups, even the trade unions no longer looked, as they once had, to Parliamentary action.

The Member of Parliament himself was becoming more and more a professional, a technician among technicians: inside the House, committee-man and vote-recorder in a legislative process that appeared increasingly preset and automated, outside it, a constituency welfare officer busy with his weekly "surgeries".

Even as the forum of national debate, Parliament was now powerfully challenged: an M.P. was merely an M.P.—a Television M.P. was something different. Winston Churchill growled his resentment at the encroachments of "this vast new robot organisation of television and broadcasting", and Parliament—much as it had once contested reporting by Wilkes and Hansard—brought in the Fourteen Day Rule forbidding electronic anticipation of the subjects of its debates within fourteen days of their scheduled occurrence.

But Sir Winston could no more hold back this tide than the tide of Asian nationalism. In Parliament, foreign voices were Voices Off; and through the Thirties, almost to the end, they had indeed been voices off. In the Fifties they were very much Voices On; the world drama eclipsed the merely national drama, not once or twice, but most of the time. And the electronic stage was a world stage.

Prague ... Berlin ... Seoul ... Dien Bien Phu ... Geneva ... Moscow ... There were no more "far-off places of which we know little". If 1954 had been the year of the Americans and Dulles, 1955 was the year of the Russians and Khrushchev—a year in which the whole future of the world seemed to be continually, and sensationally, changing before one's eyes.

As the British went to the polls in May, a Russian Mission flew to Belgrade. Hardly had the plane landed when Khrushchev —now clearly the man who mattered—waddled over to the microphone to launch upon a humble apology for Russia's earlier "slanders" against Marshal Tito and Yugoslavia, which had been due, it now appeared, to the unfortunate "errors" of Stalinism. Then, in mid-July had come the long-deferred talks "at the Summit", first mooted by Churchill after Stalin's death—and the citizens of Geneva had beheld the extraordinary spectacle of Bulganin and Khrushchev driving around the town in an open tourer, beaming like boys out of school, or presiding over prodigious parties, with much back-slapping, heavy humour, and not wholly sober folk-song.

There was a great deal of excited, hopeful, talk about "the Geneva spirit"—growing out of the truce in the Far East, which Eden had arranged the year before. But October, with the Foreign Ministers getting down to detail, brought disillusion. It was, wrote a correspondent, "the same old Molotov . . . back to his old stone-walling form. . . ."

Meanwhile, "Russian technicians" were being reported all over the Middle East. Supplied with MIG fighters, Stalin tanks, even Russian submarines, President Nasser was said to be plotting a crusade by the "free" Arab States against Iraq, the "tool of the Imperialists and the sycophants" of the Bagdad Pact.

Along the Arab-Israeli frontier skirmishing flared up again in the war that had never ceased. That year at the Guildhall dinner, Sir Anthony Eden warned his hearers of Communism's drive to "penetrate the Arab world". In November, heralded by the explosion of a Russian H-Bomb "of unprecedented size", Bulganin and Khrushchev—"B. and K". now to the British Press—toured India, wildly cheered by immense crowds as they laced their speeches with vituperation against "colonialism", with particular reference to the Power which had made the Indians "slaves".

The reaction of the *Daily Telegraph* was to denounce "B. and K." as "malicious mountebanks". The *Daily Sketch* invited its readers to decide whether the Prime Minister's invitation to them to visit Britain in 1956 ought not now to be withdrawn.

Yet if the skies were scarcely as blue as some had claimed in this extraordinary summer of 1955, at least there were now fairly frequent rifts in the overcast. In the autumn, the Four Powers' troops had marched out of their Occupation zones in Austria: ten years late, the Austrian Peace Treaty had been signed. And "mountebanks" or not, "B. and K." duly appeared in London in mid-April, sharing the front pages with Grace Kelly's Monaco wedding, and bringing with them, as a present for Princess Anne, a small brown bear named Nikki which was to become a great draw at the London Zoo.

Many less exalted Russians were now out and about. Russian delegations indeed seemed to be becoming as familiar a feature of the English scene as Breton onion sellers. There were the

Russian doctors, the Orthodox Church leaders, the teachers led by the formidable Mrs. Furtseva, the Russian farmers prodding our agricultural machinery (and pronouncing their own better), the electrical experts headed by the pudgy Malenkov himself who, despite his disgrace, seemed remarkably cheerful as he recited Burns, gave a stick of rock to a small boy on Blackpool promenade, watched the Grand National and was soundly kissed by an over-enthusiastic girl worker at a factory in the Midlands.

And there was Nina Ponomareva, the Russian woman teacher and discus champion, who endeared herself to the British public and established the "humanness" of the Russians by "lifting" five hats, total value £1 12s. 11d. from the counter of a department store in Oxford Street.

The serio-comic repercussions of the Nina Affair kept the British Press, public and Foreign Office occupied for the better part of three months. But although the Russian Press presented the matter as a counter-revolutionary conspiracy, the tide of communication continued to flow. The Bolshoi Ballet appeared at Covent Garden, the Red Army Choir at the Empress Hall, the Ukrainian State Dancers at Drury Lane. And, already, in 1954, a Russian rowing team had come to England and, with grim professionalism, had torn the last faded ribbon of Edwardian elegance from Henley, beating Leander for the Grand Challenge Cup by two and a half lengths. We were able, however, to get a little of our own back at last in mid-November when Wolverhampton Wanderers beat the Russian Spartak team 4–0 after a fierce match.

If indeed Britain's achievement in sport was any index of her well-being, there seemed more cause for optimism than for many a long year. In their Australian tour the M.C.C. had succeeded in retaining the Ashes, won for England at the Oval in 1953 for the first time in twenty-seven years. In athletics also there was much that was encouraging to report. In 1954 a medical student named Roger Bannister had become, at Oxford, the first man to run a mile in less than four minutes; an English woman, Miss D. S. Leather, the first woman to run a mile in less than five minutes. And at the White City in October of the same year the terrier-like Chris Chataway beat the formidable Russian, Kutz, and set up yet another new world record: the

5,000 metres in 13 minutes 51·6 seconds. Almost at once Kutz wrested the lead back, but next year Chataway beat him again.

V

Whatever these sporting triumphs may have done for national morale, they can have brought little comfort to the leaders of the Labour Party as they digested at their leisure the verdict of the polls.

No fewer than one and a half million of Labour's 1951 supporters had now apparently become so comfortable that they had neglected to vote at all. For a generation the Labour vote had steadily mounted at each succeeding election (save 1931) until in 1951 it had reached almost 14 million or half the votes cast. But now that majestic tide had ceased to roll in. The Labour Government, Socialists told each other ruefully, had succeeded too well. Bismarck had certainly known what he was talking about when, introducing social insurance, he had explained that "welfare is the true conservatism".

Even in the ranks of the faithful enervation, compounded in uncertain proportions of disillusion, exhaustion and ideological naïveté, was not easily overcome. The task of adjustment was not, after all, a light one. For two generations and more, the "common ownership of the means of production" had been held out as the unique, the indispensable cure for almost every social evil. Its name had been continually pronounced much as a Mohammedan pronounces the name of Allah. It had been enshrined in the party constitution since 1918 and the New Programme of that year—echoing the Social Democratic Federation programme of 1884—had called for the nationalisation of the railways, of coal and electric power, and of industrial life assurance.

Long delay had merely imparted to the vision a brighter glow, so that after the nationalising activity of 1945–50, the apocalypse had been confidently awaited. Its failure to occur had been disheartening. Problem industries had remained problem industries. Public utilities—though they now belonged to "the People"—were still somehow just public utilities. Balance-sheets were still the criteria of success.

Baffled and disillusioned, worn by the tremendous task of clearing the backlog of neglect that faces a reform party taking office in England, fretted by cold war crises and the endless nagging of the Tory Press, the Labour Government had not in fact been able to reach its first really unequivocally Socialist measure, the nationalisation of the prosperous iron and steel industry, until late in its period of office.

It then had to face opposition far more powerful and obstructive than any previously encountered. It faced it and put the Act through. But the result was that by the time the Party arrived at what might be conceived as the heart of a Socialist programme, the taking-over of those central fortresses of private financial power, the great industrial insurance companies, its nerve had gone. It cowered before the prospect of opposition from 60,000 insurance agents, organised in 400 anti-nationalisation committees throughout the country, and backed by a poster and Press advertising campaign.* It vacillated, compromised and finally collapsed.

The 1950 election manifesto had boldly proposed the nationalisation of cement manufacture, water supply, sugar refining, meat wholesaling, and the "mutualisation" of industrial assurance. On all these matters, the 1951 manifesto was resoundingly silent.

After that came the retreat into an embarrassed ambiguity. Here and there pockets of zealots continued as ever to draw up and advance at conferences their lists of industries for nationalisation, calling forth a defensive tract from I.C.I. and further sugar-bag protests by Tate and Lyle's jovial "Mr. Cube". But the Left-wing had lost its wartime potency. Sir Alexander Fleck might as well have held his peace; and Mr. Cube soon smiled again.

"Nationalisation", a word which had seemed so rich in promise in 1945, had now become so guilt—and gloom—laden that in 1951 the Party manifesto implicitly apologised for it. It would not, it explained, nationalise any successful firms or industries (i.e. because it believed in Socialism); only, perhaps,

---

* A poll of policy-holders revealed 80 per cent against nationalisation. The opposition of the Co-operative Movement, jealous for the independence of the Co-operative Insurance Society, also played its part.

the odd derelict or unsuccessful concern which might be "failing the nation".

At the Labour Party's annual conference at Margate in 1955 "rethinking" was declared to be the need of the hour. The Party, said James Griffiths, must "go back to the classroom". A three-year course was prescribed.

The difficulties of the Labour Party went much deeper than doubts about any particular dogma. The Party had owed its political effectiveness, its steady rise through the years, to two factors. One was that class-consciousness which, however mild and unbitter, had yet provided a broad and immovable organisational base. The other was something that can only be called Faith. Between them, these two factors had transmuted an extraordinary collection of shifting and disparate elements into what was justly called "the Movement".

The tragedy of the Labour Party was that both factors were now losing power at the same time, and both from long-term causes, not easily reversed. Semi-detachment on the Open Plan sapped solidarity. The deflation of politics by "scientific" economics—and the erosion of moral principle by the pervasive empiricism of the other social sciences—dissipated the Vision.

In the middle-aged, dismay was heightened by poignant memories of the Thirties, suffused by the bright orange promise of Mr. Gollancz's Left Book Club, still lit by the afterglow of the Russian Revolution, and the heroic achievement of "the Socialist Sixth of the World". The young had felt then that they held in their hands the keys to a Better World. All they had to do was to get to the doors and insert them.

But now, alas, the doors were open. And they were seen to be small prosaic doors leading to television sets and washing machines. As for the keys, they were in the care of the economists and technicians.

The God Had Failed not once, not twice, but many times over.

The young, it was said, were "contracting out of politics". At Oxford, the Union which twenty years ago had refused to fight for "King and Country" had gone Conservative. In that classic nursery of Socialism, the London School of Economics, conservative dons had taken over. By 1953 one in every three branches of the Labour League of Youth had shut down; it was the Young Conservatives who now made the pace with their dances, barbecues and house parties.

Not only had the God failed, but so also had the Devil. Already, in 1940, John Strachey, pillar of the Left Book Club and as sensitive a barometer of intellectual currents as the *Daily Mirror* was of social ones, had been taking lingering leave of Marx and preparing to cleave to Keynes. Now, eighteen years later, in *Contemporary Capitalism* he announced that instead of "plunging down into barbarism" as he had foretold in *The Coming Struggle for Power*, Capitalism was changing into something "which it would be an abuse of language to call Capitalism at all". The "fighting programme of mass struggle", would not, after all, be necessary.

The frustration and disillusion of the Radical Left were complete. Aneurin Bevan, its natural leader, while pouring Celtic scorn on those economist members of the Party—"desiccated calculating machines"—who imagined that Socialism was "an addition sum" rather than a way of life, seemed to have little to offer but barbed phrases and threats of resignation. In April, 1954, he did, in fact, resign again, this time from the Shadow Cabinet, though again the grounds of resignation, nominally the leadership's failure to oppose SEATO—were variously stated and obscure.

Having lost that vision and sense of mission by which alone it could live, the Party was sliding down miserably into faction-feuds, back-biting and bickering in a demoralised scramble for personal power.

And, in 1956, came the first comprehensive Rethought Version, a monumental book to lie like a tombstone on the moribund corpse of Socialism.

It was, inevitably, the work of an economist. And whereas the books of earlier Socialist writers, immensely varied as they were, were distinguished by the moral conviction that shone through the words of even the most academic, the voice of Anthony Crosland's "The Future of Socialism" was the voice of the scientist-in-command, measured, statistical, expertly hedging, clinical. Whereas generations of Socialists had anathematised "The System", to the economists-come-of-age Capitalism was a mechanism of intricate beauty, the necessary frame of their study as "class" was of the sociologists. Crosland's elaborately documented work was suffused by the professional economist's respect for the Market and the Price Mechanism; if this prophet in a white coat offered a hymn to anything it was to what Keynes once called "the dizzy virtues of compound interest."

Years ago, the Webbs, too, had recognised the "divorce of ownership from control" brought about by the large company with its professional managers. They had seen it as simplifying the further step to public ownership. In the Rethought Version it was held to make public ownership superfluous.

In this age of economic sophistication, the old Socialist adage about "production for use" instead of profit was exposed as largely meaningless. For what was profit but the index of efficiency in meeting needs? Far from being evidence of guilt, high profits should be welcomed, since, ploughed back, they would enable the new technology further to multiply its wondrous Abundance.

For the rest, in the new democracy of the supermarket and the union wage deal, the economists with their expertise in the use of fiscal controls could be trusted to remove any lingering social poison from the "profit motive". However nominally owned, industry could thus be left to get on with its task of producing the greatest good for the greatest number—which would, of course, be determined by the Market. How else?

The State could, if it wished, go into business itself, in a limited way, setting up "competitive public enterprises". Or by purchasing shares in the larger private concerns it could participate in the rewards of their beneficent activity while running no risk of dislocating the—in Mr. Crosland's phrase— "organic unity" of our Advanced Industrial Society.

Apostasy on so grand a scale, at once so painstaking and so bland, must be relatively rare in Radical politics. Yet in the strange mental condition of the Labour Party at this time, it roused little stir. In 1957 the Party Conference approved a new policy document, *Industry and Society*, embodying a programme "rethought" on Crosland lines, by a majority of four to one.

"The trouble with Experts," Henry Ford is reputed to have

said, "is that they know too many ways a thing CAN'T be done." The world had moved on since Ford. One might still, just possibly, choose one's expert; but one dare no longer disagree with him. The grand Ruskinian or Carlylean protest had ceased to be possible.

From another point of view the Rethought Version could of course be seen as a salutary stripping of cumbrous Utopian wrappings from that liberal empiricism which the Labour Party in practice had always pursued. Even so the shock of such sudden exposure was great and might be fatal. "The so-called Left," protested an angry Herbert Morrison, of the "so-called Right", "have swallowed this, the most Right-wing policy deviation in Labour Party history."

How wise indeed had been the traditional warnings about the unreliability of middle-class intellectuals! But the Old Guard, —the men and women for whom the Movement had been meat and drink, Life and Church, were passing. Many of the authors of the "social revolution" of 1945–50 were dead, Bevan, Cripps, Ellen Wilkinson, her successor at the Ministry of Education, George Tomlinson, Harold Laski, Arthur Greenwood. . . .

Here, too, it was the time of the New Men. In the election for the Party leadership in December, 1955, Morrison, the policeman's son, the Party's Deputy Leader and its Organiser of Victory, and Aneurin Bevan, the ex-coal miner, keeper of its Radical Conscience, were both overwhelmingly defeated. They were defeated not by one of the new 'grammar school' generation whose appearance had been noted in 1945, but by a young economist-administrator, educated at Winchester and New College, who had been in the House just ten years.

Cripps's Assistant Manager had been promoted Manager.

And Hugh Gaitskell at once set the new course with a public warning to the Party against the insidious peril of "stale slogans" "the subtle terrorism of words".

VI

The making over of the two great political parties in the course of a decade or so reflected both the patterns and strains of the process of adjustment in the nation at large.

Like Labour, the Conservative Party, "the party of the Ruling Class", was moving towards the middle socially as well as politically. Lord Woolton, brought in by Churchill in 1946 as a "modernising" Chairman, was the Tory answer to Morrison, Labour's wooer of the middle classes. Briskly warning the Party that it must "democratise or die", Woolton frustrated the purchase of Parliamentary seats by restricting candidates' donations to constituency funds to £25. But Woolton democratisation ran up against deep Tory instincts and progressed only slowly. After the 1955 election, the Party's Parliamentary ranks included fifty "Redbrick" graduates as some small counter to the weight of Eton-and-Oxbridge.* But within the Cabinet itself a lower middle-class grammar school boy was still a phenomenon rare enough to excite comment. And despite many efforts to create a Tory trade unionist movement, the Parliamentary party still had just one genuine manual trade unionist M.P.

Thus—though the public school spirit ensured that differences were better concealed—old class reflexes were apt to be no less troublesome on the Right than on the Left. "King and Country", "the Empire", "the Pound Sterling", continued to exert a "terror" as potent and as "subtle" as "the Profit Motive" or "the Capitalist System". At the thought of the impudence of that ingrate, Nehru, the insolence of the upstart Nasser, the oriental wiles of the political priest, Makarios—all shamelessly getting away with it while the honest Punjabi Mussulmans, the noble Bedouin, the simple, trusting, Sudanese were abandoned to their fate, the Party's internal pressures were apt to mount to dangerous levels.

The political picture of these years is thus curiously spectral. Between the archetypal representatives of the Conservative and Labour Parties there were still immense and fundamental differences of thinking and attitude that stretched down into almost every area of life. Yet, in the newly cohesive society which was forming, these could rarely find public expression— beyond the constituency workers' meeting or the golf club bar. All was swallowed up in functionalism, in the unreality of the larger ideological war, and the foam rubber wallow of the "Endless Middle".

* Of 1955's 334 successful Tory candidates, 260 were public school men, 23 per cent Etonians.

Perhaps indeed it was the slogans which gave the sharpest hints of the philosophic and temperamental gulf—the "Opportunity State" for the "Classless Society", the "National Minimum" (or "Safety Net") instead of "Fair Shares". But when one abandoned these airy realms, and came down to details in the here-and-now, differences were apt to shrink away to the merely marginal, to become differences not of kind but of degree. Labour might supplement the health service, offer more housing subsidies, a national superannuation scheme more generous at the lower end of the scale, more comprehensive schools, stricter use of planning, more physical "controls", steeper death duties, higher supertax. . . .

Over a period of time such changes of emphasis and priority, if persisted in, could well change the tone and direction of our society. Yet because the grand moral vision had been lost, the conviction that this would be so was largely lacking. Even the persistence of the public schools, thumbing a nose at Labour's most cherished ideal, now gave rise only to one more "rethinking" committee and the verdict that the right of parents to determine their children's education could not be set aside.

But still the young sought gropingly for cause or principle, for that moral element their natures craved. Thousands of young people now flocked into the Liberal Party for no other reason than that to this new generation it appeared fresh and uncompromised; it could still hold out hope. In the later Fifties there was a similar influx into the Campaign for Nuclear Disarmament, which not only provided a large simple cause, but also revived the temporarily lost arts of demonstration, slogan-writing and political "marching".

The Hungarian Rising and the Suez Adventure were both to show that when a major moral issue was presented, England was still not too bemused by television and the Brighter Home to be incapable of response. Suddenly flaring out of the vast greyness of Eastern Europe, the Hungarian national revolt touched forgotten springs in the British. The struggle of bare hands against tanks in the streets of Budapest quickened again the moral sense which the nuclear confrontation had only served to numb. People gathered around their radios as in war, listening anxiously for the latest scrap of news, hoping against hope again for a small nation "struggling to be free". Middle-aged intellectuals, watching the collections for Hungarian Relief Funds, the mass meetings at the universities, the young men rushing off to the Austro-Hungarian border, recalled the days of the Spanish Civil War and the International Brigade.

But the Spanish Civil War lasted three years: the Hungarian October Rising lasted merely days. Then the tide of Red Army tanks rolled over, demonstrating once again the impotence of the individual, the irrelevance of the old romantic, idealism. And, back in England, the "noble Freedom Fighters" welcomed with such fervour a few weeks before, were just one more batch of sad and seedy refugees, hanging around Nissen huts, one more dreary problem for the authorities and the ever-patient welfare-workers.

If the Spanish Civil War had been the zenith of the English Left's infatuation with ideology, the Hungarian Rising marked the final deflation, the last weary sigh in that curious "un-English" delirium which had gripped so many of the intellect-uals in the "Red Decade". The trade unions had begun to close ranks against the Communists in 1949; the electorate had rejected them in 1950, and in the same year Professor J. B. S. Haldane had secretly resigned from the Party rather than subscribe as a scientist to the new Soviet Truth of the biologist Lysenko. Yet most of the intellectual survivors of the Thirties had clung desperately on, somehow managing to accommodate themselves to the many changes of line from the Nazi-Soviet Pact on. But in 1956 Stalin-style repression, following so closely on the shocks of Khrushchev's revelations about the evils of Stalinism, proved more than even the well-trained intellect could take. If the intellect still could, the stomach couldn't.

Declining since 1948, the Communist Party's membership now plummeted. When the *Daily Worker* refused to print its own correspondent's despatches from Budapest, about a third of its staff resigned, including *Gabriel*, its cartoonist of twenty years. In Oxford, the University Communist Club met and dissolved itself: in the old Red strongholds of Scotland and South Wales the miners marched to demand the resignation of their Communist leaders; in Croydon a "former Communist", charged with being drunk in the High Street, told the court:

"It has been said that alcohol is a great salver of conscience. I was drunk last night. Let that suffice."

But it was not only Communist intellectuals who were confronting a dead end in 1956. The preoccupations of Labour's Left in these years, the "anti-American Imperialism" of the Forties, transmuting into the "anti-German rearmament" and "anti-Bombism" of the later Fifties, had been nurtured in frustration and now nurtured it. Yet the driving force of the Labour Party had always lain in its Left-wing. Without it, it became so much dough. With it, it was divided, but alive.

In the wider perspective of English history, Radicalism had been one of our deepest and most durable traditions, the vital and necessary counterpart—in the nation as in the party—to England's instinctive conservatism.

Was that great theme, too, at last exhausted—fallen victim in the end to scientific economics on the one hand, and to Marxism-gone-sour on the other?

In 1931 the economist Keynes had written that he looked forward to the day when the economic problem would be solved and could be relegated to the back seat so that "the arena of heart and head" could be occupied by "the real problems of life and human relations".

Though this point had not in fact been reached, it was interesting that people were already behaving rather as though it had. The debates which had stirred genuine passions since the war had not been the debates which stemmed from economics, where division followed recognised party lines. They had been the debates, across party lines, on such "real" problems of life and human relations as the divorce laws, the death penalty, the control of broadcasting, the problems of homosexuality and of censorship, of education and delinquency.

The so-called apathy in politics had arisen not from disinterest, but from the fact that the old political frame no longer corresponded to the living need. A new one—and with it, new terms, counters, formulations—had yet to be designed. In the process the very points at which democratic control and criticism could most effectively be applied would need redefining.

To assist this process—much less advanced in politics than

in the field of morals—the younger social sciences, sociology in particular, could now offer diagnostic instruments opening up a view of the living social body that was wider and more sharply focused than before. It was significant that the so-called "New Left", which appeared at this time, derived from "scientific" sociology rather than from "scientific" economics.

A group of youngish intellectuals, university teachers, mainly at provincial universities, sociologists, writers, architects, students, some former Communists for whom Hungary had been the end of the line, the "New Left" set out to take a long, appraising look at this new postwar society. It sought to turn attention from its quantitive to its qualitative aspects. Was poverty in money terms the only form of poverty? What would a true social democracy require in terms of culture? And how could this be achieved?

In the history of British Socialism these had, in fact, been perennial questions. But Science, the reign of the "expert", had deepened the old breach between the Movement's "heart" and "head".

Could that same Science now show how to end that fatal dualism? Could it indicate how to act and where to act without destroying in the process the will to act or that vision without which the people perish? Sociology might be capable of a synoptic view, yet its practitioners cultivated their own professional astigmatisms, tending to reject whatever could nòt be counted and neatly incorporated in a statistical table.

Nor, in the world of Admass and "two camps", was science so easily harnessed to large social purposes. Scientists, self-directing for much of the time, also, at critical moments, had masters. Similar questions to those of the "New Left" had been asked by the Common Wealth party, as recently as the war years. Society had been malleable then. But the war was over; the tide of opportunity had passed. There *was* a new society, though hardly that then sketched. There was a common culture—the international Admass culture. The "aristocratic embrace" against which the early Socialists had been warned had at least been a visible and generally also a merely intermittent peril.

The embrace of Admass was all-enveloping.

The rebel of today was the Angry Young gossip paragraph or the TV personality of tomorrow.

PART SIX

NIAGARA SHOT

"But the whole series of events comes swifter and swifter at a strange rate; and hastens unexpectedly,—'velocity increasing as the square of time'; so that the wisest prophecy finds itself quite wrong as to date: and patiently, or even indolently, waiting, is astonished to see itself fulfilled, not in centuries as anticipated, but in decades and years."

—Thomas Carlyle, *Shooting Niagara—and After?* 1867.

29. "Flying Saucers—OFFICIAL"

THROUGH THE ten years following 1947 the Great Flying
Saucer Story flashed and hummed in and out of the
headlines with a persistence that rivalled even the prewar
performance of the Loch Ness Monster—by comparison a
homely body. A retired Army officer, walking on the Yorkshire
moors, heard a "strange swishing sound" and looking up beheld
"poised at considerable height, a disc-like object"; in Liverpool, four women and one man reported to the police "a
flashing object like a large silver dinner plate, travelling eastwards"; at Malvern one evening, residents were astonished to
observe a "bluish-green bubble-like sphere" sweeping across
the sky "at tremendous speed" to vanish behind the Mendips.
At Chard, in Somerset, a saucer even put in an appearance at
a football match: "Spectators in the stand cried 'Oh!' as the

white liquid form sped inland from the direction of the English Channel"—a new peak even in the rich imagery of sports reporting.

The Astronomer Royal and other authorities poured dutiful scorn on the "Saucer Myth", explaining the "objects" as optical illusions, mock suns, meteorological balloons or merely mass hallucinations. They might as well have saved their breath. In Cumberland the small son of a local doctor, aged thirteen, and his cousin, aged eight, climbed a hillside and observed "a solid metallic thing, with a dome, portholes and three bumps underneath" coming down in front of them. He snapped it with his Kodak. At the subsequent public meeting in London, Air Marshal Lord Dowding pronounced the photographs "very interesting".

By the winter of 1950 two leading popular Sunday newspapers were running Saucer investigation series, advancing the general theory that the saucers were "space-ships", controlled by men from "other worlds" who were "watching us". This notion was confirmed in *Flying Saucers Have Landed*, a book published in 1953 by an amateur astronomer, living on the slopes of Mount Palomar, who described a brief chat he had enjoyed, by telepathic means, with a "Venusian" who had alighted from a Flying Saucer "at about 10.30 p.m. on November 20" in the Californian desert.

There was a spate of these "saucer" books, some of which sold hugely and were accorded solemn reviews in serious journals. For in the matter of "Ufo's"—Unidentified Flying Objects—most people were inclined to suspend both belief and disbelief. Was a flying saucer, after all, so much more extraordinary than nuclear fission, than supersonic flight, than those bat-like all-wing planes, or the British rocket-guided missile which, we were told in August, 1953, had achieved a speed of 2,000 m.p.h., travelling at a height of ten miles?

It was known that both the American Air Force and the R.A.F. had conducted official "saucer" investigations and had drawn the veil of "security" across the results. Could the saucers, as some hinted, be America's "Secret Weapon"? Or even—appalling thought—Russia's "Secret Weapon"? On the latter point, Mr. Gerald Heard in the *Sunday Express* was reassuring: "Discs have been seen in such numbers that very

39. New Men for New Times. In 1955 Churchill retired and so did Clement Attlee. In the Labour Party the Old Guard was in retreat. At the Party Conference at Margate (*above*) Herbert Morrison congratulates Hugh Gaitskell, just re-elected Treasurer. Two months later Gaitskell defeated Morrison in the contest for the Leadership. 40. (*Below*) At No. 10, too, roles were reversed. Sir Winston was the caller, Anthony Eden, the Prime Minister and host.

41. With Stalin's death, the iron curtain had risen—some of the way at least—
and Russians—sporting, political, technical—appeared astonishingly among us.
In April, 1956, they included Georgi Malenkov, Stalin's former right hand man,
here greeted by the Dagenham Girl Pipers at the Mansion House.

big plants must be turning them out in high quantity. Is that possible in Russia? It isn't."

"Saucers" certainly closely corresponded to the sort of thing the Old Testament would have called "a sign". A more sophisticated age could perhaps see them as a state of mind produced in normal human beings when the limits of the Possible were suddenly removed.

The Age of Steam, slowly spreading from Britain across the world, had lasted a hundred and fifty years. To its dying puffs, the Press successively proclaimed, in 72-point headlines, in a matter of ten years, the Jet Age, the Atom Age, the Synthetic Age, the Electronic Age, and now—why not?—the Space Age. . . .

The last steam locomotive, emerging in 1957 from the century-old Derby workshops—as the railways of the great Victorian engineers were at last electrified, dieselised, made-over—was still, in essentials, the engine that George Stephenson had created. Even in the inter-war years it had still seemed possible for a boy to grow up with a new invention such as the motor-car or radio. But now machines, techniques, were obsolete almost before they could be got off the drawing-board.

Aviation, the new world transport, drove the lesson home in these years brutally and at enormous cost. In 1951 when it flew over the Festival grounds, the giant Bristol Brabazon, constructed—at a total cost for the project of £12,000,000—to fly the Atlantic west-to-east non-stop, had been the object of much excitement and scores of enthusiastic articles. A little over a year later, it and the one other existing Brabazon had been sold by the Ministry of Supply for scrap.

The Brabazon had been "top priority" on the programme of airliner types for the coming "Jet Age" drawn up, at the Government's request, by the Brabazon Committee during the war. By the mid-Fifties the fate of the other types developed from the Committee's list was, with one or two striking exceptions,* hardly more encouraging. The "interim" Tudors—

* Particularly the medium-range turbo-prop Vickers Viscount which by the late Fifties was being operated by the airlines of fifty nations.

N

with the notable innovation of "the pressure cabin"—were hardly even a memory. The "Princess" flying-boats, twice as big as any previously built in Britain, lay cocooned and unwanted on their Calshot slipway—also, it seemed, on their way to the vast technological waste-bin of the Fifties. Even the star performer from the Brabazon Committee's list, the "pure jet" Comet, was now threatened by the fantastic pace of technological advance.

Global air transport itself had become a cardinal new fact so quickly that it had not been possible to grasp all its implications. 1957 was the first year in which as many people crossed the Atlantic by air as by ship. Yet only two years later, twice as many were flying to America as were sailing. Certainly few of those passengers can have recalled that up to the outbreak of war the crossing of the North Atlantic by air had the flavour of a hazardous feat—or can have remembered that the first tentative mail service, with two flying-boats, via Ireland and Newfoundland, had not been started until August, 1939. It had, in fact, been the wartime Return Ferry Service flying home the pilots who had delivered American bombers that had finally conquered the Atlantic.

Was it really true, we might ask ourselves, in some bewilderment, from our precarious perch in the subsonic Fifties that, back in 1949, we had been prepared to get excited about the feat of the B.B.C. commentator, Wynford Vaughan Thomas, in travelling around the world in eight days?

II

In the later Fifties the word "break-through"—a generation earlier a mainstay of Western Front talk—began to circulate again. To the layman, at least, it appeared that no less dramatic an expression would suffice. Scientists and technologists suddenly seemed to have acquired the power to advance into the Unknown with the precision and assurance of civil engineers building roads.

High in the sky, fusillades of supersonic bangs saluted science's new omnipotence and drove gardeners mad by shattering their greenhouse panes. The Americans had been the first to break through the "sound barrier", so long wrapped in mystery and dread. That was in the autumn of 1947. Six years later Neville Duke reached a speed of 717 m.p.h. in a Hawker-Hunter, recapturing the air speed record for Britain. After that the Americans made the pace for three years. And then in March, 1956, Peter Twiss travelled above the Sussex coast at 1,132 m.p.h. in a needle-nosed Fairey Delta 2.

The next barrier was the "heat barrier" and that, too, was, it seemed, being taken confidently in the stride. In the air, speed and power now advanced at short, regular intervals as if functions of the multiplication tables. The thrust of Whittle's first successful jet engine was 850 lb. That was in 1941. By 1945 the thrust of the jet engine had reached over 4,000 lb. Eleven years later it was 16,000 lb. in the Bristol Olympus engine, 15,000 lb. in the de Havilland Gyron.

Geared together by the urgencies of war in research on the industrial scale, science and technology were continuing their potent partnership where national need compelled or private profit drove. In the space of ten years, a vast, complex organisation to generate electric power from nuclear fission was built up from a foundation that at the outset in 1946 consisted of little but a series of equations. Many unprecedented problems had to be solved. New crafts and technologies had to be created. Yet in 1957 at Sellafield on the Cumberland coast electric power began to flow into the National Grid from what, it was proudly claimed, was the first industrial-scale atomic power station in the world. The same year, a £300,000,000 programme for the construction of twelve nuclear power stations was set on foot. And soon on the lonely coasts and desolate estuaries of Essex and Somersetshire and Gloucestershire and Dumfries strange shapes loomed: new artefacts of a new Age.

Such a world seemed to call for scientific seers rather than for mere economic planners. In 1948 the nation had resounded with talk about coal, upon which, it was given to understand, its whole future turned. The National Coal Board's expansion plans were continually assailed as inadequate. Yet ten years later, mountains of unsold coal piled up at the pitheads.

Britain had risen to power and greatness on coal. America had risen on oil. And now oil, so much more portable and better adapted to the automatic processes of the modern world—and with modern methods of exploitation in ample supply—was increasingly taking over in Britain also.

Once again ground that had been familiar beneath the feet for centuries was being cut away, it seemed, in weeks. Time was telescoped. Memory was lost. The picture, a semi-abstract, had no perspective, existing only in the single plane of the Present.

III

It was clear enough by this time that the true "Niagara leap" in these years was not Democracy's but Science's. It was applied science that, in World War II, had broken through the crust of tradition where it was thickest, compelling the sort of approach to men and machines that made 1945's "clean break" inevitable. It was economic science that, reinforcing the logic of the conveyor-belt, exorcised the spectre of slump and depression. "Social equality" was a potent idea, but it was technology through mass-production and mass-distribution that had clothed it. It was Science that, at a dozen points, had broken into the old class structure, throwing it into confusion. It was electronic science that had created the true nation-wide audience which,—thanks to the sampling techniques developed by social science,—took "count-heads" democracy to its logical—if still uncertain—conclusion.

And it was Science that was transforming—and re-transforming—the realities of Power.

And yet there were moments when it became clear that Science's forward leap was, nevertheless, also a leap in the dark. Five hundred new drugs were synthesised each year, powerful reinforcement in Medicine's armoury. But some proved to have unforeseen "side-effects"—an endearing phrase of these years which the "wonder drug" cortisone, arriving from America in 1949, had sensationally illustrated. From the mid-Fifties new tranquilliser drugs held out hope for the mentally deranged. But no one, it seemed, knew just what they did or how. The unknown perils of processes of nuclear fission reached out to generations yet unborn. In 1954 there was much alarm in the Forest of Dean over the Atomic Energy Authority's scheme to dump its radio-active waste in the district's old mine-workings. Was the concentration of strontium 90 in the bones already reaching dangerous heights as radiation mounted? There was an interesting diversity of scientific opinion.

Selective weedkillers, multiplying since the war worked wonders in the harvest fields. They also killed the bees, and much else, upsetting the process of fertilisation across wide areas, disturbing Nature's intricate balance. Intensive farming of animals boosting yields, weakened them, laying them open to infections. Special antibiotics were fed both to counter these and to speed growth. But what long-term effects these in their turn—and all the unnumerable chemical additives to manufactured foods—might have on the final human consumers none really knew.

Western Man had become the experimental guinea-pig of Science on a totally unprecedented—and indeed frightening —scale. But he was not frightened. He watched the scientists at work with calm—possibly tranquillized?—gaze in confident expectation of greater wonders to come.

Such confidence was, after all, understandable. The jubilant headlines spanned the front pages. THAT'S THE COMET, THAT WAS! Like the nuclear scientists, the aeronautical engineers were breaking through on new frontiers. No one knew what conditions prevailed up there in the stratosphere where the Comet flew at an unprecedented cruising speed of 500 m.p.h. Jet take-off, in the thinner air of the tropics, presented wholly new problems. Columbus, setting course across "boiling seas", was hardly more at grips with the unknown.

Yet the Comet's trials and development proceeded with a smoothness which suggested no more than the systematic working through of a series of equations. Three years after designing began and only five after the first practical jet-aircraft, the Gloster-Meteor fighter, had gone into action, the Comet had made her first short flight. And on 2nd May, 1952, with appropriate fanfares, the Comet embarked in B.O.A.C.'s colours on the world's first scheduled jet service—to South Africa.

Eleven months later it had brought Tokyo within 36 hours of London.

1953 was the year of Stalin's death; but for the British it was also the year of the Comet. Thousands now made their first jet flight and came home to boast about how they had stood the ritual penny on edge. By January, 1954, Comet airliners in service had completed 12 million remarkably trouble-free miles. Orders from all over the world were pouring into de Havillands. To an extraordinary degree the Comet had captured the nation's imagination and given form and brilliance to the hopes kindled at the Festival in 1951.

Then, out of a clear sky, the blow fell.

At a quarter-past ten on a Sunday morning, 10th January, Italian fishermen in their boats off the Isle of Elba, heard a high-pitched drone, succeeded by three explosions. They looked up, and saw a black plume of smoke, falling rapidly towards the sea.

It was the Comet C-ALYP which three-quarters of an hour earlier had taken off from Rome Airport en route to London with twenty-three passengers. Among them was Chester Wilmot, the B.B.C. war reporter and author of *The Struggle for Europe*.

At first there was angry talk of sabotage But then a doubt or two began to creep in. Eight months earlier disaster had overtaken a Comet as it climbed away from Calcutta in an area of sudden, violent storms. Had storms been the real trouble? Was there perhaps, after all, some hidden flaw in this vision of perfection?

For ten weeks the Royal Navy swept the seas off Elba, searching for some fragment of wreckage that might offer a clue. In Britain, in buses, pubs and offices people gravely discussed the rival theories. Might the kerosene-type fuel, highly volatile at high altitudes, have exploded? Had the power operated controls somehow led the pilot into some fatal manœuvre? Or vapour, leaking from a hydraulic line, been touched off by a chance spark?

The plane's engine was at last salvaged and flown to London. At Hatfield, de Havillands made fifty modifications in the Comet. They fitted special armour between the turbines and the fuel tanks. The Comets went back into service.

In April, three months after the disaster off Elba, another Comet, en route from Rome to Johannesburg, came spinning out of the sky, again off the coast of Italy, sixty miles north of the Straits of Messina.

This time there was no talk of sabotage on the Rome tarmac.

The Comet's certificate of airworthiness was withdrawn. At Hatfield all work on the Comet production line was stopped. This was not merely an industrial setback. It was a national catastrophe. It was like defeat in battle.

Yet even now confidence in the omnipotence of Science was not lost. In the Thirties, after the dirigible disasters, airships had been abandoned. But there was no thought now of abandoning the fantastic adventure of jet flight.

At Hatfield and at Farnborough, a whole year was occupied in the elaborate, infinitely painstaking process of elimination, testing and experiment, bringing to bear, at vast cost, all the techniques and specialisms of mid-century Science. And in February, 1955, the flaw was revealed: metal fatigue at a weak point in the airliner's thin metal skin, now exposed to the strains of pressurisation for flight at great heights—a new disaster of a new age.*

The equations were duly amended; the Comet structurally strengthened. Comet III, larger, more powerful, embarked on her flight tests. The unknown was knowable. Science, it seemed, indomitable.

Yet the delay had been costly. The "five-year lead" Britain had boasted in pure jet airliners was largely lost. In the "one world" that Science itself was making, "leads", it increasingly appeared, were merely momentary gains in a fast relay-race: technological advance developed a momentum of its own, transcending men and nations.

IV

Yet great as it was, our confidence in Science was essentially different from that of the Victorians. This Science of ours had

* The Comet's was not perhaps the first instance in which the technique of pressurisation had created a mystery of the air. In 1948 and 1949 two Avro Tudor IV airliners of British South American Airways, the "Star Tiger" and the "Star Ariel", had vanished without trace on scheduled flights over the sea between the Azores and Bermuda. "No more baffling problem has ever been presented for investigation", concluded the report of the Court of Inquiry on the "Star Tiger". The Tudors—in which high hopes had been placed—were grounded.

brilliance; but it had not the old simple grandeur. The Victorians had watched Darwin overthrow Genesis with a few fossils, microscope slides and the Scientific Method. They could, indeed, look down the microscope or, fossilising hammer in hand, read the Record of the Rocks themselves. The spectacle of the Great Engineer—or the man-on-the-footplate—in combat with the Elements had been one which all could comprehend and enjoy. The old steam locomotive, now puffing its way towards oblivion, had been, in the words often used by its mourning servitors, "almost human".

Even before the war, in the days of the Schneider Trophy races, speed was something which could be grasped, which brought a simple physical thrill. But now it had passed into the realm of pure mathematics. Add the word "electronic"—the abracadabra of the Fifties—and, for the layman, all contact with "reality" was lost.

For the non-scientists—that is, for most people—life in the Fifties often seemed to resemble an endless ride on a rollercoaster in which the landscape rushed by as a blur and a scream. Might the H-Bomb "trigger off the basic material of the Universe"? V.T.O.—Vertical Take-Off was the next thing in aviation now. Have you seen the "Flying Bedstead"? At the Harwell Atomic Research Establishment, Sir John Cockcroft announced that ZETA—the Zero Energy Thermonuclear Assembly—had produced fusion-temperatures a third those at the centre of the sun. "Stage Four would be commercial application and might be reached, if everything went perfectly, in ten years' time.". . . In gum-boots, white overalls and long white gloves, and Perspex-visored helmets, the decontamination squads stood ready. . . .

Sometimes the roller-coaster car, hurtling down an incline, drew up with a jolt at a station, and dizzily one read a name. Thus, one day in 1956, the word AUTOMATION leapt out of the headlines. Automation, it appeared, was Science's newest spell, the open sesame to the age of plenty. It would be the salvation of British industry. Alternatively, it would make half the working population redundant. AUTOMATION: TEN UNIONS TO MEET, shouted the evening newspaper contents bill. At Coventry, 11,000 workers were already out on strike because of the plan to introduce "Automation" at the Standard Motors'

Plant. Automation books followed swiftly on each other's heels; public men delivered themselves of dicta on the "vital" subject; there were "important" speeches in the House.

In fact, the first transfer machines had been installed at Morris Motors plant in the mid-twenties. And in the 'continuous processing' industries automatic control had long been in use. But now the tempo was increasing. The magic word "electronic" had been added. The newspapers were full of the miraculous feats of the "Electronic Brain", which in its two forms, the digital and the analogue computer, had in a single decade achieved such proficiency that it could be placed in control of some industrial and commercial operations.

Economists and other experts rushed in to explain, with their customary assurance, that "automation" was a beneficent force which would deliver the workers from their old bondage to the conveyer-belt, to offer them bright new lives as "programmers", electronic engineers, maintenance technicians and machine "monitors". Not all, however, found this prospect irresistible. At Derby, one, George Mee, made the headlines by quitting his job at a new "fully automated" ground mica factory. All he had to do all day, he explained to reporters, was to watch gauges, making an occasional adjustment. In six months of automated existence he had put on three stones. "Automation," declared Mr. Mee, "may be perfectly all right for some people. But it bores me."

But by 1956 there were probably few who retained the robust individualism of Mr. Mee. The tune of the year was *Che sara*, *sara*—whatever will be, will be. It was sung in tones of suitable bemusement.

V

Dr. Carl Gustav Jung—in whose province the matter clearly lay—wrote a little book about the significance of Flying Saucers. They were, he explained, a projection of man's unconscious mind—a symbol of his inner disquiet. The saucer's roundness simply expressed the mind's yearning for the wholeness it now lacked.

It was perhaps encouraging that more and more people, including even some scientists, were at last beginning to treat the point with the seriousness it deserved. In medicine, where the impact of science had been most intensive and spectacular, there was an increasing retreat from mechanistic concepts, an increasing stress on the psychological factors in illness, a move back towards the treatment—art as well as science—of the whole man. Psychiatry itself was less narrowly sectarian and exclusive, and was returning to a more social view of mental disorder, with a shift in emphasis from hospitalisation to community care.* The expression Social Medicine was now heard (replacing the older Public Health), and there was an increasing number of chairs in it. And if there was an almost total lack of machinery by which the insights of social medicine could be followed up (preventive services received a mere 1 per cent of the total N.H.S. budget), here and there some sort of a start had been made. The Clean Air Act, passed in 1956, was the first with teeth in it; that year too the B.M.A. at their annual conference voted not to smoke—in recognition of the correlation now established between smoking and lung-cancer; industrial health services were at work in several places, tracking down the true causes of most ill-health; and if the gigantic traffic-choked conurbation still seemed to present a well-nigh insoluble problem, the L.C.C., among others, had at least launched a campaign to encourage and help firms to migrate from London to the "expanding country towns" of neighbouring counties.

There were other straws in the wind. There was the new technology of "Ergonomics", which set out to design machines to fit men, rather than distort men to fit machines. After prolonged research, specialists in geriatrics, the study of ageing and the elderly, had discovered the virtues of the rocking-chair. A growing body of "organic gardeners" and compost-addicts —the newest form of 'Back to Naturism'—were mounting a revolt against the cocksure domination of the chemists.

Within the world of Science itself, new knowledge was

* In the Mental Health Act, 1958, following the findings of a Royal Commission, the framework of a Mental Health Service directed towards early locally-based preventive work—and coupled with an "open doors" policy in the mental hospitals—was sketched out. Implementation, however, was frustrated by lack of adequate local organisations and psychiatric social workers.

tending to break down the old tight compartmentalisation. Sociology—if its practitioners could somehow avoid being imprisoned in their own technicalities—might yet bring a new breadth and unity of view to the social sciences, as mathematics, nuclear physics and biology had to the physical sciences. As the "reality" of science became less and less mechanistic, some claimed that not only were scientific specialisms in process of coming together, but that Science and Religion, Science and Art, were equally comprehended in a new way of looking at the world.

These were breath-taking prospects. But for the moment the reappearance of the Universal Man would clearly have to wait on the reorientation of an educational system still largely based on the socio-cultural system of the distant Past. Parliament, still cluttered with lawyers, contained hardly a scientist in its ranks. The University of Oxford, despite much agonised debate, had not been able until 1960 to bring itself to the point of no longer requiring Latin and Greek as an entrance condition— for scientists and mathematicians.

Nevertheless, seventy years after T. H. Huxley had so vigorously pointed out the need, tentative approaches to a reorientation in education (which by this time also involved reintegration) were being made. Much thought was being given to methods of closing the gap between "the two cultures". In a Victorian mansion at Keele, near Stoke-on-Trent, in a "campus" of army huts, a new University College had come into being in 1949 under the direction of Lord Lindsay (one of the bold founders in 1921 of Oxford's "Modern Greats") dedicated to the eschewing of "disjointed specialisms" and the recreation of a cultural synthesis based on studies spread over the arts, social studies and experimental science.

As time went on, other new foundations began to make their own approaches, similarly directed towards enabling their future alumni to maintain a foothold—without magic and spells—in this "electronic" and "automated" world.

VI

If far from solved, the problems were at least increasingly recognised.

And now powerful new means of communication and education were at hand—if our society could command the social purpose to use them.

Was there, then, perhaps a chance that we should succeed in assimilating the scientific revolution at last? In this race between the forces making for disintegration and the slow groping towards a reintegration—with Man rather than Machine at its centre—was it conceivable that reintegration could win?

The chances seemed slender. To exist at all, they seemed to require some slowing down in the frantic pace of technical advance, a pause in the continuous scientific revolution in which we lived. Of this, in the Fifties, the prospects were meagre.

In 1957—the year in which the women of England were—or so the newspapers said—preoccupied by the Great Hemline Question: to Raise or not to Raise—the Americans announced plans for greeting the Geophysical Year by sending up what they called "earth satellites" to girdle our planet in ninety minutes.

FLYING-SAUCERS—OFFICIAL, announced the *Daily Express*, not unreasonably, across eight columns of its front page that morning.

The warning was timely. But the saucers, when they came, flew in from an unforeseen direction. On the 4th October, that curious, almost endearing, little word, *sputnik*, came spinning out of Outer Space into the English language and the new Esperanto of the Age.

Relayed by the B.B.C., the *bleep-bleep* of the sputnik's transmitters enlivened the British breakfast table. On Monday, 7th October, thousands of Londoners searched the sky at 7.7 a.m. when the "Red Moon" was scheduled to pass overhead on its global circuit. They saw nothing. But astronomers, tracking the satellite's 18,000 m.p.h. flight through space, appeared each day before the television cameras to chart the sputnik's progress.

Immediate reactions to this extraordinary scientific triumph were characteristic of the times, both in their complexity and perversity. The Russians—like a medieval church that had brought off a particularly potent miracle—were voted to have won a signal victory in the ideological war. Wall Street slumped.

American newspapers pointed out that, equipped with radar stations, Soviet sputniks would now enable the Reds to "keep an eye on every nation in the world".

As the "crisis" developed, it revealed once again the cleavage between American and British approaches which had been so continuous an element in these years. On one side of the Atlantic, President Eisenhower rallied the nation, appealed to Americans on TV to "close ranks". On the other, people appeared more concerned about "Little Lemon", the dog that had gone up in the second sputnik. The thought of that bright-eyed little animal up there in the sky, alone in its air-conditioned container, hurtling through space, its heart-beats broadcast to Earth, gripped a million British minds. Supported by two boxer bitches, a deputation from the Canine Defence League marched to the Soviet Embassy to deliver a protest.

But the larger implications of the sputniks were not slow to assert themselves. It would have been hard to imagine a more telling method of announcing to the world that the fecund partnership of Science and Technology was now global. The first industrial revolution had established the technical supremacy—virtual monopoly—of Western Europe, and, then of Western Europe and the U.S.A. The second industrial—or scientific—revolution had shattered it, and was now in process of shattering all the comfortable old assumptions that had gone with it.

The "Space Race" was on.

Yet if, even now, there was no escape from the stultifying ideological frame in which the world was clamped, at least the onset of the Space Age was drastically changing the picture within it. Disintegration by Intercontinental Ballistic Missiles, fired from several thousand miles away, might not appear, to the individual, notably preferable to annihilation from tank-fire at close range. Yet both the psychological and the power realities were transformed in ways more complex and far-reaching than we had yet begun to grasp. The concept of physical "disengagement" might be rejected,—even when propounded by so persuasive an advocate as Mr. George F. Kennan, who, in 1947, had originated the historic American "doctrine of containment". Yet the fact of disengagement remained. The world of the I.C.B.M.s was a scientists' world, in which truth could not be confined, "one world" in which advance in one geographical sector was now almost instantaneously transmitted to another, and espionage became largely anachronistic and not a little ridiculous.

In spite of political and commercial efforts to direct it to dubious ends, Science was still proceeding by its own method and setting its own pace. In 1957 the savage repression in Hungary, the new purges, the execution of Imre Nagy, seemed for a while to have plunged the world back into the claustrophobic nightmare of 1948. In fact, it could not: the Iron Curtain in its old sense could not exist in the Space Age. That same year at Geneva, the scientists of Russia, America, Britain, India, Japan and other nations of East and West met again at the second international conference on the Peaceful Uses of Atomic Energy, freely exchanging their findings. Despite all efforts to obscure the fact, the new triumphs in space were triumphs of humanity and of Science rather than of any single nation state or political faith. If at home Science sometimes seemed to be confronting society with the prospect of imminent disintegration, when one looked beyond national frontiers at the wider scene its power to unify was once again in evidence.

To unify—or annihilate.

30. Triumph of a Salesman

> "You're about twenty years behind
> us now, but you know with these TV
> cameras twenty years can be tra-
> versed in a single year."
> —Frederick Wakeman, American
>   author of *The Hucksters,* in a
>   B.B.C. interview.

> " 'OMO improves even on perfect
> whiteness.' 'Even on *perfect* whiteness ?'
> 'Even on perfect whiteness!' "
> —Television commercial of the Fifties.

> "The couple turned and saw the
> maniacs at the door with hatchets in
> their hands. At ——'s orders they
> returned to their seats and all four
> began to watch television."
> —*Daily Mirror* news-item, 21st Jan-
>   uary 1956.

ENGLAND AWAITED the first day of Commercial Television
rather as one might await a tidal wave, an earthquake
or some other force of nature. There was a feeling that
something somehow critical was about to befall, but only the
vaguest idea of how severe "it" might be, or of how it could
have happened.

Heralded for months by news-items about the "desertions"
of famous B.B.C. performers and producers, the "Gala Opening", on the 22nd September, 1955, was accompanied by champagne at the May Fair Hotel, State trumpeters at the Guildhall,
and, as earnest of high cultural intentions, by Sir John Barbirolli
and the Hallé Orchestra. But though the proceedings began at
7.15 it was not till after eight that the programme reached what

the 200,000 or so TV-owners able to receive it were breathlessly awaiting—the first duly authorised "commercial" in our island story. It turned out to be a tribute to a "tingling fresh" toothpaste.

Reviewing this and other offerings next day, the newspaper critics were unable to suppress a certain incredulity. But there it was. It had happened. And the only real sensation of the evening had been provided by the staid old B.B.C. which, a few minutes before Independent Television was due to make its bow, had immolated young Grace Archer (of the "Archers of Ambridge") in a blazing stable, thus cruelly bereaving her loving husband, Phil.

The day had been awaited with the more trepidation in that not only was commercial broadcasting flagrantly at variance with British tradition, but television itself was still deeply suspect. The speed with which it had swept across the land, its hypnotic grip (according to B.B.C. Audience Research it took an average family five years to break loose) had taken almost everybody by surprise. In 1950 Mr. Lionel Hale had written, echoing the official view: "Even when television is in its full stride, sound radio will more or less keep its present place." In the event, though the B.B.C. was in process of providing a chain of V.H.F. transmitters to give high quality listening, the average regular radio sound audience fell between 1954 and 1957 from around 9,000,000 to 3,500,000. The derisive term "steam radio" reflected well enough the reaction of the average family once the television set had moved into the house.

Earlier innovations in mass-communications had been cold-shouldered and kept in their lowly places for years. But TV not only reported the news, it made it. Each morning at the bus-stop, on the railway platform, in office and shop and factory, there was a new topic of conversation to replace "the weather". It was not the latest antics of Khrushchev, nor the new balance of payments crisis. It was: "Did you see So-and-So on television last night?"

In the Twenties the newspapers had for a while boycotted the B.B.C.'s programmes, and had barred it from collecting news. But times had changed. Now, their instinct for self-preservation well alerted, they leapt for the TV bandwaggon, printing acres of TV gossip, signing up TV celebrities, offering elaborate daily critiques of programmes, copying TV ideas. This did not stop television writing "finis" across the great Press boom of the postwar years. In the periodical field, in particular, the advent of full-scale TV brought the end of an era. *Picture Post* ceased publication in the summer of 1957, and, after that, the remaining illustrated general "middlebrow" magazines, which had been an important feature of the Forties, enjoying a collective circulation of several millions, sank one by one, leaving scarcely a ripple behind them.

The cinema—the first great mass-entertainment industry— was so gravely stricken that Wardour Street was driven to desperate exertions. Its first thoughts, naturally were in terms of size. In November, 1953, the Biblical "epic", *The Robe*, introduced British cinemagoers to the splendours of Cinemascope. And the screen continued to expand and explode, both visually and orally. Producers offered not only a story and stars, but a complete packaged tour. One chugged down Venice's Grand Canal with Katherine Hepburn, pitched coins into Rome's Trevi Fountain with Dorothy McGuire, climbed the Acropolis, dived beneath the blue Aegean in *Boy on a Dolphin* . . . A cinemagoer now needed a head for heights. He was continually ascending—to the top of a silo, or up Hongkong's Peak, or up in a balloon—to take in the view.

Despite all these rich and colourful experiences—and revived Horror films, Westerns, and Mr. Cecil de Mille too— mass desertion to the little grey screen continued. Indeed it gathered pace. This was the more mortifying in that technically television had apparently so little to offer. It was not a new art-form, but rather occupied a shadowy territory somewhere between the theatre and the film, borrowing from each. And yet this particular combination, coupled with a native intimacy and immediacy which came partly from the size and quality of the electronic screen, partly from the privacy in which it was watched, were sufficient to generate insights and attitudes which were soon exerting a powerful influence on both cinema and theatre.

In England the theatre now began to develop a new flexibility well suited to the talents of the rising school of "demotic" "slice-of-life" writers, while the cinema returned to black-and-white to develop a "theatrical" and even claustrophobic intensity which was far removed from the traditional cinema whose essence had always been felt to lie in freedom of movement and space.

A good many American films, like the aptly-named *Big Knife*, now introduced an all too real rawness and brutality designed to hit the audience so hard in the solar plexus that it would scarcely be able to stagger back to its TV set. At some little distance British film-makers followed this lead, on several occasions presenting British lorry-drivers, for instance, as ugly, face-smashing, racketeering brutes.

But later, the documentary strand in British film-making, which had emerged so strongly in the war years, was picked up again, purged now of Ealing whimsy, and films too had their share of "kitchen sinks" and industrial backgrounds. Many found this somewhat startling, for these were aspects of British life which had never been seen on our screens before. TV, this small lighted box, seemed indeed to have brought a new interpenetration of media in a manner worthy of a true child of this atomic world, and seen also in some other arts, such as sculpture.

It was thus not surprising that for many long troubled by the uneasy feeling that civilisation was collapsing about them, the arrival of television should seem to mark the beginning of the end. Commercial interests might be obliged to capitulate; individuals were not. A Mr. Fyfe, of Beckenham, wrote to the *Daily Telegraph* filling half a column with a picture of the mental and spiritual degeneration that swiftly followed on the acquisition of a television set. "Britain," he wrote, "is becoming full of unhappy people, who to their dismay, are steadily losing touch with everything that used to matter."

Mr. Fyfe rallied the still TV-less with a final word: "Once you waver, you are lost." There were many to say "Amen" to that. A survey in the mid-Fifties put TV "abstainers" at no less than one-sixth of the adult population*—many, consciously or unconsciously, making a last stand for the Old Society. *Après TV, le déluge.* TV, they complained, "killed civilised conversation". It turned intelligent children into morons. It induced "narcotic dysfunction". It would only enter the house, in the

* Gorer, *Sunday Times* Survey, November, 1957.

classic phrase of Sir Eric James, High Master of Manchester Grammar School, "over my dead body".*

Certainly no machine in history had so vastly and so rapidly disturbed and injured such a variety of powerful vested interests —commercial, intellectual, professional. For this offence TV was placed in the dock and kept there, more or less continuously, for five years. It was cited in divorce courts, brought into suicide notes, pleaded in extenuation of theft ("And then the monster called TV came into my life and . . .") blamed for little boys' nightmares, for typists' bad spelling, and (of course) for juvenile delinquency. Doctors diagnosed "TV Neck", "TV Crouch", "TV Dyspepsia" and "TV Stutter"; dentists issued a solemn warning against buck teeth produced in children by "viewing" from the floor, chin cupped in hands.

Innumerable anxious surveys and investigations into the effects of TV were set on foot, and the publication of each renewed the indictment. But by no means all the reports bore out the charges. After surveying 400 London TV families, a Dr. Belson reported: "The meeting of a deadline together gives form to the evening, provides a sense of achievement, and creates a feeling of togetherness."

Whatever its merits, this particular sort of togetherness continued to grow in phenomenal fashion. The nation's children, switching as one from Davy Crockett coonskin caps and Indian hunter flintlocks to Robin Hood hats and bows-and-arrows at the promptings of the Box, formed a vast infiltrating army of TV zealots. In 1955 the B.B.C. reported that among five-to-seven-year-olds 85 per cent watched TV daily; if their own home did not contain a set they insinuated themselves into one that did.

Under such relentless pressures, Abstainer after Abstainer wavered, took the first sip, and was lost. In 1949 two-thirds of the people of Britain had never seen a television set working, much less owned one. Yet by the winter of 1957–58 an average Sunday evening found almost half the adult population engaged in "viewing", while among working-class viewers 45 per cent

---

* A fascinating echo, across thirty years, of a similar remark by the Headmaster of Rugby, deploring the inroads of the wireless-set in the early Twenties.

remained in communion with the Box for an average of four hours every night of the week.

Not only was this the most extraordinary example of sustained "togetherness" in our national history, but it also opened up entirely new dimensions in "mass-communications" and startling new prospects for popular culture.

II

Though the character of "mass-communications" can now be seen to be of central importance for the future of Socialism, the Labour Government's appointment of the Beveridge Committee on Broadcasting in 1949 had, in fact, been a largely routine step dictated by the impending expiry of the B.B.C.'s Charter.

In January, 1951, after sifting and assessing a vast volume of evidence, the committee recommended that "this most pervasive and therefore one of the most powerful agents for influencing men's thoughts and actions", should remain exclusively in the tried and trusted hands of the B.B.C. There was only one dissentient to this verdict, a Conservative lawyer M.P. and Recorder of Wigan, a Mr. Selwyn Lloyd. The Labour Government, however, clearly did not consider the matter particularly urgent. It waited so long before embarking on legislation to renew the B.B.C.'s Charter that the General Election supervened. The matter thus passed unsettled to the Conservative Cabinet.

This, in turn, seems to have regarded the whole issue as an unnecessary interruption in its international and economic preoccupations. Its vague announcement in May, 1952, that "in the expanding field of television" provision would be made "for some element of competition" had the air of being a sop thrown to the party's more ardent "free enterprisers" rather than a carefully thought-out decision on a matter of central importance. If Conservatism was experiencing difficulties in "setting the people free" in other directions, at least it could liberate them here!

It was not until the great debate provoked by the Government's White Paper got under way that the fundamental issues were thrown into relief; not until the debate itself that one was afforded a sudden glimpse of the way in which, beneath the surface of the old society, the still half-hidden drives of the new one had been gathering strength for a break-through.

Like the debate over the Comprehensive School in the Forties this was a debate which might almost have been staged as a symbolic confrontation. For though in origin an historical accident, the B.B.C. had been all but absorbed into the unwritten Constitution. Under war and postwar pressures, it was true, it had relaxed a little, but its social prestige remained immense, its position apparently impregnable. The challenge to the B.B.C. monopoly was a head-on challenge to tradition, hierarchy, British received values.

At the same time the debate sharply illuminated the central dilemma of this critical stage of social transition. If, in the name of Democracy, Freedom, Equality, one delivered the people from hierarchical bondage, was one merely, in effect, surrendering them to another, and possibly worse, enslavement?

It was an issue which—particularly on the Right—cut briskly across party lines and again suggested their inadequacy to the real world of the Fifties. There were many Tories in whom the old faith in the hierarchical order and attendant authoritarian culture outweighed their party's latter-day subscription to the values of competitive commercial enterprise. To these the Government appeared, in Lord Hailsham's phrase, to be proposing to erect a Golden Calf in addition to the Established Church. There were likewise some Socialists for whom the joys of deliverance from the Squirearchy of Broadcasting House loomed larger than the perils of commercial corruption.

The spectre which haunted the debates (as it had haunted radio debates in the interwar years)* was that of final and irrevocable "Americanisation". For many, this was decisive. There was much public shuddering over horrific details brought back from the United States by hardy travellers—"Hamlet with dentifrice ads." or the awful warning of the Coronation film which had been interlarded on American TV with commercials featuring a Mr. Fred J. Muggs, a chimpanzee.

* Advertising on the air had been rejected by the Sykes Committee on broadcasting as early as 1923 as "likely to lower the standard", and this view had been reaffirmed at intervals since then.

Many devoutly agreed with the writer of a letter to *The Times*: After all, "we do not allow salesmen to walk at will into our homes nor to paste display advertisements upon our walls".

Others, however, contrasted the "vitality" and "richness" of American competitive broadcasting with the monopolistic "complacency" or "grandmotherly" attitudes of the B.B.C., death to all true art and enterprise. To Mr. Norman Collins, a former controller of B.B.C. Television (who had been refused the vacant post of Director, and was later to become Deputy Chairman of Associated Television Ltd.), commercial television appeared to belong to "those Four Freedoms which less than ten years ago we were saying we were prepared to defend with our lives".

The battle was highly organised, with heavy artillery brought up on both sides. The Popular Television Council (Lord Derby, Lord Brabazon *et alia*) exchanged salvo for salvo with the B.B.C.'s champions, the National Television Council (Lord Halifax, Lady Violet Bonham-Carter *et alia*). Meanwhile, a Gallup Poll showed that through it all, more than one-half of the population remained staunch B.B.C. loyalists, a remarkable enough figure, whether it signified satisfaction with the programmes, inertia, instinctive respect for one's betters, or patriotic preference for a *British* tradition over an American one. In addition, the Archbishops, the University Vice-Chancellors, the authoritative figures in the worlds of education, religion and the arts, were strong for the B.B.C. and its "public service" concept.

But—as Lord Beveridge observed in the House of Lords debate—"Money talks". And Money's voice had never been so well modulated or so pervasive in our society. The Parliamentary debate might be impressive, but it was not decisive. The defenders were infiltrated before the battle had begun; the campaign for "Independent"—characteristically equivocal phrase—Television was engineered with great skill and pressed home on all fronts by a camouflaged advertising-and-big-business pressure group, operating from what, in our society, was an increasingly central position of strength. Significantly, Lord Woolton, the Tories' postwar Organiser of Victory, the 'moderniser' imported into the party from the world of mass merchandising, had been commercial television's chief champion in the Cabinet.

But the outcome—so much the protests in Parliament and elsewhere had secured—was not "sponsored" television on the American model. It was a complicated compromise which, according to the *Manchester Guardian*, testified to the continuance of our "insular hypocrisy". The customary loving care was devoted to the preservation of the old façade; the "cash nexus" was decently obscured beneath the maximum number of layers of dark oak panelling. There was to be one more public authority, an I.T.A. Uncle for a B.B.C. Aunt, headed by public luminaries, and fortified by £750,000 of public money a year. This would allot time to a suitable diversity of contractors and, having done so, would ensure that they maintained "a proper balance", "good taste and decency" and a "high general standard of quality", and kept the "commercials" "recognisably separate", confined to the "natural breaks" in the programmes and conforming to "the highest standards of advertising conduct".

"The British", summed up an American commentator, "have decided to paint the gaudy thing a sombre grey to blend with the general fog."

In the years to follow a certain gaudiness was to show through all the same.

III

Its development stimulated by the great debate, by the allocation of new resources, and now by the hot breath of competition, television continued to demonstrate that as a medium of mass-communication its potentialities were both unique and tremendous.

In the second half of the Fifties TV output and technique advanced at a pace that, at any other time, would have seemed astonishing. In 1954 the B.B.C.'s newly inaugurated television "news and newsreel" service was being widely criticised for its amateurishness and dilatoriness; three years later, TV reportage had reached a high peak of immediacy in world news coverage—an immediacy the medium itself seemed to exact—

and such topical weekly programmes as Panorama (with an audience of eight or nine millions) really were opening "a window on the world" in no merely metaphoric sense. Vast numbers of citizens who had never read beyond the sports pages or travelled much further than Southend now moved around the terror-ridden cities of Algeria, watched excited Arabs in billowing burnouses haranguing crowds in the hard bright light of the Persian Gulf, or saw what it was like to stand in the bread-lines in the United States, again in recession. Nasser in his Cairo garden, Khrushchev in full spate in Moscow, Eisenhower gravely reasonable in the White House, appeared on the screen in the sitting-room, answered or parried questions, revealing in the process every grimace and inflexion.

The world was peopled as never before.

And the nation was peopled, too. The "man-in-the-street", "the workers", "the boss", were, no longer merely symbolic figures: they were there, on the screen, their opinions endlessly solicited by omnipresent television reporters. It was established that there were many accents in Britain, many idioms and standards, besides "B.B.C.", and that these were not necessarily comic. For, by its nature, television largely escaped the "We/They" dichotomy into which the popular Press sometimes seemed to fall the more deeply the more desperately it strove to be "matey".

In this way, and in some others, the logic of television as a medium added its force both to the Egalitarianism of 1945—of the "Beveridge Revolution"—and the Equality of 1955—of the conveyor-belt—to close—or at least narrow—the old social and cultural gulfs in the nation.

Thanks in part to the illustrative possibilities of the medium, in part to the strength of the B.B.C. tradition, leavened now by the more informal and 'democratic' approach of I.T.N., television was able to establish new standards in the popular exposition of serious subjects. In particular, it rescued such "difficult" and hitherto barred subjects as abortion law, prostitution and homosexuality from the plane of Sunday newspaper sensationalism and gave them humane, informed and serious treatment. Because of television's public and semi-monopolistic character, its producers were obliged to strive for balance in handling controversial issues—with the result that large numbers who read only one newspaper now habitually and willy-nilly heard "both sides" of political and other current controversies. Potentially at least, this was a development of the greatest significance in the growth of an educated democracy.

Nor was the stimulus which TV could offer confined to its explicitly informative programmes. Even a "panel game", in the face-to-face, sound-and-vision, intimacy of the small screen, *could*—rather as in an odd echo of an Oxbridge tutorial—bring stimulating contact with lively and well-stocked minds. In "Animal, Vegetable or Mineral?"—a sophisticated revival of a Victorian parlour game—or "Buried Treasure", Sir Mortimer Wheeler and his Cambridge colleague, Dr. Glyn Daniel, were able to convey the excitements of their subjects with such authenticity that a boom in popular archaeology resulted. The broadcasting don, not long ago a sort of freak, was becoming a commonplace; the academics were coming down into the market-place.

Natural history, too, proved to be a television "natural". Programmes like Peter Scott's "Look" brought the secret life of the wild into the sitting-room, renewing the jaded sense of wonder in many a townee. More surprisingly, the detail of painting and sculpture often seemed to come across in a remarkable way under the TV camera's lens. As Sir Gerald Kelly or Sir Kenneth Clark conducted viewers on tours of the galleries, or painters like Stanley Spencer or L. S. Lowry talked about their canvasses as they painted, it did not seem altogether impossible that television might yet do for Art something of what radio had done for music. When Mervyn Levy gave a series of painting lessons before the television cameras, so many housewives and others donned the smock that the sales of tubes of paint went up with a rush, and Thomas Cooks put on a new sort of tour:

PAINT ABROAD WITH MERVYN LEVY—Choice of Cézanne Country (Provence), Gauguin Country (Brittany) or Venice, the Artists' Paradise.

Obviously, much of this was ephemeral. Surveys suggested that the percentage of the audience stimulated to positive

study or action remained small. But 2 per cent*—of 20,000,000
—is no negligible number, as runs on books in libraries all over
the country now confirmed.

Yet it seemed that television's greatest service of all might
reside in its ability to chart and illuminate for the layman the
new frontiers of science—to reduce the roller-coaster ride to an
intelligible progression. For this Third Eye with which humanity was now equipped seemed able to penetrate the microcosm
as effortlessly as it embraced the macrocosm. It could expose
the cells of the human body, proliferating gaily; it could slip
the viewer into the operating theatre and take him inside the
pulsing human heart; with the aid of a medical viewing
instrument, it could send him tobogganing down the human
throat and trachea into the great vaulted cavern of the lungs.

In these and other exercises television received the sort of
co-operation from scientists that they had never been willing
to accord to the Press. The scientist—as well as the man-in-the-
street—appeared on the screen and despite his white coat was
observed to be possessed of two legs and even vaguely human.

IV

Yet so characteristic a phenomenon of mid-century Science
did not escape that science's persistent ambivalence. It was,
on the contrary, a particularly baffling example of it.

If television opened a window on the world, it shut the door
on the street; its offer of cultural integration contained a threat
of social atomisation. Its revelations were vivid—in the moment
before they were washed away in the endless flow that followed.
Its spontaneity and "sincerity" were the product of processes
so complex and of specialisms so numerous, that they were
inevitably suspect.

And yet here, too, science itself was neutral. The balance
struck depended on the manner in which the new instrument
was employed, and upon the master motives of those who

* The *Sunday Times*—Gorer Survey, 1957, with a sample of 1,246
viewers, showed that a little over 2 per cent had been stimulated by
TV to do some reading on a novel topic and 131 to put into practice
something they had learned from viewing.

employed it. Its virtues could be given full play, its dangers minimised. Or vice-versa.

As it turned out, after 1955 the unique qualities of this new gift of science provided the perfect crown to the fast-growing structure of Admass in Britain. Conjuring up its own closed-circuit "electronic" world, television offered new quick and profitable access to the subconscious. Vividness combined with ephemerality was ideal for the promotion of rapid fashion-change. Simultaneous impact on eye and ear in the relaxed privacy of the home was excellent for the impression of the new brand image, or for the stimulation of the impulse to go out and buy. The window that television opened on the world now opened also on the supermarket; the viewers became also that wonderful, unprecedented thing, a nation-wide "captive audience" counted in millions.

At the stage which Britain's social evolution had currently reached, commercial television had another immense advantage to offer the interests which employed it: it enabled them to assume the mantle of Liberators.

For as the new I.T.A. transmitters spread across the land, and more and more viewers had their old sets "converted" or bought one of the new "13-Channel" sets, an interesting social phenomenon was observed. While the upper income groups remained staunch B.B.C. loyalists, and the middle income groups were about equally divided, the lower income groups clutched ITV possessively to their bosoms, the People's Own. "In my Secondary Modern School," reported a London teacher, "to watch the B.B.C. is regarded as 'sissyfied' behaviour."

While this was to some extent an intellectual choice, as in the B.B.C.'s Light-Home-Third division,* it was also much more. It was a "political" vote-with-the-switch. For, despite the democratisation of the war and postwar years, there still clung about the B.B.C. the aura of "the Establishment", of the leadership—infinitely discreet, but nevertheless indubitable— of "officers and gentlemen". That quiet assurance bespoke

---

* This sort of choice does not, however, within its limits, appear to have worked on a predominantly class basis. According to the Third Programme's Controller in 1956 the Third's audience was then made up of 28 per cent upper middle class, 37 per cent lower middle, and 35 per cent working class.

proprietorship. But ITV was different. ITV with its cheerful announcers and breezy 'newscasters', with the London Palladium, Omo and Murraymints, the-too-good-to-hurry-mints, appeared to stand unequivocally for "no class distinctions" and the Other Ranks, still obscure, perhaps, but definitely up-and-coming and yearly more aware of it.

The advent of commercial television, announced Sir Robert Fraser, the new Director-General of the Independent Television Authority, a former Socialist journalist, formed "the fourth great revolution in public communications".

Clearly, there were elements of truth in that—although some might think that never in history had a revolution quite so quickly been betrayed.

As in other departments of the "People's Capitalism", the first and most noticeable effect of Commercial TV was the effect of superabundance. In 1956 the "toddlers' truce", the hour of television silence between 6 p.m. and 7 p.m. was abandoned. Henceforth, citizens throughout their leisure hours were offered five separate radio and TV programmes. As in the supermarket, so on the small screen, the shelves were long. Riches were offered which at any other time must have seemed fabulous. In the drama department, Tchekhov, Shakespeare, Ibsen (for a time almost a "resident script-writer"), Shaw, Sheridan, O'Casey, Eugene O'Neill, Elmer Rice and others were freely available for millions who would never otherwise have experienced them. Performances by the Hallé and other great orchestras made the viewer a participant in the excitements of the concert hall. Someone calculated that the B.B.C.'s elaborate production of Richard Strauss's opera, *Salome*—no doubt assisted by advance publicity for the Dance of the Seven Veils—was seen in a single night by more people than had seen it on the stage during the entire fifty years of its existence, or, alternatively, by an audience which would have packed the Albert Hall nightly through fourteen annual six-week seasons.

For the contemporary writer, television might appear to offer the opportunity for the first time for many years to develop a genuine popular drama. And it did indeed nourish a lively brood of naturalistic writers. But quantity, by its sheer weight and bemusement, threatened quality. The Electronic Machine had been created, had been multiplied, and now it had to be fed. (It required, for instance, 400 new plays a year.) To keep it running smoothly required a standard product, deliverable by the trainload. The formulas, as in sound radio, had been worked out across the Atlantic, and required only adaptation (and little enough of that).

At one point, commercial television was running a give-away quiz show on every day of the week, and two on Saturdays. That could pall. More reliable was the half-hour serial episode, which appeared capable of infinite multiplication and permutation. The best of these were well scripted and acted. They were highly efficient mechanisms, little machines, machine-made for the larger machine. Often they were "semi-documentary", and belonging to the same phantom world as the "fictionised fact" and "factualised fiction" on the bookstalls. They consumed life painlessly, and, in these years, in substantial slices.

Thus "culture and anarchy" were further multiplied: "all rabble-scrabble" *ad infinitum; Hedda Gabler* followed by *Wells Fargo* succeeded by *Dixon of Dock Green* played out by Sir Thomas Beecham and the London Philharmonic followed by *"Double Your Money"* and *"What's My Line?"* and *Boyd, Q.C.* followed by *Whither India?* and *Highway Patrol* and *What's the Matter with France?* followed by P.C. Dixon again and Sir Kenneth Clark lecturing on painting. . . .

The problem of choice became acute. Even for an educated and disciplined mind to navigate this flood and not be merely swept on by it, day after day, week after week, could not be easy. Science, however, had provided another small machine to make undue exertion unnecessary. Fixed to the television set in the homes of "consumers", the electro-mechanical Audimeter or Tam-meter automatically registered, minute by minute, the votes of the household, later to be transferred from tape to punched cards, grossed and analysed by other machines.

The statistics that resulted had, like those of Dr Kinsey, a merciless (if spurious) precision. NORTHERNERS REJECT SHAKE-SPEARE, announced the Nielson Survey's bulletin, impartially but decisively. The charts showed the graph line of the Audience Rating rising like Table Mountain for a give-away quiz-show like "Double Your Money" or for the half-hour episodes of "Wagon Train" or "Emergency Ward 10"; they showed them plunging to Dead Sea levels for Barbirolli and the Hallé Orchestra or for Shakespeare.

By this ingenious device, producer and consumer now appeared geared together in the final "democratic" relationship. "Count-of-heads" had been taken to that level of perfection where it acquired the continuous quality of caricature. Numbers were all; the depth and quality of the experience, its true impact, were discounted.

Democracy depends ultimately on the motivations of those who are voted into power. The votes received can be interpreted either as pointing to opportunities for service or as indicating vulnerable areas for exploitation. In this case there was little need for deep inquiry into motivation. The Tam-meter or Audimeter was primarily the means of delivering to advertisers, in the words of the Nielson Index Service, "the best possible 'cume' ["accumulated audience"] with the best possible A.C.D. ["average number of commercials delivered per home"]." Or as one of the same firm's survey leaflets put it, rather less scientifically: "Time Buying's like Trawling. The Chap Who knows Fish, NETS 'EM."

Carefully safeguarding the "British tradition", the Television Act had separated programme-making and control from direct contact with the salesman. The Tam-meters and their ever-present charts now brought the two neatly and firmly together again.

Whatever their true value, the intimidation of the figures, set out in columns, rising and falling in graph-lines, was completer and more lasting than the orange-peel which "the gods" in an earlier popular theatre showered down upon the stage in token of their displeasure.

When the figures began to show a steady desertion of the B.B.C. for ITV by those viewers now in a position to choose,*

* By the end of the first full year of Commercial Television for viewers who could choose, ITV was capturing seven hours a week to the B.B.C.'s four—and ITV's inroads were still growing. By the end of 1957, 72 per cent were choosing ITV, 28 per cent the B.B.C. (but thereafter the B.B.C. began to pull back a little).

even the B.B.C. could not resist the implication that something had to be done. For a time indeed competition between B.B.C. and ITV attained an almost gladiatoral character. This certainly stimulated the energies, but not necessarily the creative ones. As had already been fully demonstrated in journalism and, to a lesser degree in politics, this kind of competition (with millions, of both pounds and heads, at stake) tended to paralyse the creative imagination, producing a humiliating panic-stricken copy-catery. Thus, ITV's "I Love Lucy" was instantly matched and met by the B.B.C.'s "I Married Joan", the B.B.C.'s "Wells Fargo" went gunning for ITV's "Wyatt Earp", "Double Your Money" challenged "What's My Line?", "Free Speech" contended against "In the News", Formula YXZ was cunning countered with Formula XYZ.

Competition on this level was, it is true, complemented by competition (at suitably (inexpensive) late hours on ITV) in a commodity called "Prestige". Possibly this acknowledged that standards other than the statistical lingered on. But when it was accompanied by such an immense parading by both sides of audiences-in-chains, so much crowing over places in the "Top Ten" programmes, even this seemed doubtful.

Audience Research, the respectful B.B.C. "servant" of the Forties, had become the hectoring major-domo of the later Fifties. In 1957 the B.B.C. Director-General, Sir Ian Jacob, announced a new radio pattern "to meet the changing tastes and habits of a television age". There would be "less talk, more music". The Light was to be lighter yet, and extended for two hours daily. The Third was to be cut by 2½ hours daily.

The latter gesture called forth protests from many respected names in Letters, Music and the Fine Arts, deploring—through the Sound Broadcasting Society formed for the purpose—the B.B.C.'s surrender to "the Mass Audience drifting aimlessly on its tide of treacle".

Such pessimism might be excessive, arising from a failure to understand the new conditions of the cultural supermarket. Yet it seemed clear that the advent of commercial television had carried the "pop radio" revolution of the Forties into a new phase. Before the war the B.B.C., like some sort of university, had paid its performers "civil service" rates. Now it had to bid in competition for "top" stars and "top writers". Performers could achieve dazzling financial rewards, but these were strictly related to success as measured by the Rating. Figures begat figures. The B.B.C., too, had entered the Big Money orbit.

V

The very high cost of providing television programmes had been among the most telling reasons advanced for allowing commercial television to provide them "free". The result—as might have been foreseen—was that the influx of advertising millions inflated costs still further and translated television, like mass-sale newspapers, into the world of Very Big Business. Thus although under the Television Act advertising agents themselves were ritualistically excluded, financiers, newspaper bosses, electronic industrialists and entertainment czars were the logical controllers of the principal programme companies. Logic prevailed. The Empire of Admass in Britain was consolidated.

Between 1956 and 1959 expenditure on television advertising more than quadrupled, in the latter year exceeding the advertising revenue of all the national and London evening papers put together, itself at record heights. As advertisers and advertising agents became accustomed to the multi-million captive audiences delivered to them by commercial television, they were more than ever inclined to turn up their noses at the smaller, more idiosyncratic, less "efficient" units of the Press which could offer only the odd million or two variegated, not too well-off, readers, insecurely roped at that.

The range of newspapers and weeklies now rapidly narrowed.* Losses were particularly heavy in the Provinces. The 200-year-old *Birmingham Gazette* was obliged to close down at this time; so was the *Daily Dispatch* which had long been a part of the life of Lancashire; so was the *Evening News*, Glasgow. And in the autumn of 1960 the death of the *News*

* Newspapers suffered both in their circulation and advertising revenue from the advent of commercial television. By 1958 advertisers of some mass-selling commodities such as detergents, sweets, dentifrice and beer were devoting between a half and a third of their advertising budgets to TV.

42. At Edinburgh University, (*above*) pro- and anti-Eden student factions clashed in the Old Quad.

The Suez Action divided nation—and even families—with a passion and bitterness rarely known in British life.

43. *Below*, Front Page, 2nd November, 1956.

 Evening Standard

41,181 FRIDAY, NOVEMBER 2, 1956 Twopence

Israelis claim capture of Gaza

RAF SMASH NASSER'S RUSSIAN BOMBERS

His air force now practically out of action'

RENCH SAY 'CONSIDERABLE FORCES ON THE MOVE'

Allied Forces communiqué issued in Cyprus today said that widespread raids by RAF Valiant and Canberra ers continued all night against Egyptian airfields in the

'Red tanks pour into Hungary'

VIENNA, Friday.—Reports reaching Vienna today said the Soviet army in Hungary was mounting a full-scale offensive to wipe out the revolutionary forces.

Soviet troop units, including strong armoured forces, were pouring into Hungary from Russia and Rumania.

The strength of one Soviet drive towards Budapest was estimated at two full armoured divisions. The revolutionary forces are

GAITSKELL ASKS EDEN 'WILL YOU DO AS UNO SAYS?'

Premier says 'I cannot

44. In 1956 everybody was doing it. . . . But the craze for "do-it-yourself" skiffle on guitar, washboard and tea-chest presently fell away.

45. The record-player remained the essential centre-piece of the new teenage world whose wealth—and the new micro-groove records—generated a great disc-buying boom.

Chronicle, long representative of an important body of opinion and of a certain very English mental temper, suddenly deprived four million readers of their trusted daily paper. The simultaneous shutdown of the *Star* left the capital without one Left or Liberal evening newspaper.

At the same time the now irresistible logic of the Accountant was being applied to the periodical field to distribute magazines over the range of advertising market needs in such a way as to minimise costs and maximise revenues. The process got under way in November, 1958, with a bid by Mr. Cecil King, the *Mirror* Group's Chairman, for "uncle's old business", the Amalgamated Press, the many-storeyed but now somewhat dusty structure which Northcliffe had raised on the foundation of *Answers*. This formidable amalgamation was met by the mammoth Odhams Group with the absorption, in March, 1959, of the Hulton Press and, two months later, the takeover of its old rival, Newnes, thus creating the largest periodical publishing organisation in the world. The subsequent digestion of the gorged Odhams Group by the *Mirror* Group, leaving this in possession of the bulk of popular magazines in the country, and also of the *Daily Herald* and *The People*, seemed a neat enough conclusion to the massive process of Admassian "rationalisation" that had marked the decade—especially since the Canadian, Mr. Roy Thomson, having made a further fortune in Scottish commercial television, was still at the time publicly engaged in digesting the former Kemsley empire with papers in towns all over Britain.

The proliferation of "cultural" and other goods through increasing "industrialisation" at once facilitated the manipulation of the consumer and rendered more indispensable and central the offices of the manipulators. As the supermarket facilitated the "free choice" of its crowds by "loss-leaders", carefully calculated positioning, packets instantly identifiable with some massive national advertising campaign, so the sophistication and abundance of the entertainment industry now made necessary parallel devices.

The Forties were the years of the "spiv," a word which carried an implied moral condemnation. The Fifties were the

o

years of the neutral and functional "gimmick", a word which, like "teenager", had spun in from across the Atlantic, and had quickly become naturalised.

The mechanical sophistication of television brought a boom to the gimmick industry. A beard, and a striped butcher's apron were enough to make Philip Harben, "the TV cook", more famous than Escoffier or Brillat-Savarin can ever have been. The ability of a young schoolmaster to answer recondite history questions, thus doubling his money in the "Double Your Money" quiz, kept the strange name of Plantagenet Fry in the headlines for weeks. By assuming the name Sabrina, and merely remaining silent before the cameras, a Miss Norma Sykes, a Blackpool landlady's daughter, became a sort of national monument. The "radio personality" had sketched the preliminary pattern. Now TV, with its voracious appetite for new faces, new gimmicks, transcended it. Given luck, a good gimmick and a resourceful publicity man, a snack-bar girl or lorry-driver of small but particular talent could now attain, in weeks, a fame and an income far eclipsing that of a Cabinet Minister.

But gimmicks, by definition, were highly expendable; decreasing returns very quickly set in. Hence another verbal sign of the times was the extraordinary prevalence of the word "top", employed American-style, as an adjective. There were "Top" models, "Top" writers, "Top" artists. Even *The Times* now found it necessary to point out, in its advertising, that the "Top" People read it. The last, indeed, was particularly significant.

When position is no longer "understood" or determined by judgments within a social and cultured tradition, but is something to be assessed statistically, in public, weekly, daily, in terms of money received, audience rating, gossip paragraphs, total of headlines, it gains a new and obsessive attraction.

Thus the electronic box joined the electronic brain in the fragmentation of time and the erosion of memory. A dozen songs, it was sometimes pointed out, had lasted an old music hall artist, like Harry Lauder, a lifetime: they were good songs, well sung, and they gave immense if simple enjoyment. A Hit Parade or "Top Ten" song needed a good gimmick to get there, and having got there—with vast attendant publicity— would burn itself out in six weeks.

Instability, on this scale, obviously could not be confined to the world of "commercial" entertainment (now in any case so all-embracing). And as time went on there appeared to be an ever-increasing uncertainty of judgment in the worlds of literature, drama, and the other arts, also.

Other factors, of course, contributed. Nor had the gimmick been born with television, or even with Lord Northcliffe. What our times had achieved was its solemn and systematic exploitation as a technique, as an established part of a process—in short, its industrialisation.

In such a clamour a great premium was put upon novelty of any sort, and upon noise. The novelist who could make the most violent impact, or select the most sensational theme, the playwright who could blaspheme the loudest, the painter who could produce maximum immediate shock clearly enjoyed substantial advantages.

The success of the time was more than usually apt to be the *succès de scandale*.

VI

By 1957 an advertising man was able to calculate that the masterly Omo aria ("Omo adds Brightness, etc.") had been projected into the homes of Britain a thousand times to date. From the new 17-inch screens which were now becoming a "must", the People's Own Television poured out, endlessly, in the "natural breaks" in the programme (which had turned out to occur every quarter of an hour) a stream of "voice-over" invitations to continuous consumption—fevered, fantastic, breezy, portentous, or softly beguiling. The salesman was inside the house now, and (as feared by the writer of the letter to *The Times*) was pasting his advertisements on the sitting-room walls with enthusiasm and abandon. The child's first lisp was very likely to be of "Silvrikin" for Lovely Hair rather than of Little Red Riding Hood or the Three Bears. The composition of jingles, insistent variations on half a dozen notes, interspersed with cunningly placed 'booings' and boomings and echoes, had become a lucrative new branch of the many-sided publicity industry. A well-contrived jingle, repeated an adequate number of times in the course of an evening, could induce a trance-like state in which the $\frac{1}{16}$th truths looked no worse than half-truths, and half-truths looked like Eternal Verities.

"As advertised on TV" was discovered by retailers to be a potent incantation. The fickleness of fashion, the neurosis of the "Top", now broke into many simple British loyalties to articles which had "stood the test of time", and—in the older British psychology—had therefore been held in a steady affection. Cigarettes whose packaging and marketing had remained little changed for years and which had tended to cling to such symbols of "rightness" as the Royal Navy, were now suddenly a battleground of ever-changing packs and gimmicks, with advertising offering everything from sexual adventure to the assuagement of loneliness.

As a social solvent and as an accelerator of the processes of social change, television—with the commercial superchargers attached—was, in the Fifties, comparable only to the war in the Forties. Like the war it did not originate the trends it speeded; when the Set moved in, the processes of change were already well advanced. But at this critical juncture, television put the nation into a sort of trance, soft and shallow, from which it presently emerged to find itself living its dream.

As television fuelled the boom, as hire purchase debt soared towards new peaks, as the profits of the television contractors spiralled spectacularly, turn and turn about with metropolitan land values under the hands of the ever-active developers, the psychology of "the People's Capitalism" penetrated into some of the innermost strongholds of the old convention.

Even the City discovered Public Relations now. The "Big Five" joint stock banks, putting away the mahogany and stately Georgian, bronze grilles and aristocratic condescension, began to deck their branches in glass, aluminium and neon, joining the vulgar clamour of the High Street. In 1958 the Midland set a brisk pace in the wooing of the new customer with its Personal (i.e. unsecured) Loan scheme and its Personal (i.e. simplified) Cheque plan. "Social changes have brought many a working-man's income to where they ought to have a banking account," explained the Midland's Chairman, Lord Monckton, firmly. "Many of their incomes are higher than those of our existing customers."

Not to be outdone, a rival bank riposted with an advertisement showing a man gazing complacently on a modest motorcar. "What a pity to miss something good merely because the money is not immediately available . . . a Westminster Bank Personal Loan provides the answer to his kind of problem."

In this same *annus mirabilis* the joint stock banks began unashamedly, by partnership or takeover, to ally themselves with hire purchase finance houses which a very few years ago they would have considered of dubious respectability and anyhow socially far beneath them.* While the Big Five were moving into H.P. finance, infinitely dignified merchant banks were moving into the "unit trusts" which it was hoped would attract the "new class of investor".

Much was now heard of this still somewhat elusive species. In order to educate him or her it was agreed that the sacred mysteries must now be laid bare—within limits of course. The Stock Exchange built itself a public gallery, furnished it with "hostesses" and—like Lloyds and the Bank of England—had a film made about itself. (*Dictum Meum Pactum.*)

Certainly a great deal of "education" would be required to turn a very large number of English eyes from the football results (for the Pools) to the stock market prices, and even more before many English brokers felt the desire, claimed by a famous American brokerage house, "to do business in a goldfish bowl". But it was perhaps not without significance that among entrants in the *Investors' Chronicle* share-recommendation competition in 1957 were a bus driver, a miner, an iron moulder, several printing workers, a valet, two policemen and several labourers. And after 1958 small investors clubs began to spread rapidly across the country reaching a total of about 500 by 1960 (and twice that a year later) while most large public companies reported a steady increase in the numbers of very small and small shareholders on their registers.**

* Thus, Barclays, the pioneer, put £4 m. into United Dominions Trust, Lloyds nearly £3 m. into Bowmakers, the Westminster £4 m. into Mercantile Credit, while the Commercial Bank of Scotland took over Olds Discount, and National Provincial took over N. Central Wagon.

** In the later Fifties polls suggested that 10 per cent of all adults, and 3 per cent of the working class, had invested in some stocks and shares.

In the short term, and at the current stage of England's social evolution, "the People's Capitalism", "the Consumer Democracy", was inevitably democratising. The revolution might have been betrayed, but it had been a revolution none the less. Whether "fixed" or free, or however much of each, the vote was the vote, and casting it weekly, with material consequences so large, necessarily changed the social balance and tone.

The longer term effects would depend on many things. But first upon the reality of that apparent freedom of choice. And this, in no small measure, would depend on the ability to live with machines, to accommodate cultural—as well as other—industrialisation, to consume the gimmick and survive.

It was, in any case, the middle-aged, not the young, who sought refuge in cultural Luddism. The young were notably unembarrassed by the clamour of the bookstalls, the outpouring in the ether. Whether their calm bespoke familiarity with the machine, and an ability to cope with it, or was merely the result of total bemusement—of being so completely manipulated as to be unaware of manipulation—was a matter on which opinions differed. Yet it was interesting that it was the new generation, the generation born to television, who in their teens appeared to be about the only large body of people in the country in these years who could, with complete equanimity, take television or leave it—and who quite frequently left it.

31. Teenage Trajectory

> "Everybody over twenty has passed through his teens but nobody over thirty has been a teenager."
>
> —*World's Press News.*

> "I was born into an unfortunate generation. When I was a child I had to knuckle under to grown-ups, and now that I am grown up I have to knuckle under to children."
>
> —Sir Stephen King-Hall.

> "If you were given a Hottentot to bring up I think you would have a bit of a job, because I do not think you would begin to understand how the Hottentot mind works. As far as we are concerned, I think this teenage group is a Hottentot group."
>
> —Mr. G. Prys Williams, London School of Economics.

IN THE later Fifties the "Youth Question" seemed at times to be succeeding to the place occupied by the "Woman Question" in an earlier age. Never had "Youth"—with the capital "Y"—been so earnestly discussed, so frequently surveyed, so extensively seen *and* heard. The nineteen-year-old dramatist, the twenty-one-year-old pundit, the seventeen-year-old singing star became established features of the times. A young man had only to be described as "Angry" to receive, in many quarters, the most reverential attention, while to enter one's teens was to be inducted into an exclusive and privileged order, several millions strong, which those outside it observed with an uncertain mixture of envy, awe, fascination and repulsion.

Youth, it was explained, was "in revolt". But then youth

always had been—even if it had not always possessed the means of making its revolt effective. A particular blend of "rebellion" and anxious conformity—conformity, verbal, sartorial, philosophic, with one's coevals, "rebellion" against the Rest—had long been a feature of undergraduate life. What was new—and important—was that economic and other factors had now made possible the extension of this ritual declaration of independence —with much of its panache—to the youth of the nation at large.

The young were the outstanding financial beneficiaries of the postwar situation. By the later Fifties teenage real earnings were more than 50 per cent higher than before the war, a rate of increase half as great again as that achieved by adults. Mere shillings of free spending money before the war were transformed into pounds,* creating a new *jeunesse dorée* able to enjoy in these years between leaving school and marriage a freedom and an opulence which many would never know again in their lives.

In the pattern of the time this "coming into money" coincided with the breaking-up of many traditional restraints. The housing general-post, the working mother, the small, "partnership" family, now often TV-immured in a small semi-detached house or flat, the upsetting of old wage differentials so that a semi-skilled youth in a booming new industry might earn as much or more than his craft-proud father after long years of experience—all these things facilitated the assertion of the adolescent. At the same time, Nature, the Welfare State, better nutrition, were extending the period of adolescence downwards as later school-leaving extended it upwards. The L.C.C.'s Principal Schools' Medical Officer reported in 1959 that schoolchildren were around an inch taller than ten years earlier; the Boy Scout movement was about to ballot on the abandonment of short trousers. In London, eleven-year-old girls were large and enthusiastic readers of "love comics";** at thirteen they were using make-up; by the age of fifteen they now confidently expected to be "going steady".

* In 1938, the Ministry of Labour survey put the average male youth's earnings in industry at 26s. a week, average girl's at 18s. 6d. Average teenage spending money in the Fifties, £2–£5 a week (after contribution to "Mum") according to London Press Exchange surveys, was thus considerably more than prewar total earnings, even when correction is made for changed money values.

** *The Leisure Activities of School Children*, W.E.A., 1960.

These factors enabled the so-called "Revolt of Youth" to achieve expression on the national scale. But what *institutionalised* it, what ratified and confirmed the separatism of the adolescent and built his new world, was something different. The emergence of the Teenager as a new sub-species of Western Man was a tribute to the multiple skills and infinite ramifications of Admass and the first full-scale demonstration in England of its powers.

With free spending money amounting to £900 millions a year, or £2,500,000 a day, with an urgent need for assertion, an insatiable appetite for novelty, a strong imitative instinct and a lively fear of being somehow left out, adolescents offered an area in our society even more vulnerable to commercial exploitation than women. And age provided the simplest and most universal of the common denominators to which the Admass Machine could be geared.

"With new teenagers arriving at the rate of nearly half a million a year", pointed out the *Draper's Record* enthusiastically, "the teenage trade cannot be treated as a sideline. . . ." Departmental stores now set up special teenage shops, sometimes with teenage panels of advisers. One departmental store chain chief, Mr. Rudkin Jones, announced plans to redesign entire stores for the young, since it was they "who are most aware of fashion changes". Norvic, the shoe firm, noting that the average teenager bought five pairs of shoes a year while the all-woman average was only 2½, elected a "Miss Norvic Teenager", crowned her at the May Fair Hotel, and proudly proclaimed on the first page of its annual report: "Norvic in step with Teenagers."

Old industries boomed and a number of new ones were quickly run up by tapping the new teenage wealth. They ranged from the manufacture of pocket radios and the printing of American-style greeting cards ("Hi! beautiful! Wanna go steady?") to the production of teen-orientated "Rock" or "Werewolf" films. Meanwhile, that part of popular journalism which was not woman-angled, increasingly strove—with both the future and the advertiser in mind—to achieve authentic "teenage" appeal.

But it was the now central and all-pervasive entertainment industry that held up the Admass magic mirror to the greatest effect and profit, giving the Teenage Image its sharpest, most flattering definition. In the Forties, the young—not quite unveiled as "teenagers" yet—were already finding their heroes in the world of entertainment. But these heroes and "dreamboats" were in their thirties, like Johnnie Ray or Gregory Peck, and might even be veterans like Donald ("Babbling Brook") Peers. Through the first half of the Fifties, teenage favourites grew younger. "Pop" singers like David Whitfield, Dickie Valentine, Ruby Murray, were in their twenties. And, then, finally, around 1956 the accolade was reserved for entertainers who were "one of themselves".

"The kids," explained an expert, "like to have their Rock delivered by other kids. They think that when you get out of your teens you automatically become a 'square'."

The teenage world was fully emergent.

The vigour and volume of its challenge were demonstrated in 1956 by the sputnik-like ascent to fame and fortune of a nineteen-year-old Bermondsey ex-cabin boy named Tommy Hicks, aided by a guitar, a hair-cut, and an imaginative Press agent. "The Tommy Steele Story"—the title of a film he made only six months after being launched into Show Business— opened the way for a rapid succession of juvenile heroes, running down to the age of fourteen, each with his gimmick, his clamorous fans, each earning his much-publicised thousands and claiming for a while his front-page headlines.

Once, not long ago, the chief aspiration of the adolescent had been to escape as rapidly as possible from his or her dependant, indeterminate—even humiliating—status into the full enfranchisement of the adult world. Perhaps it still was; if so, the fact had never been better concealed. The "sub-teens", eager pocket-moneyed apprentices, waited impatiently for admission to this booming, neon-lit Teenage Promised Land. Advertisers went out to welcome them. The *Financial Times* reported that the foundation garment industry was beginning to direct an appeal to twelve-year-olds, while, at Broadcasting House, the stately B.B.C., having scored a success with its teenage-jiving programme "6.5 Special", was planning—after a run of nearly forty years—to abolish "Children's Hour". "Some children," a spokesman explained, "do not like being called 'children' any more."

II

The creation and functioning of the Teenage World provided a model—sometimes simplified to the point of caricature—of forces and ideas at work in society at large.

However hesitant might be the approach of the average Englishman of the older generation to the notion of Equality, for the young, born perhaps in the war years, approaching or entering their teens in the Marksian Fifties, it had an immediate and 'natural' appeal which by no means stopped at equality between age-groups.

If one was born in a New Town or had passed the Eleven Plus, the existence of a degree of Equality might now seem self-evident; if one was not and did not, the need to assert it might be acute. And the means now existed. It was indeed among the semi-skilled youths of the working class that wages were often highest and necessary expenses lowest, creating the most spectacular margin for free spending, not inhibited by any feeling of being in *statu pupillari* which might linger in middle-class youth.

And thus it came about that a brief, discreet fashion revival among young men about town in the West End in 1948— slightly narrowed trousers, a velvet collar here, a brocade waistcoat there, a very tentative riposte to the women's New Look—crossed the River and, exaggerated—almost consciously guyed—became the defiant uniform of what the newspapers were soon calling the "New Edwardians".

However called, the "Teddy" vogue, moving through its various permutations—and sometimes with a judicious mixing of cultural streams, the addition, say, of the semi-frock coat or the dangling string tie of the U.S. Frontier Marshal—reigned, in all, something like ten years and clearly answered a widely felt need in the hundreds of thousands of teenagers who persisted in it in face of parental mockery and magisterial threat.

To some, the extraordinary outfit, worn with a grim and self-conscious gravity, offered—as Methodism had in the eighteenth century—the possibility of individual assertion and identity, otherwise difficult to achieve. It offered, too, a sense of belonging, which, with variations of the uniform from gang to gang—some had *green* velvet collars for instance—fulfilled broadly the function of the School Tie in better endowed circles, and was often accompanied by similar esoteric private codes of manners and language, a similar *esprit de corps*.

But most significant perhaps, was the Teddy outfit's function as the badge of a half-formed, inarticulate radicalism (which the political Left had failed to capitalise). A sort of half-conscious thumbing-of-the-nose, it was designed to establish that the lower orders could be as arrogant and as-to-the-manner-born as the Toffee-nosed Ones across the River. From this point of view, the uniform's most important features lay, firstly, in the fact that—unlike the American "drapes" of the earlier postwar years—it was, in origin, English class-based, secondly, in its cost which —from the "blow-waves" or "Tony Curtis" hair-do to the 2-inch thick crepe "creepers" with patent leather uppers— might exceed £100.

Thus, while the contemporary millionaire now favoured the discreet Post-Impressionist, conspicuous consumption passed to the teenagers of the working classes where it functioned, not so much as a badge of arrival, but as a defiant declaration that "arrival" was superfluous because one was already there.

Conferring its dual emancipation of age and class the Teddy costume conquered district after district in these years, making the fortune in the process of many a little corner tailor—and hairdresser—astute enough to "humour the kids". But, finally, having made its point and having no further need to labour it, the uniform gave way before the blue jeans, the windcheaters, the bright raincoats, the gentler, more civilised, immensely variegated Italian and Continental styles which seemed to confirm and usher the opening society. And in England, where male fashions had always been one of those "understood" things—essentially aristocratic, fear-edged, inhibition-inlaid— nothing, it seemed, could ever be quite the same again.

The revolution of the Telly was confirmed. In the Twenties new fashions—pullovers, sports coats, wide-bottomed flannels— had been established by the rich young undergraduates of Oxford. Now, instead of percolating slowly downwards, fashion had been made at the bottom, made with a new and vulgar vigour, and was now spreading upwards. Mr. Cecil Gee, latter-day impresario of the Male Trend, extraordinary metamorphosis of the old Gent's Outfitter, having migrated from the East End to the Charing Cross Road, now moved on again to smarter parts of the West End where his colourful emporiums with "un-English" lack of inhibition laid the world under tribute for the benefit of the young and "young-in-heart"—a phrase significantly increasingly popular with admen—of all classes.

Thus stimulated, pushed on from behind and below, the English male at long last began to throw off the gentlemanly intimidations of Brummel and, emerging from his perpetual Victorian mourning, began to dress to express himself or his clique rather than merely to conform and preserve an unbroken social and moral front.

The mid-century eclecticism of the new-style men's wear shop, and the vast duffled heterogeneity of the War Surplus Stores where, in the earlier Fifties, the young often seemed largely to clothe themselves, both made it difficult to employ clothes effectively as indicators of class. And if it was still marginally possible, the lack of a firm class sense was one of the most notable things about a great many of the young. The working-class lad was no longer swallowed up into the beery fug of the working-class pub. In the new coffee bars, jazz cellars and youth clubs, grammar school and modern school rubbed Italianate shoulders; "fish-and-chip" girl and Acacia Avenue girl alike embraced the new informality of "separates" and drove holes into the floor with stiletto heels of approximately the same sharpness.

A teenager was a teenager.*

III

A word much favoured by manufacturers and traders for attachment to the new-style men's clothing and footwear was

---

* They were thus natural candidates for the Endless Middle. In 1959, a Mark Abrams-*Socialist Commentary* social survey showed that two-thirds of all young voters placed themselves in the middle classes —twice the proportion among their elders.

the adjective "casual", now very often promoted to noun. It shared its popularity with another adjective, "relaxed", e.g. "bronzed and relaxed". "Relaxed" affixed the seal of social approval, offering a warranty of well-being and virtue. Together the words signalled the final supercession of the Victorian Cult of Work by the rapidly developing "New Elizabethan" cult of Leisure.

By the end of the Fifties the five-day week had become almost universal. With this and paid annual holidays also, one-third of the average Briton's days were now his own.*

The famous English "long week-end" had been an upper middle-class institution with a narrow range of correct class occupations. The week-end of the Fifties was everybody's week-end, a vast, ever-expanding hold-all packed with an immense diversity of interests and pursuits.

Even the traditional sports of the well-to-do had become subject to "democratic" takeover bids. New materials and techniques, the cheap outboard motor, build-it-yourself kits, had created a whole bobbing world of small boatery on rivers, coastal waters, lakes, reservoirs and gravel pits. This now claimed at least one million adherents. Two million people—including many enthusiastic teenagers—went fishing. Thanks, to television's taking down the KEEP OUT signs, three times as many people as before the war were learning to ride horses. Nor was ski-ing any longer confined to a small body of *cognoscenti :* from January to March the packed "Snow Sports Specials" running each week-end out of Victoria carried off hordes of highly miscellaneous English to the robust joys of Alpine sun and nursery slopes.

Despite the alleged passivity of the "ox-faced Plebs", a trend of the time was the decline of spectator sports and the multiplication of participation. Three-quarters of a million men and youths played football seriously for their own enjoyment; there were nearly 3,000 amateur teams playing in local Sunday leagues. The theatre in the provinces might seem finished; yet Birmingham alone had almost 200 dramatic societies. Dancing,

* Survey, 1959, Industrial Welfare Society. Among industrial companies it was found that fewer than one in a hundred now offered less than a fortnight's paid holiday. However, persistent overtime still ate into leisure.

in its many styles, was approaching the level of a national obsession. Five million people engaged in it each week, sustaining 5,000 dancing schools and 450 Palais, Locarnos and Meccas, not to mention a further 2,000 halls where dances were regularly advertised.

The nation's six million teenagers were the natural trailblazers of this oncoming Age of Leisure. While "Dad" might persist in the old firmly working-class pursuits like pigeonracing, darts or the Dogs, or in things rooted in regional cultures, like the cultivation of pot-leeks on the Tyne or houndtrailing in the north-west, his children grew up into leisure occupations that were classless, international, and embraced the whole proliferating mid-century world of the hobbyists—those new minorities of the modern State whose importance the B.B.C. recognised in 1957 in the creation of Network Three. New Towns like Harlow or Crawley boasted hundreds of clubs and societies in which people were brought together by dedication to chrysanthemum-growing or weight-lifting or bagpiping, in which class was transcended by common possession of the deeper secrets of judo, the spirit of folk-dancing, or the Greater Truth of Hi-Fi.

Nor, despite ever-advancing urbanisation, was outdoor life neglected. Caravans multiplied. Youth Hostels anywhere near industrial centres were packed every week-end. Each summer was loud with the click of cameras: there were 11 million of them now, more than twice the prewar number, and by 1960 every fourth camera-owner had a ciné-camera, too. The primitive old box camera had all but disappeared. Even the cheapest models were made to look like miniatures or reflexes and often fitted with flash-guns, while the more expensive were increasingly "automated" and foolproof. In the Fifties flash-bulb sales mounted from $1\frac{3}{4}$ million to 20 million: by the end of the decade one in every four amateur films was in colour.

IV

Amongst teenagers, in particular, leisure now often revolved around some fairly sophisticated item of "contemporary" mass-produced machinery—the Vespa scooter or the fast motor-bike—each with its following and panache—the record-player, the "transistorised" pocket radio, the tape-recorders which by 1958 were selling at the rate of 1,500 a week. . . .

Record-player, note: the term "gramophone" was now officially pronounced by the industry's spokesman to be obsolescent. For with the arrival from the United States in 1950 of the lightweight micro-groove plastic disc the mid-century democratic revolution, the revolution of the Great Market, had arrived here also and, this time at least, was certainly a revolution in quality as well as quantity. As the dignified old "brown-paper-and-Caruso" days faded into antiquity, the windows of booming record shops spilled over with the new glossy, multicolour "L.P." record sleeves that were soon to become almost a new popular art-form. By 1954 disc sales had reached four times their prewar level and were still growing fast.

"The kids," explained the producer of the B.B.C.'s jiving programme "6.5. Special", "start buying their records at 11 or twelve." And for some years after that the ritual weekly decision on whom to bestow, and from whom to withhold, their love and their money appeared one of the most important in life.

Nine out of every ten London teenagers spent some of their leisure listening to records. In the making of the new teenage society the record-player appeared to have a catalytic role, similar, if more complex and subtle, to that of the motor-car in the adult world. While not creative in any direct sense it nevertheless permitted selection and, like that other characteristic instrument of the times, the tape-recorder, thus offered a sort of electronic enlargement of private and group personality.

Every week-end and lunch-hour the self-service "Browseries" and "Melody Bars" were packed with abstracted teenagers, 'winkle-picker' toes tapping, pony-tails swinging; and as the disc-jockeys, the High Priests of the cult, made their offerings to the Great God Turntable, the talk of a million homes was hushed as the young inhabitants sought to divine whether this was—or was not—"today's sound".

Once again, the new superabundance. Once again, the acute problem of selection—which, however, was here seized upon and gloried in.

How the choice was in fact made was not easy to say—perhaps some form of internal radar was involved. At any rate, the beam seemed to be picked up, its deviations followed. And then, somehow, suddenly a landing had been made. The nature of the process invited close psychological and sociological study, but seemed almost certain to defeat it. Clearly, commercially calculated gimmicks—the echo chambers, the tremolos, the carefully fabricated ambiance— were heavily involved. Yet for this knowing Admass-nurtured generation there could be connoisseurship of gimmicks, too. Certainly, connoisseurship, nothing less, was the aspiration. And if superabundance invited the gimmick-men, in the long run it might also defeat them. Particularly since the record-player was a "social" as well as a "musical" mechanism, serving the mysterious processes of teenage adjustment, of individual to group, of group to society, of one sex to the other, of adolescence to adulthood, so that while manipulation was undeniable, the relation of manipulators and manipulated had more than its usual ambivalence.

In 1956, the great "Rock' n 'Roll" wave, sweeping across the Atlantic from the United States, broke over the British dance-halls. With its elemental shouts and pile-driver beat, Rock 'n' Roll produced something which—visually at least—resembled a children's uprising. When the Bill Haley film, *Rock Around the Clock*, was generally released in September, teenagers leapt from their seats and rocked and rolled in the cinema aisles. In a number of towns they flooded the dance-halls at midday, to gyrate non-stop through the school lunch-break. Nothing like this had ever been seen in Britain before. Parents were baffled and, sometimes, not a little worried.

Commercial interests seized their opportunity, building up the vogue, harnessing it to propel their teenage protegés to wealth and stardom. But though teenagers responded to the gimmicks, it remained something of a question who was using who.

Moreover, the guitar, the generator of this mass-produced delirium, stayed on to become the instrument of a freer, more individual and humanised expression. "Rock 'n' Roll GUITARS —Professional Style—SENT FOR 5/-" ran the advertisements. "FREE! Beginners' Guitar System. STRUM IMMEDIATELY!" Many did. By the summer of 1957 it seemed hardly possible to move more than a mile or two in urban England without coming upon some little band of troubadors on a suburban street corner, under a railway arch, in pub or coffee bar, below pier or promenade, confidently "doing it themselves" on guitar, domestic washboard and double-bass made from tea-chest and clothes prop. By this time over 500 regular "skiffle groups" were in action. Male skifflers affected fringe beards, bold checked open-neck shirts and a nostalgic melancholy, the girls cultivated a look of folksy simplicity with loose sweaters, black stockings and longish, judiciously disordered hair. Both sexes sought, earnestly and sometimes successfully, to make up for what they lacked in musicianly skill by the freshness and *élan* of their approach.

It was an astonishing phenomenon—a nation-wide movement for amateur music-making which had sprung up, in a matter of months, without organisation or premeditation. The brass band movement of Victorian times, a rough parallel that springs to mind, serves mainly to indicate the essentially "contemporary" nature of skiffle. Brass bands were profoundly proletarian, rooted in place, male. Skiffle—somewhat ironically in view of its origins—was classless, international, and embraced both sexes. Its simplicity, unlike that of the brassbanders, was a cultivated, sophisticated simplicity; its regional culture was imported from half across the world. While the brass bands were middle-aged, a little pompous and enduring, skiffle was youthful, earnest and transitory.

A correspondent of *The Times* reminded his readers that the 'great art of the English music hall' had begun with amateurs singing in public houses. Was it conceivable that, even now, in this age of "mass culture" and canned music, a new popular art was about to be born?

Skiffle—authoritatively defined as "folksong with a beat"— shortly afterwards offered an answer of a sort by fading away almost as rapidly and as mysteriously as it had arisen.

But even if it was doubtful whether an English popular art could be conceived in the simulated accent of aboriginal Kentucky, and even if the materials for more indigenous creation seemed lacking, there were now other alternatives to the supine acceptance of the dictatorship of Tin Pan Alley.

In the Thirties "true" jazz in Britain had been the cult of a very small intellectual minority. In the Forties it expanded and exploded in the "modernist" frenzy of the so-called "Bop rebellion" and in the enthusiastic revival of the "true gospel" of New Orleans.

Though the sects assailed each other, all were united by a determination to conquer the—in the phrase of a jazz historian —"prewar desert of moribund commercialism". They enjoyed remarkable success. Jazz clubs proliferated, moved into central London, spread across England. They were packed with young people of all classes, avidly listening to home-grown jazz groups.

Way back in the unsophisticated Thirties, a normal (non-intellectual) young person had merely been required to accord his or her favour to one or other of a few big "Name" dance bands, Harry Roy, Jack Payne, Ambrose. . . . Now, as the "groups" multiplied, and their leaders attached themselves to this or that dogma and password, "trad", "non-trad", "mainstream", etc., the possibilities of heresy and deviation became infinite. But however much the sects might dispute and splinter, like those of Nonconformity before them, they had, one great bond in common. They were "agin" Them, the Establishment (which for some *aficionados* might coincide with the adult world). Their Truth was not *received* from the Hierarchy, but divined by gospel reading and the inner light.

Ruled Humphrey Lyttelton, Old Etonian King of British Jazz: "Call it what you will—jiving, bopping, skiffling, rock 'n' rolling—it is all basically the same. Its most significant characteristic, which it shares in varying degrees with all the different musical styles which accompany it, is improvisation."

Only the basic pattern was "given"; the total outcome had something of the unpredictability of an Action painting, its objectivity as elusive, meaning different things to different people, nothing to some.

And again there were those strange social echoes of the randomness of nuclear collision—with the momentary glimpse of emergent pattern as in some physicist's dream of the play of the particles.

For the teenage society, bringing to a focus the social trends of the times, also seemed to project the shape of the future. It foreshadowed a society not so much of "Masses and Classes" as of "Masses and Groups", the groups large and small and immensely miscellaneous, self-electing through common inclination, hobbyism, shared interests, the whole in continuous flux, the residual classes increasingly self-elective also, more subjective than objective, emerging from the "Masses" at one moment, for one purpose, then, at another, vanishing back into them, leaving only a smile like the Cheshire Cat.

V

In face of the formidable Admassian "processing" to which the young were now subjected, the survival of a capacity to reject and of an eagerness to improvise was encouraging.

Yet any freedom achieved in this setting was freedom achieved at a price. The waves of fashion, extending over wider areas of life, succeeded each other at an ever swifter pace. "There's an entirely NEW kind of girl around," announced a woman's writer in the *Sunday Express* in 1958. "Awkward and angular, pouting and petulant, history has seen nothing like her before." Much material had flowed through the multiple dress shops since the "New Look" burst upon Austerity Britain in 1946. For the last few years, an "entirely NEW kind of girl" seemed to have appeared on the pavement every few months. The *gamine* look, wide-eyed and elfin, inspired by the rising star of Audrey Hepburn—*Roman Holiday* had been released in 1953—had in due course given way to the Juliette Greco "squalid" look—and then, suddenly, the streets were full of Bardot-type waifs-in-trenchcoats, advancing precariously, placing one foot three inches in front of the other in the manner of disdainful sleepwalkers.

"The Sack", with its long bead-string echoes of the Twenties, appeared in 1957 and, with teenage *élan*, was speeded through a wondrous variety of permutations, the Trapeze-line, the H-line, the Tulip-line, the Chemise. . . . The Sack brought a return to power of the legs, but no longer merely as a move in the historic cycle of display. For this entirely new kind of girl was a maker of history. She had discovered, according to another fashion authority, how "to bare her shoulders, accentuate her bust, pull in her waist, and show her legs" all at the same time.

Fully interpreted, each successive new look, now rapidly multiplied by a highly efficient ready-to-wear industry, was not merely a matter of the odd garment, but of a head-to-toe, heart-and-soul, transformation, involving stance, walk, philosophy of life, and crowning glory. The hairdressers reaped a magnificent harvest, opening salons at every other corner, as styles and effects grew more wondrous and complex, proliferating endlessly . . . the poodle-cut, the Bardot dishevelled, the top-heavy hay stack, the "beehive", the rats' tails, the "gold lights", the pink rinse, the silver streak, the judiciously piebald. Once not long ago, the question had been whether a woman's hair was dyed or natural. Now the assumption that hair could be merely hair *simple* was beginning to appear naïve.

Adolescents, in their commercial role as pacemakers, bore much of the strain of this mounting "sophistication", with its attendant burden of self-consciousness.

"What the kids want to hear," said the Expert, "is *today's sound*." But what was today's sound? More important, what was tomorrow's?

What was "vital", what was "urgent" now? The question which worried the young artist, the writer, the entertainer, nagged at the teenager also. One had to be not only "in" with the group, but up with the national gimmick of the hour, and mounted, however precariously on the crest of the Wave of the Future.

No wonder that Sir John Wolfenden, Vice-Chancellor of Reading University, noted "a sort of excitement, a kind of emotional, hectic flush about many young people today—as if their metaphoric pulse-rate had to be high to keep pace with the speed of what was happening around them".

As anthropologists have shown in recent times, the manner in which a society resolves the problem of accommodating its restless adolescents can be critical for its character and future. In Britain, the traditional restraints of Guild and indentures, the stern authority of the Victorian paterfamilias, the uncertain blend of reason, cajolery and threat in the small modern "partnership" family, had all served their turn. In the Forties, with the widening social responsibility that followed the war, came a large extension of social provision. Municipally staffed and subsidised, youth centres and youth clubs multiplied.* In Birmingham, the City Youth Committee recognised twenty-five youth organisations, with 1,500 "units"; over Britain as a whole, four in every ten between the ages of fourteen and eighteen now belonged to some sort of youth club.

And yet these Welfare State efforts to accommodate the young and gently guide them, now had to contend not only with youth's natural restiveness, but also with the commercialism which found immense profit in flattering and exploiting it.

The hiving-off of the teenagers in these years was not, however, merely the result of a combination of their own affluence and business opportunism. This was the first generation to grow up beyond the long shadow of Victorian morality. These were the children of Dr. Kinsey. The "basic pattern" upon which they improvised was the pattern, not only of Admass and the Organisation, but also of Science.

It was not remarkable therefore that their attitudes and interpretations should sometimes arouse, in the older generations, not only puzzlement, but also alarm. Drink, it was conceded, was not a major peril: so far jive and Coca-Cola had seemed tipple enough. The "pint" was no longer the badge of manhood. But in matters of "sex"—a term which—whether from moral precision, the prevailing clinicism, or premature cynicism—teenagers were apt to prefer to "love"—it was observed that they could affect—and even have a casual post-Kinsey offhandedness and frankness which could startle their elders. Especially since earlier maturity was moving the age of sex interest down almost to the gates of the primary school. "Children of twelve, thirteen, and fourteen know all about birth control", a London social worker assured a conference in the late Fifties. Not quite enough, it appeared, however, for the nation's Unmarried Mothers had never been

* Municipal provision of Youth Centres was urged by Whitehall in 1939, the duty of ensuring adequate social and recreational provision for young people enjoined on local authorities by the Education Act, 1944.

so young (in Manchester the number of those under fifteen had doubled between 1954 and 1959) and, of the married mothers under twenty, the Registrar-General ungallantly revealed, in 1955, that 60 per cent were pregnant on their wedding-day. As "offences" by male teenagers against female teenagers under the statutory sixteen crowded the courts, the age of consent was already beginning to look oddly dated.

The prewar grammar schools, like the public schools they often aped, had maintained a monastic regime: as far as they were concerned the opposite sex did not exist. If the existence of a nearby girls' school threatened this thesis, it was not unknown for starting times to be changed so that the two schools never met. Sexually, as in other ways, many of the middle-class young had thus led an extremely sheltered existence; it was upon this narrow foundation that middle-class morality had been erected. This system was now breaking down. But what probably most disturbed the older generation, as they uneasily watched its dissolution, was, first, the absence in the young of what they regarded as appropriate feelings of guilt and shame, and, second, linked with this, their growing disinclination to take on trust the moral system and values— the Rules—handed down by the adult world.

In the words of the Crowther Report, there had been a "substitution of the public opinion of the peer group for the wisdom of ages".

In the world of the Fifties, so drastically made over by science and technology, the "wisdom of ages" (whatever this might be) might seem, however, to have limited relevance. But the young were not so practised at paying lip-service as their elders. This indeed was their merit; this was their social function, their so-called "revolt". To their fresher eyes some of the monumental inconsistencies of our society stood out in a way that could not be covered by conventional phrases. And these were not only inconsistencies between the rulings of the Church and the actual conduct of the people. A society which called for teenage continence appeared to revolve, commercially, around the continuous exploitation of sex. A society which had proclaimed Equality had demonstrated it with the massive rejection of "Failed Eleven Plus", and with the Public School System. A society which held out, as its most wondrous prize, the vote of the consumer democracy, went to enormous pains behind the scenes to rig that vote. A technological society which offered a man fulfilment in his leisure, took away his dignity and sense of purpose at work.

Thus, many teenagers, having so successfully asserted themselves, having "arrived", found that they had in fact arrived at nowhere. Nor could "revolt" satisfy for long when repressive Authority was so hard to pin down and the ever-understanding psychiatrist never far away. Hence the familiar postwar flatness or "apathy", which some sought to dissipate by shrillness and violence.

The collapse of Authority—religious, social, familial—was bound to bear most heavily upon the young. They sought guidance, realistic and honest, in which they could have confidence. They rarely received it. Since few adults—with one part of their lives in the old world and the other in the new— could articulately resolve current confusions, the burden of groping towards a new morality fell upon the young. "No society," wrote Ruth Benedict in *Patterns of Culture*, "has yet attempted a self-conscious direction of the process by which its new normalities are created in the next generation." Yet it was a task something like this which, in the Age of Dr. Kinsey, confronted the young. In a scientific age it was not remarkable that their attitude should be experimental; that they should ask for proof. What was remarkable and what, as ever, renewed hope for the future, was that they did not lapse into total cynicism and apathy, but retained the confidence to inquire and the will to improvise in the restricted space available.

Within the four walls of the jazz club, the theory ran that the improvisation transcended the "given" pattern. Whether this could also be true in the larger world remained one of the larger "open questions" of the future.

32.   The End of the Beginning

"All that remains is the Future,
Georgie."
—Jane, of the *Daily Mirror*, in final
post-election strip, October, 1959.

"You might as well fall flat on your
face as lean over too far backwards."
—Motto from Thurber, appearing
on title-page of Catalogue of
Royal Academy, 1959, which
admitted Bratby and other Avant-
Gardists.

THERE ARE events in the history of nations which gather
about themselves such a weight of significance that they
are conveyed in a single word. The Fifties added to
their number the word 'Suez'.

"For the first time in history," Arthur Koestler had written
in his autobiography, in 1954, "we see an Empire gradually
dissolving with dignity and grace. The rise of this Empire was
not an edifying story: its decline is."

He wrote, alas, two years too soon: the story was not over.

By the mid-Fifties, it was true, the decline of British power
had been intellectually accepted by most people capable
of consecutive thought. But for nations as for individuals,
there is much which cannot be said to be known until it
is known, through the impact of experience, emotionally.
Suez provided that experience and with it the necessary, the
final, catharsis.

Though like Munich so largely the work of one man, the
Prime Minister of Great Britain, the event, seen in retrospect,
has a certain inevitability. A nation cannot escape the defects of
its qualities. Nor can persona-change be accomplished in a
decade. Behind the crisp façades of Festival "Contemporary"

there still appeared, faint but persistent, the grandiose Imperial domes of Wembley; the Ealing comedy giggle had been underlain by the *Amethyst* cheer. The intellect might dictate the freeing of Nkrumah, the evacuation of Egypt, retreat before Mossadeq. But beneath the surface the old John Bull truculence lingered. Patriotism did not easily find new forms, and patriotism, amongst the ordinary people, still went deep. There were so many memories, persistent echoes, names that still rang, things taught long ago at school. . . .

Sometimes, resentment, accumulating beneath the surface of realism and acceptance, broke through. It was particularly intense in March, 1956, when General John Glubb, "Glubb Pasha"—builder of the modernised Arab Legion and almost the last of the long line of British Arabists—was abruptly expelled from Jordan by young King Hussein, Old Boy of Harrow and Sandhurst.

That seemed the final, the symbolic, insult. Emotion, overflowing, sought blindly for an outlet.

By the summer it had found one.

Colonel Gamal Abd-el Nasser and the junta of young officers who had ruled Egypt since mid-1952 were in some ways well fitted to marshal that large-scale attack on Arab poverty and ill-health which Ernest Bevin had, in 1945, discerningly declared to be the first condition of Middle Eastern peace. Energetic, incorruptible—by money at least—capable of inspiring and harnessing the spirit of the people, they had, in fact, rapidly set on foot a large programme of social and land reform and reclamation.

Crucial in these plans was the much-deferred project for a High Dam at Aswan. And although this would require massive foreign aid, it was the very type of project—many-sided, far-reaching, concentrating imagination and energies on a constructive programme—that a West which had the true needs of the Middle East at heart would surely have hastened to under-write.

But the West, unfortunately, saw the Middle East mainly as a chequer-board in the Power game. It could not resist trying to place upon its finance for the Dam the price of military alignment—a price no new ex-"Colonial" nation like Egypt could now conceivably accept.

Baulked in the project which had become a central symbol of Egypt's Revolution, and needing to maintain dynamic and keep its followers in heart, the régime turned to such well-established activities of Pan-Arabism as Imperialist-baiting on Cairo Radio, aid for "rebel" Algerians, tirades and threats against Israel (that "agent of Western Imperialism"), arms-deals with the ever-ready Russians. . . .

When the torrents of Arab invective were translated into sober English, when the myth about Britain's numerous "friends" and high standing in the Middle East was sedulously preserved, it is not hard to understand how many in Britain came to see in Nasser a sort of darker-skinned Hitler and in his vague and adolescently idealistic *Philosophy of the Revolution* a sort of Middle Eastern *Mein Kampf*. Instead of merely canal-ising the virulent nationalistic, anti-Western, anti-Colonialist emotions sweeping over the entire area, he was seen as person-ally creating them.

The spectacular psychosis of the Arab World whose splendid Pan-Arab Dream was visibly fading before its eyes at what should have been its moment of triumph—not only by reason of the "betrayal" of Israel but also because of the Arabs' own all-too-obvious inadequacies—was well matched by the psychosis of the ex-Imperial Power, still secretly mourning its vanished glories and hugging its accumulating humiliations to its bosom.

They fed upon each other.

In much of the British Press at this time every development injurious to British interests over a large part of the globe was unhesitatingly ascribed to Nasser's machinations. As a scape-goat Nasser indeed left little to be desired. His caricature, the great hooked nose, the flashing teeth, loomed larger and larger in the newspapers. He was conspiring with the Russians. He was employing ex-Nazis. He was planning an Egyptian Empire. Like the Mahdi before him—for this was by no means a wholly new vein—he was everything that was evil and un-Englishly indecent.

Along the Israeli Border, that ever-sensitive barometer of Middle Eastern pressures, the tension mounted. Then, on

19th July with the abruptness of a slap in the face, John Foster Dulles announced that American finance for the High Dam would not now be forthcoming.

Next day, the British echo.

Egypt's dependency had been humiliatingly exposed before the world. In the current state of Arab nationalism the sequel was predictable. Seven days later, at the climax of a 2½-hour speech at Alexandria, Nasser announced the immediate nationalisation of the assets and installations of the Suez Canal Company. The Canal dues would finance the High Dam. The Revolution was invincible. Far from being defeated, the Dream was on the verge of fulfilment.

If internationally-owned, the Suez Canal Company was Egyptian-registered. As the sovereign nation she was so eager to prove herself, Egypt was within her rights. Shareholders were to be compensated at pre-nationalisation market prices, and in any event, the Canal's company's concession expired in 1968.

But if the High Dam symbolised the Arabs' New Dawn, the Suez Canal—as every schoolboy had been taught and as a whole generation of politicians had echoed—was the "lifeline of Empire". The conflict of national psychoses was deepened by the clash of national symbolisms. The impudence of Mossadeq, the treason of Makarios, the ingratitude of Nehru, the insults of Farouk, and Mintoff and Peron and Khrushchev and the rest seemed monstrously and finally accumulated in the insolence of Nasser.

The potent little word "wog" had been officially suppressed; now it came welling forth again on a gale of the old John Bullish anger. The Tory Irreconcilables, "the Gun-boat Tories", came at last into their own. But in the House on that first day after Nasser's bombshell it had been a Labour Member, R. T. Paget, who had inquired of the Prime Minister whether he was aware of the consequences of not meeting force with force until it was too late.

The Prime Minister said he was aware. Three aircraft carriers were being despatched to the Eastern Mediterranean. The troopship *Dunera*, outward-bound for Hongkong, was being recalled. Useless for "Nasser"—even *The Times* had dropped the prefix now—to "guarantee" the free passage of the Canal.

The notion that the Egyptians could efficiently operate this intricate waterway themselves was considered laughable, a typical example of "wog" presumption.

Nevertheless, by August, Nasser had, predictably again, rejected the 18-Nation plan for an international Suez Canal Control Board (outcome of the London Conference of maritime Powers) on the ground that this must constitute an affront to Egypt's sovereignty and "the dignity of nations".

Clearly the time had come to cut this "mountebank" down to size. "EDEN GETS TOUGH", headlined the *Daily Sketch*, "TELLS NASSER: Ike's with us and we're taking over OUR Canal. The next step armed convoys. Let the crybabies howl! It's GREAT Britain again."

In this demonstration of continuing "greatness" Britain was now more than ready to join that other frustrated ex-Imperial Power, France, whose chauvinistic delusions in Indo-China and Syria she had but lately, from the heights of her Commonwealth liberalism, rebuked.

But "Ike" was not "with us"; the Anglo-French could get no American support for plans for military intervention.

"The Prime Minister's course can only lead to disaster," warned the still small ('crybaby') voice of the *Manchester Guardian*.

It was not heeded. At the end of October, three months after the Canal's nationalisation and the failure of the first Franco-British attempt at disciplining Egypt, the newspapers reported that the Israeli Army was moving fast and in force across Israel's southern frontier.

A full-scale "preventive war" against Egypt was under way.

As the U.N. Security Council met next day to consider this act of aggression, the British and French delivered to the belligerents their twelve-hour ultimatum. It was a curious document. It had an appearance of bland cynicism that seemed worthy of a Bismarck. It demanded that Egypt, in the middle of a clear attack upon her, should cease fire and retire for ten miles on either side of the Suez Canal within her own territory. It required her to accept a "temporary" Anglo-French Occupation Force in Port Said, Ismailia and Suez.

Such terms were clearly impossible for Egypt honourably to accept. At 1 a.m. on Wednesday, 31st October, Nasser rejected the Franco-British ultimatum. By 7.30 a.m. the first British raids on Egyptian airfields had begun.

Now the black headlines came thick and fast . . . R.A.F. VENOMS BLAST EGYPT'S AIRFIELDS . . . INVASION FLEETS NEAR . . . BLOW UP OIL LINES, CAIRO CALLS. It was as if by some curious freak the pages of history had slipped back and one was again in that Imperial chapter which opens with Mr. Gladstone bombarding Alexandria in the name of International Order, and, incidentally, to break the rebel, Arabi.

"How good it is to hear the British Lion's roar . . ." wrote a reader to the *Daily Telegraph*. And millions echoed that satisfaction. But not all. In Petts Wood, on the morning of the first air strike, a housewife sat down and wrote a letter to the *News Chronicle*: "After the children had left for school this morning, I couldn't help it, I wept. I wept with shame and humiliation."

And there were many who understood those tears, and shed their own. If the Russian snuffing of the Hungarian rebellion had united the nation, Suez tore it apart. At Westminster the House was suspended amid an uproar such as had not been heard there since before the First World War. The division of opinion cut across party lines: the lowest as well as highest strata of society tended to react in traditional "British" fashion. Its circulation hit by its onslaught on Eden, the *Daily Mirror* was compelled by the logic of the mammoth sale to soften its attack. But two Tory Ministers resigned in protest. The Archbishop of Canterbury recorded his Christian disapproval; the Bishop of Exeter praised Eden's "superb moral courage". At Oxford, thirty professors and two college heads and 350 senior members of the University, signed a protest against the Government's aggression. But Professor Gilbert Murray, lifelong liberal and League pioneer, came to the Prime Minister's support.

Letters from people who appeared to speak mutually incomprehensible languages poured into the newspaper offices. Many who had never written to a newspaper in their lives wrote to one now. EDEN MUST GO! meetings attracted large and excited crowds all over the country.

But what was most extraordinary was the "un-English" bitterness. The word "traitor" was flung about with alien abandon. Friend cut friend. In a restaurant a man knocked off his mother's wig during a Suez argument. In pubs, clubs and not a few homes, "Suez" had to be rigorously forbidden. Many thousands of people cancelled orders for newspapers they had taken for many years, sometimes all their lives. "It would give me great pleasure to hear of your ceasing publication," a fifty-year-old reader wrote to the *Observer* which had condemned the Government's "folly and crookedness".

Such disruption of the normal deep-rooted unity of the British had not been seen since the fight over the passing of the Parliament Act, in 1911. The parallel was no accident. For now, as then, the emotional turmoil represented not a fight in the last ditch, but the sudden shocking realisation that the last ditch no longer existed.

This was the experience that teaches—or destroys. It taught. In the clash of Past and Present which had troubled and confused us now for so many years, the Present had triumphed, and triumphed decisively and irrevocably.

"Public Opinion" was no longer made across a few dozen dinner tables and club carpets—or even wholly in Western Europe. Yet diffused as it might be, world opinion could now be electronically focused and brought to bear with a speed and clarity that could make it a moral force of a power unknown before in history.

One day after the paratroopers' landing, the Anglo-French advance was halted in mid-course.

In the Commons the Cease-Fire was cheered as if it were some famous victory. It had, said the *Sunday Express* been "the proudest week we have known for years".

In the current state of auto-hypnosis it took a little time for the truth to go home.

Yet go home it did. In that ghastly Morning After, humiliation was piled on humiliation. Our soldiers were left stranded, in an untenable position, sniped at by Egyptians, waiting impotently for the United Nations Force to relieve them. The Royal Navy, surveying the Canal, assembling its wreck-raising vessels, issuing masterful statements, was not allowed to carry through the clearance. The British Prime Minister, broken in health, flew away to seek the sun in Jamaica. The gold reserves ran down again, and one more sharp credit squeeze was hurriedly imposed to save the pound. As the tankers slowly made their way round the Cape, the country returned to petrol rationing. Until April, 1958, when the Canal was cleared of the last obstruction and reopened under Egyptian auspices, every time a British motorist filled his tank he paid a special tax, "the Suez Shilling".

Briefly, we found a scapegoat in the Americans, who in their gross dollar-love, had "let us down". One hundred and twenty Conservative M.P.s put down a motion accusing America of "gravely endangering the Atlantic Alliance". In Tring, Hertfordshire, a car-dealer made the point more briskly with a sign: NO AMERICANS SERVED HERE.

But it was perhaps the last flare-up of this particular sort of anti-Americanism. The truth had to be faced now. The "Lion's Roar" that had proved so gratifying to the reader of the *Daily Telegraph* was all too plainly that poor beast's last.

In the Middle East the pressures of Arab Nationalism, dangerously heightened by Suez, were breaking through the artificial pattern of frontiers drawn by the Western Powers in 1919. In June, 1958, that antiquated structure toppled in Iraq, pivot of the West's Middle Eastern illusions and of its Baghdad Pact. In another "Nasser-type" officers' coup, King Feisal was killed, the British Embassy sacked, the veteran Nuri es-Said—last of the older generation of Arab "pasha" politicians, as Glubb had been of the British Arabists—torn to pieces by the mob.

The once great British position in the Middle East was reduced to the "protection" of a few steamy Persian Gulf sheikdoms. In March, 1957, Archbishop Makarios was released from exile on the Seychelles; and, less than two years later, Cyprus achieved that sovereign independence which not long before a British Colonial Secretary had stated could "never" be conceded. The British Empire, which in 1945 had held sway over 600,000,000 people was now rapidly and visibly being reduced to a scattering of small islands, "bases" whose function appeared yearly more dubious.

ABC OF £SU

—to help you understand the jargon

By DEREK DALE
Mirror City Editor

Mirror City Office,
24, Old Broad Street,
London, E.C.2.

POET and essayist Alexander Pope wrote 250 years ago: "A little learning is a dangerous thing."

And that is certainly true when it comes to investing money.

To enrich both your vocabulary and, I hope, your pocket, the City column will present, over the next four weeks, an Investor's Alphabet.

My aim: A simple, basic guide for you to keep handy for future reference.

So start your investment scrapbook this morning with ... A.

A is for

Account

THE Stock Exchange has a special calendar of its own divided into what are called "Accounts." These usually run for "two weeks."

When you buy shares on the Stock Exchange, you do not have to pay cash down for them.

Payment becomes due on what is called "Settlement Day."

This arrives eleven days after the end of the Account in which you bought the shares.

So if you buy shares on the first day of an Account, you would have a run of twenty-five days' grace before having to pay for them.

To help your broker, don't overrun your time.

The system works also in reverse. When you sell, you receive a cheque from your broker by Settlement Day.

Move on now to ...

B is for

FOURTH LINE. Finally comes the Government stamp duty of 2 per cent. This is a charge of £2 for every £100 worth of shares bought.

It is levied only on a share buyer — NOT on the seller.

A further fee of 2s. 6d. is also usually charged by the company in which the shares were bought, for transferring the ownership of their share register to the new owner.

As the purchase price in our example was £100, the final entry on our contract note would be:

Transfer, Stamp and Fee:

Total 103 8 6

The contract note also carries on it the words—"Bought for Settlement," followed by a date. This is the next Settlement Day by which the broker's bill must be paid.

Now you've found your broker — invested £100 in tiddlywinks — and you're ready for D-Day.

D is for

Dividend

DIVIDEND is the reward

scale of fees charged by brokers, based on the stock market price of shares they are asked to buy or sell:

On stocks or shares costing more than £10 each, the broker's charge is 15s. for every £100 worth bought or sold Stockbrokers are not allowed to advertise for business. But you can get in ...

46 and 47. Mirror indeed! From Zec's "Fair Shares" Election cartoon of 1945 (*left*) to the first *Stocks and Shares* page of 1960 (*right*). The *Mirror's* advice on "How to Get the Goods" had been supplemented.

48. *Above*, the L.C.C.'s Peckham Secondary School for Girls, a "comprehensive school" opened in 1957, realising an educational philosophy often paid lip-service, but rarely acted upon.

Contrasts between the New Britain emerging and the Old Britain lingering on were nowhere sharper than in the schools.

49. *Below*, the L.C.C.'s Tower Bridge School, erected in 1895 and still in use.

In London, in an access of masochism, crowds flocked to John Osborne's new play, *The Entertainer*, where against the background of a tawdry Britannia, Union Jacks and a row of "nudes", the British Empire was equated with the squalid self-delusion of a worn-out tenth-rate music hall performer and ritualistically spat upon.

On the pavements outside the Canada Immigration Offices the queues were longer than they had been at any time since the dark days of 1948.

II

Like the Suez Débâcle, the General Election of October, 1959, had the air of a logical conclusion, the ruling of a firm red line across these postwar years. Defeated for the third time in succession after its half-century-long climb to power, the Labour Party seemed not merely excluded from office, but despatched into political limbo. The tide of Collectivism, having reached highwatermark in 1945, seemed already on the ebb.

But if, again, the book appeared to be closing on a famous chapter in English history, it also appeared to have opened, almost at once, upon a new one.

The 1959 election really was the "first TV election" that 1955's had prematurely been proclaimed to be. Even more significantly, it was the "first ITV election".

For a year or more before the event, the small word "image" had been percolating, from the advertising and public relations world, via the smarter commentators into daily political usage. For in the era of the new Consumer Democracy, or People's Capitalism, it was, it now appeared, naïve to think that what mattered was a political party's Message, i.e. something it believed in, so gave forth. Montgomery's putting the men "in the picture", Cripps' "telling the people", were beginning to appear crude and primitive exercises indeed. As Chairman of the Conservative Party Organisation, Lord Woolton, the leading Conservative advocate of commercial television, had, as he himself boasted, introduced into its operations the methods of big business merchandising which he knew so well.

But the possibilities were not fully demonstrated until after Suez, when a leading advertising and P.R. firm was engaged to

P

refurbish the Conservative Party's image. First, the market was surveyed by the usual sampling techniques to outline its most "receptive" areas. These having been identified as women, the young and the better-off workers, a two-year £500,000 Press and poster advertising campaign was then directed towards enabling these groups to identify the Conservative Party with Prosperity and Opportunity. "YOU'RE LOOKING AT A CONSERVATIVE", advised the caption over the portrait of a prosperous but cloth-capped worker.

The dissolution of the old frontiers characteristic of the Admass society in full bloom now made it possible for the great industrial federations, and even for large individual concerns, to participate in such a campaign without the crudeness of overt political commitment. The costly and accomplished advertising of the Iron and Steel Federation was mainly directed towards "reporting" (often under the names of journalists secured for the purpose) the efficiency and happiness of the— denationalised—Steel Industry. IN THIS WORKS ONE MAN IN THREE DRIVES TO HIS JOB, a characteristic "human story" was headlined.

Hitherto, the B.B.C. had narrowly confined the political employment of radio in order not to disturb too greatly the time-honoured forms of the hustings. But in 1959 the pressures of "democratised" broadcasting—heightened by the force of television as a medium—broke through. The electronic hustings were erected. The old embargo on political news in the election "closed season" was lifted, the contest televised on a round-the-clock blow-by-blow basis. The Press now found itself playing a secondary, though still essential and complementary, role.

The old hustings—so long the stout and durable prop of the British political tradition—had offered a rough-and-ready trial by ordeal rather as the old pre-supermarket market had enabled the customer to come to grips with both goods and supplier. They might enfranchise the demagogue. But the old demagoguery was an art and true demagogues rare. They cannot be made to measure and may be politically creative. The electronic hustings, by contrast, interposed the whole mid-century world of specialisms, of producers, camera-experts, make-up artists, script-writers, statisticians, market-researchers between the politicians and the public. Both parties now set up their own closed circuit television schools where the requisite sincere approach could be perfected. Demagoguery was scientific now and, possibly, automated.

In 1945 the public opinion poll had been so novel that few paid much attention to it. By 1959 it had become an institution. During the campaign itself rival opinion polls were published on no less than four days of each week. To these were added the audience ratings of the Party broadcasts, the tell-tale, intimidating curve of switch-offs. Meanwhile, both during and between elections, a small but increasingly influential body of social scientists and "psephologists"—a word, significantly, of postwar coinage—industriously processed every available statistic.

Because of the Party's old atmosphere of earnestness and faith, the change was most striking on the Labour side. Labour's election campaign on television was cast in popular magazine form, complete with TV Personalities, animated cartoons and diagrams, on-the-spot interviews, inset films, jingles, sound-effects and signature tunes. The Party's high-gloss pre-Election "book", *The Future Labour Offers* YOU, which enveloped its very few specific details in multi-colour layouts and euphoric photogravure, was likewise a far cry from the poky, crowded, serious manifestoes of earlier years.

In yet another central, tradition-ruled area of British life the technicians appeared to be finally taking over. Their preoccupation with packaging and images, with the "audience-impact" of a policy rather than with its importance or worth, showed through in the tone of the election itself, which some very experienced observers pronounced to have been "the most materialistic in recent history". The Labour Party—apart from the odd reference to Stock Exchange gamblers, expense accounts and the needs of the Old—did not seriously seek to transcend the new "never-had-it-so-good" semi-detachment. It merely suggested that, under Labour, the "percentage" would be even better. To that end, Mr. Gaitskell gave a pledge on no account to increase income tax. The proposal to renationalise Iron and Steel and Road Haulage had, in the circumstances an air of inexplicable pedantry.

The impression that emerged with devastating clarity from the contest was that of two large rival commercial concerns, manufacturers of detergents or breakfast cereals, competing for the same carefully researched market, pension plan for pension plan, new schools against new schools, slum clearance and easier house purchase for the same in a different coloured packet, a Youth and Leisure Programme against a Youth and Leisure Programme. When seen on TV, the echoes of the familiar rivalry of Daz and Omo were irresistible.

"It is not thus," said *The Times* disapprovingly, on the eve of the poll, "that a great people are summoned to yet another session in their endless appointment with history."

But *The Times* was behind the times. In the age of Vital Statistics, all appointments were made with the Market.

An electorate as sagacious and as experienced as the British might yet demonstrate that it could see through the processed "image" to the men and motives behind, and thus call—in this field at least—the bluff of Admass. That done, TV, with its characteristic ambivalence, could serve uniquely to inform* rather than to pander.

But, for the present, the efficiency of the new catering mechanisms with their built-in monitors, graph-lines, mirror-devices, feed-backs, was both impressive and intimidating. Ownership, snowballing, as hire purchase debt leapt by 70 per cent in pre-election year, had continued to erode the old working-class solidarity. Savings rose steeply. Life insurance boomed. On the housing estates of the Midlands and the South —a prime source of Labour gains in 1945—the newest generation joined the multiplying army of "Don't Knows" and "Won't Tells".** In these areas of the new semi-detachment and among the free-spending women and young, the swing to Conservatism was the greatest.

It was least (or non-existent) in the old industrial areas of Lancashire and Lanarkshire. But these were already beginning to wear the air of places that "History" had passed by.

* In the Trenaman and McQuail investigation into the 1959 election, it was found that of all media and sources of political persuasion, only television added significantly to electors' knowledge.

** The "Don't Knows" were a continuous and much-commented-on phenomenon of the political scene in the late Fifties. In March, 1959, the Gallup Poll put them at no less than 22 per cent of the electorate.

The change bore all the marks of permanence. In May, 1945, two months before the first election of peace, the *Daily Mirror* had attached to its masthead the brave slogan: FORWARD WITH THE PEOPLE!

On the Monday following the 1959 election it took it down.

In the fifteen years between these gestures the pages of the *Mirror*, the Soldiers' Voice of 1939-45, offer dramatic evidence both of the potency and the deadly limitations of the Admass mirror process brought to final perfection in the Fifties.

In January, 1949, still riding on the crest of the wave of postwar social revolution, the sales of the *Mirror*, of the Universal (but strictly postwar) Housing Estate, passed those of the *Daily Express* of the Endless Suburb, which had gloried in the top place for years.

The Common Man had triumphed.

But not, now, be it noted, too common a Common Man. For if, after this realignment, there was discernible in the *Express* a broadening of tone and heightening of headline, there was, in the *Mirror*, a certain retreat from the bloodier "Radicalism", a tendency—increasing through the Fifties—to allow that the younger readers might sip a Tio Pepe as well as sink a pint.

Behind the "contemporary" curtains and rustic name-plates, Suburb and Housing Estate were merging where they met.

As the Fifties ended, this process moved on apace. In one grand obeisance to the *Zeitgeist*, the *Mirror* not only dropped its "old hat" Radical slogan, but also proclaimed a FUN FORTNIGHT ("The accent is on Youth, the accent is on Gaiety") and dismissed "Jane", veteran of the war years, in favour of a teen-ager named Patti. In the New Year, as the industrial share index broke through its all-time high, as car manufacturers came out with multi-million pound expansion plans and Fords issued their first "two-car family" advertisement in Britain ("FOUR BEDROOMS . . . THREE CHILDREN . . . TWO FORDS"), the *Mirror* introduced a City Page to instruct its readers, in simple terms, on how to join the shareholder state. "A is for Account . . . B is for Broker . . . D is for Dividend . . ." its City Editor advised. In a strip below, "Uncle Forsyte" explained the value of 'takeover' deals.

Meanwhile, another leading Labour economist, after further "rethinking", advanced the suggestion that not only should "nationalisation" be publicly drummed out of the party, but that that dreary name "Labour" might go as well.

III

The "pendulum" was not the only piece of political imagery that was now beginning to seem outmoded: there were also the metaphors of political control. In England, Lord Attlee had said, Labour's function was to be the accelerator, Conservatism's to act as the brake. But it was becoming evident that the Machine now installed had a fuel-feed and momentum of its own, and that anyone who sought to predict its course, had better look, not to Whitehall but—as an increasing number of businessmen were now doing to their great profit—across the Atlantic.

From hula-hoops to Zen Buddhism, from do-it-yourself to launderettes or the latest sociological catch-phrase or typographical trick, from Rock 'n' Roll to Action Painting, barbecued chickens rotating on their spits in the shop windows to parking meters, clearways, bowling alleys, glass-skyscrapers, flying saucers, pay-roll raids, armoured trucks and beatniks, American habits and vogues now crossed the Atlantic with a speed and certainty that suggested that Britain was now merely one more offshore island. Strip-tease clubs completed the "Fordisation" of sex, supermarkets of shopping and Wimpy bars of eating. As if by some automatic process every successful American stereo or gimmick duly appeared in British version—a Dors for a Monroe, a Steele for a Presley, a Shirley Bassey for an Eartha Kitt. The freeing of Lawrence's *Lady Chatterley* which took place in Britain in 1960 was preceded by her liberation in the United States in 1959. American drug-houses furnished our tranquillisers, American publishers our excitants, with the co-operation of British publishers who found the recommendation "sweeping the U.S." ever more compulsive. A second Canadian financier now continued the Americanisation of our Press which the first had some time before begun. And there was *still* an American musical on the boards at Drury Lane—G.B.S. triumphantly re-exported in the expert packaging of *My Fair Lady*.

W. T. Stead's warning book, *The Americanisation of the World,* had appeared in 1901. Between the first strains of ragtime before the First World War and the coming of the super-market in the late 1950's, Americanisation might be considered to have been completed, and the 1959 election was duly fought by the Government on a slogan taken over from the Democrats' campaign of 1952. The Left, too, was now drawing such few new ideas as it had from American sources like the sociologist C. Wright Mills or the economist J. K. Galbraith.

Yet, again, the end of a long process also implied a point of departure. Whereas earlier "Americanisms" were often im-portations primarily stimulated by America's "glamour", the reproduction in postwar England of basic American conditions —"count-heads" democracy, mass production-distribution, nourished by and nourishing the Moneyed Masses, tech-nology applied to the full in a country short of labour—was creating parallel phenomena, directly, on our own soil. The comprehensive school which England had now discovered, initially with such alarm, was not merely a copy of the native American High School, but also a native product of our own democratic pressures. The new interest in sociology, now cropping up even in radio serials, was the natural consequence of a more "made" society. Consumer testing, a new phenomenon in the England of the late Fifties,* though modelled on the veteran U.S. Consumers' Union, was a response to the more sophisticated mass market, as monopoly-busting was to an evolving managerial society. That feature of American life, the "working" undergraduate, had likewise appeared over here as a logical social development. So, more spectacularly, had the whole "teenage" business.

Having lost the monopoly of her particular revolution—as Britain before her had lost her own long start with the steam engine and the factory system—America no longer monopolised that "secret", that vaunted "know-how" from which had flowed so much of her unique prestige and magnetism in the Forties. The spell was broken. The sputniks were in orbit and that orbit was global. Meanwhile, America's old position as the standard-bearer of Freedom (in the face of both Imperialism and

* The Consumers' Association, financed by members' subscript-ions, was founded in 1957 and grew rapidly into a movement with far-reaching possibilities.

Communism) was progressively eroded by the actual achievement of freedom by the countries of Asia and Africa, particularly
when these formed a Third Force which, however nebulous, was
on occasion a powerful moral presence. In the blaze of this
younger, fiercer revolution, America's "Permanent Revolution"
began to appear pale and jaded. The American Century which
in 1946, in the face of Europe's debility, had seemed so unchallengeable—and so galling—fifteen years later, in the face of
Europe's re-equipment, consolidation and resurgence, was
already over.

Americans themselves were not unaware of these facts.
The American Way of Life which had been trumpeted with
such brazen confidence in the Forties was now being subjected
to increasingly critical examination. Meanwhile, in the "one
world" which American technology had brought about, and
more particularly in Western Europe, entering a new era of
affluence, free movement and leisure, it would perhaps have
been an exaggeration to say that the American title-deeds were
forfeit; but certainly the patent-rights had run out. Blue jeans
were no longer American blue jeans but just jeans; the juke-box
was no longer an American juke-box, and it was even possible,
on a propitious day, to see Tommy Steele not as a mere copy of
Bill Haley or Elvis Presley, but—like the Teddy boys—as
Britain's and Bermondsey's own.

As the conveyor-belts gathered pace and the lights on the
automation panels blinked more swiftly, England, with the
rest, was increasingly involved in an international "culture"
which, on the blue-jeans-and-Coca-Cola-ICI-GAS-OIL-SNACK
background, might impose Italian-styled scooters and suits,
Spanish holidays, Scandinavian furniture and light fittings,
Scotch whisky, Chinese and Indian restaurants, Sartre, Sagan,
Henry Moore and Jackson Pollock, Anna Magnani and Tommy
Steele, Beckett and Osborne, Tennessee Williams and T. S.
Eliot, cheap French wine and French Impressionists, calypsos
and espresso bars. . . . Europe, in short, was at last giving hints
that she might yet succeed in assimilating the Americans as
America had assimilated Europeans.

As for England, Suez at least had delivered us from the
burden and falsity of an Empire that had ceased to be either
morally or financially supportable: we were purged at last of

the slow poison of that particular sort of anti-Americanism which is based in jealousy and self-pity; and thus free to seek our own particular accommodation with technological society while holding on to our own lifeline of continuity in these seas of change.

33.   Fog Lifting

"So, it is quite possible that the porter
who carries your cases at Waterloo or
Victoria has just returned from San
Sebastian or the South of France. . . ."
—Article in *The Times*, 1956.

"Try Pizza and Chips—the Italian
Welsh Rarebit."
—Notice in London café window.

"The question often put by friends in
Europe is: 'Do you think Britain is
part of Europe?' The answer is 'Yes'
. . . We are part of Europe. But that
is not the whole question. We are
more than part of Europe. . . ."
—Mr. Selwyn Lloyd, House of Commons debate on the European
Common Market, February,
1959.

ALL THE way from Aldgate to Notting Hill and beyond the
tower cranes thrust their slender jibs against the sky.
Pneumatic drills jibbered, pile-drivers thudded against
steel driven deep into the London clay. By 1959 London was
rebuilding fast—in the last five years most of the bomb-torn
gaps had gone. Not all though; almost twenty years after the
great fire-Blitz of 1940 that laid them bare, the cellars of the
Barbican were still open to the sky and gay with ragwort and
rose-bay willow-herb and the odd plum tree. But a block to
the north now soared the grey-and-yellow tower of the City
Corporation's Golden Lane flats, its seventeenth storey crowned
by a curving windroof like a Mikado's hat. And across the
river, on the old Festival site, a great hole gaped in the earth
from which presently a steel-and-concrete tower would rise to

a height only a few feet lower than St. Paul's. After centuries of expanding outwards, the Great Wen, as powerful a magnet as ever, was thrusting skywards.

A new streetscape as well as a new skyline was shaping. Everywhere one looked the new architectural language, patently a language as universal as blue jeans and the juke-box and ballistic missiles, asserted its idiom, stark and strong, over the time-honoured observances of cornice and moulding, pediment and column. And if rumbles of that old rearguard action against the modern movement in architecture could still from time to time be heard, after the defeat in 1956 of the "neo-Georgians" in their fight for Renaissance colonnades for the new precinct of St. Paul's, they grew more distant. Before the decade was out Cambridge had engaged Sir Basil Spence to build on its hallowed Backs and Oxford commissioned Arne Jacobsen, an *avant-garde* Dane, to design St. Catherine's College.

A character in an Evelyn Waugh novel once traced England's character and greatness to her shroud of fog. "We had," he cried, "a foggy habit of life and a rich, obscure, choking literature. . . . Out of a fog we could rule. . . . We designed a city that was meant to be seen in a fog."

But not any more: not these bright blue plastic panels, these gleaming curtain walls of glass, these aluminium grids. The fog, the last protection of our insularity, was lifting. The process consciously inaugurated in 1951 by the Festival of Britain had moved on apace. The striped umbrellas had blossomed and multiplied, and here and there, Englishmen and women were to be observed actually sitting, not too self-consciously, at tables on the London pavement.

But the most calculated and astonishingly successful exercise in the new "un-Englishness" was the espresso bar. The espressos, which arrived from Italy in the mid-Fifties, found their most enthusiastic clientele amongst the young and put a high polish on the contemporary veneer of international sophistication. They were also one more pointer to the opening age of leisure. For in a Britain whose furnishings were still largely those inherited from the Victorians, there had been no place for the ordinary non-clubman to sit and talk or sit and stare but the dreary working-class "caff" or the pub where drinking was still perpendicular and fog-and-fug often impenetrable. The prewar milk bar and the postwar clattering self-service tea-shop were designed for speed, not leisure. The espresso bar was at least a token acknowledgment of this large gap in Britain's urban pleasures.

In its décor, its key element, it gave possibly the boldest expression yet to the new "democratic" eclecticism, somehow combining the relative austerity of Festival Contemporary with a dash of Mediterranean colour and abandon. One dallied not over the once inevitable slab-cake and iced pastries but over *Apfelstrudel*, Danish pastries, cheese-cake, chocolate *torte*, dispensed by sophisticates in swinging skirts and large brass ear-rings or black-jersied gamines with Audrey Hepburn hairdo's.

Exuberant and, at times, bizarre, as the espressos might be, they clearly—like Teddy costume—corresponded to some felt need—for from their heartland in Chelsea and Kensington, the Mocambos, the Tarantellas, the Blue Danubes, the Romas, the Venezias, the Piccolos, the Boccaccios, and the rest now spread like some exotic rash across the Metropolis, then across the country, and finally reached Manchester. By the winter of 1957 there were over a thousand of them.

They afforded striking evidence, not only of the highly—some might say, virulently—infectious character of the new "international culture", but also of its brilliance and its shallowness and its magpie ability to snatch from the surface of scores of cultures in order to feed its appetite for novelty and change. For this was something different from earlier foreign "influences", from, say, the eighteenth-century cult of chin-oiserie, or the nineteenth-century European "Tea Room and American Bar". This eclecticism was total. "Wider still and wider, shall thy bounds be set . . ." From the pseudo-peasant to the pseudo-intellectual, from the colourful gaucho blanket to the colourful Existentialist coffin, from Vienna to Rome, from Monte Carlo to the South Seas, was now but a step.

And yet wafer-thin as the veneer might be, the factors behind it now had strength and permanence. Furthermore, in England at this juncture the ability of superficial change to stimulate deeper change, as a pebble starts an avalanche, could be considerable. Even that hallowed institution, the English pub, was in places now being made over, its dark mahogany and frosted glass retreating before the "contemporary" wallpaper, perforated hardboard and red metal funnel lamps.

"We are not thinking of the future in terms of saloon and public bars," announced Mr. Edward Thompson, Chairman of Ind Coope, the brewers.

And it was in 1958 too that one of the largest and hitherto most tradition-bound of British motor makers brought out a new popular model styled—and very clearly so—on the drawing boards of Signor Pinin Farina of Milan.

II

One of the most potent agents of this international "rabble-scrabble"—as the good Dr. Arnold would undoubtedly have called it—was tourism, now numbered among the most important and fastest-growing of Britain's industries.

In 1952 the airlines had introduced the first "Tourist" fares. Cut-price night flights followed. We seemed to be moving at last towards an era of cheap mass air travel. Travel agencies, multiplying and expanding at a great rate, brought costs down again by chartering aircraft. The fortnight on the Costa Brava or the Ten Days at Nice became as cheap and a good deal easier than the holiday in Bridlington or Bournemouth. At the same time, for the more elderly and cautious the luxury motor-coach, apotheosis of the old working-class "chara", boarded with one's pals or family virtually on one's own doorstep, so thoroughly removed the perils of "Abroad" that the inhabitants of a good many towns of Western Europe became inured to sudden eruptions of solid, mackintosh-carrying British citizens, descending upon them like visitants from another planet.

By 1958 the number of Britons travelling abroad for their holidays had reached two million, almost twice the prewar peak,—still small enough percentage-wise, but rising fast. The Automobile Association reported that two-thirds of their members had taken their cars abroad in the Fifties: the Channel car-ferries were jam-packed.

The Continental Holiday, in short, was now well on the way to establishing itself as a basic ingredient of the "new standard of living". But it was more than that. For some, hemmed in by the managerial society, debunked and deflated, it brought back, by stealth, the lost dream of Paradise or Utopia; there was, after all, a happy land, far, far away—if only one could find the right little beach and hotel. Each January, as the newspapers brought out their advertisement-crammed Holiday Supplements, and the rain lashed against the bus windows, the brochures were studied, the delicious speculation got under way. Would it be Naples again this year? The six days in Salzburg and seven on Lake Garda? Peseta was set against franc, lira against schilling, route against route. In the late Forties, the poverty of Austria brought a Tyrolean holiday boom; then Italy, with Chianti at 2s. a bottle, and a wealth of warm, romantic associations, moved into favour; then came the turn of Majorca and Spain, whose Mediterranean coast-line, bursting into a wild rash of new building, seemed cast for the part of a "democratic" or cut-price Riviera, even, in places of a sort of "picturesque" Blackpool, with flamenco, stewed octopus, and dark brown tan.

The first wave of middle-class tourists, in Victorian times, had merely colonised Switzerland and the Riviera. The new wave of the Endless Middle could not be thus confined. All around the Mediterranean, "snorkel" tubes thrust from the azure waters, British mouths beneath them. And each year the scouting parties of the tourist agencies pushed out a little further opening up some new "delightful little beach", some still—but not for long—"unspoiled island".

There were many, of course, for whom the people of the places concerned never really emerged from the travel posters; the organised tour cushioned them well enough against contact with reality. But it was also true that many of the young of all classes, introduced by National Service or by the war to travel, were thoroughly at home in Europe, for ever hitch-hiking, scootering, cycling and jaloppying their way around it. Something like a democratic version of the Grand Tour was evolving, but this ex-Imperial generation, no Milords they, were notably lacking in the old insular arrogance, willing to accept Europeans on their own terms, and even to regard themselves as belonging among them.

And even for those who were couriered in packs, there might

be a certain loss of island innocence. Eighty Derbyshire miners who travelled to Riccione on the Adriatic cautiously took with them their own beer and cook, but were subsequently reported to have decided that "wine and spaghetti are not at all bad". Foreigners might remain odd, but no longer seemed *totally* inexplicable.

And back in Britain, the "innocents abroad"—completely innocent no longer—nourished, husbanded, and pondered their memories. There was a run on foreign cook-books—*La Cuisine Française*, Portuguese, *Espagnole*, Vietnamese, Roman, Viennese, Venetian, Yugoslav. . . . Neapolitan *pizza* appeared in the milk-bars, while *scampi* became, for a while, *de rigueur* in every restaurant or small hotel with any pretensions to modishness. Spanish baskets thrust hard corners into passengers on London's buses or tubes. The sales of Continental-style lager beers soared and we were drinking more than twice as much coffee, three times as much wine as before the war. The demand was no longer for expensive vintages, but for ordinary light wines at 8*s.* or less a bottle from whatever country could best provide them. Wine was ceasing to be an upper-class or conspicuous consumption drink, and was moving into the Endless Middle. Old and aristocratic—but still awake—wine merchants like Harveys of Bristol now embarked on a "Marksian revolution" of their own. Formerly British wine-stores had been dark and dingy, and often carefully screened in as if to hide some guilty secret. In the made-over stores all was bright and open to view.

There were many other signs of a less insular "mild-and-bitter" habit. Delicatessens, once confined to Soho and the more Germanic areas, were now spreading elsewhere. Foreign restaurants flourished and multiplied, and Indian and Chinese ones opened up in the most sober and moderate-sized northern towns. Even holiday camps now boasted of being "Continental-style". Butlins ran their own foreign travel agency for their campers, while football fans, once the most fiercely parochial of Britons, casually bandied the names of Di Stefano of Spain, of Puskas, the Hungarian, Pele of Brazil, and Yashin, the Russian goalkeeper.

"Up for the Cup" no longer represented the ultimate horizon.

III

The fact that Tourism was now enjoying a world boom made it a particularly potent addition to the influences undermining the old English cult of the familiar—the same old boarding-house, same sticks of rock, and same old jokes every year—and installing the new international cult of novelty and fashion-change. It slashed carelessly across the old class lines also: the cheap night flight now offered as wide a cross-section of English society as the launderette.

And if Tourism were regarded cynically, as one more para-sitic and voracious growth incubated by Admass, its parasitism was, nevertheless, of a unique order in that the "host" of one day was the parasite the next.

Thus while British women in bikinis or tartan trews out-raged the Spanish sense of propriety and embarrassed the Civil Guard, foreign tourists in Britain—whose numbers trebled during the Fifties—used Guardsmen sentries at Buckingham Palace as background for their portait "snaps" and, with the enthusiastic aid of the British Travel Association, brought a new gloss to the Ancient British Tradition Industry.

In the later Fifties new hotels were rising all over London, where American luxury establishments were about to challenge the British Savoy-Claridges tradition as directly as Italian men's wear styling was now challenging the conservatism of Savile Row. But Tourism was not the only cause of London's growing cosmopolitanism. Grey pavements were lightened by the flutter of silken saris or lent sudden dignity by the majesty of Kente cloth. From all over the Commonwealth, and indeed the world, students were flocking to Britain at their Govern-ment's expense to enlist their nations in the "one world" of technology and science.

Every year, too, there now arrived from the countries of Europe 20,000 "home helps" or *au pair* girls who came to bridge the gap left by the disappearance of the English "domestic", while introducing a few new spices to the kitchen and learning our now indispensable language. Less happily, the traditional inflow of refugees also continued. After 1956 Britain had six times as many Hungarians as before the war.

In London, certainly, none of this was wholly new. But now the "alien" wave travelled further and wider. There were many Poles in Birmingham, Wolverhampton and Glasgow; a large colony of Latvians and Ukrainians kept the woollen mills of Bradford going; Italians supplied a large part of the labour in the Lea Valley nursery industry and in the brickfields of East Anglia: every tenth Bedfordian was an Italian now. Nor were the newcomers necessarily manual workers. In the Sheffield Region's hospitals half the junior doctors were foreigners, a roll-call which included twenty-nine nationalities.

These were educational experiences—a sort of tourist continuation course—but hardly likely unduly to ruffle our insular complacence.

The West Indian "invasion" struck deeper.

By the early Fifties Londoners had grown accustomed to the sight of loose-limbed Jamaicans strolling nonchalantly along in groups, strange hats perched on the backs of their heads, bright blue suits flapping about them, dazzle ties and black-and-white brogues bringing a touch of zaniness to the postwar scene. It was a gaiety, alas, which did not last.

Again this was something which had developed out of the war when 8,000 West Indians had served in the R.A.F. and many others in British arms plants. The accounts they had sent back home of a "Mother Country" where there were jobs for all, where education was free, and (especially in the Forces) there was little colour discrimination, had launched the peacetime movement of work-seekers eastwards across the Atlantic.

By 1956 the annual influx had reached 26,000, and by the end of the decade there had grown up in Britain a West Indian community of around 150,000. These were still not large numbers. But hitherto English experience of "colour" had been largely confined to the great ports. Now dark faces appeared in increasing numbers on the streets of a score or more of towns all over Britain where they were startlingly visible. Birmingham, in particular, with its great variety of industries became a Mecca of West Indians. It attracted 30,000 of them. And at the same time, there were the parallel, though much smaller, arrivals of coloured Commonwealth subjects from Africa,

Pakistan and India. A Birmingham Clean Air leaflet had to be printed in Urdu, Hindi and Arabic, as well as English. By the end of the decade the city's coloured immigrants—immigrants no longer—were estimated to own £5 million of Birmingham property.

A temperament and way of life adapted to sun-bathed Caribbean islands did not necessarily accord well with the habits and prejudices of some damp, grey, parochial English town. In the best circumstances assimilation must have had its difficulties. The severe housing shortage ensured that the circumstances were the worst possible. Too often the coloured immigrants fell into the gaps still left by the Welfare State. Too often a process dismally familiar in other countries set in . . . fantastic overcrowding, rack-rents . . . "blacks" moving in, "whites" moving out . . . bitter accusations about dirt, noise, vice, black-men-and-white-women (for in the earlier years— this corrected itself later—there were few West Indian women).

Officialdom—Whitehall, employers' organisations, trade union chiefs—continued to insist that in Britain no distinctions based on colour were ever made or even conceivable. No statistics of "coloured" labour could be supplied since, officially, "colour" did not exist.

Practice unfortunately fell a long way short of this admirable, but possibly unrealistic, attitude. In many places of employment there developed some sort of tacit "colour quota". According to surveys analysed by the sociologist, Anthony Richmond, one-third of the British were "extremely prejudiced" against coloured persons and wished to exclude them, one-third were tolerant and approved their coming to Britain, a third vacillated.

In Sheffield, Bristol, West Bromwich, Wolverhampton and some other towns there was a good deal of trouble with local transport workers over the employment of "the darkies" on the buses. Sometimes politely veiled discrimination in lodgings, pubs or workplace would be forced into the open, hardening into an ugly colour bar. One such case at the Scala Ballroom in Wolverhampton in 1958 became the centre of a national row, leading to the boycott of the dancehall concerned by the Musicians' Union and the—unsuccessful—promotion of a Bill by a local M.P. to make colour bars in public places illegal.

In an egalitarian society, those whose "equality" is most

shaky are not unaware of the reassurance to be derived from having some group to occupy the social basement. Coloured immigrants are ideal candidates for this position. Should they display a certain reluctance to accept it, the vicious circle of prejudice forcing them into squalid housing conditions, the squalid housing reinforcing prejudice, can be trusted to confirm their candidature.

In August, 1958, rising tension in Nottingham and North Kensington exploded in disturbances which brought the sinister phrase "race riots" into the headlines. Violence was, in fact, confined to a relatively small number of trouble-seeking toughs, often youths. But for some days it was unsafe for coloured people to venture on to the streets in these areas in the evenings, and a number of pathological "fringe" racist groups who found here a promising alternative to prewar Jew-baiting were permitted, in the name of Free Speech, to exacerbate and capitalise a situation they had done a good deal to create.

Racial affrays in port towns in Britain were not new, and the "Notting Hill Riots" were probably less virulent than those that had followed the First World War in Cardiff and Liverpool and on Tyneside. But the world—and Britain—had moved on apace. These coloured immigrants of London and the Midlands were no longer so many anonymous dark faces. They were citizens, not only of the "multi-racial Commonwealth", but of independent nations with a powerful voice in the world—and sometimes with an "anti-colonial, anti-White" colour consciousness as rabid as the Western *Herrenvolk* approach that had produced it.

The arclights of world publicity were switched on to the festering slums of Notting Dale. For days the attention of the world's Press, radio, television, was focused on this mess which the "Mother Country" appeared to have been concealing underneath her neat official carpet. Suddenly, the British at home—these insular British who had been content to remain abysmally ignorant* of the Commonwealth—found themselves at the heart of one of the central and most intractable problems of the modern world.

* As illustrated, for instance, by the Social Survey's inquiry in 1948 on behalf of the Colonial Office. This found that one-half of those questioned could not even name a single colony correctly.

The experience was unpleasant, but salutary. TV, radio and Press poured out a stream of reportage that was often detailed, serious and constructive. West Indian Ministers came to London and were taken into consultation by Britain's Prime Minister. A few details were added to the new view of the world revealed at Suez. Welfare organisations were strengthened, joint inter-racial community committees formed. The existence of a "colour problem" was admitted; it was dispassionately examined and analysed; and something at least was done about it.

The situation would inevitably remain an uneasy one. But apathy had been shaken. And the sensational headlines gave no hint of the innumerable friendly working relationships that had been established. We needed the coloured workers; and there were many who esteemed their obviously valuable services and were anxious to make this clear. The timidity of retailers might prevent their employment as shop assistants,* but in the hospitals—whether as nurses or maids, porters or doctors— in the Post Office and on the railways they had become indispensable. By the end of the Fifties the coloured drivers and clippies on the buses, the stationmen and women and guards on the Underground, were a well-established feature of the London scene, while West Indian writers were contributing to the literary menu a *sauce piquante* all their own.

IV

But there were still patches of English landscape to which the fog lovingly clung. An insularism nourished during nine centuries inviolate behind our Moat, buttressed for another four or so by the commodiousness of church, the cosiness of chapel and the valour of the Royal Navy, supported for another two by a world-girdling Empire made over in our image, then prolonged by Watt's steam-engine and Stephenson's railway trains, cushioned by Victorian opulence and confirmed by victory, against great odds, in two world wars—such an insularism was scarcely to be dissipated overnight. It had, after all, been born of experience, and had served us well.

* The first coloured (Jamaican) J.P. was appointed in Nottingham in 1962.

Foreigners, if no longer automatic candidates for the proverb-ial "'alf a brick", were still apt to appear invaders. The miners' reluctance—despite Labour's theoretic internationalism and the pledges of their union—to accept the Hungarian refugee trainees (as they had earlier refused the Italians) was repro-duced, more discreetly, on the Governmental level, in White-hall's continued shuffling of feet before the renewed invitations of Europe.

When in March, 1957, the six West European Powers signed the Treaty of Rome, seeking to extend the economic integra-tion successfully inaugurated in the European Coal and Steel Community six years earlier, Britain had again found herself excluded. Once again negotiations had pursued a long and dispiriting course as French "principle" vainly sought to grapple with English empiricism, and the British tried, with a touch of desperation, to reconcile their old vision of themselves as a great world-ranging Power—with a special relationship to the United States—and the novel, and still somewhat disconcerting, idea that they were, after all, a part of Europe.

It was possible, all the same, to detect a marked difference of quality between the withdrawal of 1951 and that of 1958. For events, in the meantime, had been making points of their own. In O.E.E.C. and its companion economic planning agen-cies co-operation had been continuous; in NATO and W.E.U. commitments to Europe had been accepted; in fact if not in theory "sovereignty" had been compromised.

As the impoverishment of the immediate postwar years receded, as Western Europe re-equipped and production surged forward, the old economic nationalism was increasingly outdistanced. If American firms were increasingly acquiring branches and partners in England, British firms were doing the same in both America and in Europe. The logic of world development was at last moving towards that ideal of freer, wider, trade which had been written into the Atlantic Charter and the immediate postwar documents. Mass production demanded large mass markets; in the later Fifties the new assembly lines and the vast industrial organisations they re-quired, were transcending narrow political frontiers to outline that United States of Europe for which statesmen like Briand, using merely political tools, had so long struggled in vain.

A Europe with a common market of 170,000,000 consumers, already the world's largest importer, and still developing at an exhilarating rate, was plainly not one from which the most insular of British businessmen could any longer stand aloof. Though politicians still zealously fostered the illusion that the Great Decision whether or not to "join Europe" was theirs, in the longer perspective of history, it is unlikely that freedom of choice at this point will appear very large.

Back in 1946, despite our Occupation Forces in Europe, and a world-ranging war just over, our insular fog had still richly enwrapped us. Perhaps it was fortunate that it did so: it enabled us to survive the multiple shocks of those months and years. But now the fog was lifting. The Labour Party, that uniquely British secular church, could no longer visualise with its old sublime confidence the creation of the New Jerusalem-in-one-island, much as it might try. The failure of our protective fog was, indeed, one of the major sources of its difficulties. Meanwhile, the Church of England, that other unique and long-enduring buttress of our insularity, was considering opening relations with Rome, and the Commonwealth, less and less made in the Westminster image, was now shedding the "British" prefix in fact as well as form, becoming a vague world grouping for which London might be a convenient exchange and service centre, but was scarcely, as it had been accustomed to boast, the Hub.

Even in the most literal sense we might soon cease to be an island. Out in the Channel in the last year of the Fifties boats were taking soundings to chart the course of a tunnel which would link Britain physically to the land mass of Europe. Derisory a protection as it might be in the nuclear age, that twenty miles of water still possessed an immeasurable psychological significance. The treason of a tunnel had been resisted for three-quarters of a century. Now it was accepted as one accepts the inevitable.

In the same year, 1959, the first full-length motorway, M.1, was opened, cutting a 70-mile swathe through the fine mesh of the English countryside between Birmingham and London.

Across the Channel, under the auspices of E.E.C., other motorways were building, a network of express highways sweeping over national frontiers with little more ceremony often, than if they had been mere county boundaries. On the new E.E.C. Motorway map of Europe, "E.1" would link London to Palermo, "E.5" Glasgow to Istanbul, by way of Cologne and Vienna.

34. The Heart of the Matter

"Architecture is the will of an epoch translated into space—living, changing, new."
—Mies van der Rohe, 1925.

"Nor need we fear that as the pattern changes life in England will lose its peculiar flavour. England will still be England, an everlasting animal, stretching into the future and into the past, and like all living things, having the power to change out of recognition, and yet remain the same."
—George Orwell, *England, Your England*, 1941.

"If the pessimism of the philosopher is a valid attitude, the duty of the militant humanist to go on hoping against hope is no less valid. . . ."
—Arthur Koestler, *Arrow in the Blue*, 1952.

As in the grey old city of London office "slab" and "tower" outbid spire and turret, the break with the past which had once seemed so continuously present appeared complete and irrevocable. The much vaunted new architectural materials, the vast gleaming curtain-walls of glass and aluminium, the alloys and the plastics, bright, sterile, precision-machined, seemed to belong not merely to a different period but to a totally different universe from the mellowed brick of the Bloomsbury squares, the Regency stucco, the Victorian pomp and idiosyncrasy, the velvety sooty Portland stone, gently shading under the rain. Each year the familiar old London now seemed more fragmented, well on the way to becoming a series of quaint museum or tourist pieces.

As in the moral field, some found the new "honesty" at the best ungentlemanly, at the worst brutal and shameless. In any event, it had to be admitted that the "Engineer's Aesthetic" had failed to ensure, automatically and inevitably, the Utopian consequences foretold by Le Corbusier and so many others in thirty years of preaching and prophecy. Once again the process of transition from Cause to inadequate reality had brought that sense of deflation and puzzlement which had already overtaken Feminists, Socialists, Imperialists, Internationalists, Educationists, Humanists, and which was so much a part of the flavour of these years. What had been long visualised and striven for as ends were now seen to have been merely means, and sometimes dubious means at that. Meanwhile, the Present now imposed itself with a velocity and an impact that left little place for the consolations of "the Future".

To many, indeed, the new architecture of the towns, these great rectilinear slabs and blocks, these vast bureaucratic hives with their "structure-revealing" grids, seemed to advance with a peculiar starkness the central question—at once hackneyed and inescapable—of the time: Could we bring Technology and Science under social control, preserving, somehow, the human scale, harnessing them to serve our chosen and necessary ends— or must we be dominated, pushed about and ultimately enslaved by them?

Could we still improvise upon the pattern they had imposed with increasing power since the war?

Or were we numbly and hopelessly clamped within it?

The years which had so insistently posed the question had not supplied an answer But they had offered a few random notes towards one. And they had demonstrated our peril.

In the Forties an attempt had been gropingly made in the creation of the National Health Service to bring together the proliferating specialisms of science in the service of individual and community, thus reconciling art and science. In the Fifties architects and town-planners also found themselves heavily involved in this key task of our time. In both cases the result was powerfully distorted by factors carried over from the old situation: the "little businessman outlook" which dictated the N.H.S. capitation fee system was parallelled by the "Big

Business" outlook which saw the land of our cities primarily as a counter in a central money-making process.

In approaching their task the architects, despite a fierce sectarianism, had one powerful advantage over the doctors. A sociological element in their training, greatly strengthened in the war years, offered a breadth of vision and a unifying technique not accessible to the G.P.s, still steeped in the nineteenth-century individualism of the Professional Man.

In 1940, the Barlow Committee (whose appointment had arisen out of the old scandal of the Depressed Areas) had reported that only a new concept of *positive* planning, "national in scope and character", could prove adequate to coping with our advanced state of urban obsolescence and squalor. This verdict, hailed with enthusiasm in the atmosphere of the war years, inspired both the plan for New Towns and the Town and Country Planning Act of 1947, the first to impose compulsory planning control for the whole country, requiring all counties and county boroughs to prepare comprehensive twenty-year development plans.

In the war and immediate postwar years the great regional surveys and reconstruction plans, prepared with an almost superhuman thoroughness and imaginative breadth, by Professor Abercrombie and others on the basis of detailed study of social habit and need, not only gave definition to social purpose, but were clearly approaching the heart of the problem of achieving civilised living in an advanced industrial society.

The postwar provision of Green Belts, of National Parks and protected "Areas of Outstanding National Beauty" appeared to mark an encouraging advance in the assertion of the claims of community and a developing concern for the quality of life.*

And in the first years of peace, British architects, under the Labour Government's licensing régime, were almost wholly engaged on building for public authorities—schools and housing estates and New Towns and flat-blocks—where modern architecture's social approach was nourished and developed,

* By 1959 ten National Parks, stretching from Dartmoor to Northumberland, had been created under the National Parks and Access to Countryside Act, 1949, and a number of Nature Reserves and other protected areas had been delineated—a quiet, little noticed, but far from insignificant advance.

serving to integrate and discipline the new technologies and techniques.

Writing a brief guide to modern British architecture as it existed in 1938, Hugh Casson found British schools "typical of an out-of-date outlook". Twenty years later, authors of similar guides found in the several thousand new schools that had gone up all over Britain since the war a most promising sign of the times. True to the Machine Aesthetic, many of them were yet notably civilised and human places, spacious, yet not dwarfing, sane, unpompous, even gay. To the old Architecture's preoccupation with Tradition, its pursuit of weight and gravitas, they opposed—sometimes with brilliant success—the new Architecture's special qualities of lightness and poise and integrity. Here, at least, it sometimes seemed that Science and Technology, purposively controlled, both embraced Art and inspired Faith.

Here, and in the new public authority housing—the other notable achievement of postwar British architecture—increasing attention was being given not merely to preserving, but also to *using*, the natural landscape, trees, slopes, the "lie of the land". Technology was not only made to serve social need but was now sometimes accommodated to the larger unity of Nature. At Roehampton the "points-blocks" of the L.C.C.'s Alton Estate rose like white cliffs from gardens which had once formed the grounds of private mansions, as if seeking to realise Le Corbusier's vision of *La Ville Radieuse*. People were living now, as well as working, high in the air. From the dreariness of the Harrow Road area, the sudden drama of the Hallfield Estate, its tall grouped blocks poised on *piloti*, captured the eye. In once grim Pimlico, the bright new world of Churchill Gardens, housing 6,500 people, and created by Powell and Moya, the young architects of the Festival's skylon, appeared mirage-like beside the river.

But, in general, there was little drama. These postwar buildings did not represent the heroic vision of some Master Architect. They were designed rather than conceived, the product of teams of architects, engineers, manufacturers, planners, social scientists, educationists. This indeed was their importance—and it was no small one. It meant that here at least the central and immensely complex task of integration and social direction was being tackled to some purpose: science had been enlisted to harness Science.

In the New Architecture English social democracy indeed discovered in these years both an apt instrument and an effective ally—as was again demonstrated in the creation of the New Towns. Sited by a national committee, by the mid-Fifties fifteen New Towns were half-built, at a public cost to date of £100 million,* and were drawing streams of pilgrims from all over the world. At home, however, enthusiasm was far from unalloyed: again there was the familiar postwar consciousness of the gap that yawned between vision and fulfilment. With few flat-blocks, the New Towns sprawled over large areas; despite their terraces, they sometimes seemed the ultimate expression of contemporary semi-detachment. Perhaps the truth was that they reflected the weaknesses as well as the strengths of English social democracy—having grown out of the earlier English Garden City movement with its Arcadian overtones of "back-to-the-land" and the simple life. These notions had become increasingly impracticable and irrelevant; but young architects now yearning to create a new "urbanism" continued to be democratically frustrated by the romantic individualism of the Englishman, by his resolute attachment to the rustic name-plate and 12 by 12 yards of carefully fenced-off garden, and by his entire failure to perceive the truth of the great Corbu's dictum that *la maison de famille est une illusion demagogique.*

But if Utopia had again eluded us, the New Towns nevertheless were, as the Reith Reconstruction Committee in 1946 had hoped they would be, "an essay in civilisation". After the First World War the New Towns movement had urged that the chance be taken to "make a fresh start in a fresh place". Thirty years later that fresh start had been made on an impressive scale. People had been delivered from the bricks-and-mortar wilderness of the Great Wens without being simultaneously condemned to the fate of the commuter. Reviving the pedestrian precinct, the New Towns had piloted the assimilation of the motor-car. They had transformed work as well as leisure.

---

* However, on the longer term they would represent an extremely lucrative investment—with the profits, for once, accruing to the community.

The factories on their industrial estates in their clean simple lines, their lightness and airiness, were worlds away both from the dark satanic mills and from the Egyptology of the Great West Road. In the New Towns there had at least been a clear breakaway from the old Drain's Eye-view of the Victorian Borough Engineer; there was at least a glimpse of the new horizons of common life which technology, under social control, could open up.

Yet, as the Fifties ended, the New Towns were already beginning to look like lonely monuments to Good Intentions. The generous social impulse of the war years had worked itself out. The fearful weight of the *fait accompli*, of the vast urban sprawl which the bulk of Britain's population inhabited, reasserted itself. "Subtopia" was as indispensable a piece of contemporary verbal coinage as 'Butskellism'. Except perhaps in industrial location, positive planning on the regional scale—and in an island of Great Wens plainly nothing else would serve—was failing. The nation had willed the end, but had neglected to will the means. The grand designs of the postwar planners were enmeshed in endless complexities of sectional interest, and dissipated in the opportunist pursuit of private profit.

The achievement of the New Towns had been made possible by the fact that their land was publicly owned (i.e. by the Development Corporations) and the town-planners were thus free to make the best provision they knew how, unhampered by the bidding up of site values. Unfortunately, this common-sense state of affairs was rarely seen elsewhere. For though the Uthwatt Committee, reporting during the war, had suggested that land nationalisation offered the only completely effective means of safeguarding public interests, it had also pronounced it to be politically impracticable. The Labour Government had therefore adopted the Committee's intricate compromise, an attempt to reconcile, or at least to balance, private property rights and public interest through the device of "development charges".

Like prewar "English compromises" between public and private interest on the railways and in the mines this proved to be an arrangement of self-defeating complexity. It was formally abandoned by the Conservatives in 1953-54. By the time the rebuilding of the central areas of the cities got under way there was thus little to restrain the spiralling of site values, which quickly passed beyond the range of even large and wealthy public authorities, who henceforth lived—in the heart of their own domains—in the long shadow of the financier-developers, the "Property Kings".

In theory, public control was to be achieved by a partnership between the public architect-planner and the commercial architect-developer, the first laying down an "outline plan", the second filling it in. But it was a curious, forced—and symbolic—partnership, often necessarily of mutual frustration, the one side intent on maximising private profit, the other on minimising public harm. And there could be little doubt where the initiative lay: the creative impulse behind the new townscape was the multiplication of private wealth rather than the enrichment of the common life.

This was something which could not be concealed. For even more than the old architecture of the street, the new architecture of the slab and tower and block, depending on the relationship of buildings and spaces over a large area, demanded the unifying vision, the large public aim. Except in towns like Coventry, where German bombs had promoted a radical approach, it rarely received it. Instead the great towns succumbed to that now familiar process of financial inflation already vividly demonstrated in the area of the Press and broadcasting, that postwar translation from the public and quasi-public domain to the special world of Very Big Business with its relentless accountant's logic and its statistical dazzle. Free or rigged or both, the Market took over again, confirming that bizarre scale of values which placed on a teacher a fraction of the monetary valuation of the producer of some deodorant or laxative's invitation to neurosis. By the later Fifties it was the Property Kings—the Cottons, the Clores, the Samuels and the rest—and the speculators' values they represented—who made the pace and the headlines, not the architects and the planners—the Gibberds and the Spences and the Aslins, the Holfords and Abercrombies—and the values they represented.

Meanwhile, as the ever-present accountant exacted from each square yard of urban England its full financial due, the Proper

Return on the Money Employed, architects sighed in vain for the clean slate afforded by the noble landlords of the eighteenth century and the chaos and clamour of our towns, choked or torn open by the brutal individualism of the private motor-car,* remained the most revealing failure of the "mixed-economy-Welfare-State" in these years, rawly exposing its moral and mechanical inadequacies and the unresolved conflict at its heart.

II

Was the "essay in civilisation" embarked on in such high hope in 1945 finally to collapse then in an acquisitive free-for-all? Had the skills which architects and planners had acquired in *using* science and technology in the service of human needs been learned too late?

In England on the threshold of the Sixties the answer returned was very apt to depend, almost literally, on where one stood. The future viewed from one of the many fine new schools, or from a flat in a new council block, or from Coventry's main shopping precinct, was very different from the view from the pavement's edge in some traffic-ravaged city centre, walled in by the concrete cliffs of the "property developers". Yet in 1960 both views were valid; in England an old society stood at the crossroads.

Although the Labour Government had confirmed the social revolution that the war had made it had been unable or unwilling to back it by the economic revolution that socialist theory required. The once-and-for-all opportunity of 1945 was largely consumed in clearing up capitalism's messes and repairing its worst defaults, greatly enlarging the public sector in so doing, yet stopping short of the main concentrations of corporation profits and the mainsprings of financial power. Moreover, whenever that "social justice" and "individual freedom" which it was Mr. Attlee's declared purpose to reconcile appeared, nevertheless, to conflict, the Labour Party's native liberalism

* Per mile of road Britain now had more motor-vehicles than any other country in the world. In London the number of cars had grown from 400,000 in 1948 to one million in 1958 and was continuing to grow at the rate of 8 per cent per annum.

generally ensured that the new "equality" took second place to the older "liberty". The public schools remained inviolate, and if the Government now sought to regulate the economic climate, its power to do so—much less to *create* a climate—remained severely limited.

Yet "social revolution" had been a fair enough term. In 1945 the promise of social democracy had been confirmed in the guarantee of full citizenship for all. This notion had still been so novel in England that the move towards it—in the health service, in education, in industry—had generated much friction and heat. Yet the general utility of the new arrangement had been demonstrated—it was nice, after all, to have a good supply of public library books not coated in grime. New norms of social decency had been established. And if the guarantee of 1945 had not been fully met, it had been sufficiently built into the social structure for deficiencies henceforth to carry their own indictment. Powerful social pressures had been released. If the Eleven Plus denied equality, it asserted it also—and staked a claim on the future. Through the Fifties, despite heavy defence expenditure and continual demands on a Conservative Government for tax cuts, expenditure on the social services in fact rose by about 40 per cent in real terms, reaching in 1960 a new peak of 20 per cent of the national income.

The "contracting-in" of the war and immediate postwar years remained more important than any subsequent limited "contracting-out". Nor were the values of 1945 necessarily at once cancelled by the advent of the People's Capitalism of 1955. The Marksian Revolution had indeed complemented the Beveridge revolution. Both were in the logic of the times. Both were founded on science and technology and democracy and together they closed at last the dark and ugly gulf opened up in British society by the first industrial revolution.

But as the mass market expanded and the People's Capitalism moved into high gear, it became increasingly evident that the equality of the tick on the market researcher's sheet might still fall somewhat short of the equality of man. Emancipating as it might be at first, the "consumer democracy" was a democracy that was rigged and that had to be rigged because the vastly capitalised mass-production machine demanded the predictable: sufficient "wrong" votes could bring the economy crashing.

50. The economists and market researchers might have taken over politics, and the voice of the churches might be muffled, but the young still sought a Cause and a Faith. In 1958 some found both in the Campaign for Nuclear Disarmament which spread across the country with remarkable speed, reviving the lost arts of slogan-writing and marching. On Easter Monday, 1959, 50,000 took part in the Aldermaston March; in 1960, almost 100,000.

51. The familiar old London was being swallowed up by the new international
streetscape. In September, 1959, Thorn House (*above*) was opened, towering
austerely over the Victorian frontages of the Charing Cross Road area. In 1951,
its architect, Basil Spence, had been one of the Festival's bright young men, the
comparatively unknown designer of the Ships and Seas Pavilion. Now he was one
of the busiest of British architects, giving a new look to our universities, town halls,
rehousing developments and churches. Some liked this new look, others hated it;
many just felt lost. One thing alone was certain: there could be no going back.

Yet the danger lay not so much in the fact of the rigging—which was scarcely new—as in its advanced Admassian techniques, the apparatus installed at the centre, commanding immense resources, over-running all the old barriers, and pervading society in a way no mere political gerrymanderer could ever have done.

In this situation the balance and relationship between public and private sectors became crucial; upon it depended whether or not society could retain the freedom to control its destinies. The Conservative Government, succeeding Labour in 1951, had accepted the Welfare State, the much enlarged public sector and—however haltingly—the notion of public planning. Yet perhaps its most important single act had been its admission of commercial television in 1954. This, ironically, had been in large measure an accident, though a characteristic modern accident in that it had been commercially contrived. Oddly enough the creation of the B.B.C. in the Twenties had been something of an accident too. But whereas the B.B.C. accident, with minor "democratic" adjustment, fitted well enough into the hierarchic structure of the old society, ITV at a critical point of transition, confirmed the rule of numbers in a central social area, completing the Admassian structure which sustained the People's Capitalism. Lord Northcliffe, though he had based journalism on advertising, had yet always resented the advertisements in his papers, sometimes throwing the more obtrusive ones out. No such proprietary resentment survived into the Fifties and by the end of them it was evident that not only was the whole shape of the Press mainly determined by its merchandising function, but that the market ruled in politics also.

We were all "in the picture" certainly. The only question was: "*Whose* picture?"

There were no visible tyrants or suborners—only the contemporary "sophistication", the endless, gentle, gently loaded questions, the powerful logic of the accountant, the automated tyranny of numbers.

Nothing appeared more democratic than the audience rating, the net sales certificate, the opinion poll, the box-office figure, the twice daily vote in the supermarket. And it was here, perhaps, that the greatest danger lay. For in the conditions of

Q

the Fifties continuous automated count-of-heads represented not democracy's completion, but its devitalisation, stifling the genuine creative impulsive at birth, and turning society in upon itself in diminishing circles of enervation.

Meanwhile, still further advancing this result, an increasing proportion of society's scarce stocks of talent and intelligence were diverted to trivial ends and the systematic manipulation of Them, which was the others.

This was the invisible price on the goods in the supermarket and it did not seem a negligible one.

III

England was undergoing these novel experiences at a time when she was peculiarly vulnerable. "An Englishman," said Nathaniel Hawthorne, "likes to feel the weight of all the Past on his shoulders." In the years since the war that comfortable old burden had lost its reassurance, and had on several occasions been ritually discarded. But we still felt uneasy without it. There was a tendency not merely to utter our famed "English understatements" but actually to believe them. Press and ether were full of anxious and un-English self-examination, conducted under titles like "What's Wrong with Britain?" From the hoardings huge posters offered the reassurance which authority apparently now felt necessary: BE PROUD OF BRITAIN! BRITISH ACHIEVEMENT SPEAKS FOR BRITAIN!

Within, as without, there was no longer anything clear and simple to set against the rule of the market or challenge the sovereignty of the accountant. Social and cultural authoritarianism had followed moral and religious authoritarianism into final dissolution. After the death of George VI monarchy itself, at the social apex, had shed its authoritarian aura, and in 1958, as if to provide a serio-comic curtain, even the Royal Academy grew tired of trying to keep up the old pretence, and visitors to its 190th summer exhibition were startled to find churning Action paintings and vast demoniac Bratbys, sprawling wastepipe by jowl with the usual polished aldermanic portraits. The old pyramid had crumbled: a new society of complex and shifting relationships was in being. Its values had not yet clearly emerged; for all that, after the clearance and re-surveying of these years, the foundations were sounder than before. An expert committee of social investigation convened by the Archbishop of Canterbury could report in 1958: "The modern family is in some ways in a stronger position than it has ever been at any period of our history. . . ."

Perhaps the new values would come into focus in the suburbs, at that critical point where white collar met blue in the new world of hobbyism and leisure and domestic do-it-yourself, and the new egalitarianism of 1945 was bizarrely transmuted in the widening competitiveness of an opening society. As yet they showed few signs of emerging in politics. For the Conservative Party was incongruously divided between the few eager young who increasingly espoused the American-type mobile, money-assessed economists' society and the instinctive adherents of the old English class tradition. The Labour Party was likewise bewildered by a deep conflict of old and new values.

The values that emerged would not, in fact, emerge from doctrine, nor would they be based on a sharp choice between "old" and "new". They would emerge from the character and history of an old but resilient people, once again responding to large-scale change. For at deeper levels continuity remained. Even in the "Age of Automation" English society was not machine-made, but was organic, retaining its ability ultimately to extrude that which it could not assimilate. If we installed American "picture windows" in our houses, the odds were we shrouded them with curtains or built a screening wall. We still enthroned not the dollar or the pound sterling or the production index but—in a variety of forms—the Tea Break. Salesmanship was not yet the highest virtue, "City Hall" not merely a rival faction. If statistics and cash went to ITV, on important occasions most people still turned to the B.B.C. If Authority with the capital "A" had gone, there remained in our society a sort of phantom authority, the consensus of informed opinion. Drawn now from many sources and various social levels, from "Any Questions" to, say, the speeches of Prince Philip, this was less sharply defined than formerly because the new society only very spasmodically and uncertainly provided the means to bring it to a focus. Yet despite the multiplying distractions of the times and the 'wonder' years of television, this widening highest common factor—which had been real enough to bring a revolution to book publishing—was not cancelled by the concurrent broadening of the lowest common denominator enforced by the logic of mass media and mass market; just as the formation of the "mass society" did not destroy the minorities that proliferated within it, but might shelter and promote them.

"There is one difficult exercise to which we may accustom ourselves as we become increasingly culture-conscious," wrote Ruth Benedict in *Patterns of Culture*. "We may train ourselves to pass judgment on the dominant traits of our own civilisation".

Though the age of the prophets was over, by the end of the Fifties there were signs, here and there, that our new and often dubious "sophistication" might yet stretch to this. There was a growing consciousness of the gap between social possibilities, given the tools that social science and science-technology now provided, and social performance. There was a developing watchfulness about advertising and public relations and some other aspects of Press and television. Public protest over the property developer, Mr. Jack Cotton's, design for the capitalisation of one side of Picadilly Circus had forced a public inquiry and finally the calling in of Professor Gropius himself.

More fundamental was a dawning awareness of the dangers of "leaving it to science". The benefits brought by science-and-technology in these years had been spectacular and immense. In one way or another they had opened up life for the elderly, for married women, for the young. They had penetrated both the old class system and the Iron Curtain. And yet the equivocal nature of science in its application to society had also been strikingly demonstrated. If it had materially enlarged life for millions it had also devised new techniques of enslavement. Science had penetrated to the heart of matter, yet fragmented human experience. Technology broke down the old class system, but brought its own sterilities and new divisions which, if less visible to the eye, could, it seemed, be even more complete and final.

If, in an earlier phase, science had destroyed one sort of faith, it had replaced it with another hardly less strong: faith in science itself and the invincible rationality of the Scientific

Method. Now it merely destroyed faith and replaced it with an idiot's confidence or a numbed acceptance. And if possibly less numbed, scientists themselves often seemed to share that acceptance.* Scientists too worked for the highest or hardest bidder: the satellites girdled the world, but the satellites were also missiles. The social sciences brought new insights and new possibilities of shaping society to man's needs; but in their concentration on narrow factors, torn from their living context, they also bred inertia. Their practitioners not only studied "the given", but succumbed to it. The amorality of science subtly reinforced the amorality of the accountant for whom also ultimate truth was contained in numbers.

IV

The perils of ideology, amply demonstrated in the Thirties, had been further underlined through the postwar years by the sterile confrontation of the U.S.S.R. and the U.S.A., both sustained by dogmas which bore only minimal relation to realities.

In post-Imperial Britain, by contrast, ideology had been at a low ebb; with the aid of science we had been gropingly seeking to redefine reality, moral, political, social. The exercise had been salutary. But now the suspicion grew that "the Facts"—"truth to materials" as the architectural slogan went—were not enough. They did not, of themselves, confer a sense of direction or afford that vision without which the people perish.

Our society needed, above all, a frame in which qualitative as well as quantitative criteria would become visible; within which informed opinion could challenge the rule of the market and the neutrality of the laboratory; within which social, as well as immediate monetary, costs would be counted.

* Varying, of course, with the branch of science. Physicists and biologists, dealing with large "abstract" worlds, seem to have produced a quite impressive quota of Communists. It may, of course, be objected that the social sciences are not, in fact, sciences. But the point is that their practitioners behave as though they are and scientific assumptions, however untenable, permeate them, thence infiltrating into a vast area of life.

Within such a frame, for instance, the need to clear the slums and renew the vast twilight areas of our cities would take precedence over unnecessary demolition and redevelopment of office blocks or luxury flats, even though the return on the capital was "inadequate"; human quality would receive acknowledgment without the certification of I.Q. rating or five-figure salary; and it might just be possible to start with human needs and work outwards instead of submitting humanity as raw material to be processed by the machine, according to *its* needs.

Such a framework of social priorities had been erected in the war years and strengthened and broadened in 1945. It had not proved strong enough. For the drive of the machine, geared to the mass market, had become immensely powerful and—as the economists, poised between admiration of its wonders and nervous prostration, pointed out almost daily—to interfere radically with its complex design and functioning was to court economic disaster. Such was the machine's need to keep up the revs. that it pushed out relentlessly into all areas of life. Increasing leisure might seem to offer a private area where new social values could freely develop. But as the sudden bodying forth of the "teenage world" showed, leisure also was a market, with a prospect of prime yields. Already stockbrokers were recommending their clients to switch from engineering to "leisure and entertainment shares—the growth investment of the future". Whether or not people actually wanted to own three times the number of cars in the years ahead, they would have to have them. For the alternative to "affluence" was no longer modest comfort, but bankruptcy and economic disaster.

It was indeed in the very extremity of the situation that the best hope that social control might yet be achieved now lay. The vast *reductio ad absurdum* of our traffic-jammed towns proclaimed only a little less clearly than the nuclear race to annihilation the catastrophic possibilities now inherent in science and technology when harnessed merely to sectional interest and driven by the calculus of private profit.

The point had in fact been taken. In town and countryside the planners' compromises of the Fifties, clumsy and ineffective as they might often be, had yet continued to assert the claims of the community with a certain quiet doggedness: and in a few cities there had been purposeful reconstruction on a scale and with a breadth of vision not seen for many years.

The public sector which, in the new conditions, could alone offer the strength of base to uphold a national frame of values had continued, in the widest sense, to grow. For this too was in the logic of the times. Both the tripartite organisation of the postwar society and democratic pressures—with the two great parties still in equipose—required it. So indeed did technology itself. The costs of designing nuclear reactors—or supersonic aircraft—transcended the risk-bearing capacity of private enterprise. An efficient health service required immense resources which only the State could now effectively provide.

And whatever might have happened in the newspaper world, television was now seen to be so potent and costly a medium that no British Government which did not wish to abdicate could disavow responsibility.

But whereas technical necessities might ensure a strong centre they did not also ensure a sense of values and a working democracy to nurture it. Surrender to the bureaucratic paternalism of technocracy in return for relaxed semi-detachment, fringe benefits, TV serials and continental holidays appeared equally possible. Whether it would take place depended on many things. It would depend on the multiplication and renewal in our society of points where the issues could be exposed as they arose and submitted to wide-ranging criticism —whether at public inquiries, in town councils and works committees, by local radio and local journals, in parent-teacher associations, consumer movements or elsewhere. It would depend upon the evolution of television—which *could* provide a genuine national forum and *would* do much to set the tone of the new society. It would depend upon curbing the growth of large gaps between income-groups—for the appeal to equity and reason cannot succeed in a too patently inequitable society or in one whose heart resides in the Stock Market. It would depend not only on the maturation of the public sector in the widest sense, but more particularly on the outcome in the (next to the entertainment and electrical power industries) most rapidly and continuously expanding part of it—the public educational system.

This had been the scene, in these years, of the most bizarre confusions, contradictions and time-lags. Even at the end of the Fifties a central part of it still lay more in the old society than the new, more "contracted out" still than "contracted in". Yet, as the coining and frequent usage of the word "Oxbridge" suggested, the anomaly was at least now recognised and no longer considered a part of the order of Nature. But though debated as never before, the great issues here remained unresolved. In the Forties the old radical "anti-feudalism" issue had been transmuted from the familiar "Gentlemen v. Players", "Privileged and Dispossessed", through the great comprehensive school row, into the somewhat newer and more complex issue of "Alpha-types v. the Others" with its overtones of Huxley's *Brave New World*.

And as the Fifties ended and the new universities proliferated —with the needs of technology providing the driving force— the issue was yet further complicated and restated in terms of the supposed conflict between science and the humanities. Were we aiming to produce machine directors, servicers and minders —or the educated nation the 1944 Act had promised? Efficient functions, with the schools offering mainly 'career-tickets'—or whole men and women?

Before the war the complaints of "businessmen" about the waste of money on education had been a continuous note in the sound-track of the times. Now business pressed for educational expansion. The change was a welcome one; yet it might be here that the dilemma of "take over or be taken-over" confronting our society as a whole would assume its most acute and critical form.

In the meantime, the nation's secondary schools, still broadly divided between grammar schools where one stayed on and inadequately staffed modern schools where one left at fifteen, continued to threaten the re-creation of "the two nations" in cultural and occupational terms.

Inevitably, the schools mirrored society more than society reflected the schools. Yet in some areas the new schools had already become focal points of the life of the community and neighbourhood in a remarkable way. And clearly it was here, in the schools and universities, if anywhere, that the validity and fruitfulness of the theme of human equality, proclaimed in 1945, would be demonstrated. It was here that what chances remained to democracy would be lost or won. It was here that the ability to pierce the Admassian envelope and to know and own one's own motives and achieve a genuinely critical appraisal of our society must be developed and sustained. And it was here, upon the schools and universities, that must fall the main burden of reabsorbing science into the mainstream of life and human history—the indispensable prelude to its social control. For at least by the end of the Fifties many had come to realise that to exchange the effortless superiority of our Philosopher-Kings for the clinical detachment of Scientist-Kings would be a bleak exchange indeed. If the moral vacuum was to be filled it would no longer be filled from above in any such simple manner.

V

These were immense and complex issues. But Britain did not now face them alone. Other old societies of Western Europe had, with differing emphases, undergone in these years since the war similar vast processes of change. They too had experienced their postwar "social revolutions", had widened their public sectors, built up their welfare states and reached their own versions of "Butskellism" and the Mixed Economy. The Great Market which had set the tempo in the later Fifties embraced not ourselves alone but the peoples of Western Europe and the social direction it called for would be direction in which we must join, but could not wholly determine.

All the old landmarks were gone. With the dissolution of Empire collapsed the old assumption of the Anglo-Saxon mission and the accompanying notion of our special relationship to the United States, our "lost dominion". The obstinate old illusion of "cousinhood" had helped build the bridge between America and Europe across which regenerating aid had flowed. But now the last shred of verisimilitude was gone. The new patterns and the new politics that would emerge would emerge in the fullness of time from the mingling of European traditions, all adapting in their various ways to "American" mass market technology and to a new relationship with the ex-Colonial world. If the outcome was unknown, those traditions were still strong and were more likely to find rebirth than death. The landmarks might be lost to view, but the lie of the land remained. For if, on one level, technology and the market transcended nationalism, on another, equally clearly, the nations—peoples—transcended technology. The new international surface, the curtain-walls, the blue jeans, the Scotch, the Coca-Cola, the jazz and the rest could not conceal the depth and strength of the old immense inward differences that grew from national history, from language, climate, temperament, literature, region and work—and from unique and durable amalgams of all these.

In England, so much longer exposed to the tyrannies of the machine than other European countries, erosion of character and culture might have been expected to have progressed further and in some ways—as seen for instance in pop singers' styles or lack of them—might indeed have done so. Yet, though the boy might wear a "Latin"-stripe shirt and pointed "Milano" shoes, the girl might wear jeans and try to look like Bardot, when either opened their mouths and spoke, they spoke—despite a generation of B.B.C. English and American films—in the accents and with the idiom of their native heath and thought as it thought.*

Here, in the genius of people and place lay, as ever, our true strength against the tyranny of the machine and the final victory of averages. For if, in England, the weight of the Past had shifted, its steadying touch could still be felt upon the shoulders. Atomic research piles might rise on the edge of Hardy's "Egdon Heath", looms might fall silent in a Lancashire heavy with the hulks of great cotton mills which had once clothed half the world; electrification might lift the protective smoke pall, as well as destroy the familiar skyline, of Arnold Bennett's Five Towns. Yet the texture of regional life remained tough and deeply woven. Not the least astonishing thing in these astonishing years of vast and rapid social change was the way in which the riches of character rooted in soil and scene and work and speech and climate endured. Could Defoe have returned to resume his Tour in the late Fifties he would still have found

* Those inclined to discount the durability of national, regional and even local character in modern conditions might consider the evidence of the massive national survey, *The Lore and Language of Schoolchildren* by I. and P. Opie, O.U.P. 1959.

men building ships in the "coaly Tyne", making chairs in vast quantities among the Buckinghamshire beechwoods, controlling "prodigious engines" to drain the Fens, and weaving woollen cloth in the narrow West Riding valleys that wind up into the Pennines, and there would be a good chance that —after more than two centuries—the Yorkshiremen and Northumbrians and East Anglians and Cornishmen he met would still bring the gleam of recognition to his eyes.

As modest travel and observation would rapidly establish, there was not one England or two, but many still; and yet beneath all there somehow lay, as an iceberg lies eight-ninths invisible, the essential enduring Englishness. Nor had anyone observed that the Welsh had yet ceased to be Welsh or the Scots, Scots or that there had been any cessation of the extraordinary alchemy by which peoples so dissimilar came together to make up the British nation.

Nor was it now any longer true that *all* forces were inevitably making for the sapping of such regional roots. It was the demands of a "standardising" technology which was now forcing the development of provincial universities. Television, a prime agent of the international espresso culture, had also, transcending the limitations of print, brought back into the national scene regional settings and accents—just as tourism showed signs of stimulating a new interest in *English* as well as foreign cooking. If, hitherto, when boy or girl addressed not local friends but the wider world, the accent had often been hesitant or pseudo-American that had been in large measure because of the class-based character of "posh" or so-called "standard English". If now, as communications developed, as movement upwards from many directions outran the capacity of the old tidy monotone ruling class apparatus to absorb and sterilise, the strong springs of the national life—no longer cut off by this hard south-based intrusion of class—would flow through clear to the surface. Then England's Past—and not merely its pomps and pageantry—and England's Present could join hands and England would know herself again.

But as the "affluent" Fifties turned into the uncertain Sixties most of this was speculative. The processes of change were massive, many-sided and intricately interacting and it would be a rash or much-blinkered man who would attempt to measure the logic of technology against the force of ideas and human aspirations or strike a statistical balance between the power to corrupt and the power to resist corruption. There can have been few periods in English history when life has been lived in the presence of so many vast open questions. A contemporary social history can perhaps show some of these questions forming. It may, on occasion, contain a hint or two of possible answers.

But only the future can write them.

BIBLIOGRAPHY

If THE special quality of "contemporary history" as a genre lies in its being history savoured, so to speak, in the making, it follows that printed books are by no means its only or even its most important source. The files of newspapers and periodicals, personal experiences and memory, the observations possible to a journalist who, like myself, has moved about the country in these years, the innumerable polls and surveys now so much a part of our times, Hansard, the distillations of the cartoonists, White Papers and Blue Books, public exhibitions, TV and radio programmes, the manifestoes and reports of the numerous voluntary associations for this and that and of such research bodies as P.E.P., the Fabian Society and the Bow Group must clearly all be grist to the mill. The reports and volumes of evidence of the major or more controversial Governmental committees and Royal Commissions of the period are of great value in charting currents of opinion as well as identifying current facts. Among these must be included the Beveridge Report on Social Insurance, of 1942, the Fleming Report on the Public Schools and the General Educational System, 1944, the reports of the Royal Commission on the Press, 1949, the Broadcasting Committee, 1949, the Royal Commission on Population, 1949, the Royal Commission on Betting, Lotteries and Gaming, 1951, the Royal Commission on Capital Punishment, 1953, the Royal Commission on Marriage and Divorce, 1955, the Committee on Homosexual Offences and Prostitution, 1957, *15-18*, a Report of the Central Advisory Council for Education (England) ('Crowther Report') Vol. I, 1959; Vol. II, 1960. For statistics I have drawn on two wide-ranging compilations of current material: G. D. H. Cole's *Postwar Condition of Britain* (Routledge, 1956) and *A Survey of Social Conditions in England and Wales* by A. M. Carr-Saunders, D. Caradog Jones and C. A. Moser (O.U.P., 1958) in addition to the usual Governmental sources.

A bibliography of a book such as this might include almost

everything published in the period, but among works consulted either for their factual or for their evocative content or for both, have been the following:

POLITICAL

C. R. ATTLEE: *As It Happened*, Heinemann, 1954
—— and FRANCIS WILLIAMS: *A Prime Minister Remembers*, Heinemann, 1961
ROSE and HINDEN ABRAMS: *Must Labour Lose?* Penguin, 1960
JOHN BONHAM: *The Middle Class Vote*, Faber, 1954
ROBERT BOOTHBY: *I Fight to Live*, Gollancz, 1947
JOHN BOWLES: *Minos or Minotaur?* Cape, 1956
D. E. BUTLER: *The British General Election of 1951*, Macmillan, 1952
—— *The British General Election of 1955*, Macmillan, 1956
—— and RICHARD ROSE: *The British General Election of 1959*, Macmillan, 1960
LORD BEVERIDGE: *Power and Influence*, Hodder and Stoughton, 1953
JANET BEVERIDGE: *Beveridge and His Plan*, Hodder and Stoughton, 1954
HARRY BOARDMAN: *The Glory of Parliament*, Allen and Unwin, 1960
ARTHUR H. BOOTH: *The British Hustings, 1924–50*, Muller, 1956
VINCENT BROME: *Aneurin Bevan*, Longman, 1953
MARGARET COLE: *The Story of Fabian Socialism*, Heinemann, 1961
COLIN COOKE: *The Life of Richard Stafford Cripps*, Hodder, 1957
C. A. R. CROSLAND: *The Future of Socialism*, Cape, 1956
R. H. S. CROSSMAN ed.: *New Fabian Essays*, Turnstile Press, 1952
—— ed.: *The God That Failed*, Hamish Hamilton, 1950
CUMMINGS: *The Uproarious Years*, MacGibbon and Kee, 1954
HUGH DALTON: *The Fateful Years*, Muller, 1957
—— *High Tide and After*, Muller, 1962
ERIC ESTORICK: *Stafford Cripps*, Hodder and Stoughton, 1949
TREVOR EVANS: *Ernest Bevin*, Allen and Unwin, 1946
ROY HARROD: *John Maynard Keynes*, Macmillan, 1951
J. E. D. HALL: *Labour's First Year*, Penguin, 1947
ARTHUR HORNER: *Incorrigible Rebel*, MacGibbon and Kee, 1960

LESLIE HUNTER: *The Road to Brighton Pier*, Barker, 1959
ROY JENKINS: *The Labour Case*, Penguin, 1959
—— *Attlee, an Interim Biography*, Heinemann, 1955
DAVID LOW: *Autobiography*, Joseph, 1956
—— *Low Visibility, a Cartoon History,1945–53*, Collins, 1953
—— *The Fearful Fifties*, Bodley Head, 1960
R. B. McCALLUM and A. READMAN: *The British General Election of 1945*, O.U.P., 1947
R. W. G. MACKAY: *Britain in Wonderland*, Gollancz, 1948
NORMAN MACKENZIE ed.: *Conviction*, MacGibbon and Kee, 1958
HAROLD MACMILLAN: *The Middle Way*, Macmillan, 1938
KINGSLEY MARTIN: *Laski*, Gollancz, 1953
R. J. MINNEY: *The Private Papers of Hore-Belisha*, Collins, 1960
HERBERT MORRISON: *Autobiography*, Odhams, 1960
RALPH MILIBAND: *Parliamentary Socialism*, Allen and Unwin, 1962
H. G. NICHOLAS: *The British Election of 1950*, Macmillan, 1951
JOHN PARKER: *Labour Marches On*, Penguin, 1947
HENRY PELLING: *The British Communist Party: A Historical Profile*, Black, 1958
ENOCH POWELL and ANGUS MAUDE: *Change is Our Ally*, Conservative Pol. Centre, 1954
EMMANUEL SHINWELL: *Conflict without Malice*, Odhams, 1955
SOCIALIST UNION: *Twentieth Century Socialism*, Penguin, 1951
DIANA SPEARMAN: *Democracy in England*, Rockcliff, 1957
JOHN STRACHEY: *Contemporary Capitalism*, Gollancz, 1956
R. H. TAWNEY: *Equality*, 4th Edition, Allen and Unwin, 1952
VICKY: *Stabs in the Back*, Reinhardt, 1952
FRANCIS WILLIAMS: *Ernest Bevin*, Hutchinson, 1952
—— *The Triple Challenge, the Future of Socialist Britain*, Heinemann, 1948
NEAL WOOD: *Communism and British Intellectuals*, Gollancz, 1959
LORD WOOLTON: *Memoirs*, Cassell, 1959

SOCIAL AND GENERAL WAR AND POSTWAR BACKGROUND

PEARL BINDER: *The Peacock's Tail*, Harrap, 1958
ARTHUR BRYANT ed.: *Triumph in the West: The Alanbrooke Diaries*, Collins, 1959

ASA BRIGGS: *Friends of the People*, Batsford, 1956

BUREAU OF CURRENT AFFAIRS: *The First Eighteen Months*, Penguin, 1947

W. S. CHURCHILL: *The Sinews of Peace* (Postwar Speeches), Cassell, 1948

—— *Second World War*, Vol. 6: *Triumph and Tragedy*, Cassell, 1954

VIRGINIA COWLES: *Winston Churchill, the Era and the Man*, Hamish Hamilton, 1953

—— *No Cause for Alarm*, Hamish Hamilton, 1947

J. W. DRAWBELL: *The Long Year*, Wingate, 1958

JOYCE EGGINTON: *They Seek a Living*, Hutchinson, 1957

C. A. FURTH: *Life Since 1900*, Allen and Unwin, 1956

HAMILTON FYFE: *Britain's Wartime Revolution*, Gollancz, 1944

BRIAN GLANVILLE: *Soccer Nemesis*, Secker and Warburg, 1955

RUTH GLASS: *The Newcomers*, Allen and Unwin, 1960

G. GORER: *Exploring the English Character*, Cresset, 1955

R. GRAVES and A. HODGE: *The Long Weekend*, Faber, 1940

TOM HARRISSON: *Britain Revisited*, Gollancz, 1961

J. L. HODSON: *The Way Things Are* (*Diary 1947–9*), Gollancz, 1949

HULTON PRESS: *Patterns of British Life*, 1950

DANIEL JENKINS: *Equality and Excellence*, S.C.M., 1961

L.C.C.: *Postwar Housing*, 1950

L. J. LICKORISH and A. G. KERSHAW: *The Travel Trade*, Practical Press, 1958

WILFRED MARCH: *The Story of the Lynskey Tribunal*, Redman, 1949

DAVID MARSH: *The Changing Social Structure of England and Wales 1871–1951*, Routledge, 1958

HERBERT and NANCY MATTHEWS: *The Britain We Saw*, Gollancz, 1950

DREW MIDDLETON: *The British*, Secker and Warburg, 1957

B. L. MONTGOMERY: *Memoirs*, Collins, 1958

C. L. MOWAT: *Britain Between Wars*, Methuen, 1955

VIVIAN OGILVIE: *Our Times: 1912–52*, Batsford, 1953

ERIC PARTRIDGE: *Here, There and Everywhere*, Hamish Hamilton, 1950

P.E.P.: *The Economics of Domestic Pets*, 1957

J. A. R. PIMLOTT: *The Englishman's Holiday*, Faber, 1947

L. G. Pine: *The Story of the Peerage*, Blackwood, 1956
Alan Pryce-Jones: *The New Outline of Modern Knowledge*, Gollancz, 1956
A. H. Richmond: *The Colour Problem*, Penguin, 1955
B. S. Rowntree and G. R. Lavers: *Poverty and the Welfare State*, Longmans, 1951
—— —— *Life and Leisure*, Longmans, 1951
Alan Ross: *The Forties*, Weidenfeld and Nicolson, 1950
J. D. Scott: *Life in Britain*, Eyre and Spottiswoode, 1956
David Thomson, ed.: *The New Cambridge Modern History*, Vol. XII: *The Age of Violence, 1898–1945*
The Times: *The History of* The Times, Vol. IV
This England, 1946–49; 1949–53; 1953–57, Turnstile Press
Warren Tute: *The Grey Top Hat, the Story of Moss Bros*, Cassell, 1961
Ernest Watkins: *The Cautious Revolution*, Secker and Warburg, 1951
James Wickenden: *Colour in Britain*, O.U.P., 1958
Earl Winterton: *Fifty Tumultuous Years*, Hutchinson, 1955
M. Young and P. Wilmot: *Family and Kinship in East London*, Routledge, 1957
Ferdynand Zweig: *The British Worker*, Penguin, 1952
—— *The Worker in the Affluent Society*. Heinemann, 1961

HEALTH AND WELFARE SERVICES

S. M. Ferguson and H. Fitzgerald: *Studies in the Social Services* (Official History of Second World War, civil series), 1954
James Halliday: *Psychosomatic Medicine*, Heinemann, 1948
R. J. Hammond: *Food* (History of Second World War, civil series), 1956
Katharine Hood: *Room at the Bottom: National Insurance in the Welfare State*, Lawrence and Wishart, 1960
S. Leff: *Social Medicine*, Routledge, 1953
Mass-Observation: *Meet Yourself at the Doctors*, Naldrett Press
Ffrancon Roberts: *The Cost of Health*, Turnstile Press, 1952
M. Sheridan: *Rowton Houses, 1892–1956*, Rowton Houses, 1956
Frank Slaughter: *Science and Surgery*, Perma, New York, 1956
Stephen Taylor: *Good General Practice*, O.U.P., 1954

RICHARD TITMUSS: *Problems of Social Policy* (Civil History of the War), Longmans, 1950
—— *Essays on the Welfare State*, Allen and Unwin, 1958
E. S. TURNER: *Call the Doctor*, Michael Joseph, 1958
PAUL VAUGHAN: *Doctors' Commons*, Heinemann, 1959
KENNETH WALKER: *Patients and Doctors*, Penguin, 1957

THE "CLASS SYSTEM"

ACTON SOCIETY TRUST: *Management Succession*, 1956
D. V. GLASS ed.: *Social Mobility in Britain*, Routledge, 1956
FLOUD, HALSEY and MARTIN: *Social Class and Educational Opportunity*, Heinemann, 1956
R. LEWIS and A. MAUDE: *The Middle Classes*, Phoenix, 1949
—— —— *Professional People*, Phoenix, 1952
NANCY MITFORD: *Noblesse Oblige*, Hamish Hamilton, 1956
T. H. PEAR: *English Social Differences*, Allen and Unwin, 1955
MARGARET STACEY: *Tradition and Change: A Study of Banbury*, O.U.P., 1960
H. THOMAS ed.: *The Establishment*, Blond, 1959
P. WILMOTT and M. YOUNG: *Family and Class in a London Suburb*, Routledge, 1961
M. YOUNG: *The Rise of the Meritocracy*, Thames and Hudson, 1959

EDUCATION AND YOUNG PEOPLE

W. H. G. ARMYTAGE: *Civic Universities*, Benn, 1955
PETER CHAMBERS and AMY LANDRETT: *Called Up*, Wingate, 1955
COUNCILS AND EDUCATION PRESS: *Teenage Morals*, 1961
H. C. DENT: *Growth in English Education, 1946–52*, Routledge, 1954
—— *Secondary Education for All, Origin and Development*, Routledge, 1949
W. D. FURNEAUX: *The Chosen Few*, O.U.P. for Nuffield Foundation, 1961
G. C. T. GILES: *The New School Tie*, Pilot Press, 1946

GALLUP POLL: *Youth Survey*, News Chronicle Publications, 1959
MARGERETA BERGER-HAMMERSLAG: *Journey Through a Fog*, Gollancz, 1955
Inside the Comprehensive School, Symposium, Schoolmaster Publishing Co., 1958
PEARL JEPHCOTT: *Rising Twenty*, Faber, 1948
G. W. JORDAN and E. M. FISHER: *Self-portrait of Youth*, Heinemann, 1955
A. V. JUDGES: *Looking Forward in Education*, Faber, 1955
G. A. N. LOWNDES: *The British Education System*, Hutchinson, 1955
VIVIAN OGILVIE: *The English Public School*, Batsford, 1957
ROBIN PEDLEY: *Comprehensive Education*, Gollancz, 1956
W. O. LESTER SMITH: *Education*, Penguin, 1955
JOHN VAIZEY: *The Cost of Education*, Allen and Unwin, 1958
—— *Education for Tomorrow*, Penguin, 1962
REX WARNER: *English Public Schools*, Collins, 1945
FRANCES STEVENS, *The Living Tradition*, Hutchinson, 1960
W.E.A.: *The Leisure Activities of Schoolchildren*, 1960

ECONOMIC, INDUSTRIAL, TECHNOLOGICAL

P. H. ADY and G. D. H. WORSICK ed.: *The British Economy 1945–50*, O.U.P., 1952
G. C. ALLEN: *British Industries and Their Organisation*, Allen and Unwin, 3rd edn., 1951
Automation, H.M.S.O.
G. E. BALDWIN: *Beyond Nationalisation—Problems of the Coal Industry*, Harvard University Press, 1955
G. BULL and A. VICE: *Bid for Power*, Elek, 1958
H. A. CLEGG and T. E. CHESTER: *The Future of Nationalisation*, Blackwell, 1953
P. H. GENAULT and J. M. JACKSON: *The Control of Monopolies in the United Kingdom*, Longmans, 1960
ALDOUS HUXLEY: *Brave New World Revisited*, Chatto, 1959
K. E. B. JAY: *Britain's Atomic Factories*, H.M.S.O., 1954
DE JOUVENAL: *Problems of Socialist Britain*, Batchworth, 1949
J. B. JEFFREY: *Retail Trading in Britain, 1850–1950*, Cambridge, 1954

R. Kelf Cohen: *Nationalisation in Britain*, Macmillan, 1958
J. H. Dunning and C. J. Thomas: *British Industry*, Hutchinson, 1961
L. Landman Goodman: *Man and Automation*, Penguin, 1956
Roy Lewis and Rosemary Stewart: *The Boss*, Phoenix, 1958
J. C. Naylor and E. Ower: *Flight Today*, 4th edn., O.U.P., 1957
W. W. Rostow: *The Stages of Economic Growth*, Cambridge, 1960
Dudley Seers: *The Levelling of Incomes Since 1938*, Blackwell
Andrew Shonfield: *British Economic Policy Since the War*, Penguin, 1958
N. A. H. Stacey and A. Wilson: *The Changing Pattern of Distribution*, Batsford, 1958

LABOUR

V. L. Allen: *Trade Union Leadership*, Longmans, 1957
—— *Trade Unions and the Government*, Longmans, 1960
G. Cyriax and R. Oakeshott: *The Bargainers*, Faber, 1960
The Dock Worker, Liverpool University Press, 1954
P. Sargent Florence: *Labour*, Home University Library, 1949
Joseph Goldstein: *The Government of British Trade Unions*, Allen and Unwin, 1952
M. Harrison: *Trade Unions and the Labour Party Since 1945*, Allen and Unwin, 1960
K. G. J. C. Knowles: *Strikes*, Blackwell, 1952
David Lockwood: *The Blackcoated Worker*, Allen and Unwin, 1958
G. R. Taylor: *Are Workers Human?* Falcon Press, 1950
Eric Wigham: *Trade Unions*, Home University Library, 1956
Francis Williams: *Magnificent Journey*, Odhams, 1954
Ferdynand Zweig: *Men in the Pits*, Gollancz, 1948

MORALS, RELIGION, CRIME

Nina Epton: *Love and the English*, Cassell, 1960
Anne Lyon Height: *Banned Books*, Allen and Unwin, 1954
The Family in Contemporary Society, Report of a Group set up by the Archbishop of Canterbury, S.P.C.K., 1958

JAMES HODGE: *Famous Trials*, vol. 5, Penguin, 1952
CYRIL GARBETT: *In an Age of Revolution*, Hodder, 1952
SIR ERNEST GOWERS: *A Life for a Life*, Chatto, 1956
MARGARET KNIGHT: *Morals without Religion*, Dobson, 1955
O. R. MCGREGOR: *Divorce in England*, Heinemann, 1957
LORD RADCLIFFE: *The Censors*, C.U.P., 1961
R. J. E. SILVEY: *Religion on the Air*, B.B.C., 1956
SIR HAROLD SCOTT: *Scotland Yard*, Deutsch, 1954
N. ST. JOHN STEVAS: *Obscenity and the Law*, Secker and Warburg,
    1956
E. S. TURNER: *A History of Courting*, Joseph, 1954
G. WILLIAMSON: *Morality Fair*, Watts, 1955
BARBARA WOOTTON: *Social Science and Social Pathology*, Allen
    and Unwin, 1959

WOMEN AND FASHION

CECIL BEATON: *The Glass of Fashion*, Weidenfeld and Nicolson,
    1954
VERA BRITTAIN: *Lady into Woman*, Dakers, 1952
CHRISTIAN DIOR: *Dior by Dior*, Weidenfeld and Nicolson, 1957
MADGE GARLAND: *Fashion*, Penguin, 1962
MARGARET LANE: *Half a Century of Fashion*, Dennis Yates, 1951
A. MYRDAL and V. KLEIN: *Women's Two Roles: Home and Work*,
    Routledge, 1956
FERDYNAND ZWEIG: *Women's Life and Labour*, Gollancz, 1952

MASS COMMUNICATIONS, ENTERTAINMENT, AND THE ARTS

T. W. R. ADAMS: *Modern Town and Country Planning*, Churchill,
    1952
E. and D. ALLAN: *Good Listening*, Hutchinson, 1951
KENNETH ALLSOP: *The Angry Decade*, Owen, 1958
WILLIAM ASHWORTH: *The Genesis of Modern British Town
    Planning*, Routledge, 1954
IAN BEVAN: *Top of the Bill*, Muller, 1952
ASA BRIGGS, *The Birth of Broadcasting*, O.U.P., 1961
ARTHUR CHRISTIANSEN: *Headlines All My Life*, Heinemann, 1961

502   THE NEW LOOK

HUGH CUDLIPP: *Publish and be Damned*, Dakers, 1953

—— *At Your Peril*, Weidenfeld and Nicolson, 1962

DAVID DAICHES: *The Present Age*, Cresset, 1958

EDWARD J. DENT: *A Theatre for Everyone*, Boardman, 1945

ROYSTON ELLIS: *The Big Beat Scene*, Four Square, 1961

R. FINDLATER: *The Unholy Trade*, Gollancz, 1952

MAURICE GORHAM: *Sound and Fury*, Percival Marshall, 1948

—— *Broadcasting and Television Since 1900*, Dakers, 1952

ERNEST GREEN: *Adult Education: Why This Apathy?*, Allen and Unwin, 1953

GILBERT HARDING: *Along My Line*, Putnam, 1953

REX HARRIS: *Jazz*, Penguin, Revised 1956

HOWARD HARTOG ed.: *European Music in the Twentieth Century*, Routledge, 1957

PATRICK HERON: *The Changing Forms of Art*, Routledge, 1955

STUART HIBBERD: *This is London*, Macdonald, 1950

HAROLD HOBSON: *The Theatre Now*, Longmans, 1952

RICHARD HOGGART: *The Uses of Literacy*, Chatto, 1957

TED KAVANAGH: *Tommy Handley*, Hodder, 1949

JOHN KENNEDY: *Tommy Steele*, Souvenir Press, 1958

OSBERT LANCASTER: *Pillar to Post*, Murray, Revised edn. 1956

JOHN LEHMANN: *The Craft of Letters in England*, Cresset, 1956

ROGER MANVELL: *On the Air*, Deutsch, 1953

—— *The Film and the Public*, Penguin, 1956

T. S. MATTHEWS: *The Sugar Pill*, Gollancz, 1957

FRANCIS NEWTON: *The Jazz Scene*, MacGibbon and Kee, 1958

P.E.N.: *The Author and the Public—Problems in Communication*, Hutchinson, 1957

P.E.P.: *Television in Britain*, 1958

W. PICKLES: *Between You and Me*, W. Laurie, 1949

R. G. G. PRICE: *History of Punch*, Collins, 1957

J. B. PRIESTLEY: *Journey down a Rainbow*, Heinemann, 1955

—— *The Writer in a Changing Society*, Hand and Flower Press, 1956

J. M. RICHARDS: *Introduction to Modern Architecture*, Penguin, Revised edn. 1956

EDOUARD RODITI: *Dialogues on Art*, Secker and Warburg, 1960

M. ROSENAUER: *Modern British Offices*, Batsford, 1955

EDWARD SACKVILLE WEST: *Graham Sunderland*, Penguin, Revised 1953

H. H. WILSON, *Pressure Groups, the Campaign for Commercial Television*, Secker, 1961

LORD SIMON: *The B.B.C. from Within*, Gollancz, 1953

THOMAS SHARP: *Exeter Phoenix*, Architectural Press, 1946

JOHN SPRAOS: *The Decline of the Cinema*, Allen and Unwin, 1962

DAVID CLEGHORN THOMSON: *Radio is changing Us*, Watts, 1937

J. TRENAMAN and D. McQUAIL: *Television and the Political Image*, Methuen, 1961

J. C. TREWIN: *The Theatre Since 1900*, Dakers, 1951

—— ed.: *Theatre Programme*, Muller, 1954

E. S. TURNER: *The Shocking History of Advertising*, Joseph, 1952

Unsound Broadcasting—publ. The Sound Broadcasting Society, 1957

FRANCIS WILLIAMS: *Dangerous Estate*, Longmans, 1957

RAYMOND WILLIAMS: *Culture and Society, 1780-1950*, Chatto, 1958

SIR WILLIAM EMRYS WILLIAMS: *The Penguin Story*, 1956

ALAN WOOD: *Mr. Rank*, Hodder, 1952

T. C. WORSLEY: *The Fugitive Art*, John Lehmann, 1952

EXTERNAL AND COMMONWEALTH

HERBERT AGAR: *The Unquiet Years, 1945–55*, Hart-Davis, 1957

MAX BELOFF: *New Dimensions in Foreign Policy*, Allen and Unwin, 1961

JAMES F. BYRNES: *Frankly Speaking*, Heinemann, 1947

WILLIAM CLARK: *Less than Kin*, Hamish Hamilton, 1957

LUCIUS D. CLAY: *Decisions in Germany*, Heinemann, 1950

GORDON CONNELL-SMITH: *The Pattern of the Postwar World*, Penguin, 1957

DUFF COOPER: *Old Men Forget*, Hart-Davis, 1953

J. H. DUNNING: *American Investment in British Manufacturing Industry*, Allen and Unwin, 1958

ANTHONY EDEN: *Full Circle*, Cassell, 1959

J. H. HUIZINGA: *Confessions of a European*, Heinemann, 1958

J. HAMPDEN JACKSON: *The Postwar Decade*, Gollancz, 1955

GEORGE F. KENNEN: *The Atom and the West*, O.U.P., 1959

SIR IVONE KIRKPATRICK: *The Inner Circle*, Macmillan, 1959

SIR R. BRUCE LOCKHART: *Your England*, Putnam, 1955

MALCOLM MCKEE: *The History of Anglo-American Relations in Brief*, E.S.U., 1958

JULIAN MOCKFORD: *Seretse Khama*, Staples, 1950

ALAN MOOREHEAD: *The Traitors*, Hamish Hamilton, 1952

H. SETON-WATSON: *Neither War nor Peace*, Methuen, 1959

HOWARD K. SMITH: *The State of Europe*, Cresset, 1950

FRED VANDERSCHMIDT: *What the English Think of Us*, Quality Press, 1948

BARBARA WARD: *The West at Bay*, Allen and Unwin, 1948

ALAN WOOD: *The Groundnut Affair*, Bodley Head, 1950

K. ZILLIACUS: *I Chose Peace*, Penguin, 1949

RURAL ENGLAND

V. BONHAM-CARTER: *The English Village*, Penguin, 1952

E. W. MARTIN: *Where London Ends*, Phoenix, 1958

W. B. MERCER: *British Farming*, H.M.S.O., 1951

CICELY MCCALL ed.: *Our Villages*, W.I., 1956

W. M. WILLIAMS: *The Sociology of an English Village*, Routledge, 1956

—— *The Country Craftsman*, Routledge, 1956

ACKNOWLEDGMENTS

MY THANKS are due to the following sources for permission to reproduce photographs: *Radio Times* Hulton Picture Library,—1, 2, 7, 9, 10, 28, 36. Keystone Press Agency,—11, 24, 29, 39, 40, 41. Central Office of Information,—20, 21, 22, 23. Imperial War Museum,—3, 5. Planet News,—4, 44. *Express* Newspapers,—13, 18, 19, 32. London News Agency,—14. Barrat's Press Agency,—30. B.B.C.,—16, 17, 34, 35. *Daily Mirror*,—46. *Glasgow Herald*,—42. Odhams Press,—45. Angus McBean,—37. Houston Rogers,—38. Henry Grant,—49. Lyons, Israel and Ellis, architects,—48. Thomson Newspapers, —8, 6. Associated Press,—26. Stevenage Development Corporation, W. Sushitzky,—25. Feature Photography Howell Evans,—50.

[Numbers refer to the List of Illustrations on pages 9 and 10.]

Index

Abdullah, King of Transjordan, 279
Abercrombie, Sir Patrick, 24, 474
Acland, Sir Richard, 29
Accountants, 160, 219, 233, 481
Adair, James, 205
Adam, Mary, 322
Adenauer, Dr. K., 257
Admass, arrival, 231-2, 246, 251, 299, 308, 336, 380; I.T.V. crowns, 411, 416; 406, 417, 425, 436, 438, 450, 452, 464, 488, 489
Advertising, 158, 231, 316-17, 371, 405-6, 417; expansion, 416, 419, 449, 450
Africa, 282, 361; Afro-Asian, 281; groundnuts, 69-72; Seretse Khama, 281-2
Agriculture, New Deal for, 177-8, 180, 181n, 364; mechanisation, 178, 180; landlords, 181-2; science in, 178-9; workers, 115, 184
Air travel, 386-7, 461
Altrincham, Lord, 299
Amery, Leopold, 31
Amethyst, H.M.S., 274, 280, 442
Amis, Kingsley, 244
Andrews, Eamonn, 234
Anne, Princess, 290
Architecture, 160; school, 165, 477; Festival, 272, 277; "modern", 459, 472-3, 475f.
Armed Forces, "citizen army", 18-21, 462; leave, 34; A.B.C.A., 21, 24, 25, 65, 68, 171, 247; demobilisation, 36, 44, 45; vote, 27, 29
Armitage, Kenneth, 250
Arts Council, 33-4
Asian nationalism, 59, 280, 281
Attlee, C. R., 11, 13, 24, 27, 28, 30, 38, 40, 54, 63, 73, 78, 91-2, 117, 185, 203n., 256, 262, 265, 280n., 286, 288, 359, 360, 361, 454
Automation, 392-3
Aviation, civil aircraft types, 276, 385, 386, 391n.; jet engines, 277, 387; industry, 276-7, 374; Comet, 386, 389-91; airlines, 55, 389; speed, 387

Baillieu, Sir Clive, 56
Bairnsfather, Bruce, 19n.
Ballpoint pens, 50
Banks, new approach of, 335, 420, 421; and trade union, 343
Bank of England, 53, 311, 421
Bardot, B., 436, 437
Barnes, Dr., Bishop of Birmingham, 212
Bannister, Roger, 369
Barlow Report, 476
Barrington-Ward, 32

B.B.C. (see also Radio and Television), prewar, 15, 355; wartime, 14, 21-22, 227; changing, 210, 227, 226-9, 231, 415-16; and politics, 367, 450; and class, 411; Beveridge Committee, 404; impact commercial TV on, 399; abolishes Children's Hour, 426
Beaverbrook, Lord, 232
Beckett, Samuel, 251, 456
Bedford, Duke of, 298
Beer, 331, 335, 439, 453, 463
Belcher, John, 100, 102
Benedict, Ruth, 440, 484
Bentley-Craig murder, 215
Bergman, Ingrid, 223
Berlin Blockade, 80-1, 257
Betjeman, John, 275
Bevan, Aneurin, 129, 137, 156, 160n., 220; resigns, 268, 285, 365, 373
Beveridge, Sir William, 24, 25, 63, 154, 159, 287
Beveridge Plan and effects, 24, 25, 28n., 29, 53, 93, 126-8, 132, 133, 136, 272, 287, 311, 346, 408; deficiencies, 349
Bevin, Ernest, 38, 40, 41, 57, 60, 61, 62, 92-3, 113, 285, 365, 442
Birmingham, 347, 465-6; Gazette, 416
Black Market, 97-9
Blitz, 22, 46, 143, 458
Book, publishing, 231, 240, 246; reading, 239f.; and TV, 410; paperbacks, 239-40, 244, 248; war books, 240-1; best sellers, 241-3; novels, 243, 356; American, 195, 454; history, 244
Boothby, Robert, 42
Bournemouth, 341, 461
Bratby, John, 355, 482
Britain can Make It, 51
British Empire, power, decline in, 11, 59, 278-80, 297, 360-1, 448; Argentine railways, 59; Persian oil, 278-80; Egypt, 279-80, 361, 442; Suez, 441f.; Cyprus, 448; Palestine, 59, 279
Brittain, Vera, 322
Britten, Benjamin, 249, 296
Buchman, Dr. Frank, 221
Burgess, Guy, 264
Burma, 62, 260
Butler, Reg, 250
Butler, R. A. B., 286, 310, 363, 366
Butlin, Billy, 298, 463
"Butskellism", 464

Calvert, Eddie, 346
Canterbury, Archbishop of, 203, 205, 446, 483,
Capital Levy, 187
Capital Punishment debate, 213-17
Casson, Sir Hugh, 294, 475

Catering, war and post war, 34–5, 44, 56; Wages Act, 115; Forte's, 44, 351–2; Lyons, 34, 164, 351; Edwardian restaurants, 207, 352n.; Wimpy bars, 454; espressos, 456, 459–60
Censorship, 197–8, 408
Chadwick, Lynn, 250
Chamberlain, Neville, 17, 31
Charles, Sir John, 142
Chataway, Christopher, 297n., 369–7
Children, 201; physique, 339, 340n., 424; and TV, 403, 419; clothing, 315; "sub-teens", 426; and sex, 438–9
China, 259–60, 265, 272; at Geneva, 362
Christian Action, 212
Christie, Agatha, 242
Church of England (see also Religion), 199, 297, 301, 470; and women, 321; and contraception, 202; and divorce, 203; and homosexuality, 204–5
Churchill, Winston, 15, 16, 17, 18, 19, 23, 25; election, 1945, 27–8, 30; 39, 40, 58; at Fulton, 65; 105, 255, 261, 271, 286, 360, 365, 367
Cinema, in decline (see also Films), 331–2
City of London, 176, 188, 189, 240, 421, 458
Civil Service, 172, 322, 343
Clark, Colin, 178, 366
Clark, Sir Kenneth, 409
Class (see also Upper, Middle and Working) consciousness, 142, 149, 354; erosion of, 339–41, 344–55, 358–60, 376, 429, 431, 434, 461, 464
Clean Air Act, 394
Clore, Charles, 359
Coalition Reconstruction Committee, 24, 28
Coal-mining, nationalisation, 53–4; vesting day, 72–3; crisis, 74f.; socialist emulation, 88–9; miners, 116, 331; N.C.B., 117, 121, 122; slump, 387
Cockneys, 326, 327n., 347
Collier, John, shops, 315
Collins, Canon John, 212
Collins, Norman, 406
'Colour Problem', 465–8
Common Wealth Party, 29
Commonwealth, the, 283, 360–1, 362, 470; "new multi-racial", 61, 62, 69, 271, 280–1; and monarchy, 302; students from, 464; workers from, 465–8
Communism in U.S., 259; in Far East, 259f.; British attitudes to, 67, 263, 264, 265; in trade unions, 80; and Commonwealth, 281
Communist Party, British, 29, 48, 256, 256n., 378
Conscription, 18, 60, 208, 462; industrial, 22
Conservative Government, dismantles controls, 310; policies, 286–7, 363–5, (1955) 359, 377, 378, 480–1; and commercial TV, 404; and Empire, 361; image-making, 450f.; social composition, 172

Conservative Party, pre-war record, 31, (1945) 28, 55; and Empire, 60–1, 69; and Americans, 68, 448; and health service, 131; and public schools, 172, 175; and Industrial Charter, 287; the "new Conservatism", 360–1, 363, 383; Young Conservatives, 373; "democratising", 376; and Suez, 446, 448; vote, 452
'Conspicuous Consumption', 352, 353, 428, 463
Consumer Durables, 309, 320, 325, 327
Consumer Movement, 455, 487
Conurbations, 141, 476
Cotton, Jack, 478, 484
Coventry, 313, 478, 479
Coward, Noël, 35, 167, 196
Cowes, 356
Crawley, 431
Crazy Gang, 325
Crime, 207; deserters, 97; juvenile, 207, 215, 403, 440; big money raids, 208, 454; research, 217
Cripps, Sir Stafford, 74; Chancellor, 82, 94, 95, 97, 99, 114, 123, 124, 172, 187, 212, 258, 268, 285, 288, 319, 364, 366, 448
Crosland, C. A. R., 358, 373–4
Crossman, R. H. S., 61
Crowther Report, 163, 439
Cudlipp, Hugh, 221, 233n.
Culture, 234–50; international, 456, 490
Cunningham, John, 276
Czechoslovakia, 79–80, 362

Daily Dispatch, 416
Daily Express, 27, 28, 53, 69, 78, 89, 91, 205, 215, 222–3, 301, 396, 453
Daily Herald, 69, 73, 118, 143, 222, 313, 417
Daily Mail, 18, 23, 27, 40, 69, 74, 85, 89, 125, 205, 280
Daily Mirror, 18, 23, 24, 32, 116, 129, 205, 221, 222–3, 299n., 301, 417, 446, 453
Daily Telegraph, 93, 98, 246, 280, 446, 448
Daily Worker, 52, 378
Dalton, Dr. Hugh, 38, 53, 56, 69, 181, 311
Dancing, 431, 433
Daniel, Dr. Glyn, 409
D.D.T., 16
Deakin, Arthur, 114, 121, 124
Death Duties, 181–2, 379
Debenham and Freebody, 350
Debutantes, 298
Demobilisation and redeployment, 36, 44–5
Denning Committee, 201
Depressed Areas, 312, 474
Derby, Lord, 189, 406
Design, 238, 270–2, 329, 330, 453, 460–1; of motor-cars, 335, 460; Council of Industrial, 51, 335
Detergents, 325
Devonshire, Duke of, 181
Diet/Dieting, 326, 336, 453, 463
Dior, Christian, 94, 284
Divorce, Royal Commission on, 202–3

Do-it-yourself, 332, 334
Docker, Sir B., 352
Docks, decasualisation scheme, 118, 120
Dowding, Air Marshal, 384
Driberg, Tom, M.P., 266
Dramatics, amateur, 430
Duff-Cooper, A., 20
Duke, Neville, 387
Dulles, John Foster, 361-2, 443

Eady, Sir Wilfred, 58
Ealing Studios, 273-4, 402
Economic crises, Lend-Lease, 41; 1947,
    78; 1949, 90; 1955, 309; Suez, 448
Economic planning, 32, 83-87, 94; and
    Depressed Areas, 312; and Conserva-
    tive Party, 364-5; and Europe, 62, 469
Economic Survey, The, 256
Economist newspaper, 86, 116, 298, 364
Economists, influence of, 38, 83, 94, 199,
    311, 365-6, 372, 373, 375, 379, 483
Eden, Anthony, 27, 172, 203, 361, 362
Edinburgh, Duke of, Philip Mountbatten,
    engagement, 51-2, 283, 290, 296, 300,
    303, 483
Education (see also Universities), "Secon-
    dary—for All", 142-52; Butler Act,
    24, 241, 488; technical, 19, 159, 341;
    Adult, 246; Eleven-plus, 150-2, 153,
    439; G.C.E., 150; grammar schools,
    19, 149-50, 154, 162-4, 172, 174, 185,
    344, 356, 375, 429, 439; secondary mod-
    ern schools, 164-6, 411, 429; compre-
    hensive schools, 146-7, 152, 165, 245,
    377, 455
Edward VII, King, 299, 303
Eisenhower, President, 14, 362, 397, 408,
    445
Elections, General (1945), 27-31, 39;
    (1950), 254-5; (1951), 286; (1955),
    358-9, 370; (1959), 455, 449f.
Electronic, industry, 276, 385; 'brain',
    393
Eliot, T. S., 155, 199, 288, 356, 456
Elliot, Sir John, 318n.
Ellis, Ruth, 216
Elizabeth, Princess and Queen, 51, 283,
    284, 287f.; Coronation, 292-6, 299,
    300, 302-3, 303n.
Emmett, 274
Emigration, 91, 449
Epstein, 103, 195
Ercolani, Lucian, 329
Espresso bars, 459-60
Eton, 171, 350, 376
Equality, 123, 124, 128, 185-90, 408, 439,
    480, 483; financial, 99, 181-2, 186-8;
    and manual workers, 116; in education,
    143, 480, 488; in rural life, 181-2; and
    monarchy, 296; of sexes, 320-4; and
    science, 388, 480; and youth, 427;
    Tawney on, 111, 338, 354
Europe, British relations with, 61, 62,
    456, 458, 469-70, 489; economic
    co-operation with, 61, 364; N.A.T.O.,
    258; E.D.C., 362; W.E.U., 363, 469
Evacuees, wartime, 22, 46

Evans, Lincoln, 287
Evans, Stanley, 176, 178

Fabian Society, 38
Family, "decline" of, 193; working-class,
    313; post-war, 200-2, 200n., 424
Farouk, King, 279
Fascists, British, 50, 467
Fashion, 335, 418, 421, 436, 490; men's,
    315, 428, 430; New Look, 94-6, 315;
    female teenage, 425, 429, 432, 436, 437;
    male teenage, 428, 432; foundation
    garments, 232, 232n., 426
Feminists, 290, 321, 323, 328, 473
Festival of Britain, 253, 269f., 441, 459-60
Field, Sid, 35
Films, 231, 232; wartime, 33; documen-
    tary, 33, 273; Continental, 33, 196;
    X Certificate, 197, 219; sex and, 207;
    Third Man, 264; Ealing, 273-4; 3-D,
    277; Cinemascope, 401; 'kitchen-
    sink', 402; teenage, 425
Financial Times, 182, 426
Fleck, Sir Alexander, 159
Flying saucers, 383f.
Food, Ministry of, 43, 56, 57, 103-4;
    British restaurants, 35, 56 (see Diet)
Football, 105, 331, 369, 430, 463
Football pools, 351, 351n., 421
Ford, Henry, 305, 310
Foreign influences, Scandinavian, 271,
    272, 275; films, 195, 196; restaurants,
    463; Italian, 429, 461; espressos, 460;
    immigrants, students, 103, 464-5;
    tourism, 461f.; hotels, 464 (see also
    U.S.)
Forester, C. S., 242
Forever Amber, 35, 224
Forte, Charles, 44, 351-2
Fortnums, 189
France, 61, 362, 445, 469
Fraser, Sir Robert, 412
Frozen foods, 326
Fry, Christopher, 236
Fuchs, Klaus, 259, 264
Full Employment, 24, 25, 29, 93, 311, 317
Furniture, 45, 329-30
Fyfe, Sir D. Maxwell, 216

Gaitskell, Hugh, 38, 93, 172; Chancellor,
    268, 286, 451
Galbraith, J. K., 455
Gambling, gaming law reform, 200;
    Premium Bonds, 211n.
Garbett, Dr. Cyril, 32, 208
Gardening, 333; organic, 394
Gee, Cecil, 429
George VI, King, 253, 269; death, 283-4,
    291, 482
George, Lloyd, 17, 28, 126, 129, 297n.,
    365
German prisoners, 103
Germany, starvation in, 43, 57; dismant-
    ling, 58, 257; war crimes trials, 49-50;
    zones fused, 59; rejoins Europe, 257;
    rearmament, 361
Gibberd, Frederick, 326, 478
Gibson, George, 100

Giles, 78, 333
Gimmicks, 418, 422, 433
Glasgow, 347, 416
Glubb Pasha, 442
Goddard, L.C.J., 208, 213, 217
Gollancz, Victor, 58, 372
Goldwyn, Sam, 33
Gorer, Geoffrey, 209
Gorham, Maurice, 228
Gort, General, 18
Graham, Dr. Billy, 211
Gramophone/records, 236, 432–3
Greco, Juliette, 436
Greece, 60, 65
Greene, Graham, 243
Greenwood, Arthur, 288, 375
Grieve, Mary, 320, 328
Griffiths, Jim, 56, 372
Gropius, Professor, 484
Guards, brigade of, 298
Guillebaud Report, 137n.
Guilty Men, 31
Guinness, Alec, 273, 274

Hailsham, Lord, 405
Haldane, J. B. S., 378
Haley, Bill, 433, 456
Haley, W. J., 227, 245
Hallé orchestra, 399, 414
Hancock, Tony, 247
Handley, Tommy, 23, 227, 247
Harben, Philip, 418
Harding, Gilbert, 229, 230, 231, 234
Harlow, 319, 326, 431
Harrods, 189
Harrow School, 172, 175, 442
Hayworth, Rita, 223
Health, war and post-war, 16, 56; vital
    statistics, 47, 139, 140, 339; T.B., 138;
    obesity, 336n.; psychological illness,
    140–1; current diseases, 140–2, 394;
    school children, 339 (*see* Medicine)
Health Service, National, N.H.S.,
    128–142, 185, 473; White Paper, 24;
    hospitals, 31, 135; B.M.A. and, 128–9,
    133; early days, 129f.; dental care,
    132; health centres, 136–7; private
    health insurance, 133n.
Heath, N. C., murder case, 50, 51
Herbert, A. P., 106
Hepburn, Audrey, 436, 460
Heraldry, 121, 292
Heyworth Committee, 55
Hibberd, Stuart, 15, 22
Hillary, Edmund, 295
Hillary, Richard, 241
Hill, Dr. Charles, 36
Hire Purchase, 317–18, 332, 345, 421, 452
Hobbies, 430–31
Hoggart, Richard, 238
Holidays-with-pay, 341, 342; abroad,
    355, 461f.
Hollis, Christopher, M.P., 31
Home, modern, 324–34
Homicide Act, 217
Hooper, Frederick, 45
Hore-Belisha, Leslie, 17, 18, 20
Horner, Arthur, 80, 117, 118, 120

Housewives' League, 55
Housing, post-war situation, 45–7; pre-
    fabs, 46; rent control, 47, 313; home
    ownership, 348; new estates, 256, 324,
    346, 452; flats, 475; slum clearance,
    347, 466–7, 486
Hoyle, Fred, 212
Hughes, Emrys, 289, 299
Hungarian Rising, 377–8, 398
Hunting, 183
Hussein, King, 442
Hyndley, Lord, 74

Ibsen, 412
I.C.I., 159, 188
Ideology, 249
Immigrants, 464–8
Incentives, 86–9
India, 59, 62, 265, 281
Ind Coope, 461
Industry, growth, 311; takeovers, 157;
    personnel officers, 160; and grammar
    schools, 164; and public schools, 172;
    training in, 169–70; technologists and
    managers, 159; new for old, 276–7,
    276n., 312, 340
Innes, Hammond, 242
Insularism, 195, 272, 280, 407, 456, 459,
    461–71
Insurance companies, 188, 343n., 371,
    452
Isaacs, George, 37, 99

Jacob, Sir Ian, 415
James, Dr. Eric, 403
Jenkin, Rev. D., 210
Jon's 'Two Types', 19n.
Jones, Tom, 35n.
Japan, war with, 16
Jazz, 432, 435–6, 440, 454
Jehovah's Witnesses, 211
Jung, Dr. C. G., 393

Kaye, Danny, 108, 109
Kelly, Sir Gerald, 409
Kennen, George F., 397
Keynes, J. M., 34, 41, 66, 77, 83, 85, 189
Keynesianism, 84, 93, 94, 287, 363, 365,
    373, 374, 379
Khama, Seretse, 281–2
Khrushchev, 172, 308, 367, 368, 378, 408
King, Cecil H., 23, 233n., 359, 417
Kinsey Report, 194–5, 199, 209, 213, 219,
    224, 413, 438, 440
Knight, Mrs. Margaret, 212n.
Koestler, Arthur, 67, 441
Korean War, 260–7, 361; economic
    effects, 268, 281, 311; armistice, 308

Labour, direction of, 87, 99
Labour Government takes office, 37; and
    Commonwealth, 62, 280, 361; and
    Press, 89, 221; and Middle East,
    279–80; and B.B.C., 404; achievements
    and shortcomings, 91–4, 113, 286, 311,
    370–1, 474, 479–80

Labour Party, 1945 programme, 29; parliamentary, 38; electoral vote, 31, 39, 181, 286n., 370, 425; and health service, 132; foreign policy, 40, 60–3, 64–8, 256, 279–80; and middle classes, 39, 153–4; and Communists, 80, 256; and 'consolidators', 284; and youth, 372–3, 452; and 'class-conflict', 358–9, 372, 452; doctrine, 82–3, 365, 370–5, 377, 451, 453, 455, 470, 483
Lancashire, 276, 342, 347, 348, 452, 490
Land boom, 364, 478
Laski, Harold, 28, 375
Laski, Marghanita, 236, 268
Laundrettes, 352
Lawrence, D. H., 195, 210, 218, 454
Lawther, Will, 117
L.C.C., 147, 238, 246, 321n., 395, 424, 475
Leather, Miss D. S., 369
Le Corbusier, 473, 475, 476
Legal Aid Service, 127–8
Leisure, 424, 430–1, 440, 450, 452, 456, 460, 483
Leslie, S. C., 88
Levy, Mervyn, 409
Liberal Party, 377
Lighting, 329
Lindsay, Lord, 395
Lloyd, Selwyn, 404, 458
Local Government, 49, 122, 321, 418
London, 141, 207, 347, 456, 458–9, 465, 466, 468, 473, 475, 484
Lords, House of, 297–8, 321
Low, David, 342
Lubetkin, Berthold, 326
Lynn, Vera, 46
Lynskey Tribunal, 100–3

McCarthy, Senator Joseph, 258–9, 268
MacArthur, General, 263, 265
Maclean, Donald, 264
Macmillan, Harold, 30, 359, 366
MacPherson, Stewart, 228
Mailer, Norman, 195
Makarios, Archbishop, 448
Malenkov, 261, 308
Managerial society, 56, 94, 344
Manchester Guardian, 91, 155, 246, 342, 407, 445
Manchester, 323, 347, 460
Margaret, Princess, 296, 300–2
Market research (*see also* Opinion polls), 232, 316, 450, 480
Marks and Spencer, 314–15, 480
Marriage, modern, 201, 323, 332; divorce, 194, 202–3; family planning, 200, 202; marriage bureaus, 142n.; marriage guidance council, 202
Mary, Queen, 291, 293
Masyryk, Jan, 80
Mau-mau, 282
Maugham, Somerset, 206, 356
May, Dr. Alan Nunn, 67, 259
Medicine (*see also* Health), advances, 16, 17, 139; new drugs, 138, 388, 454; G.P.s, 133, 137, 135, 473–4; College of, 140; consultants, 133n., 134, 160;

psychiatry, 134, 394; mental illness, 214, 327, 388, 394; social medicine, 142, 394
Metaphysics, 199, 249
Middle class, "plight" of, 152–6; changing, 156–61; and schools, 148, 162–4, 172; and politics, 39, 376; and culture, 235; and Press, 223; and medical care, 132, 345; and trade unions, 343–5; and home ownership, 342; and morals, 439; rural, 184
Middle East (*see also* British power), 59, 278–80, 368, 443, 448
Middleton, Mr., 333
Mikolajczyk, Stanislaw, 78
Milk bars, 44, 460
Miller, Arthur, 107, 195
Mitford, Nancy, 354
Mobility, social, 162, 163, 170, 173–5
Molotov, 41, 65, 68, 261, 308, 368
Moore, Henry, 165, 238, 250, 456
Monarchy, 188n., 284; popularity, 288f.; situation, 296–303
Monckton, Sir Walter, 287, 420
Money, Sir Leo Chiozza, 187
Montgomery, General B. L., 15, 19, 87, 449
Morals, sexual, 194, 206, 209, 214, 438–9; homosexuality, 197, 200, 204–5; prostitution, 200, 207; strip-tease clubs, 454
Morgenthau Plan, 58
Morris, Dr. J. N., 140n., 340n.
Morris Minor, 335
Morrison, Herbert, 38, 93, 153, 269, 280, 281, 375, 376
Mosley, Sir Oswald, 50n.
Moss Bros., 298
Motor-car, ownership, 318–19, 351; design, 335; effects, 319, 432, 453, 460
Motorways, 470–1
Muff, George, 121n.
Muggeridge, Malcolm, 285, 357
Munnings, Sir A., 237
Murder, 216
Murray, Professor Gilbert, 446
Music, 236, 245, 249, 413; amateur, 433–34
Music hall, 107–8, 434

Nagy, Ferenc, 79
Nagy, Imre, 398
Nasser, President, 368, 376, 408, 442–5
National Parks, 474
Nationalisation, doctrine, 54, 55, 370–75; and trade unions, 114–15; and strikes, 117–18; coal, 53, 54, 72–3, 370; airlines, 53, 311; Cable and Wireless, 53; Bank of England, 53, 311; gas, 54; electricity, 54, 55, 370; iron and steel, 53, 285, 287, 297, 371, 451; insurance, 371; road haulage, 55, 287; railways, 118, 370; de-nationalising, 287
Navy, Royal, 247, 447, 468
Nenni telegram, 80
New Left, the, 380
News Chronicle, 152, 416, 446
News of the World, 221, 225, 246
New Statesman, 65, 285

New Towns (see also Place-names), 24, 50, 53, 238, 324, 327, 347, 427, 431, 474, 476–7
Nkrumah, Kwame, 282, 442
Nonconformity (Dissent), 160, 211, 427, 435
Nuclear weapons, 40, 79, 258, 265, 361, 368; energy, 53, 275, 387; dangers, 388–9, 486; disarmament, 377, 379; Civil defence, 262
Nuri es-Said, 448
Nylon(s), 49, 99, 324–5

Obscene Publications Act, 218
Observer, the, 246, 447
Office-workers, 116, 156, 343
Oil power, 387–8
Olivier, Laurence, 34
Olympic Games, 104
Opinion polls, 231, 235, 414, 451, 481; Gallup, 25, 148, 406; B.B.C., 228, 230–1, 234, 415; Tam, 413
Orwell, George, 67, 167, 224, 345
Osborne, John, 449, 456

Packaging, 316, 335, 351n., 353
Painting, 33, 237, 246, 249, 250, 254, 409, 419, 454, 482; Royal Academy, 441, 482
Paoluzzi, E., 251
Parliamentary democracy, dual vote, 12; enlargement sphere of Government, 54; tripartitism, 84; professionalised, 367, 451; decline of, 365–6; House of Lords reform, 297; women in Parliament, 321
Parnell, Val, 108
Pasmore, Victor, 249
Pawnshops, 345
Penal Reform, 213f.
Penguin books, 234, 247–8
Penicillin, 16, 139
Persian oil débâcle, 278–9
Peterlee, 326
Pets, 327, 332–3, 397
Pickles, Wilfred, 229, 240
Picture Post, 153, 224, 291, 401
Piper, John, 33
Planning (see Economic and Town and country)
Plastics, 325
Polish Resettlement Corps, 103
Ponomareva, Nina, 369
Pontecorvo, Dr., 264, 269
Pop singers, 418, 426, 454, 456, 491
Pornography, 218, 219, 224–5
Potteries, the, 340, 490
Poverty, 186, 187, 349
Powell and Moya, 475
Prefabs, 46
Press (see also titles and Admass), Royal Commission on, 220, 222, 225, 232; economics of, 189, 221–4, 417, 454; and sex, 194–5, 196, 219, 224, 225; quality, 246; Press Council, 225–6, 301; and Royalty, 288, 299–301; and women, 336; effects of TV on, 400–1, 410, 416, 450; closures, 416–17
Priestley, J. B., 32, 64, 91, 231, 236, 245
Profit motive, 219, 299, 374

Property developers, 364, 420, 478, 484
Psephologists, 451
Psychologists (and psychiatrists), 194, 198–9, 216, 394
Public relations, 20, 87, 158, 234, 316, 420, 449
Public Schools, 162, 171–3, 176, 298, 377, 439
Pubs, 332, 429, 459, 461
Punch, 167, 274, 357
Puritanism, relaxation of, 194f., 197–8, 272, 408

Radicalism, 23, 25, 373, 360, 379, 428, 453, 488
Radio, personalities, 229–30; Third Programme, 227, 235, 247, 356, 411n., 415; Light, 227, 228, 235, 246, 356, 415; Network Three, 431; V.H.F., 400; transistors, 432; effects of TV, 400; Brains Trust, 21, 227; first soap opera, 16, 227; Archers, 180, 247, 400; Dick Barton, 208; ITMA, 23; T.I.F.H., 286; Mrs. Dale, 180
Reith, Sir John, 226, 228
Religion (see also Churches), 193, 199, 211–12, 210, 439, 454
Reveille, 225, 246
Rhee, Syngman, 260
Richards, Gordon, 296
Richardson, Professor A. E., 269
Richardson, Ralph, 34
Road hauliers, 55, 287
Rolls-Royce, 277, 352n.
Rothermere, Lord, 225
La Ronde, 196
Roosevelt, F. D., 26, 67, 69
Rossellini, Roberto, 223
Rowntree, Seebohm, 186, 206
Rowse, A. L., 244
Rowton Houses, 349–50
"Ruling Class", 188, 360, 376, 491
Rural Life, 182–5
Russell, Jane, 207
Russia, relations with, 16, 25–6, 40, 41, 57, 64, 65; visitors from, 368–9; and Czechoslovakia and Eastern Europe, 65, 68, 79; Berlin blockade, 80–1, 257; and Korea, 261; explodes A-bomb, 258; East Berlin rising, 308; "peaceful co-existence", 308; and Middle East, 368; and Hungarian rising, 378

Sabbatarianism, 210
Sabrina, 418
Sanders, Edgar, 264
Salisbury, Lord, 297
Schools (see Education)
Schuman, Robert, 62n.
Science, pace of change, 385, 386, 391, 395; social effects, 12, 18, 20, 174, 218, 297, 324–5, 380, 388–9, 392–3, 396, 410, 438, 473, 484, 486; and art, 109, 248, 251, 275, 395, 475, 476; and religion, 199, 212, 395; and the housewife, 324–6; and power politics, 397–8; and the law, 216–17; and agriculture, 179; and trade unions, 123; at schools and Universities, 164, 172, 394, 489

Scientists, 159, 485, 485n.; social, 127, 200, 365, 372, 374, 380, 451, 476, 484
Scooters, Vespa, 353, 431
Scotsman, 189
Scott, Peter, 409
Scottish nationalism, 282, 289, 289n.
Sculpture, 238, 250–1, 272, 402
Seers, Dudley, 186, 364
Selfridge, Gordon, 335
Servants, 155, 155n., 464
Service occupations, 159
Sex (*see* Morals)
Shaw, G. B., 234, 365, 454
Shawcross, Sir Hartley, 101
Shinwell, Emmanuel, 53, 74, 77, 118, 153, 154, 156
Shops, re-styled, 315, 316; chain stores, 314–15; Co-ops., 350, 371; wine, 463; supermarkets, 353, 417, 481
Shrewsbury, Earl of, 182
Shute, Nevil, 242–4
Silicones, 325
Silverman, Sidney, 217
Silvey, Robert, 228
Skiffle, 433–4
Skills, changing, 157
Slums, 347, 466–7, 486
Smith, Aubrey C., 274
Smith, Sir Ben, 43
Sociologists (*see also* Scientists, Social) 162, 380, 455
Space Age, 385; sputnik, 396–8, 455
Spectator, The, 54, 280
Speech, accents, 163, 350, 355, 478, 490–1
Spence, Basil, 51, 277, 459, 478
Spinsters, 323
Spivs, 98–9, 417
Sports, 105f.; athletics, 104, 369; football, 105, 331, 369, 463; rowing, 369; boxing, 105; Channel swimming, 105; ski-ing, 430; cricket, 104, 369; tennis, 104; participant, 430
Squatters, 48
Stable, Mr. Justice, 193, 198
Stalin, 25, 261; dies, 307
Standard of living, 12, 304, 310, 311, 324, 327, 333, 342, 358, 453, 461, 462
Stanley, Sidney, 95f.
Star, The, 31, 417
Steele, Tommy, 426, 454, 456
Stevenage, 50, 165
Stock Exchange, 321, 406, 451, 453, 486, 487
Stockwood, Canon Mervyn, 210
Stopes, Marie, 202, 213
Strachey, John, 53, 58, 70, 71, 373
Straus, Oscar, 196
Streeter, Fred, 333
Strikes, 358; miners, 117–19; dockers, 120, 358; automation and, 393; teachers, 344–5
Strip-tease clubs, 454
Suez, 377, 441f., 468
Summerskill, Dr. Edith, 56, 93
Sunday Dispatch, 224, 291
Sunday Times, 189, 195, 205, 246, 303n.
Sunday Pictorial, 51, 225, 246, 301, 303
Sutherland, Graham, 33

Take-overs, 189, 359
Tailoring, multiple, 315
Tape-recorders, 432
Tate Gallery, 237
Tate and Lyle, 371
Tawney, R. H., 111, 338, 354
Taxation, 181–2, 186, 187, 286, 310, 364, 377
Technology, colleges of, 168; diploma in, 168
Teachers, emergency, 144–5; grammar school, 155, 344; N.U.T., 344–5
Teddy Boys, 427f., 456, 460
Teenagers, 164n., 201, 418, 424–40, 432–3, 453
Television (*see* Television, commercial, below) as a medium, 160, 291, 452; development, 76, 256, 295, 309, 400; content, 412–16: abstainers, 402–3; social effects, 309, 331, 351, 400–3, 407f.; and politics, 359, 367, 449, 487; personalities, 230, 418, 451
Television, commercial, begins, 399–400; debate on, 404–7; I.T.A., 407; effects, 408, 411–16, 419–20, 481
Terylene, 325
Theatre, war and post-war, 34, 35; American invasion, 107–9, 195, 454; verse drama, 236; Old Vic., 34, 236; "slice of life" school, 356, 401, 449; Whitehall farce, 356; effects of TV, 402; in provinces, 34, 430
Third Force, 61, 64, 80, 271, 281, 282, 362, 456
Thomas, Dylan, 235
Thomas, Wynford Vaughan, 227, 386
Thomson, Roy, 189, 233n., 417, 454
The Times, 32, 52, 301, 336, 418, 419, 434, 452, 458
Tito, Marshal, 80, 293, 367
Tolpuddle, 182
Tomlinson, George, 38, 375
Tourism, 461–5, 491
Tovey, Admiral Lord, 267
Town and Country Planning, Act, 177, 312, 474; Greater London Plan, 24; achievement, 312, 474, 486–7; failures, 477–9
Townsend, Group-Captain P., 296, 301
Toynbee, Arnold, 244
Trade unions, M.P.s, 38; Trade Disputes Act, 113–14, 287; new status, 113–15; and wages, 85, 87; unofficial strikes, 117–21; and workers' control, 115; block vote, 39, 121; and industrial democracy, 121–3; and Conservative Government, 287; women and, 322; white collar, 343–5; at Buckingham Palace, 298; T.G.W.U., 113, 120, 121; N.U.M., 121; A.E.U., 122; N.A.L.G.O., 116; N.U.A.W., 184
Trade, world, 66, 469
Trades Union Congress, 123
Tramps, 127
Travel allowance, 89, 286
Truman, President, 41, 59, 261, 265, 361; Doctrine, 60, 65, 259, 397
Tuberculosis, 138–9; bovine, 179n.

Turner, James, 183
Twiss, Peter, 387
Tyneside, 312, 348, 431, 466, 491

Unemployment, 312, 359, 364
United Nations, 27, 278, 445, 447
United States, Loan, 41, 42, 66, 77, 78; Marshall Plan, 68; takes over in Greece and Turkey, 60; Forces in Britain, 66, 103; in sport, 105, 109; conflicts over foreign policy, 262, 265, 266, 361–2; British attitudes towards, 64–8, 109–10, 267, 275; influences, 107–9, 195, 228 405, 425, 454–6, 464; and Suez, 445, 448
Universities, places at, 167–8, 173; controversy over, 169; 'Redbrick', 159, 168, 174, 376, 395, 488, 491; Keele, 395; L.S.E., 373; Oxbridge, 167, 174, 350, 376, 488, Oxford, 173, 317, 320, 321, 323, 372, 378, 395, 446, 459; Cambridge, 45, 173, 317; women at, 233.
Upper Class/Aristocracy/Peerage (see also House of Lords), 133, 181–2, 297, 298, 342, 350, 354
Ustinov, Peter, 33
Utility scheme, 45, 46
Uthwatt Report, 477

Vanderschmidt, F., 109
Vansittart, Lord, 58
Vaughan Williams, Dr., 249

Wales, South, 312
Walker, Kenneth, 137
Wallpaper, 329
War and planning, 83; and social philosophy, 22, 32, 47; and the arts, 33–4; and trade unions, 113–14; and psychiatry, 199; and social hierarchy, 31, 298; and income redistribution, 186
Washing machines, 309, 320, 325, 327
Watson-Watt, Sir R., 275
Waugh, Evelyn, 293, 459
Webbs, the, 55, 93, 160, 374
Wedgwood, C. V., 244
Welfare State, 12, 32, 86; 'inaugurated', 125–6, 127, 208, 359, 370, 467, 479, 480
Wells, H. G., 234, 326

West Indians, 465–8
Wheeler, Sir Mortimer, 409
White, Mrs. Eirene, 203n.
Whittle, Sir Frank, 275, 288, 387
Williams, Eric, 240
Williams, Tennessee, 107, 195, 456
Williams, Tom, 118
Williams, Sir W. E., 247
Wilkie, Wendell, 26
Wilmot, Chester, 227, 244, 390
Wilmot, John, 52
Wilson, Angus, 244
Wilson, Harold, 38, 90, 255
Wilkinson, Ellen, 144, 375
Windsor, Duke and Duchess of, 291, 301
Winchester College, 171
Wine, 462; shops, 463
Winter Crisis, 1947, 74–8
Winterton, Lord, 183
Wolfson, Isaac, 317, 318, 359
Woodcock, Bruce, 106
Woolton, Earl of, 307, 377, 406, 449
Wolfenden, Sir John, 171, 437; Report, 204–5, 213, 221
Women, equality, 201, 320–4, 324f.; as consumers, 335–7; Women's Institutes, 185; W.V.S., 127n.
Women's magazines, 196, 221, 291, 328–9, 332, 334, 336
Woodham-Smith, Mrs. Cecil, 244
Wootton, Barbara, 212n.
Working class (see also Class), changing, 167, 187, 327, 332, 339–42, 347, 360, 421; incomes, 313; skilled, 156, 157; unskilled, 163, 340, semi-skilled, 156, 167, 340; home-ownership, 348; car-ownership, 318; time-lags, 163, 348–9; and schools, 162–3; and TV, 403, 411; and tourism, 461; youth, 167, 424, 427
World War I, contrasts, 17, 18, 47, 54

Young, Dr. Michael, 355
Youth, 423–40; and politics, 372, 373, 377; clubs, 438; and travel, 462; and TV, 422 (see also Teenagers and Crime)

Zilliacus, Konni, M.P., 63, 80
Zola, works of, 197
Zoo, London, 256, 368
Zweig, F., 157n., 201, 322, 348